THE COMMON CORE OF EUROPEAN
ADMINISTRATIVE LAWS

General Editors

GIACINTO DELLA CANANEA

MAURO BUSSANI

General Principles and Sector-Specific Rules in European Administrative Laws

THE COMMON CORE OF EUROPEAN ADMINISTRATIVE LAWS

General Editors:
Giacinto della Cananea, Professor of Administrative Law at Bocconi University; and Mauro Bussani, Professor of Comparative Law at the University of Trieste and Adjunct Professor of Comparative Law at the University of Macau

OTHER TITLES IN THE SERIES:

Tort Liability of Public Authorities in European Laws
Edited by Giacinto della Cananea and Roberto Caranta

Administrative Justice Fin de siècle
Early Judicial Standards of Administrative Conduct in Europe (1890–1910)
Edited by Giacinto della Cananea and Stefano Mannoni

Judicial Review of Administration in Europe
Procedural Fairness and Propriety
Edited by Giacinto della Cananea and Mads Andenas

Procedural Requirements for Administrative Limits to Property Rights
Edited by Martina Conticelli and Thomas Perroud

The Austrian Codification of Administrative Procedure
Diffusion and Oblivion (1920–1970)
Edited by Giacinto della Cananea, Angela Ferrari Zumbini, and Otto Pfersmann

erc
European Research Council
Established by the European Commission

The Common Core of European Administrative Law (CoCEAL) project has received funding from the European Research Council (ERC) under the Horizon 2020 Research and Innovation Programme 'Advanced Grant' Excellent Science (Grant Agreement No 694697).

General Principles and Sector-Specific Rules in European Administrative Laws

Edited by

GIACINTO DELLA CANANEA

and

JEAN-BERNARD AUBY

OXFORD
UNIVERSITY PRESS

OXFORD
UNIVERSITY PRESS

Great Clarendon Street, Oxford, OX2 6DP,
United Kingdom

Oxford University Press is a department of the University of Oxford.
It furthers the University's objective of excellence in research, scholarship,
and education by publishing worldwide. Oxford is a registered trade mark of
Oxford University Press in the UK and in certain other countries

Published in the United States of America by Oxford University Press
198 Madison Avenue, New York, NY 10016, United States of America

British Library Cataloguing in Publication Data
Data available

Library of Congress Control Number: 2024931143

ISBN 978–0–19–886757–9

DOI: 10.1093/oso/9780198867579.001.0001

Printed and bound by
CPI Group (UK) Ltd, Croydon, CR0 4YY

General Editors' Preface

This is a new book in the series entitled '*The Common Core of European Administrative Laws*' (CoCEAL), based on comparative research for which the European Research Council has awarded us an Advanced Grant. From the outset, it was decided that this research would have two major themes. The first concerns the methodology of comparative analysis. Our intent is to compare a plurality of legal systems, going beyond the mainstream scrutiny of the more influential ones and seeking to understand the role of various legal formants therein. Secondly, and more importantly, this comparison has a particular end in view. Our intent is to launch a large-scale debate not only on commonalities and diversities within the European legal space but also, and more importantly, on how commonality and diversity have extended and interact with one another, within and across legal systems, both diachronically and synchronically, in the past and today.

From the first point of view, the methodology adopted in our research owes a great deal to the pioneering seminars held at Cornell Law School during the 1960s and to the 'Common Core of European Private Law' project, launched in 1993. This methodology is based on a 'factual analysis' insofar as it is based on hypothetical cases that are first subjected to scrutiny during workshops with experts from the legal systems selected for comparison in order to ascertain whether the proposed cases are plausible and meaningful. Only at a later stage are these cases forwarded to the experts, who formulate their responses based on all the pertinent legal formants. A further step consists in comparing the answers obtained, with a view to understanding the relevance and significance of both the commonalities and the diversity that emerge.

From the second point of view, this new research focuses heavily on administrative procedure and thus examines various types of administrative action, including adjudication and rule-making, without overlooking the importance of traditional sets of issues, such as those relating to judicial review and government liability in tort, which are considered both 'classic' and important. Collectively, these topics allow us to duly acknowledge the contributions of those who have gone before, using legal comparison as a means to various ends. They enable us to call for increased attention to what is new and original in the European legal space, where national legal systems interact with one another and with the two regional organizations, namely the European Union and the Council of Europe.

The website dedicated to our comparative research, www.coceal.it, provides information on both the results of the research and the next steps to be taken.

Giacinto della Cananea and Mauro Bussani

Editors' Preface

This book examines the relationship between general principles and rules from a comparative perspective. It is a particularly interesting relationship since, in the field of administrative law, there is no systematic body of rules similar to those characteristic of European civil codes. General principles are therefore of fundamental importance. The comparative perspective, while limited to some legal systems, is a privileged one, because it allows a better understanding of how principles and rules interact in modern societies. In brief, both principles and rules are relevant for the solution of the problems that lawyers and, in our case, government officials and judges have to face. In some cases, existing rules will determine the decisions of government officials, with no leeway for a contrary decision, such as when, for example, an application for public funding lacks an important requisite. In other cases, recourse will have to be made to general principles. Thus, for example, the question that often arises is not simply whether the public authority has given reasons for its decision, but whether concise or stereotyped motivation provides adequate justification for it. This example shows that, when principles are used to determine whether a certain decision is legally valid, the evaluation entails a margin of judicial discretion.

We engage in a comparative inquiry considering both a set of problems and their solutions, always seeking to understand their common and distinctive traits. Attention to both is one essential feature of the craft. In this respect, the crucial empirical question is whether general legislation on administrative procedure has a tangible impact within the legal systems where it has been adopted. In brief, do codes (of administrative procedure) make a difference? This explains the importance of another essential feature of our comparative enquiry, namely the use of hypothetical cases. Some of them might look 'extreme', where injustice is manifest, while others are closer to ordinary administration: ie the normal discharge of administrative functions and authority. In either case, we seek to understand whether the existence of general legislation on administrative procedure actually leads to distinctions between European legal systems.

The structure of the book is as follows. Part I explains the purposes and scope of our analysis. Part II illustrates some general features of the legal systems included in our comparative enquiry. Part III includes the responses of the national experts concerning the hypothetical cases at the heart of our 'factual' analysis. Part IV serves to examine the answers in comparative terms, with a particular need in view; namely to ascertain not so much whether a 'common core' exists but how it is shaped and evolves, also in response to the influence exerted by supranational legal orders.

A brief mention regarding the jurisdictions and issues examined in this study is in order at this point. While our research primarily focuses on Europe, we have also explored other regions of the world to gain a deeper understanding of both the commonalities and the differences among modern legal systems. As part of this effort,

China and Venezuela have also been included. Japan and the US were initially intended for inclusion, and their suitability for our hypothetical cases was confirmed during the workshop held in Milan in 2019. However, the problems arising from the pandemics made their participation difficult. We are aware that other legal systems are equally important and might lead to different results, so further examination is certainly necessary.

Finally, we owe a considerable debt of gratitude to many people. CoCEAL's research team (including Mauro Bussani, Martina Conticelli, Angela Ferrari Zumbini, and Marta Infantino) contributed to the design and fine-tuning of the questionnaire. Hiroko Kudo and the late professor Richard B Stewart made thoughtful remarks concerning both the methodology and the questionnaire during the workshop. Adrian Bedford and Paola Monaco reviewed all the chapters in terms of language editing and the OUP guidelines, respectively. We duly acknowledge the support of Bocconi University (and Paola Calogero especially) in the management of the project as a whole.

Giacinto della Cananea and Jean-Bernard Auby

Contents

Detailed Contents

PART III CASES

The authors of the respective country reports in cases 2–10 are the same as in Case 1 unless otherwise noted

PART IV COMPARATIVE ANALYSIS

Table of Cases

NATIONAL COURTS (CHRONOLOGICAL ORDER EXCEPT WHERE OTHERWISE SPECIFIED)

Austria

China

France

ADMINISTRATIVE COURT OF APPEAL (*COUR ADMINISTRATIVE D'APPEL*)

ADMINISTRATIVE COURT (TRIBUNAL ADMINISTRATIVE)

Greece

COUNCIL OF STATE

Italy

CONSTITUTIONAL COURT (*CORTE COSTITUZIONALE*)

Romania

HIGH COURT OF CASSATION AND JUSTICE (*CURŢI DE CASAŢIE ŞI JUSTIŢIE*)

COURT OF APPEAL (*CURTEA DE APEL*)

OTHER COURTS

Spain

CONSTITUTIONAL COURT (*TRIBUNAL CONSTITUCIONAL*)

SUPREME COURT (*TRIBUNAL SUPREMO*)

OTHER COURTS

Switzerland

SWISS FEDERAL COURT DECISIONS (*BUNDESGERICHT*)

USA (alphabetical order)

US Supreme Court

INTERNATIONAL COURTS (ALPHABETICAL ORDER)

European Court of Justice

European Court of Human Rights (ECtHR)

International Court of Justice (ICJ)

Table of Legislation

GERMANY

GREECE

ITALY

ROMANIA

SERBIA

SPAIN

SWITZERLAND

UNITED KINGDOM

VENEZUELA

INTERNATIONAL LEGISLATION

European Union

Other international legislation

List of Abbreviations

AC	Law Reports, Appeal Cases (Third Series)
Admin L Rev	Administrative Law Review
AE AO	*Anwendungserlass zur Abgabenordnung* (Administrative ruling on the execution of the taxation code) (Germany)
AG	Advocate General
AHG	Amtshaftungsgesetz (Austria)
AJCL	American Journal of Comparative Law
AJDA	Actualité juridique, droit administratif
All ER	All England Law Reports
Am Pol Sc Rev	American Political Science Review
Am Un L Rev	American University Law Review
AMF	*Autorité des marchés financiers (*financial markets authority) (France)
ANCOM	*Autoritatea Națională pentru Administrare și Reglementare în Comunicații* (National Authority for Administration and Regulations in Communications) (Romania)
AO	*Abgabenordnung (*procedural code for cases concerning taxation*)* (Germany)
APA	Administrative Procedure Act
ART	*Autorité de régulation des transports* (transport regulatory authority) (France)
ART	*Autorità di regolazione dei trasporti* (transport sector authority) (Italy)
art/arts	Article/s
AsylA	*Asylgesetz* (Federal Asylum Act) (Switzerland)
ATF	*Arrêts du Tribunal fédéral suiss* (Swiss Federal Court Decisions)
AVG	*Allgemeines Verwaltungsverfahrensgesetz* (General Administrative Procedure Act) (Austria)
B-VG	Bundes-Verfassungsgesetz, B-VG (Federal Constitutional Law) (Austria)
BAO	Bundesabgabenordnung (Federal Tax Law) (Austria)
BDG	Federal Act for Civil Servants (Austria)
BDiszG	*Bundesdisziplinargesetz* (Federal civil service) (Germany)
BeamtStG	*Beamtenstatusgesetz* (The fundamental law on the civil service) (Germany)
BGBl	Bundesgesetzblatt (Federal Law Gazette) (Austria)
C Env	*Code de l'environnement* (Environment Code) (France)
CAA	*Cour administrative d'appel* (Administrative Appeal Court) (France)
CADA	*Commission d'accès aux documents administratifs* (Commission for access to administrative documents) (France)
CE	Conseil d'Etat (Council of State) (France)

CE	*Constitución Española* (Spain)
CESEDA	Code for the entry and residence of foreigners and the right to asylum (France)
CFR	EU Charter of Fundamental Rights
CJEU	Court of Justice of the European Community
CGPPP	*Code général de la propriété des personnes publiques* (general code of property of public persons) (France)
Colum J Eur L	Colum J Eur L
Common L Rev	Common Law Review
concl	conclusions
Cons const	*Conseil Constitutionnel* (France)
Cornell L R	Cornell Law Review
CRBV	*Constitución de la República Bolivariana de Venezuela* (Constitution of the Bolivarian Republic of Venezuela)
CRPA	*Code des relations entre le public et l'administration* (Code of relations between the public and the administration) (France)
CSA	*Conseil supérieur de l'audiovisuel* (High audiovisual council) (France)
Cst	Constitution (Switzerland)
DDHC	Declaration of the Rights of Man and of the Citizen (France)
DJC-CADA	*Dispositions Juridiques Communes—Accès aux documents administratifs—Règles générales* (Common legal provisions—access to administrative documents—general rules) (France)
DPA	Data Protection Act (Switzerland)
EEA	European Economic Area
EBEP	*Estatuto Básico del Empleo Público* (Spain)
ECHR	European Convention on Human Rights
ECJ	European Court of Justice
ECtHR	European Court of Human Rights
ed(s)	editor(s)
edn	edition
eg	exampli gratia
EGO	Emergency Governmental Ordinance (Romania)
EGVG	Einführungsgesetz zu den Verwaltungsverfahrensgesetzen (Introductory Act to the Administrative Procedure Acts) (Austria)
EIA	Environmental Impact Assessment
EisbG	*Eisenbahngesetz* (Railroad Act) (Austria)
ERDAL	European Review of Digital Administration & Law
Eur Rev Public L	European Review of Public Law
ff	following
FinfraG	*Finanzmarktinfrastrukturgesetz* (Federal Act on Financial Market Infrastructures and Market Conduct in Securities and Derivatives Trading) (Switzerland)
FinStrG	*Finanzstrafgesetz* (Federal Tax Penal Law) (Austria)
FSA	*Autoritatea de Supraveghere Financiara*) (Financial Supervisory Authority (Romania)
GAJA	Grands arrêts de la Jurisprudence Administrative

GDPR	EU General Data Protection Regulation
GelverkG	*Gelegenheitsverkehrs-Gesetz* (Federal Act for public transport) (Austria)
GEO	Government Emergency Ordinance (Romania)
GewO	*Gewerbeordnung* (Trade, Commerce and Industry Regulation Act) (Austria)
GG	*Grundgesetz* (Germany)
Harvard L Rev	Harvard Law Review
ibid	ibidem
ie	that is
Indiana J Glob Leg St	Indiana Journal of Global Legal Studies
It J Publ L	Italian Journal of Public Law
KB	Law Reports, King's Bench Division
L	Law
L	*Loi*
LG	*Ley 50/1997, del Gobierno* (Spain)
LGAP	Law on General Administrative Procedure (Serbia)
LGBl	*Landesgesetzblatt* (Provincial Law Gazette) (Austria)
LGS	*Ley General de Subvenciones* (Spain)
LPAC	Act on General Administrative Procedure (*Ley del procedimiento administrativo común de las Administraciones Públicas*) (Spain)
LPF	Book of taxation procedures (*Livre des procédures fiscales*) (France)
LQR	Law Quarterly Review
LRJSP	*Ley 40/2015 del Régimen Jurídico del Sector Público* (Spain)
LTBG	*Ley 19/2013 de Transparencia, Acceso a la Información Pública y Buen Gobierno* (Spain)
LTBG	*Ley 19/2013 de Transparencia, Acceso a la Información Pública y Buen Gobierno* (Spain)
Maastricht J Eur & Comp L	Maastricht Journal of European and Comparative Law
Modern L Rev	Modern Law Review
No(s)	number(s)
NPC	National People's Congress (China)
Ofpra	*Office français de protection des réfugiés et apatrides* (Office for the protection of refugees and stateless persons) (France)
OJLS	Oxford Journal of Legal Studies
para(s)	paragraph(s)
Pol Sci Q P	Political Science Quarterly
PTSR	Public and Third Sector Law Reports
Public L	Public Law
QB	Law Reports, Queen's Bench
R	Règlement
RDLGS	Royal Decree 887/2006 (Spain)
Rec	Recueil des décisions du Conseil d'Etat
Rec	Recital (Austria)

Rev fr adm publ	Revue Française d'Administration Publique
Riv trim dir pub	Rivista trimestrale di diritto pubblico
Sect	*Section* (France)
SGB	*Sozialgesetzbuch—Verwaltungsverfahren* (Administrative procedure in social security matters) (Germany)
Stmk ROG	Steiermärkisches Raumordnungsgesetz (Styrian Regional Planning Act) (Austria)
TA	*Tribunal administrative* (Administrative Court) (France)
TEU	Treaty on the European Union
TFEU	Treaty on the Functioning of the European Union
Tulsa L Rev	Tulsa Law Review
UK	United Kingdom
UKSC	United Kingdom Supreme Court
Un Chicago L Rev	University of Chicago Law Review
US	United States
UVP-G	*Umweltverträglichkeitsprüfungsgesetz* (Environmental Impact Act) (Austria)
VfGH	*Verfassungsgerichtshof* (Austrian Constitutional Court)
VfSlg	*Ausgewählte Entscheidungen des Verfassungsgerichtshofes* (Selected Judgments of the Constitutional Court) (Austria)
Virginia L Rev	Virginia Law Review
vol	volume
VStG	*Verwaltungsstrafgesetz* (Administrative Penal Act) (Austria)
VwGH	*Verwaltungsgerichtshof* (Supreme Administrative High Court) (Austria)
VwGO	*Verwaltungsgerichtsordnung* (Laws on administrative procedure) (Germany)
VwGVG	*Bundesgesetz über das Verfahren der Verwaltungsgerichte* (Federal Act on Proceedings of Administrative Courts) (Austria)
VwVfG	*Verwaltungsverfahrensgesetz* (Federal law on administrative procedure) (Germany)
WLR	Weekly Law Reports
Yale L J	Yale Law Review

List of Contributors

Mads Andenas Professor of Law, University of Oslo (Norway) and Institute of Advanced Legal Studies, School of Advanced Study, University of London (United Kingdom)

Gordon Anthony Professor of Public Law, Queen's University Belfast (United Kingdom)

Jean-Bernard Auby Emeritus Professor of Public Law, Sciences Po Paris (France)

Nicola Berti Assistant Professor of Administrative Law, Faculty of Political and Social Sciences, Università Cattolica del Sacro Cuore di Milano (Italy)

Isaac Martín Delgado Professor of Administrative Law, University of Castilla-La Mancha (Spain)

Giacinto della Cananea Professor of Administrative Law, Bocconi University (Italy), and Principal Investigator of the CoCEAL project

Dacian-Cosmin Dragoş Jean Monnet Professor of Administrative and European Law, Babes Bolyai University (Romania)

Angela Ferrari Zumbini Professor of Administrative Law, University of Naples Federico II (Italy)

Alexandre Flückiger Professor of Public Law, University of Geneva (Switzerland)

Theodoros Fortsakis Professor Emeritus of Public Law, School of Law, National and Kapodistrian University of Athens (Greece)

Conor McCormick Senior Lecturer, School of Law, Queen's University Belfast (United Kingdom)

Marko Milenković Senior Research Fellow, Institute of Social Sciences Belgrade (Serbia), Jean Monnet Fellow, European University Institute (EUI) and Affiliated Research Fellow, Center for Constitutional Studies and Democratic Development (CCSDD), School of Advanced International Studies (SAIS), Bologna (Italy)

Flavia Pesci-Feltri Professor of Administrative Law, Faculty of Law and Political Sciences, University of Venezuela (Venezuela)

Sébastien Saunier Professeur agrégé des Facultés de Droit, Droit public, Université Toulouse Capitole (France)

Dian Schefold Emeritus Professor of Public Law, University of Bremen (Germany)

Mauro Silvestri Associate Professor of Administrative Law, University of Firenze (Italy)

Stefan Storr Professor of Public Law and Public Economic Law, Institute of Public Law and Political Science, University of Graz (Austria)

Xiaowei Sun Associate Professor of Public Law, Centre de Recherches Juridiques de Franche-Comté (CRJFC), Université de Franche-Comté (France)

Stefano Vaccari Associate Professor of Administrative Law, University of Milano-Bicocca (Italy)

PART I
GENERAL PRINCIPLES AND COMPARATIVE STUDIES

1
Introduction

Giacinto della Cananea

I. The object and nature of this book

The questions addressed in this book can be expressed as follows: a public authority[1] is granted the power to decide on specific matters, such as evaluating asylum applications or alleged staff rule violations, or defining a policy or rule, like setting new tariffs for public utilities. This public body derives its legal authority from two sources: firstly, the powers it exercises are established by legal rules and, secondly, they are assigned to it by authority, meaning that its decisions fall within its jurisdiction or area of competence. But the legal rules for this type of action do not encompass all the requirements for administrative action to be valid. For instance, they may not provide aggrieved individuals or social groups with a substantial opportunity to be heard before a final decision adversely affecting them is made. Considering that the right to be heard is acknowledged and protected in relation to other types of administrative activities, the question arises whether public authorities are generally required to uphold principles of procedural fairness and propriety, as well as of transparency, even in the absence of explicit requirements stipulated by legislative and regulatory provisions.

Certainly, the nature and extent of these duties of procedural fairness and propriety may, and often do, vary from one legal system to another, as does the level of scrutiny that courts and other public agencies—such as audit institutions or ombudsmen—exercise in the discharge of their administrative functions and powers. The questions that thus arise are: (i) Do general principles apply? (ii) If so, are they employed only to fill the gaps left by legislative and regulatory provisions, or do they have a foundational value, as some argue?[2] (iii) And if the administration violates a general principle, what are the consequences for the validity of administrative action? These are important issues in contemporary societies. As observed by Craig, 'legal systems have to decide on criteria for the applicability of procedural norms, and the content of procedural

[1] Although several academic works use the term 'administrative agency', we prefer the term 'public authority' for various reasons: (i) it is more widespread among European legal cultures; (ii) it has a legal foundation, particularly in national administrative procedure acts, as has been pointed out elsewhere (G della Cananea and L Parona, 'Administrative Procedure Acts in Europe: An Emerging Common Core?' (2023) AJCL forthcoming; (iii) it is often used by supranational legal orders, including the EU framework governing public procurements since Directives No 71/305, 77/62, and 92/50. For further remarks, see A von Bogdandy, 'Common Principles for a Plurality or Orders: A Study on Public Authority in the European Legal Area' (2015) 12 I-CON 980.

[2] A Stone Sweet and G della Cananea, 'Proportionality, General Principles of Law, and Investor-State Arbitration: A Response to Alvarez' (2014) 46(1) NYU JILP 911.

Giacinto della Cananea, *Introduction* In: *General Principles and Sector-Specific Rules in European Administrative Laws*. Edited by: Giacinto della Cananea and Jean-Bernard Auby, Oxford University Press.
DOI: 10.1093/oso/9780198867579.003.0001

protection if it is deemed to be applicable'.[3] They are, in particular, a matter of fundamental importance for any comparative analysis of administrative law.[4]

In the past, a (diminishingly relevant) strand of legal thought concentrated mainly on the nature of the courts and their proceedings rather than the impact of their decisions on administrative action. Consequently, excessive emphasis was placed on the differences between national systems, depending on whether justice was dispensed by ordinary or administrative courts. In contrast, scant attention was devoted to similarities. However, some similarities did exist. Interestingly, in his attack on French *droit administratif*, Albert Venn Dicey not only argued that some general ideas could be traced for distinguishing it from the law in England, but he also acknowledged some similarities between them. The main differences were, according to him, the existence of a special 'body of rules' regulating the relationship between the government and private citizens (unlike the 'laws which govern the relation of one private person to another') and the creation of special administrative courts in France and other countries of Continental Europe.[5] There were also some similarities however. On the one hand, certain characteristics of administrative functions and powers had emerged in previous periods of English history, principally before the Glorious Revolution.[6] On the other hand, when considering French *droit administratif* as it existed at the close of the nineteenth century, Dicey acknowledged that 'in the method of its formation it resemble[d] English law because it was essentially judge-made law'.[7] Accordingly, its precepts were not to be found in a code or other types of legislation, but they were based upon precedent.

It might have been both interesting and significant to delve further into the content of these precepts, exploring what the French refer to as *le fond du droit*. But this step was not taken, at least not systematically. Nevertheless, the few truly comparative studies conducted in subsequent decades highlighted significant similarities between the standards of administrative action that courts enforced on both sides of the English Channel. Hence, we began our comparative research by examining the judicial evolution of standards of conduct for public authorities between 1890 and 1910.[8] This research not only affirms the value of comparative analysis in gaining a better understanding of administrative laws,[9] but it has also highlighted that there exist not

[3] P Craig, 'The Human Rights Act, Article 6 and Procedural Rights' (2003) 58 Public L 753. See also P Strauss, *Administrative Justice in the US* (3rd edn, Carolina Academic Press 2016) 59 (same remark). On the distinction between process and substance, see G della Cananea, *Due Process of Law Beyond the State. Requirements of Administrative Procedure* (OUP 2016) 9.

[4] See F J Goodnow, 'Review of E. Laferrière, Traité de la juridiction administrative et des recours contentieux (Berger-Levrault, 1881)' (1889) 2 Pol Sci Q 709 ('one of the most important questions that the science of administrative law has to solve is how shall the administration be controlled in its action by judicial bodies'); P Craig, 'Judicial Review of Questions of Law: A Comparative Perspective' in S Rose-Akermann and P Lindseth (eds), *Comparative Administrative Law* (2nd edn, Elgar 2017) 449.

[5] A V Dicey, *Introduction to the Study of the Law of the Constitution* (McMillan 1884; 10th edn, 1954) 339.

[6] ibid 369.

[7] ibid 373.

[8] See G della Cananea and S Mannoni (eds), *Administrative Justice Fin de siècle. Early Judicial Standards of Conduct in Europe (1890–1910)* (OUP 2021). The main lines of the new comparative research are explained in G della Cananea and M Bussani, 'The Common Core of European Administrative Laws: A Framework for Analysis' (2019) 26 Maastricht J Eur & Comp L 217. See also the research's website: <www.coceal.it> accessed July 2023.

[9] See J Rivero, *Cours de droit administratif comparé* (Les cours de droit 1956–57) 5; E Schmidt-Aßmann and S Dagron, 'Les fondements comparés des systèmes de droit administratif français et allemand' (2008)

only numerous significant differences among European legal systems but also certain shared elements, including principles of legality and procedural fairness, forming a sort of common core across systems.[10]

This new book stems from our curiosity to delve deeper into the relationship between commonality and diversity and to understand whether, and to what extent, things have changed over the course of a century. Before embarking on the project, we formulated a conjecture and fine-tuned research methodology, which we discussed with several experts in the field. We conjecture that the shared elements and connections among European administrative laws, together with numerous and significant differences, extend beyond broad ideals such as justice or legality. They also encompass some specific procedural aspects related to administrative fairness and propriety, such as the right to be heard and the obligation to give reasons. To test our hypothesis, instead of simply collecting a series of national reports,[11] we adopted a 'factual' analysis approach, asking experts to discuss a series of hypothetical cases in order to compare their answers and seek to understand the underlying reasons, namely the various legal formants at play.

The chapter is divided into three sections. Section 2 explains why the relationship between general principles and sector-specific rules is an interesting terrain for comparative analysis. In Section 3, I will address some methodological issues, including the nature of our 'factual analysis' approach and the selection of legal systems for our comparative structure. I will also outline the overall structure of the book.

II. Background and issues

A. Principles *versus* rules: the nature of the distinction

To provide some context to the following remarks and make the discussion readily intelligible to a broader readership, it may be helpful to start by summarizing the outcome of five prominent cases that have already addressed the distinction under consideration in this discussion:

1. King's Bench, *James Bagg* (1615). James Bagg was a burgess in Plymouth. After criticizing the mayor and his fellow burgesses, he was removed from office. Seeking justice, Bagg turned to the courts. The King's Bench—led by Chief

127 Rev Fr Adm Publ 525; F Bignami, 'Comparative Administrative Law' in M Bussani and U Mattei (eds), *Comparative Law* (Cambridge UP 2012) 153; J S Bell, 'Comparative Administrative Law' in M Reimann and F Zimmermann (eds), *The Oxford Handbook of Comparative Law* (OUP 2006) 1259.

[10] On the concept of common core, see R B Schlesinger, 'Introduction' in R B Schlesinger (ed), *Formation of Contracts: A Study of the Common Core of Legal Systems* (Oceana 1968) 5; R B Schlesinger, 'The Common Core of Legal Systems: an Emerging Subject of Comparative Study' in K Nadelmann, A T von Mehren, and J N Hazard (eds), *Twentieth Century Comparative and Conflicts. Law, Legal Essays in Honor of Hessel E. Yntema* (Sijthoff 1961) 65 (observing that it gained plausibility from historical studies concerning the common roots of legal institutions).

[11] M Shapiro, *Courts. A Comparative and Political Analysis* (University of Berkeley Press 1981) vii (for whom too often 'comparison consists of presenting descriptions of a number of legal systems side by side, [...] with no particular end in view').

Justice Cook—affirmed its jurisdiction over the decisions of local bodies and found that Bagg's removal from office was unlawful and reinstated him. What is important in this case is not only the ruling itself but the court's reasoning. Firstly, Cook considered the public office of a burgess as a freehold and thus recognized the property in office. This was the basis of protection against arbitrary removal. Secondly, the removal was deemed arbitrary because it violated the law of the land, as established by the Magna Carta, as well as what later came to be recognized as one of the fundamental maxims of natural justice, later known as *audi alteram partem*. To support this point, Coke cited a line from Seneca's *Medea*: 'the man who judges, one side unheard, were hardly a just judge, though he judge justly'. In essence, depriving someone of office without granting them a hearing is considered unlawful.[12]

2. *Conseil d'État, Sieur Aramu* (1945). Gaston Aramu, like James Bagg, was a civil servant and held the position of police commissioner. However, following the liberation of France in 1944, he was stripped of office and pension as part of the legal purge known as '*épuration légale*'. This purge targeted public officers who had collaborated with the Vichy government and were accused of pro-German activities. In this case, the decision makers, a special commission, were not required to provide the individuals in question with access to the evidence against them. The *Conseil d'État* found this exercise of power to be wrong because it breached the unwritten general principle of law that no one may be subjected to punishment without having the opportunity to present their case beforehand. What matters, once again, is not only the principle itself but also the fact that, for the first time, the French administrative judge articulated the doctrine of the '*principes généraux du droit applicables même en l'absence de texte*'. The court annulled the contested decree.[13]
3. US Supreme Court, *Mathews v Eldridge* (1976). While the cases mentioned above concerned deprivation of office, *Mathews v Eldridge* regarded the withdrawal of benefits. Under the US social security-funded disability scheme, applicants not only had to show their inability to work but also to continue to show, presenting medical evidence, that their impairment was of such severity that they could carry on neither their previous occupation nor any other. The agency that managed the disability scheme could, however, arrange for an independent medical examination, resulting in an assessment that differed from that of the interested person. As a result, it informed the recipient that his benefits would end in a month's time. Instead of requesting reconsideration of the assessment,

[12] See Seneca's *Medea* (paras 190–202): 'He who decides an issue without hearing one side has not been just, however just the decision.' The original text, quoted by Coke, is the source of the maxim: '*Qui statuit aliquid parte inaudita altera, aequum licet statuerit, haud aequus fuerit*': see *The Reports of Sir Edward Coke* (The Lawbook Exchange 2002) II, 174. For further discussion of this case in light of natural justice, see P Craig, 'Natural Justice in UK Law: Continuity and Change from the 17th Century' in *Liber Amicorum Marco D'Alberti* (Giappichelli 2022) 9. See also, on the citation of Seneca's Medea (§§ 190–202), G della Cananea, *Due Process of Law Beyond the State* (n 3) 36.

[13] *Conseil d'Etat, Assemblée*, 26 October 1945, *Aramu*. For further details, see B Jeannaeu, *Les principes généraux du droit dans la jurisprudence administrative* (Sirey 1954) 124 (examining the precedents) and R Drago, 'The General Principles of Law in the Jurisprudence of the French Conseil d'Etat' (1964) 11 Am U L Rev 127.

the recipient brought an action, challenging the constitutionality of the procedures for terminating disability benefits under the Due Process Clause. Both the District Court and the Court of Appeals endorsed his claim. A few years after the celebrated *Goldberg v Kelly* ruling, the Supreme Court limited its effects, affirming that procedural due process of law must be evaluated using a balancing test that takes into account: i) the interest of the affected individual, ii) the interest of the government in limiting procedural burdens, and iii) the risk of error in redefining benefits, as well as the additional procedural burden, which would help reduce this risk. In other words, due process requirements depend on the nature of the interest at stake and the weight of that interest, balanced against the opposing government interests. This implies that applying these standards depends heavily on the facts of each case.[14]

4. European Court of Justice, *Transocean Marine Paint Association v Commission* (1974).[15] This case differs from the previous ones in more than one respect. Firstly, the issue at hand involves the alleged violation of the right to be heard, specifically in relation to an action taken by a supranational authority rather than a national one, namely the European Commission (EC), in relation to a specific firm. When the firm applied to renew an exemption from competition rules, the Commission complied but with some limitations, which, according to the applicant, adversely affected its interests without affording it an opportunity to be heard. On the other hand, the complexity of finding a solution was heightened by the fact that the doctrine developed by the European Court of Justice (ECJ) refers to general principles that are also 'common to the legal orders of the member States'. Before the ECJ deliberated on the case, Advocate General Jean-Pierre Werner observed that

> there is a rule embedded in the law of some of our countries that an administrative authority, before wielding a statutory power to the detriment of a particular person, must in general hear what that person has to say about the matter, even if the statute does not expressly require it. '*Audi alteram partem*'. [. . .] I say that the rule applies in general because it is subject to exceptions, as are most legal principles.[16]

He went on to analyse the laws of the Member States and found that the same general principle existed there too, albeit under a different name.[17] The Court followed the Advocate General. Not only did it affirm that, 'notwithstanding

[14] US Supreme Court, *Mathews v Eldridge* 424 US 319 (1976). Furthermore, it is worth noting the dissenting opinion of Justice Brennan, who argued that Eldridge should be entitled to an evidentiary hearing of the same nature as that required for beneficiaries before their benefits are terminated, as established by *Goldberg v Kelly*, 397 US 254 (1970). For further analysis, see J L Mashaw, 'The Supreme Court's Due Process Calculus for Administrative Adjudication: In Search of a Theory of Value' (1976) 44 Un Chicago L Rev 26 and *Due Process in the Administrative State* (Yale UP 1985) 22 (discussing the growth of due process litigation). See also M D Bayles, *Procedural Justice: Allocating to Individuals* (Law and Philosophy Library 1990)(discussing more generally how procedural requirements confine discretion).

[15] Case 17/74 *Transocean Marine Paint Association v Commission* [1974] ECR 1063.

[16] ibid Opinion of AG Warner, delivered on 19 September 1974.

[17] ibid Opinion of AG Warner, delivered on 19 September 1974.

the cases specifically dealt with' the Regulation applied 'the general rule that a person whose interests are perceptibly affected by a decision taken by a public authority must be given the opportunity to make his point of view known', but it also added that the undertaking 'must be informed in good time of the essence' of the measures that might affect its interests.[18]

5. European Court of Human Rights, *Taskin and others v Turkey* (2004). Unlike the previous cases, which focus on decisions adversely affecting individuals or firms, *Taskin*[19] goes beyond administrative adjudication in two ways. Firstly, it concerns the consequences on a social group, specifically a local community, of issuing a permit to exploit a gold mine. Secondly, it addresses the broader environmental impact resulting from the permit. Only after the initial operating permit had been granted (for a duration of ten years) did the competent administration initiate the procedure for preparing an environmental impact report as mandated by national legislation. Although the report pointed out several critical aspects, the government decided to issue a permit to operate the gold mine. The court challenged the permit, and the Supreme Administrative Court eventually quashed the contested decision. Although national legislation stipulated that the Court's ruling would result in suspending execution of the decision, this provision was not enforced and, as a result, allowed operations to commence, with significant consequences for both human lives and the environment. A claim was brought before the European Court of Human Rights (ECtHR) in Strasbourg, which determined that Turkey had failed to fulfil its obligation under the European Convention on Human Rights (ECHR) with regard to both Article 8, protecting the right to family life, and Article 6, due to failure to comply with the judgment of the administrative court in a reasonable time.[20] The court thus awarded the applicants damages.

It should be evident that general principles played a significant role in all these cases. Sometimes they were derived from constitutional provisions, such as the Due Process Clause of the US Constitution; more often, they arose as unwritten doctrinal constructions that became institutionalized as case law. The most important principles thus materialized in judicial decisions. Higher jurisdictions, such as the English House of Lords and the French *Conseil d'Etat*, applied the principles as unquestioned constituent elements inherent to their legal systems. The role of particular legal doctrines, such as natural justice in the UK and the '*principes généraux de droit sans texte formel*' in France, can only be adequately assessed within such a framework. The case-by-case development of principles was by no means confined to these legal systems, as similar trends emerged in other parts of Europe, including Austria, Germany, and Italy.[21] Since 1950, the ECJ has largely drawn from those legal systems. We can infer from these developments that the problem of resolving disputes on the

[18] ibid para 15.
[19] *Taskin and others v Turkey* App no 46117/99 (ECtHR, 10 November 2004).
[20] ibid paras 126 and 137.
[21] See G della Cananea and S Mannoni (eds), *Administrative Justice Fin de siècle. Early Judicial Standards of Administrative Conduct in Europe (1890–1910)* (OUP 2021).

basis of general principles is not confined to the legal relations that exist within a given municipal system but is universal. Such problem has an even greater significance beyond the state, because legislation is less extended. The EC/EU is partially an exception. However, the ECJ has elaborated a body of general principles of administrative law, including legality, due process, and proportionality. In this respect, it may be helpful to consider once more the opinion of AG Warner in *Transocean Marine Paint Association*, where he observed that:

> In the law of England the [*audi alteram partem*] rule is centuries old, firmly established and of daily application. It is considered to be a 'rule of natural justice', a somewhat flamboyant and sometimes criticized phrase, embodying a concept akin to what is, in French-speaking countries, more soberly and, I think, more accurately, referred to as 'les principes généraux du droit'. [. . .] The most often cited expression of the rule is in the judgment of Byles J. in *Cooper v. Wandsworth Board of Works* (1863), where he said that 'although there are no positive words in a statute requiring that the party shall be heard, yet the justice of the common law will supply the omission of the legislature'. In England today there is no scope for controversy about the existence of the rule, but only about the circumstances in which it may be held inapplicable and about the manner in which it is to be applied in particular instances. [. . .] In French administrative law [. . .] it matters little whether the applicable rule is subsumed under the title '*audi alteram partem*' or [. . .] under the concept of the 'droits de la défense'. What is undoubted is that French administrative law does acknowledge the existence of these 'principes généraux du droit' [. . .] which are applicable even in the absence of any specific legislative provision.[22]

His approach shows five points of general interest. The first concerns the term 'general principles of law'. Although other terms such as 'general rules' or 'standards' were sometimes used, it should be evident that the courts referred to principles and conceived them as norms, distinguishing them from ethical precepts or political guidelines. As such, general principles have a broad scope of application, unlike sector-specific rules applicable to a certain issue or sector and their relevance and significance is not hindered by the fact they are unwritten principles. As observed by George Vedel, unwritten principles have an increasing importance in public law.[23]

The second point is that general principles have a variety of functions. Around a century ago, a strand of legal thought (whose significance would diminish over time) held that judges could rely on unwritten principles only when written rules were either absent or ambiguous: ie when there was a gap, which had to be filled.[24] The underlying

[22] Opinion of AG Warner (n 16).

[23] G Vedel, 'Les règles et principes non écrits en droit public. Réflexions finales' in *Actes du colloque organisé par l'Université de Paris II et l'*AFDC (Éditions Panthéon-Assas 2000) 254. See also F Delpérée, 'La place des principes non écrits dans les avis et les decisions des Conseils d'État' (1999) 52 Revue admin 122 (returning to Vedel's remark that referring to unwritten principles obviates to their lack of solemnity) and C Perelman, *Logique juridique. Nouvelle rhétorique* (Dalloz 1978)(observing that, below legislation, there is a substratum of general principles of law).

[24] See C Perelman (ed), *Le problème des lacunes en droit* (Bruylant 1968) and L Siorat, *Le problème des lacunes en droit international (contribution à l'étude des sources du droit et de la function juridictionnelle)* (LGDJ 1959) 63 (distinguishing a lacuna from a doubtful provision).

assumption was that only legislatures were capable of making laws. However, this vision was too narrow. Both national and international courts have used general principles to address 'hard cases', which arise when existing rules are either obsolete or likely to result in morally and socially unacceptable outcomes.[25] Accordingly, more recent scholarship emphasizes that general principles are 'foundational', as they embody the fundamental values upon which modern legal systems are built.[26] We will return to this point in the next section, exploring the different types of relationship that exist between principles and rules.

A third point of general interest regards both the scope of principles and their effects. Some years ago, legal theorists debated the 'logical' distinction between principles and rules. For example, even for positivists such as Hart, variable standards have 'a fringe of open texture',[27] while Dworkin argued that, while rules have an all-or-nothing character, principles have an undetermined scope of application,[28] and Alexy objected that even principles have exceptions.[29] This is, of course, an important debate, and much may be learnt from it. However, for our purposes, Warner's pragmatic approach well captures the essence of the issue: the discussion about general principles does not regard so much their existence but the circumstances in which a certain principle may be considered inapplicable, on the one hand, and the manner in which it is to be applied in particular instances, on the other. From the first perspective, for example, the principle of proportionality is said to be applicable whenever a balance must be struck between competing rights, with the notable exception of cases concerning human dignity, considered an absolute right. From the second perspective, although public authorities are increasingly required to give reasons for decisions with negative effects on individuals, there is ongoing debate as to whether reasons may be given only partially or to the court alone should a public interest so require—eg in cases involving national security.

Fourthly, all the five cases mentioned earlier clearly show that general principles are among the norms with which courts ensure compliance. Accordingly, legal consequences follow from any deviation from general principles, such as due process. They are normally discussed under the heading of 'annullability', meaning that administrative acts not compliant with those principles will be invalidated. In some legal systems there is, however, a distinction between mandatory and directory norms. This distinction does not impinge on the legal significance of norms but on their consequences from the point of view of validity. Although all breaches of procedural requirements are legally significant, only some will result in annullability (or even nullity). In contrast, others will result in an 'irregularity', namely a defect or weakness that does not

[25] See R Dworkin, *Taking Rights Seriously* (Harvard UP 1977) and A Barak, *The Judge in a Democracy* (Princeton UP 2009).

[26] See H Kelsen, *Principles of International Law* (1948; The Lawbook Exchange 2003), VI (for whom 'principles . . . are the most important norms') and W Lorenz, 'General Principles of Law: Their Elaboration in the Court of Justice of the European Communities' (1964) 13 AJCL 1, at 3 (for whom 'experience has proved that such principles may turn out to be practically the most important').

[27] H L A Hart, *The Concept of Law* (2nd edn, Clarendon Press 1994) 132.

[28] See Dworkin (n 25) 24 (arguing that 'the difference between legal principles and legal rules is a logical distinction').

[29] R Alexy, 'On the Structure of Legal Principles' (2000) 13 Ratio Juris 294.

undermine the act's validity and can thus be remedied by the public authority that adopted it. The German Administrative Procedure Act (APA) of 1976 is grounded in this idea, which is also not alien to the Italian legal system, as well as to others.[30]

Fifthly, and finally, the fourth and last cases share both common and distinctive features. The common features revolve around the fact that both cases are adjudicated by supranational courts, established through treaties in which the Member States agree to limit their sovereignty by accepting the jurisdiction of such courts in accordance with those treaties. There are also two important distinctions. On the one hand, while both the ECJ and the ECtHR have comprehensive jurisdiction to settle disputes concerning the exercise of power by Member States, the former also defines the powers of common institutions, thus 'taking the form of an administrative court'.[31] On the other hand, although the Treaty of Paris (1952) did not include a provision similar to Article 38 (1)(c) of the Statute of the International Court of Justice, which refers to the 'general principles of law recognized by civilized nations',[32] the ECJ drew extensively from national legal systems. Following the Treaty of Rome (1957), it exercised its legislative power through two general provisions, one empowering the Court to ensure adherence to the 'law' in the interpretation and implementation of the treaties, and the other establishing that the grounds for judicial review included compliance with any 'rule of law' relating to the treaties. There was also a more specific clause concerning the non-contractual liability of EC institutions and their employees in the execution of their duties. In this regard, the Court was called upon to adjudicate in accordance with 'the general principles common to the laws of the member States' in order to provide compensation for any damage caused to third parties. This reinforced the Court's tendency to use the comparative method already employed in tracing both procedural and substantive principles of administrative law, such as legal certainty and the annulment of unlawful acts.[33]

B. Principles *and* rules: a complex relationship

After clarifying the distinction between general principles and sector-specific rules, it must be added that the relevance and significance of general principles extend beyond

[30] In the German APA, Articles 46 and 47 regulate the consequences of defects in procedure and form and the conversion of a defective administrative act, respectively. According to Article 46, the infringement of procedural rules does not give rise to annulment 'where it is evident that the decision has not infringed the decision on the matter'. Likewise, in the Italian APA, Article 21-octies (2) excludes the annulment of administrative acts 'if it is evident that the provisions it contains could not have been other than those actually adopted'.

[31] W Lorenz, 'General Principles of Law: Their Elaboration in the Court of Justice of the European Communities' (1964) 13 AJCL 5.

[32] For a recent appraisal, see M Andenas, M Fitzmaurice, L Chiussi, A Tanzi, and J Wouters, 'General Principles and the Coherence of International Law: Setting the Scene' in M Andenas, M Fitzmaurice, L Chiussi, A Tanzi, and J Wouters (eds), *General Principles and the Coherence of International Law* (Brill 2019) 1 (raising the issue whether general principles 'are about filling gaps, or much more'); C Redgwell, 'General Principles of International Law' in S Vogenauer and S Weatherhill (eds), *General Principles of Law. European and Comparative Perspectives* (Bloomsbury 2017) 21 (accepting the approach for deriving principles bases on the 'representative legal system' approach).

[33] See Lorenz (n 31) and T Tridimas, *General Principles of EU Law* (OUP 2008).

the traditional conflict-of-laws approach.[34] There are several ways in which a legal system can shape the relationship between general principles and sector-specific rules. Firstly, a specific rule may be considered to be an application of the general rule in a given circumstance.[35] Thus, for example, the rule established by the EU with regard to antitrust procedures requires the Commission to provide 'undertakings [with] the opportunity to be heard',[36] in full coherence with Article 41 (2)(a) of the Union's Charter of Fundamental Rights, which recognizes and protects 'the right of every person to be heard, before any individual measure which would affect him or her adversely is taken'. Secondly, and alternatively, the specific rule may be regarded as an exception to the general principle. This situation arises when there is a conflict between the general and the particular precepts, and when a higher norm, such as a constitutional provision, establishes that the latter takes precedence over the former. The exclusion is normally regarded as a consequence of the *lex specialis* principle (more precisely, *lex specialis derogat legi generali*), which in some legal systems constitutes also an exception to the preference for the rule enacted later. Thirdly, the general rule can be considered to establish a sort of baseline above which particular rules may define other standards, which may be more favourable to private individuals, for example.

Of these three types of relationships, the second is one that lawyers more frequently take into account since the *lex specialis* maxim, together with the hierarchical criterion, serves to resolve conflicts between norms. This maxim originated in Roman law and has since become an established principle of legal reasoning in domestic law. As far as the regulation of administrative procedure is concerned, an interesting example is the Finnish Administrative Procedure Act, which provides that 'if another act contains provisions that deviate from those in this Act, the provisions of the other act shall prevail over those of this Act'.[37] Since subsequent legislation would prevail over the APA based on another general criterion, that of *lex posterior*, it can be inferred that the criterion established in Article 5 is that of *lex specialis*.

The exclusion can, however, operate in the opposite way if a higher norm stipulates that a certain matter must be exclusively governed by general principles. A slightly different circumstance occurs when the higher norms refer to general norms, meaning that they apply to all interested natural and legal persons. Thus, for example, the Italian Constitution provides that the legislature 'may introduce general provisions for the disclosure of financial sources of periodical publications'.[38] Similarly, the New York Constitution prohibits passing private or local bills in a series of cases, including regulating the interest rate on money and the opening and conducting of elections.[39]

A different type of relationship arises when a particular rule applies the general principle in a specific circumstance. In this case, the former defines the requirements of the latter in the given circumstance. For instance, if the general principle states

[34] In continental Europe, legal scholarship has elaborated the concept of 'antinomies': see C Huberlant, 'Antonomies et recours au principes généraux' (1964) 18 Dialectica 204.

[35] See Dworkin (n 25) 27 (noting that a legal system may prefer a rule supported by principles).

[36] EU Regulation No 1/2003, art 27 (1).

[37] Finnish APA of 2003, as modified in 2015, § 5 (1).

[38] Italian Const, art 21. For further analysis, see M Cartabia and N Lupo, *The Constitution of Italy. A Contextual Analysis* (Hart 2022) 229.

[39] NY Const, art III, § 17.

that all persons adversely affected by a certain administrative activity are entitled to be heard before the final decision is taken, the rule governing disciplinary procedures may, and generally does, allow them to be assisted by an expert, eg a trade union representative.

There is yet another type of relationship where general principles complement sector-specific norms. We might recall that this issue had already arisen in the civil codes of the early nineteenth century. Thus, in response to what many citizens and lawyers perceived as the arbitrary conduct of the old tribunals (*parlements*), the French Civil Code not only prohibited denial of justice but also prescribed penalties in this case. Consequently, judges had to administer justice even when the law was either deficient or unclear in this regard.[40] The 1811 Austrian Civil Code adopted another method. It recognized the importance of the similarity of cases decided according to the law and the 'tenets of similar laws'. However, it took care to prevent *non-liquet* by providing that, in a 'doubtful case', the judicial decision should be made in accordance with the 'principles of natural law'.[41] These principles served as a supplementary source of norms, as only positive rules could be interpreted by analogy. Nonetheless, the coexistence of two normative sources, positive law and natural law, ensured a dialectical relationship.[42] The Croatian Administrative Procedure Act (2009) also establishes a similar dialectical relationship between general and sector-specific rules. According to Article 3 (a), it is precisely because the APA contains general legislation that it 'shall apply in proceedings in all administrative matters'. The Act allows 'individual issues of administrative procedure' to be regulated differently if two conditions are respected, namely that it is necessary and is not 'in violation of the basic provisions and the purpose of this Act'.

Finally, general principles may furnish a sort of baseline without preventing sector-specific rules from providing higher standards of protection. Thus, for example, the Italian APA recognizes that regional legislation may contain different provisions. However, it clarifies that they 'may not establish lesser guarantees than those ensured for private parties' by those established by the APA with regard to citizens' participation in administrative procedures and access to files. They may, instead, 'provide for higher levels of protection'.[43]

The questions that arise encompass the following: (i) Is there any constitutional provision laying down either variable or invariable standards concerning the discharge of administrative functions and powers? (ii) Regardless of whether there is a legislative provision authorizing them to do so, do the courts rely on general principles if there

[40] French Civil Code (1801), art 4 (providing that 'judges who refuse to decide a case on the pretext of silence, obscurity or insufficiency of the law are liable to be prosecuted for a denial of justice').

[41] Austrian Civil Code (1811), art 7 ('If the case still remains in doubt, it shall be decided according to the *principles of natural law*, taking into careful consideration all the circumstances of the case') (emphasis added). See also the Egyptian Civil Code, art 1(2) (referring to 'Muslim law' and natural law).

[42] See the Portuguese Civil Code (1867), art 16 (establishing that if doubts persist, 'regard shall be had to the principles of natural law'), and the Colombian Civil Code (1887), art 32 (referring to the '*natural equity*') (emphasis added). For a survey of less recent provisions, see B Cheng, *General Principles of Law as Applied by International Courts* (1953, Cambridge UP 2006) Appendix 2.

[43] Italian Administrative Procedure Act (1990), as amended in 2005, art 29 (2-*ter*). For further remarks, see D Sorace, 'Administrative Law' in J S Lena and U Mattei (eds), *Introduction to Italian Law* (Kluwer 2002) 125.

are gaps in the written law? (iii) Do they do so also when the law is obscure or obsolete? (iv) And, if so, do they generalize existing rules, or do they use unwritten general principles?

C. Do 'codes' (of administrative procedure) actually make a difference?

A further question requires separate treatment. It concerns the role of legislation in administrative law. Although previous works within our historical and comparative enquiry have shown the importance of judge-made law, especially with regard to general principles, a caveat is necessary about court-centred legal analysis, focusing mainly—if not only—on courts and the processes of judicial law-making.[44] It is precisely for this reason that some of the examples discussed above refer to one type of general legislation on administrative procedure or another. Although they are frequently called 'codes of administrative procedure', this term is not entirely satisfactory. On the one hand, administrative procedure legislation is highly differentiated since it includes both statutes with few provisions of a general nature and others with hundreds of detailed ones. On the other hand, neither the latter nor, more significantly, the former possess a structure comparable to the systematic architecture typically found in civil and criminal codes. With this caveat in mind, one question requires particular consideration: Does the existence of general legislation on administrative procedure make a difference?

In this regard, it is worth noting that general legislation on administrative procedure has become increasingly common over the years. It first emerged in Austria and other countries in Central Europe, followed by the United States, and eventually in almost all regions of Europe. It is important to mention, however, that not only Britain and Ireland but also Belgium still do not have legislation of this kind in place. On the contrary, all countries previously under Soviet rule have adopted some kind of code of administrative procedure. In a few legal systems, alongside general legislation enacted by national institutions, there are also rules developed by sub-national authorities, such as the German Länder, the Italian regions, and the Spanish autonomous communities, and there are instances where national legislation has been implemented by state or regional legislation, as in the case of Italy.

On the other hand, there are situations where sub-national rules existed before the national legislation was enacted. For example, in the United States, California adopted its Administrative Procedure Act in 1945, before the Federal APA came into force in

[44] See E A Purcell, 'Paradoxes of Court-Centered Legal History: Some Values of Historical Understanding for a Practical Legal Education' (2014) 64 J Legal Educ 229, at 234. See also J Beerman, 'Common Law and Statute Law in Administrative Law' (2011) 63 Adm Law Rev 1 (pointing out the 'largely statutory appearance of U.S. Administrative Law', with specific regard to the Federal APA), and S Cassese, *Le basi del diritto amministrativo* (6th edn, Garzanti 2000) 80 (pointing out the growth of legislation concerning administrative functions and powers in modern legal systems), and P Badura and others, *Besonderes Verwaltungsrecht: Herausgegeben Ingo von Munch* (De Gruyter 1979) (showing the growth of sector-specific administrative rules).

1946.[45] The development of the various types of procedural norms represents a significant investment of expertise, power, and resources to achieve more predictable and potentially more efficient administrative behaviour. However, the empirical evidence regarding the actual impact of general legislation on administrative procedure to date has been relatively limited. For instance, there seems to be an apparent paradox, as the Austrian legislation of 1925 was overlooked in Germany. Similarly, the procedural requirements set forth in Scandinavian legislation have seldom been examined systematically.

The increasing adoption of general legislation regarding administrative procedure raises two related but distinct questions. The first concerns its effectiveness. It is not uncommon to read that administrative procedure legislation is sometimes no more than a rhetorical exercise or a public relations stunt. In the past, especially under authoritarian governments, codes were not only ineffective but could actually reduce the administration's credibility still further in the eyes of the general public. Others view administrative procedure legislation as having greater potential, at least because the courts can use it to handle future disputes that cannot be solved based on sector-specific rules. Even though administrative procedure legislation may be vague concerning a certain issue, it can offer guidance for situations and questions that might, at best, be only vaguely anticipated at the time of enactment. Of course, enforcement mechanisms can, and often do, make a difference. As Auby notes, the crucial question is, therefore, whether general legislation on administrative procedure has a tangible impact within the legal systems where it is implemented.[46]

The question also has a comparative aspect, namely, whether the existence of general legislation on administrative procedure actually leads to distinctions between European legal systems. In this respect, it is not enough to acknowledge that one legal system has adopted such legislation while another has not. Further research is necessary before it will be possible to reach a firm conclusion regarding the actual impact of this regulation and the conditions under which it operates. For example, one legal system without general legislation on administrative procedure may have implemented several sector-specific codes containing very similar provisions, if not identical to, those of another. Additionally, its courts may have developed and elaborated general principles of legality, due process, and proportionality that produce outcomes similar to those established by legislation elsewhere.

Last but not least, the importance of international treaties must not be overlooked. Article 6 ECHR is of fundamental importance in this respect because it imposes a duty to provide a hearing when 'civil rights and obligations' are at stake. While early interpretations tended to exclude public law disputes, Article 6 has been found to be applicable to administrative matters such as issuing licences for serving alcoholic beverages and permissions for building work in more recent cases.[47] For example, in the

[45] M Asimow, 'The Influence of the Federal Administrative Procedure Act on California's New Administrative Procedure Act' (1990) 32 Tulsa L Rev 297.

[46] For this remark, see J-B Auby, 'General Report' in J-B Auby (ed), *Codification of Administrative Procedure* (Bruylant 2014) 27 ('Living without a GAPA').

[47] See, respectively, *Sporrong and Lönnroth v Sweden* App nos 7151 and 7152/75 (ECtHR, judgment of 23 September 1982) and *Microintelect Ood v Bulgaria* App no 34129/03 (ECtHR, judgment of 4 March 2014).

jurisprudence of the ECHR, this requirement is not satisfied if the court or tribunal is biased or is not independent of political power.[48] Similarly, EU law sets demanding standards regarding judicial independence[49] and due process of law.

Another interesting example is the Aarhus Convention, which acknowledges the importance of access to information and public participation in environmental decision-making.[50] It requires that 'the public be informed [...] early in an environmental decision-making procedure, and in an adequate, timely and effective manner' and in such a way as to allow the public to submit comments and evidence concerning the proposed activity. All this suggests that living without a code may not necessarily make a difference.

III. In search of the 'common core'

The remainder of this chapter is structured as follows. Firstly, we examine the relationship between commonality and diversity. Then we outline the nature of our comparative exercise, which is a 'factual analysis'. The chapter concludes with a discussion of how the legal systems in question were selected.

A. A common core research

For several decades, comparative studies have often emphasized either commonality or diversity. For example, Dicey was aware that

> a comparison between the administrative law of France and our English rule of law, if taken from the right point of view suggests some interesting points of likeness, no less than of unlikeness.[51]

[48] *Ringeisen v Austria* App no 2614/65 (ECtHR, judgment of 16 July 1971) (rejecting the claim that a regional commission did not satisfy the requirement); *Benthem v Netherlands* App no 8848/80 (ECtHR, judgment of 23 October 1985) (endorsing the applicant's claim, which led to a change in Dutch administrative law). For further analysis, see P Craig, 'The HRA, Article 6 and Procedural Rights' (2003) 48 Public L 753.

[49] Case C-286/12, *Commission v Hungary* [2012] ECLI:EU:C:2012:687 para 80 (endorsing the Commission's view that Hungarian legislation establishing the early retirement of judges infringed the principle of proportionality). For further remarks, see G Halmai, 'The Early Retirement Age of the Hungarian Judges' in F Nicola and B Davies (eds), *EU Law Stories* (Cambridge UP 2017) 471. See also the more recent judgment of the Grand Chamber of the ECJ, Joined Cases C-585/18, C-624/18, and C-625/18, *A.K. and others v Sad Najwzszy* [2019] and, for further comments, M Ziolkowski, 'Two Faces of the Polish Supreme Court after Reforms of the Judiciary Systems in Poland: The Question of Judicial Independence' (2020) 5 European Papers 347 (observing that while a first judgment of the Polish Supreme Court sought to fully enforce the ruling of the ECJ, another limited its impact).

[50] Convention on access to information, public participation in decision-making and access to justice in environmental matters, signed at Aarhus, Denmark on 25 June 1998, arts 4 and 6. See M Lee and C Abbot, 'The Usual Suspects? Public Participation under the Aarhus Convention' (2003) 66 Modern L Rev 80; A K Mangold, 'The Persistence of National Peculiarities: Translating Representative Environmental Action from Transnational into German Law' (2014) 21 Indiana J Glob Leg St 223 (pointing out the difficulties that arise within some national legal systems).

[51] Dicey (n 5) 369.

However, he emphasized the contrast between England and France, holding that *droit administratif* had no equivalent in the common law world. For him, it was 'in its content utterly unlike any branch of modern English law'.[52] In the same years, the scholar considered to be the founder of German administrative law, Otto Mayer, pointed out the strong influence of French administrative law either indirectly, when it was adapted to the realities of the host state, or directly, when it was simply copied ('*simplement copié*').[53] In sum, the two approaches emphasized diversity and commonality, respectively.

Our intention in this book is not to assert that any of those approaches was inherently right or wrong. Rather, we argue that any approach that solely highlights analogies or differences is questionable from both the descriptive and normative perspectives. Descriptively, there is a significant risk that only the legal realities that align with the chosen perspective are examined.[54] The normative validity of any approach that emphasizes only commonality or diversity is equally flawed. On the one hand, supranational courts have acknowledged the importance of national traditions within certain limits. For instance, the Court of Justice of the EU has referred to national procedural autonomy.[55] The ECtHR has frequently invoked the concept of the margin of appreciation when dealing with 'hard' cases. On the other hand, rights are safeguarded not only by the ECHR but also by 'common constitutional traditions', to borrow the phrase elaborated by the ECJ and subsequently codified by EU treaties.[56] Accordingly, an accurate comparative analysis must consider both commonality and diversity[57] and seek to explain their origins.

B. A 'factual' analysis

Some consideration must be given to both the research methodology and the questions themselves. The research is part of a wider project focused on analysing the

[52] ibid 373.

[53] See O Mayer, *Deutsches Verwaltungsrecht* (1894), French translation by the author, *Le droit administratif allemand* (Giard et Brière 1903–1906) 12. See also the review of Mayer's treatise by E Freund (1906) 1 Am Pol Sc Rev 136 (observing that it was 'primarily an attempt to construct a scientific system', rather than a description of the law) and, on Mayer's role, E Forsthoff, *Lehrbuch des Verwaltungsrecht* (1966), French translation by M Fromont, *Traité de droit administratif allemand* (Bruylant 1969) 91 (distinguishing two phases: before and after Mayer).

[54] For similar remarks, see M Adams and J Griffiths, 'Against "Comparative Method": Explaining Similarities and Differences' in M Adams and J Bomhoff (eds), *Practice and Theory in Comparative Law* (Cambridge UP 2012) 279.

[55] For further analysis, see D U Galetta, *Procedural Autonomy of EU Member States: Paradise Lost?* (Springer 2014).

[56] Article 6 (3) TEU provides that: 'Fundamental rights, as guaranteed by the European Convention for the Protection of Human Rights and Fundamental Freedoms and as they result from the constitutional traditions common to the Member States, shall constitute general principles of the Union's law.' For further analysis, see S Cassese, 'The "Constitutional Traditions Common to the Member States" of the European Union' (2017) 66 Riv trim dir pubb 943. The Court's elaboration of this phrase is illustrated by M Graziadei and R De Caria, 'The "Constitutional Traditions Common to the Member States of the European Union" in the Case-Law of the European Court of Justice: Judicial Dialogue at its Finest' (2017) 66 Riv trim dir pubb 949.

[57] See P Craig, 'Comparative Administrative Law and Political Structure' (2017) 37 OJLS 947.

'common core' of European administrative laws. The methodology employed in this research is consistent with that used in three previous books in this series.[58] There will be no attempt, therefore, to proceed from general moral propositions, *à la* Fuller.[59] Nor will there be an attempt to establish that, as all European legal systems—with the exception of the Russian Federation, after 2022—are included within the Council of Europe and many of them are bound by closer integration within the EU, and both these organizations are founded on the respect for the rule of law and fundamental rights, then all those legal systems should ensure the respect of certain general standards of administrative conduct. Quite the contrary, our assumption is that all those legal systems have to decide on the conceptual foundation for certain problems concerning public bodies or, more precisely, the discharge of administrative functions and powers, but the solutions may, and sometimes do, differ. Only experience can show, for example, whether all legal systems establish a general requirement to give reasons or exclude any general cloak of immunity for actions damaging individuals and firms. In short, what follows is an attempt to examine legal realities by experimental work.

Specifically, we formulated hypothetical cases and consulted leading public lawyers from each legal order to provide insights into how these cases would probably be resolved in their system after ascertaining that they would be relevant to all of them.[60] Thus, we can consider this to be a 'factual' analysis, drawing inspiration from the comparative inquiry developed and conducted by Schlesinger in the 1960s. The aim is to identify both the shared and distinctive elements of the legal institutions within a group of states. Its primary characteristic was precisely this: rather than seeking to describe the specific legal institutions, the focus was on understanding how a particular set of problems would be addressed within the selected legal systems. The problems therefore 'had to be stated in factual terms'.[61] In practice, this implied that, using the materials concerning various legal systems, Schlesinger and his colleagues formulated hypothetical cases to see how they would be resolved in each of the selected legal systems. Interestingly, it turned out that these hypothetical cases were formulated in terms that were comprehensible in all those legal systems. The validity of this

[58] G della Cananea and R Caranta (eds), *Tort Liability of Public Authorities in European Laws* (OUP 2020); G della Cananea and M Andenas (eds), *Judicial Review of Administration in Europe. Procedural Fairness and Propriety* (OUP 2021); M Conticelli and T Perroud (eds), *Procedural Requirements for Administrative Limits to Property Rights* (OUP 2022).

[59] See L L Fuller, *The Morality of Law* (2nd edn, Yale UP 1969) 39 (discussing various ways that make the law fail, in the sense that without the requirements discussed, the result is not simply that there is a 'bad system of law' but, rather, 'something that is not properly called a legal system at all'). See also J Boyle, 'Legal Realism and the Social Contract: Fuller's Public Jurisprudence of Form, Private Jurisprudence of Substance' (1993) 78 Cornell L R 371 (observing that, though Fuller owed much to legal realism, he examined 'a set of criteria that . . . *are deduced* from the very meaning of law') (emphasis in the original).

[60] A two-day workshop was held in Milan in October 2019. The pandemics delayed the research's completion.

[61] See O Kahn-Freund, 'Review of Schlesinger, Formation of Contracts. A Study of the Common Core of Legal Systems' (1970) 18 AJCL 429 (pointing out that 'the hypothesis itself hardly needs verification, but the extent to which it applies, the extent it can be used as a working tool does so very much') and M Rheinstein, 'Review of R. Schlesinger, Formation of Contracts: A Study of the Common Core of Legal Systems' (1969) 36 Univ Chicago L Rev 448, at 449.

methodology was later confirmed in the context of the Trento project on the common core of European law.[62]

In our view, this type of analysis is particularly valuable within the field of administrative law itself. First and foremost, as observed earlier, unlike private law, administrative law has emerged as an uncodified area of law. The courts have gradually developed its principles, often in conjunction with scholars, and the executive branch has played a significant role through its regulations. Secondly, the recent emergence of general principles in common with the laws of EU Member States is primarily of judicial input. And thirdly, while we recognize the potential impact of administrative procedure legislation, that it can make a difference cannot be taken for granted and must be verified.

The questionnaire sought to gather basic information about each legal system, including the presence of constitutional or legislative provisions laying down general principles of administrative law. Additionally, it aimed to explore how the hypothetical cases would be examined and resolved within those systems. Collectively, those hypothetical cases concern three categories of procedural requirements. There are, first of all, certain requirements pertaining to administrative adjudication, which include the right to be heard and the duty to give reasons with regard to the adoption of individual acts, such as licences and orders.[63] Secondly, some requirements concern administration outside of adjudication. These include consulting stakeholders and citizen participation. Participation is increasingly important 'to prevent a failure of justice', when public authorities shape their procedure in light of the 'purpose of presenting "public" views not otherwise adequately represented' within administrative decision-making.[64] Lastly, there is a case concerning administrative digitalization, specifically a refusal to grant access to an algorithm used by a public authority.

We are aware that this type of study is not without difficulties. Firstly, it goes without saying that answers to the hypothetical cases will not always be easy to find. Secondly, the task of comparing solutions is already difficult enough when dealing with a limited number of legal systems originating from a common source, as seen in the states established following the dissolution of the Habsburg Empire in 1919. Finding common ground within a broader and more differentiated sample is even more problematic as our research must yield more than vague generalizations, such as 'justice' or 'transparency'. However, as observed earlier, we are equally interested in commonality and diversity. On the other hand, if one were to define a theory so all-embracing that no observations could possibly refute it, it would not be scientifically interesting. Thirdly, as De Smith put it, 'to prophesy the view that a court will take of the powers or duties of an administrative authority in a particular case must inevitably remain a hazardous undertaking'.[65] Similarly, during one of our workshops Ziller observed that it is not

[62] See M Bussani and U Mattei, 'The Common Core Approach to European Private Law' (1997–1998) 3 Colum J Eur L 339; J M Smits, 'Convergence of Private Law in Europe: Towards a New Ius Commune?' in E Örücü and D Nelken (eds), *Comparative Law: A Handbook* (Hart 2007) 219.

[63] See M D Bayles, *Procedural Justice. Allocating to Individuals* (Kluwer 1990) (examining three 'traditional principles': ie impartiality, opportunity to be heard, and grounds for decisions).

[64] E Gellhorn, 'Public Participation in Administrative Proceedings' (1972) 81 Yale L J 359.

[65] S De Smith, 'Wrongs and Remedies in Administrative Law' (1952) 15 Modern L Rev 189, at 190. See also P H Schuck and E D Elliot, 'Studying Administrative Law: A Methodology for, and Report on, Empirical Research' (1990) 42 Admin L Rev 519.

easy to see how principles and rules applied to a limited number of cases can be applied universally. Our goal is, rather, to seek to understand how the case would be handled and the underlying reasons for it. Even when legal requirements cannot be derived directly from the cases or when they may constitute unreliable indicators, discussing background theories can shed light on how procedural values are balanced against other values.

C. The choice of legal systems

There remains one more choice that requires explanation. It concerns a fundamental element to any comparative inquiry, namely, which legal systems to select for comparison. As mentioned at the outset of our research, we had to steer a course between two contrasting options: either limiting the comparison to the usual three or four legal systems, based on the questionable assumption that they are the most important ones or trying to cover a broader range of legal systems. In our endeavour to reach a reasonable balance between these options, we chose to examine a dozen selected legal systems.

These include both the traditional 'major' legal systems—such as Britain, France, and Germany—and others already examined in previous research: Italy, Poland, and Spain, for instance. They also include Austria, which played a pivotal role in codifying administrative procedure in Central and Eastern Europe, and Switzerland, as its Civil Code has often been considered a sort of model due to the broad discretion it affords to judges when confronted with challenging cases: ie with the same powers of the legislator.[66]

We also attempted to compare the solutions envisaged by European legal systems with those found in three other regions of the world: Japan, the United States, and Venezuela. Interestingly, the experts from those legal systems confirmed that the hypothetical cases would be relevant, but regrettably, some were unable to provide national reports.

IV. The structure of this book

The structure of this book, in its essence, does not differ from that of the previous volume in this series. It is divided into four parts, with the first part including this chapter.

The second part comprises the reports pertaining to the legal systems selected for our comparative analysis. This includes the responses given by our colleagues to some general questions concerning the role of generalist and special courts as well as the

[66] According to Article 1 (2) and (3) of the Federal Civil Code: '2. In the absence of a provision, the court shall decide in accordance with customary law and, in the absence of customary law, in accordance with the rule that it would make as legislator. 3 In doing so, the court shall follow established doctrine and case law.' For further remarks, see P G Picht and G Studen, 'Civil Law Principles and Family Law' in M Thommen (ed), *Introduction to Swiss Law* (Sui Generis 2022) 239 (observing that Article 1 establishes both the principle of legality and the prohibition of arbitrariness in the exercise of judicial powers).

scope of judicial review, for example, whether there are nonreviewable administrative actions and whether there is some rule requiring exhaustion of administrative appeals before a case may be brought to the courts.

The third part includes their answers regarding the hypothetical cases, constituting the core of our factual analysis and serving as the basis for the actual comparative analysis. The disaggregation of these responses is designed to facilitate the analytical process.

For the final part, we asked some experts to discuss whether the answers given to the hypothetical cases suggest that the underlying problems are either shared among all those jurisdictions or are more widely shared among only some of them, offering reflections on the possible causes of the similarity and diversity of the answers. There is, therefore, a chapter confronting national answers. Two further chapters focus on the relevance of administrative procedure legislation and the principles established by the EU and Council of Europe, respectively. These comparisons form the basis for the concluding chapter.

PART II

THE LEGAL SYSTEMS SELECTED FOR COMPARISON: BACKGROUND AND PERSPECTIVES

2
Austria

Stefan Storr

I. General principles

The '*Rechtsstaatsprinzip*', or rule of law principle, is one of the fundamental guarantees of Austrian constitutional law and the source of several principles related to administrative procedures.[1] However, there are also some particular constitutional guarantees which provide specific administrative procedural principles, or at least principles of relevance for administrative procedures.

Article 18 (1) B-VG (Federal Constitutional Law) entails the principle of legality: 'The entire public administration shall be based on law', and, in this context, the word 'entire' is given a broad interpretation. The requirement of lawfulness applies not only to so-called intervening administration, ie, the administration that intervenes in the subjective rights of the citizens ('*Eingriffsverwaltung*'), but also to authorities involved in the so-called administration of services ('*Leistungsverwaltung*', ie, social security). However, there is a denotative restriction for authorities acting in the sphere of private law ('*Privatwirtschaftsve rwaltung*'), to which the principle of legality does not apply.

Article 83 (2) B-VG states: 'No one may be deprived of his lawful judge.' Although the wording of this provision refers only to the 'judge', the Austrian Constitutional Court ('*Verfassungsgerichtshof*, *VfGH*) interprets this provision in the broader sense of a right, namely that no one may be deprived of access to a legally competent administrative authority.[2] This constitutional provision guarantees different kinds of protection: An authority violates Article 83 (2) B-VG if it claims a competence that it does not have; for example, if it employs coercion without having the competence to do so.[3] Such an authority also violates Article 83 (2) B-VG if it refuses to accept the competence that has been assigned to it.[4] Other forms of violations are, for example, if a collegial authority is not correctly constituted,[5] if an authority decides *ex officio* even though the law requires a person to bring a case before an administrative proceeding can begin,[6] and if an administrative penalty is imposed despite the statutory limitation period having already expired.[7]

[1] The '*Rechtsstaatsprinzip*' as a fundamental principle of Austrian constitutional law ('*Baugesetz*'): S Storr, 'Allgemeiner Teil' in B Raschauer, D Ennöckl, and N Raschauer (eds), *Grundriss des österreichischen Wirtschaftsrechts* (4rd edn, Manz 2021) 65.
[2] VfSlg 17967/2006.
[3] VfSlg 10020/1984.
[4] VfSlg 9696/1983.
[5] VfSlg 11.336/1987.
[6] VfSlg 5685/1968.
[7] VfSlg 2093/1956.

Stefan Storr, *Austria* In: *General Principles and Sector-Specific Rules in European Administrative Laws*. Edited by: Giacinto della Cananea and Jean-Bernard Auby, Oxford University Press. © Stefan Storr 2024.
DOI: 10.1093/oso/9780198867579.003.0002

The principle of equality in Article 7 B-VG prohibits any authority from acting arbitrarily. According to the Constitutional Court, it is arbitrary to misjudge frequently, to refrain from investigating the facts or doing so in a decisive manner. This applies in particular in connection with ignoring parties' statements and carelessly deviating from the details contained in official files or disregarding the facts of a case.[8]

The Constitutional Court derives—and this is significant for the Austrian legal doctrine of constitutional law—the principle of objectivity from the principle of equality, meaning that the legislator may not create any regulations that are not objective. It violates the principle of objectivity if, for example, a statutory provision is not reasonable or coherent with other provisions. Regarding party rights, the Constitutional Court has specified that, in principle, there is no constitutional provision to the effect that party rights must be guaranteed to a certain extent or even at all.[9] However, the granting of subjective rights regularly requires party rights to be granted. Depending on the purpose of the proceedings and the nature and significance of the legal position affected, the refusal to assign party status may also be appropriate if the proceedings are primarily intended to protect the interests of another party.[10]

A unique Austrian constitutional principle is the 'exclusivity of legal sources' ('*Geschlossenheit des Rechtsquellensystems*'). This principle entails that legal protection is only provided against specific administrative-legal sources. In general, Article 130 B-VG provides that judgments on complaints by the administrative courts:

- against rulings ('*Bescheid*') by administrative authorities for unlawfulness,
- against the exercise of direct administrative power and compulsion for unlawfulness ('*Ausübung unmittelbarer verwaltungsbehördlicher Befehls- und Zwangsgewalt*'), and
- for breach of the duty to reach a decision by an administrative authority ('*Säumnisbeschwerde*').

This means that any authority may only use forms of action against which legal protection by courts is admissible. This affects administrative procedures insofar as they may only be concluded by a specific form of action, namely, a formal ruling.

Article 130 (3) B-VG limits the administrative courts' ability to review an administrative decision insofar as an administrative decision cannot be deemed unlawful if the law permits the authority to apply discretion, and the authority has done so in harmony with the intent of the law. However, it must be noted here that there is an exception for administrative penal proceedings and legal matters coming within the competence of the Federal Administrative Court for Finance.

Other constitutional provisions include the principle that subordinary organs are bound by the instructions of superior bodies[11] and the principle of official confidentially (there is not yet a general principle of transparency in Austrian procedural law). An constitutional amendment will become effective in 2025 which will provide

[8] VfSlg 20.185/2017.

[9] VfSlg 8397/1978; VfSlg 9451/1982.

[10] VfSlg 11.934/1988.

[11] Article 20 (1) and (2) *Bundes-Verfassungsgesetz*—B-VG (Austrian Federal Constitutional Act), Orig Vers: BGBl No 1/1930.

transparency as a principle and official secrets as an exception, Article 22a B-VG. A Freedom of Information Act will substantiate this Act.[12] However, there is a principle of imparting information, although this is regulated by statuary law.[13]

The B-VG does not explicitly guarantee the principle of fairness. However, Article 6 of the European Convention on Human Rights (ECHR) guarantees fairness in court proceedings, and, in this respect, it should be highlighted that the ECHR has constitutional status in Austria. In addition, the Supreme Administrative High Court ('*Verwaltungsgerichtshof*, *VwGH*) has extended this fairness requirement to administrative proceedings beyond the actual scope of application of Article 6 ECHR to include judicial proceedings.

II. Administrative procedure legislation and government guidance: adjudication

Several other provisions of inferior rank impose duties of due process and fairness and—to a certain extent—transparency on public authorities. This concerns, for example, a conflict of interest between administrative bodies,[14] rules about communications between the authorities and the persons involved in an administrative proceeding,[15] the obligation to settle a case in as simple, fast, and cost-saving manner as possible, as well as to record the material contents of proceedings, if required, in minutes or a memorandum.[16]

The purpose of an investigation procedure is to ascertain the facts relevant to processing an administrative matter and enable the parties to claim their rights and legal interests.[17] Transparency is ensured by the parties' right to inspect files[18] and the possibility (not the obligation) of the competent authority to conduct an oral hearing.[19] To schedule an oral hearing, the persons involved must be notified either personally or by publishing an announcement on the official bulletin board of the municipality, in the newspaper serving as a channel for the official announcements of the authority, or by publication in the official electronic gazette of the authority. There are further applicable rules for large-scale proceedings.[20] In general, a ruling ('*Bescheid*') must demonstrate a line of reasoning summarizing the results of the investigation procedure, the arguments determining the evaluation of the evidence, and the opinion on the legal issue dealt with clearly and concisely.[21] The final aspect to mention is that the addressee of a ruling must be informed of his right to appeal ('*Rechtsmittelbelehrung*').[22]

From the foregoing, it needs to be emphasized that rules concerning duties of due process and fairness and—a certain extent—transparency are also regulated in sector-specific laws that govern administrative procedures, such as the Procedure at

[12] ibid art 20 (3).
[13] ibid art 20 (4).
[14] § 7 *Allgemeines Verwaltungsverfahrensgesetz 1991*—AVG (General Administrative Procedure Act), Orig Vers: BGBl No 51/1991.
[15] ibid §§ 13ff AVG.
[16] ibid § 18 AVG.
[17] ibid § 37 (5) S 1 AVG.
[18] ibid § 17 AVG.
[19] ibid § 40 AVG.
[20] ibid § 45 (3) AVG.
[21] ibid § 60 AVG.
[22] ibid § 58 (1) AVG in connection with § 61 AVG.

Administrative Courts Act,[23] the Administrative Penal Act,[24] The Federal Tax Act,[25] and the Federal Tax Penal Act.[26] The Supreme Administrative High Court pointed out that general procedural principles derived from the rule of law apply in fields where the General Administrative Procedure Act ('*AVG*') or other procedural laws do not apply.[27] Even the provisions of the AVG must be applicable by analogy, such as those on reopening a proceeding and the reinstatement of the previous legal position. Other comprehensive principles concern the right to be heard, the conflict of interest, and the obligation to provide the reasoning for a decision.

III. Administrative procedure legislation and government guidance: rule-making

Regarding the adoption of regulations, Article 18(2) of the Federal Constitution simply provides that every authority must be based on law, issuing regulations (ordinances) within its sphere of competence. There are no rules about a general procedure except those on publishing the regulation. However, particular legislative provisions envisage consultations with stakeholders. For example, before the maximum tariffs for chimney sweeps can be fixed by decree, the competent national guild of chimney sweeps, the competent Chamber of Workers and employees, the competent Chamber of Agriculture, and the municipalities concerned must be consulted.[28] Similar regulations exist for tariffs in the Traffic Act[29] and the determination of a local market.[30]

There are, of course, specific possibilities for the public to participate in procedures, such as when a municipality adopts a development plan that involves local zoning. Procedural issues are regulated by relevant state laws and provide, for example, the preparation of an explanatory report and the publication of a draft plan.[31] Those who have raised objections must be informed, irrespective of whether or not their objections have been considered valid.[32] Lastly, in this regard, there are further requirements for environmental law procedures based on European provisions stemming from legislation such as the Environmental Impact Assessment Act.[33]

[23] *Bundesgesetz über das Verfahren der Verwaltungsgerichte*—VwGVG (Federal Act on Proceedings of Administrative Courts), Orig Vers: BGBl I No 33/2013.

[24] *Verwaltungsstrafgesetz 1991*—VStG (Administrative Penal Act), Orig Vers: BGBl No 52/1991.

[25] *Bundesgesetz über allgemeine Bestimmungen und das Verfahren für die von den Abgabenbehörden des Bundes, der Länder und Gemeinden verwalteten Abgaben—Bundesabgabenordnung*—BAO (Federal Tax Law), Orig Vers: BGBl No 194/1961.

[26] *Bundesgesetz vom 26. Juni 1958, betreffend das Finanzstrafrecht und das Finanzstrafverfahrensrecht—Finanzstrafgesetz*—FinStrG (Federal Tax Penal Law), Orig Vers: BGBl. No 129/1958.

[27] VwGH 23. 1. 1950, 0273/49.

[28] § 125 (2) *Gewerbeordnung*—GewO (Trade, Commerce and Industry Regulation Act), Orig Vers: BGBl No 194/1994.

[29] *Bundesgesetz über die nichtlinienmäßige gewerbsmäßige Beförderung von Personen mit Kraftfahrzeugen—Gelegenheitsverkehrs-Gesetz 1996—GelverkG* (Federal Act for Public Transport), Orig Vers: BGBl No 112/1996.

[30] § 290 GewO.

[31] § 38 (4) *Steiermärkisches Raumordnungsgesetz—Stmk ROG* (Styrian Regional Planning Act), Orig Vers LGBl No 49/2010.

[32] § 38 (8) Stmk ROG.

[33] *Bundesgesetz über die Prüfung der Umweltverträglichkeit—Umweltverträglichkeitsprüfungsgesetz 2000*—UVP-G (Environmental Impact Assessment Act), Orig Vers: BGBl No 697/1993.

3
China

Xiaowei Sun

I. General principles

Unlike American law which affirms the principle of 'due process' in constitutional amendments, the Chinese Constitution has not enshrined such a specific principle. Indirectly and symbolically, three constitutional articles recognize the rights of citizens of the administration.

Thus, Article 2 of the Constitution enshrines the principle of citizen participation in 'the management of state, economic, cultural and social affairs'. In the light of this constitutional provision, Article 67 of the Legislation Law provides that 'the opinions [. . .] of citizens must be heard during the development of administrative regulations, in the form of forum, conference-debate or consultation'. In application of this law, the Ordinance concerning the Procedures for the Formulation of Administrative Regulations,[1] which was amended on 22 December 2017, incorporates the legislative provision previously mentioned, specifying that the time limit for publicly soliciting opinions from society must generally not be less than thirty days.[2]

Article 27 of the Constitution provides that 'all state organs and functionaries must rely on the support of the people, keep in close touch with them, heed their opinions and suggestions, accept their supervision and do their best to serve them'. This provision could be analysed as a constitutional basis of the Hearing system.

Lastly, Article 41 of the Constitution provides:

> Citizens of the People's Republic of China have the right to criticize and make suggestions regarding any State organ or functionary and have the right to make to relevant State organs complaints or charges against, or exposures of, any State organ or functionary for violation of law or dereliction of duty, but must not fabricate or distort facts for purposes of libel or false incrimination.
>
> The State organ concerned must ascertain the facts and deal with the complaints, charges, or exposures made by citizens. No one may suppress such complaints, charges, and exposures or retaliate against the citizens making them.

[1] 行政法规制定程序条例. Chinese only footnotes are translations of the English in the main text.
[2] Art 13 of the Ordinance.

Xiaowei Sun, *China* In: *General Principles and Sector-Specific Rules in European Administrative Laws*. Edited by: Giacinto della Cananea and Jean-Bernard Auby, Oxford University Press.
DOI: 10.1093/oso/9780198867579.003.0003

Citizens who have suffered losses as a result of infringement of their civil rights by any State organ or functionary have the right to compensation in accordance with the provisions of law.[3]

This article gives citizens a right of inspection over administrative organs and their staff. When the applicant citizen is the victim of a violation of his constitutional rights, he must be compensated.

However, the institutional concept of the People's Republic does not allow judges to base their judgments on the Constitution.[4] The application of these principles depends on the lawmaker and the will of the administrative authorities.

II. Administrative procedure legislation and government guidance: adjudication

The Chinese legal system has no general legislation or government code on administrative procedure, but procedural rules dispersed in the various administrative matters. Thus, from the beginning of the 1990s, a series of laws and regulations were instituted regarding relations between citizens and the administration: the Administrative Litigation Law[5] on 4 April 1989, the State Compensation Law[6] on 12 May 1994, the Administrative Penalty Law[7] on 17 March 1996, the Administrative Reconsideration Law[8] on 29 April 1999, the Administrative Authorization Law[9] on 27 August 2003, the Regulation on Open Government Information[10] on 5 April 2007 and so on. The substantive and procedural rules do coexist in these texts.

Among these texts, the Administrative Litigation Law, described as a 'Silent Revolutionary Act', was the most decisive step in the development of the protection of individual rights facing administrative authorities. During the first five decades of the People's Republic of China, procedural rules were established with the aim of better guaranteeing the efficiency of administrative activities rather than controlling and limiting the discretionary power of the administration. With the will to establish the rule of law,

[3] Art 41 of the Constitution.
中华人民共和国公民对于任何国家机关和国家工作人员，有提出批评和建议的权利；对于任何国家机关和国家工作人员的违法失职行为，有向有关国家机关提出申诉，控告或者检举的权利，但是不得捏造或者歪曲事实进行诬告陷害.

对于公民的申诉，控告或者检举，有关国家机关必须查清事实，负责处理. 任何人不得压制和打击报复.

由于国家机关和国家工作人员侵犯公民权利而受到损失的人，有依照法律规定取得赔偿的权利.

[4] The National People's Congress (NPC) exercises both constituent power and legislative power. As the supreme organ of the state, it is the source of all public authority. Jurisdictions are submitted to (and not separate from) the NPC; they cannot control administrative acts according to the Constitution, whose sole interpreter is the NPC Standing Committee.

[5] 行政诉讼法.

[6] 国家赔偿法.

[7] 行政处罚法.

[8] 行政复议法.

[9] 行政许可法.

[10] 政府信息公开条例.

since the end of the 1980s, both ideological and cultural changes were made at the top of the state: administrative legislation no longer aims only to guarantee the efficiency of the administration, but more and more to protect individual rights. The reform of Administrative Litigation Law is fully in line with this new policy. Separated from civil litigation since the legislation of 4 April 1989,[11] the administrative suit has acquired its place with regard to civil and criminal suits, and was to constitute the main instrument both for the protection of individual rights and for the judicial review of the administration.

Furthermore, the Administrative Litigation Law was significantly modified by an amendment on 1 November 2014.[12] Firstly, this reform widened the list of administrative acts liable to appeal before the courts.[13] It also opened up the possibility of controlling 'abstract administrative acts'[14] (which previously escaped judicial review).

In addition, the reform of 2014 intensified the judicial review of administrative acts by introducing the notion of 'manifestly inappropriate' administrative act in administrative litigation.[15] Until then, the judge could annul all or part of an administrative decision both for error of law or lack of proof, as well as for some procedural flaw, incompetence, or abuse of power.[16] It was, if we use the French term, a '*contrôle minimum*', because judges were limited to verify the material accuracy of the facts (with regard to the evidence) and formal compliance with the law. In principle, the administration exercises a discretionary power in the assessment of the facts.[17] In this regard, the reform of 2014 deserves its 'revolutionary' reputation, by allowing the judge to review 'manifestly inappropriate' administrative acts.[18] Henceforth, mere compliance with legislative provisions is not sufficient to justify a 'manifestly inappropriate' administrative decision.

In addition to the aforementioned changes, the reform of 2014 brought other changes, such as the time limits for appeal[19] and enforcement,[20] the establishment of proof,[21] cases requiring a new trial,[22] the intervention of the Public Prosecutor's

[11] Before the legislation on 4 April 1989, the administrative suit was governed by the Civil Procedure Law (on an experimental basis). Under Article 3 of this law (repealed) the rules of this law apply to administrative litigations ('民事诉讼法（试行）第3条第2款：'法律规定由人民法院审理的行政案件，适用本法的规定)'.

[12] For an analysis of the general scope of this reform, see X Sun, 'La réforme de la loi sur le contentieux administratif de la République Populaire de Chine' in *Annuaire Européen d'Administration Publique 2015* (Presses Universitaires d'Aix-Marseille 2016) 294–96.

[13] Arts 12 and 13 of the Administrative Litigation Law.

[14] 'Abstract administrative act' (抽象行政行为) is a Chinese doctrinal concept used to denote all non-individual administrative acts, specially the government regulations and secondary legislation. According to Article 53 of the Administrative Litigation Law:

> Citizens, legal persons or other organizations who believe that a regulatory act formulated by the State Council or local people's government on which the administrative act is based are illegal, may request the review of the regulatory act when a lawsuit is filed against the administrative act. (公民，法人或者其他组织认为行政行为所依据的国务院部门和地方人民政府及其部门制定的规范性文件不合法，在对行政行为提起诉讼时，可以一并请求对该规范性文件进行审查.)

[15] 明显不当. See Sun (n 12) 302–03.

[16] Former Art 54, No 2, of the Administrative Litigation Law on 4 April 1989.

[17] Only in matters of administrative police, the judge could discuss the proportionality of the sanction pronounced, when this was 'manifestly unjust' (显失公正).

[18] Art 70, No 6, and art 77 of the Administrative Litigation Law.

[19] Art 46.

[20] Art 47.

[21] Arts 33 to 43.

[22] Art 91.

Office during the administrative trial,[23] and mediation.[24] The will of the legislator was to erect the Administrative Litigation Law into a real instrument for the protection of individual rights.

At the fourth meeting of the Thirteenth National People's Congress, in March 2021, the Legislative Affairs Commission of the National People's Congress Standing Committee announced the start of a codification project in administrative law. The codification of administrative procedures may be considered by the public authorities.

Beyond these constitutional and legislative protections, another principle—of doctrinal and political origin—also conditions administrative activities: the principle of legality.

A fundamental principle in most Western legal systems for more than two centuries, the principle of legality was introduced into the legal system of the People's Republic of China only in the 1980s. This principle was firstly supported in the legal literature, then accepted by the Chinese Communist Party,[25] to be finally confirmed by the Constitution in a general perspective of establishing the rule of law.[26]

The constitutional recognition of the principle of the rule of law was more than a symbolic act in the development of administrative procedure. From then on, it was not enough to limit the discretionary power of the administration by the requirement of procedural regularity; the legislator tended to rebalance the relations between citizens and the administration by the growth of subjective rights and the protection of fundamental rights. Thus, all the previously mentioned laws on administrative procedures have been amended in this sense.[27]

However, the principle of legality and its application in Chinese doctrine and by the authorities calls for some clarifications. Indeed, the Chinese term translating the 'principle of legality'[28] can have two meanings, one broad, the other strict.

In the broad sense, the principle of legality obliges the administration to exert its power in accordance with legal rules. This requirement implies the existence of legal rules delimiting and conditioning administrative activities, but it does not specify the relationship between these rules. In other words, it does not take into account the hierarchy between the rules applied to the administration. Legality, in the broad sense, refers to all the sources of administrative law, regardless of whether they are constitutional, legislative, or government regulations. This is what the Chinese public authorities retain, supported by a part of the doctrine which emphasizes the efficiency of administrative action more than respect for strict legality. In this sense, the principle of legality has been concretized by regulatory acts, of which a decision on 22 March 2004 of the State Council on the Program relating to the general implementation of the principle of legality in the administrations[29] was particularly significant. This text specifies, in Article 5, six fundamental principles implied by the application of the

[23] Art 93.
[24] Art 61.
[25] The 15th National Congress of the Chinese Communist Party, 1997.
[26] The constitutional amendment of 15 March 1999 introduced the principle of the rule of law in Article 5 of the Constitution.
[27] The Administrative Litigation Law, the State Compensation Law, the Administrative Penalty Law, the Administrative Reconsideration Law, the Administrative Authorization Law, etc.
[28] 依法行政, which can be literally translated as 'administering according to legal rules'.
[29] 全面推进依法行政实施纲要.

principle of legality to administrative activities: 1. 'Be lawful';[30] 2. 'Be fair';[31] 3. 'Due process';[32] 4. 'Be efficient for citizens';[33] 5. 'Be honest and trustworthy';[34] and 6. 'Be responsible'.[35]

Most of the principles known to Western systems can be observed in this list. However, compliance with these principles heavily depends on the administrative authorities themselves. Such self-control is not sufficient to guarantee the respect of these principles, according to most of the contributors to legal scholarship, who mainly advocate the strict acceptation of the principle of legality.

Strictly speaking, respect for legality presupposes the compliance of administrative acts, whether material or normative, with the law. It is about applying the principle of the hierarchy of legal norms inherent to the rule of law. Moreover, such a principle is based on Article 67 of the Constitution, according to which the Standing Committee of the National People's Congress has the power to 'annul those administrative rules and regulations, decisions or orders of the State Council that contravene the Constitution or the statutes'[36] and to 'annul those local regulations or decisions of the organs of state power of provinces, autonomous regions, and municipalities directly under the Central Government that contravene the Constitution, the law or the administrative rules and regulations'.[37]

There is therefore parliamentary control of constitutionality and legality over administrative acts. However, in practice, such control is only exerted before the enactment of administrative acts. There has never been an administrative act annulled by the Standing Committee of the National People's Congress. The real control of administrative acts is exerted by the courts.

III. Administrative procedure legislation and government guidance: rule-making

As observed earlier with regard to judicial review, the judge cannot base his or her judgments on the Constitution. Therefore, constitutional acts do not come within the realm of legality, which is strictly limited to legislative acts. However, not all administrative acts can be checked by a judge. Thus, according to Article 12 of the Administrative Litigation Law, the courts may not accept suits against 'government regulations, internal government regulations, or decisions and orders with general binding force formulated and announced by administrative organs'.[38] It is only after the reform of 2014 that the applicant can seize a court to check the legality of a

[30] 合法行政.
[31] 合理行政.
[32] 程序正当.
[33] 高效便民.
[34] 诚实守信.
[35] 权责统一.
[36] Standing Committee of the National People's Congress.
撤销国务院制定的同宪法，法律相抵触的行政法规，决定和命令.
[37] Standing Committee of the National People's Congress.
撤销省，自治区，直辖市国家权力机关制定的同宪法，法律和行政法规相抵触的地方性法规和决议.
[38] Art 12 of the Administrative Litigation.
行政法规，规章或者行政机关制定，发布的具有普遍约束力的决定，命令.

government regulatory act as a defence,[39] internal government regulations excepted. According to Article 64 of the same law, if a judge determines that the regulatory act is illegal, he must set it aside and propose a suggestion of regularization to the administrative authority.

It should be noted that according to the Judicial Interpretation of the Supreme People's Court relating to the application of Administrative Litigation Law, the courts can check the compliance of the contested individual or regulatory act to a superior regulatory administrative act.[40] It is an extension of the principle of legality and a way to guarantee the respect for the procedural rules determined by the administration itself, such as the Regulation on Procedures for the Formulation of Administrative Regulations,[41] the Regulation on Procedures for the Formulation of Administrative Rules,[42] and the Provisional Regulation on Major Administrative Decision Making Procedures.[43]

39 Art 53 of the Administrative Litigation Law.
40 Art 148 of the Judicial Interpretation.
41 行政法规制定程序条例.
42 规章制定程序条例.
43 重大行政决策程序暂行条例.

4
France

Sébastien Saunier

I. General principles

The French law of administrative procedure possesses a system of sources which is neither perfectly identical to, nor totally different from, those of other legal areas or legal systems. It has long accorded great procedural freedom to the public authorities and rested on quite dispersed sources.

One category of sources has, however, made it possible to bridge the gaps of the written law that only since the late 1970s has provided a framework for general administrative procedure with laws on transparency and the rights of citizens in their relations with the authorities, namely case law. The case law source has sought to give the area the cohesion it lacked.

Since 1945, availing itself of its creative power, the *Conseil d'Etat* (Council of State—CE) has identified a series of case law principles, endowed with generality, abstraction, and binding character, '*applicable without text*' or '*in the absence of text*', whose contribution has been decisive for general procedure, albeit coming late compared with other rights. By way of example, we may mention, among the '*general principles of law*', the obligation to respect the rights of defence,[1] the principle of non-retroactivity of administrative measures,[2] the principle of impartiality required of any administrative body,[3] the right of citizens to apply to the authorities to reverse their decisions via hierarchical appeal.[4]

A second volley of principles were recognized in the 1990s, such as the obligation to repeal an unlawful regulation,[5] the obligation to publish regulations within a reasonable time,[6] and the principle of legal certainty.[7] It was only in 2011 that the *Council of State* consecrated the edifice's crowning principle:

> the principle according to which administrative measures must be effected in accordance with the forms and in keeping with the procedures prescribed by laws and regulations.[8]

[1] CE, 5 May 1944, *Dame Veuve Trompier-Gravier, Rec* p 133, *GAJA*; CE, ass, 26 October 1945, *Aramu, Rec* 213; *S. 1946.III.1*, concl Odent.

[2] CE, ass, 25 June 1948, *Sté Journal L'Aurore, Rec* 289, *GAJA*.

[3] CE, 29 April 1949, *Bourdeaux, Rec* p 188; CE, 7 July 1965, *Féd Nationale des transporteurs routiers, Rec*, 413.

[4] CE, 30 June 1950, *Quéralt, Re* 413.

[5] CE, ass, 3 Feb 1989, *Cie Alitalia, GAJA* no.

[6] CE, 31 Dec 2003, *Syndicats des commissaires et hauts-fonctionnaires de la police nationale, Rec* 506.

[7] CE, ass, 24 March 2006, *Société KPMG et al, GAJA*, no.

[8] CE, ass, 23 December 2011, *Danthony et al*, No 335477, *Rec* 649.

Sébastien Saunier, *France* In: *General Principles and Sector-Specific Rules in European Administrative Laws*. Edited by: Giacinto della Cananea and Jean-Bernard Auby, Oxford University Press.
DOI: 10.1093/oso/9780198867579.003.0004

The Danthony ruling also consecrates a new function of the French administrative judge in the neutralization of non-substantial procedural irregularities.

The end of the twentieth century also saw the completion of a movement of diversification and multiplication of the sources of this law, as with general administrative law. The constitutionalization of the area has progressed under the influence of constitutional case law. However, there are still few rules applicable to administrative procedure. The Constitution of 4 October 1958, unlike other constitutions, says nothing of administrative procedure. The constitutional procedural rules stem mainly from the Declaration of the Rights of Man and of the Citizen (DDHC) of 26 August 1789 (Articles 8, 9, 15, 16) and from the fundamental principles recognized by the laws of the Republic (PFRLR).

In any event, the constitutionalization of procedural principles is neither general nor absolute. For example, the Constitution does not require administrative rulings to be made on formal grounds.[9] Citizens' rights to information and to participation in the preparation of administrative decisions affecting the environment are guaranteed by article 7 of the *Charte de l'environnement* ('environment charter'), but the notion of a decision affecting the environment is conceived strictly, thus limiting the scope of application of such participation. The requirement—as a constitutional rule—for the principles of the rights of defence and the right to a fair hearing is confined to criminal matters and to punitive sanctions.[10] It does not concern measures that do not pursue a punitive aim. The constitutional principle of impartiality stemming from Article 16 of the DDHC applies only to those administrative authorities that can be likened to 'tribunals' and above all bears significant implications for the independent administrative authorities.[11]

Some progress has recently been made. The *Conseil constitutionnel* (Constitutional Council) has recognized a constitutional right of access to public records,[12] then to administrative documents.[13] However, as prescribed in constitutional case law, limitations may be imposed by the legislator, provided, on the one hand, they are grounded in other constitutional requirements or a reason of public interest and, on the other hand, that they are proportionate to the objective pursued.

II. Administrative procedure legislation and government guidance: adjudication

French procedural law has long been characterized by patchy and dispersed written law as regulations are specific to a given area (one exception is the codification procedure for expropriation in the public interest under the law of 1810), or even to a given authority, so there was no general statutory law or regulation of administrative procedure until the end of the twentieth century. The state bodies themselves have

9 *Conseil Constitutionnel*—Constitutional Council, Cons Const, CC, 27 November 2001, dec No 2001-451 DC.

10 Cons Const, 17 January 1989, No 88-248 DC § 35; Cons Const 20 May 2021, No 2021-817 DC, § 30.

11 Cons Const, 12 October 2012, dec No 2012-280 QPC concerning the competition authority.

12 Cons Const, 15 September 2017, No 2017-655 QPC, *M François Graner*.

13 Cons Const, 3 April. 2020, No 2020-834 QPC, *Union nationale des étudiants de France*.

produced numerous rules of procedure, calling upon their regulatory and para-regulatory powers (circulars, directives, guidelines etc).

Since the late 1970s, however, the legislator has taken hold of the area, protecting citizens at a time of developments in the information sciences and technology (Law No 78-17 of 16 January 1978 on information technology, files, and freedoms), allowing access to administrative documents (Law No 78-753 of 17 July 1978 establishing measures to improve relations between the authorities and the public, and various administrative, social, and tax provisions), access to records (Law No 79-18 of 3 January 1979 on the public records), and a general rule for the justification of administrative measures (Law No 79-587 of 11 July 1979 on the justification of administrative measures and the improvement of relations between the authorities and the public). These regulations were supplemented by Decree No 83-1025 of 28 November 1983 concerning relations between public administrative bodies and users, which, in the absence of a code of administrative procedure, represents significant progress. The law of 12 April 2000 on the rights of citizens in their relations with administrative bodies took a further important step by targeting all that is meant by the term 'Administration', thus going beyond the restricted organic field of the 1983 decree to apply to the entire set of legal persons, public and private, providing an administrative public service.

It was, however, becoming a matter of the utmost urgency to coordinate the whole and give homogeneity to the regulations. Despite several attempts (in 1996 and 2004), the codification projects did not attain their goal. The law of 12 November 2013 enabled the government to 'regroup and organise the general rules relating to non-litigious administrative procedures'. After two years of work, the 'Code of relations between the public and the administration' (CRPA) was published (as a result of ordinance No 2015-1341 of 23 October 2015 and decree No 2015-1342 of the same day), which has constituted the *lex generalis* of administrative procedure since 1 January 2016.

Essentially borrowing the previous transversal procedural norms from established law, a good number of its rules frame the procedure applicable to individual decisions. Whilst the administrative procedure theoretically covers unilateral and contractual acts, as per tradition, an initial separation is carried out by codification. The CRPA is a code for unilateral administrative acts, while the public procurement code governs contractual procedures (the result of ordinance No 2018-1074 of 26 November 2018 and decree No 2018-1075 of 3 December 2018, in effect from 1 April 2019).

The code makes a second essential distinction between the procedures for drafting individual decisions on the one hand and impersonal measures on the other (CPRA, Article L. 200-1). In conformity with the codified texts, primacy is given to the individual decision, probably because the need to protect the citizen is particularly important. But this also corresponds to the strong tendency current in the law of administrative procedure to favour the development of citizens' subjective rights and the growing individualism that underpins these rules.

For example, its *Livre premier* (Book I), which frames the exchanges between administrative bodies and the public, begins with a Title devoted to the regulation of a citizen's 'request' (CRPA, Article L. 110-1 to D. 114-15), which is revealing. The point of view thus focuses on the rights of the requesting citizen. Title II regulates the procedures preliminary to the advent of certain decisions, and subjects individual decisions to adherence to a preliminary adversarial procedure (Article L. 121-1 to L. 121-2). Book II, addressing the administrative bodies' unilateral acts (Article L. 200-1 to L. 243-4), prioritizes individual decisions subject to the obligation to state grounds (Article L. 211-2), the rules of signature (Article L. 212-1), the rules on entry into effect (Article L. 221-8), the significance of silence (Article L. 231-1), and cessation of effect (Article L. 242-1 f). The primacy of the individual decision is also found in the regulation of access to administrative documents (Article L. 300-2) and the provisions for the framework of administrative appeals (Article L. 411-2). More precisely, it will be noted that within the category of individual decisions, the regulation focuses on unfavourable individual decisions and individual decisions creating rights.

III. Administrative procedure legislation and government guidance: rule-making

The general law of administrative procedure rather broadly excludes regulatory acts from its material field of application. Numerous provisions also do not apply to what in French administrative law are called '*décisions d'espèce*', such as declarations of public interest. These 'decisions based on particular facts' are neither regulatory nor individual but often take their characteristics from the regulatory act, particularly by reason of their impersonal effects. For example, the obligation of accompaniment of signature by the rules prescribed in article L. 212-1 is not incumbent on regulatory acts but in conformity with prior case law. The CRPA excludes regulatory acts from the requirement of stating grounds, as did the law of 1979 (Article L. 211-2 and L. 211-3). Consequently, such acts are not subject to adherence to a preliminary adversarial procedure (Article L. 121-1). The non-application of these general rules of administrative procedure can be explained by the strongly subjectivist orientation of French procedural law.

However, the CRPA does not exclude these acts altogether. In several instances, the *lex generalis* prescribes applicable rules of procedure.

Firstly, this is the case when the code gives a framework for the modes of 'involving the public in decisions taken by the authorities' in a dedicated title designed to group together the general rules for public participation. The CRPA then presents itself as a code centred on the procedures for drafting regulatory decisions and *décisions d'espèce*. The modification of the field of application of the law of procedure is logical in view of the goal pursued, which is to allow the public to assert their point of view in the regulatory process. The condition for using these procedures is the issuance of an act of general import. Therefore, the authorities can envisage holding an open consultation on the Internet only prior to the issuance of a regulatory act (Article L. 132-1 to R. 132-10). The new general procedure for public consultation created by the CRPA (Article L. 131-1) is meant to involve the public in 'the conception of a reform or the drawing up of a project or an act', which again concerns measures with an impersonal effect. The CRPA also governs public inquiries (those falling under neither the expropriation code nor the environment code) and procedures for the public's participation in local decisions (Article L. 135-1 to L. 135-2), which again concern impersonal decisions. It will be noted that in all these cases it is an option and not an obligation for the authorities (except for the procedures of public inquiries), and that the procedural framework is hardly precise.

The *lex generalis* also addresses regulatory acts and *décisions d'espèce* when it comes to regulating their entry into effect (Article L. 221-2 to L. 221-6 on the general rules on entry into effect of regulatory acts; Article L. 221-7 for decisions that are neither regulatory nor individual; Article L. 221-9 to L. 221-17 for particular rules on publication) and on cessation of effect of the same (Article L. 243-1 to L. 243-4 on the repeal and withdrawal of regulatory acts and non-regulatory acts that do not create rights). Thus, here is found one of the most important practical issues regarding the distinction between regulatory decisions and individual decisions.

Finally, the CRPA now contains, in its Book III devoted to access to administrative documents, the specific rules on the dissemination of instructions and circulars (Article L. 312-2 to D. 312 -11) intended to increase access and the ability to rely on such texts formally.

5
Germany

Dian Schefold

I. General principles

According to the principle of the rule of law (*Rechtsstaat*), guaranteed under Articles 20 and 28.1 of the German Constitution (Basic Law, *Grundgesetz, GG*), the powers of the administration are ruled by law. The administration is bound by it, and citizens therefore have the right to see these foundations and limits of powers observed. The essential clause to ensure this is Article 19.4 *GG*: 'Should any person's rights be violated by public authority, he may have recourse to the courts.'[1] This clause is linked to guaranteeing fundamental rights and, thus, their legally established limitations: it must be seen in the context of the ruling of the Basic Law. It distributes powers at Federation, Länder, and local authority levels, guaranteeing the field of Federal civil law,[2] in this way limiting ruling by public law and providing either a public law regulation or a reference to private law[3] in some fields. Furthermore, according to constitutional case law, the essentials of all state activities must be regulated by the law, which enshrines the rights of citizens. Therefore, administrative activity is open to judicial review, which protects citizens' rights.

II. Administrative procedure legislation and government guidance: adjudication

The Constitution does not prescribe the general legal regulation of administrative procedure, although there were some tendencies in this direction (tax administration since 1919, Thüringen 1926, the 1931 Württemberg project) in the pre-Nazi period. Nevertheless, in the Federal Republic, after enacting laws on administrative procedure (*Verwaltungsgerichtsordnung—VwGO* 1960), it appeared congruent to regulate administrative procedure, also looking to the jurisprudence. Therefore, after a long preparation and generalization of the model for an administrative procedural law in Schleswig-Holstein (1968), the federal law on administrative procedure was enacted in 1976 (*Verwaltungsverfahrensgesetz—VwVfG*). However, in light of the power of the Länder in various spheres, and executing Federal legislation, they are competent to regulate their own administrative procedure. Thus, preparation of the law on

[1] Art 19.4 GG.
[2] Art 74 No 1 GG.
[3] See arts 87–90 GG.

Dian Schefold, *Germany* In: *General Principles and Sector-Specific Rules in European Administrative Laws*. Edited by: Giacinto della Cananea and Jean-Bernard Auby, Oxford University Press. © Dian Schefold 2024.
DOI: 10.1093/oso/9780198867579.003.0005

administrative procedure was a task shared by representatives of the Federation and the Länder, and all the Länder enacted their laws on administrative procedure simultaneously. They are all very similar to the Federal law, or simply refer to it. Furthermore, all changes to the law are standardized. In practice, there is almost virtually uniform legislation whose interpretation is subject to the Federal Administrative Court,[4] but it is formally based either on Federal or Länder-level authority.

These laws include guarantees of due process for those participating in the procedure, such as legal representation, the exclusion of personally involved officials, bias, the requirement to investigate the facts, the rights of the participants, and especially the right to be heard, in addition to rules concerning administrative acts, their form, reasons, enactment, and validity. The same holds for administrative contracts. These rules, based on the case law of the administrative courts, have stood the test of time for nearly 50 years and have been supplemented by new rules on e-government and digital administration.

Nevertheless, some of these rules have been criticized. In general, one may doubt whether an administration seeking to discharge its function will be neutral towards a citizen who defends his standpoint. In this sense, judicial review will constitute effective control, and one might ask whether the 'proceduralization' of administrative action will not impose an impossible task on the administration. In terms of some more specific aspects, the participation model in administrative procedure may be too narrow and exclude persons with an interest in the case despite not being legally involved. Limitations on the right to be heard may appear too narrow, especially in cases involving many interested parties.[5] The question of protecting the administration's secrets and those of other participants in a procedure is delicate. Lastly, it must be borne in mind that, regardless of the general law of administrative procedure, there are exceptions concerning its applicability, and specific sectors have special regulations. These include tax administration and social security legislation. However, these regulations are influenced by the general law on administrative procedure and are similar to it.

III. Administrative procedure legislation and government guidance: rule-making

The administrative procedure laws regulate the operations of public authorities vis-à-vis private individuals for the enacting of administrative acts or administrative contracts.[6] Therefore, the number of subjects involved with the right to be consulted remains very limited.[7] Even more so, as mentioned earlier, if administrative acts concerning a generally defined circle of concerned individuals (§ 35.2: the so-called '*Allgemeinverfügung*') are enacted, the right to be consulted, to which the concerned citizens are usually entitled, is excepted.[8]

4 § 137.1 No 2 VwGO.
5 See § 28.2 No 4 VwVfG.
6 § 9.
7 § 13, see esp § 13.3.
8 § 28.2 No 4.

The situation is different when planning certain public enterprises. If a law prescribes a planning procedure (*Planfeststellung*, §§ 72–78 *VwVfG*), the competent local authorities must submit a draft plan and all relevant documents to the public and the interested or involved authorities for a certain period; this form of public consultation is regulated in great detail. Any objections from the concerned parties must be discussed individually, sometimes in assemblies, and the reasons for the decision concerning the plan must be stated. The final decision on the plan must take into account the objections; it constitutes the administrative act to be adjudicated in the event of recourse to the administrative courts.

Besides this procedure, which is important for enterprises and projects, it should be borne in mind that town planning falls to local authorities and is enacted in the form of local statutes. The procedure is not regulated by the law of administrative procedure but by the code of constructions (*Baugesetzbuch*), enacted first in 1960 and now applied in a version of 2017. This code lists a large number of interests and aims which have to be respected and balanced. Again, ample public consultations and talks with all the interested authorities are required.[9] Therefore, the situation is similar to that of administrative planning, but the sources are different.

In Germany, administrative rules are not legal rules with direct *erga omnes* effect like the ordinances.[10] They are enacted by the heads of administration and are binding on the subordinated administration. They are either interpretative or concretize the discretionary power of the administration; otherwise, they regulate administrative activities that do not need a legal basis. For all these administrative rules, there is no general principle of consultation. Whereas, in relations between the Federal government and the Länder, authorization by the Bundesrat is required,[11] but for administrative rules, no consultation is prescribed at the single-entity level. This does not prevent *de facto* consultations and the influence of lobbies—especially in matters such as subsidies—but no juridical principle guarantees such consultations.

9 §§ 3–4a.
10 cf art 80 GG.
11 Art 84.2, 85.2 GG.

6
Greece

*Theodore Fortsakis**

I. General principles

According to the Constitution of the Hellenic Republic (from now on 'the Constitution') and case law—mainly that of the Greek Council of State—three basic principles govern the functioning of public administration.

Firstly, the principle of legality, whereby the administration may not carry out legal acts, nor material actions, except on the basis of the competence granted to it by the rule of law and within the limits thereof. The public administration is bound by all the legal rules that govern its organization, operation, and its activities in general, from whatever source these rules may originate (the Constitution, European law, generally recognized rules of international law, ratified international treaties, statutes, regulatory acts, individual administrative acts, and general principles of administrative law).

Secondly, the satisfaction of the public interest, which the public administration must seek in all its activities. The general definition of 'public interest' is provided by the Legislator, as the law regulates the organization and activities of the various agencies of the public administration and determines the objectives it must pursue. These agencies proceed to a more detailed definition of the public interest through the exercise of their regulatory competence or by issuing or refusing to issue individual acts.

Thirdly, the requirement to protect individuals and private legal persons, which, on the one hand, obliges the administrative bodies not to impinge on the rights and legal interests of the person and, on the other, to act through material actions and legal acts in accordance with the principle of respect for the person's rights and interests. The basic principle of protection of the person can be broken down into a number of individual principles, such as the equality of all persons in dealings with public services (equality before the public), reasonable administration, and the principle of good functioning of the administration, etc.

Moreover, the Constitution explicitly protects certain rights of a procedural nature, which are necessary to protect other rights enshrined in it and to exercise control over administrative action.

The first of these is the right to judicial protection under Article 20, para 1 of the Constitution, which entitles every person to receive legal protection by the courts of justice and plead before them their views concerning their rights or interests, as specified by law. Access to independent and impartial courts forms part of the fundamental

* The author would like to thank Nicholas Vadivoulis, LLM (NYU) for his great contribution to the editing of this paper.

Theodore Fortsakis, *Greece* In: *General Principles and Sector-Specific Rules in European Administrative Laws*. Edited by: Giacinto della Cananea and Jean-Bernard Auby, Oxford University Press. © Theodore Fortsakis 2024.
DOI: 10.1093/oso/9780198867579.003.0006

principle of the rule of law, involving three forms of judicial protection: (i) the requirement that a decision be issued on the substance of the matter, that is, that there be a genuine judicial examination of the facts of the case; (ii) the requirement that the judicial decisions or other entitlements actually be enforced; and (iii) the requirement that effective provisional measures be taken until the legal remedy being applied has been resolved.

The second is the right of petition, under Article 10 of the Constitution, which entails an obligation on the administrative authorities to take all necessary action to satisfy lawful petitions and provide a reasoned response to the petitions submitted, known as administrative appeals. There is a general right to receive information from the administration and to take cognizance of documents related to individual cases.

The third is the right to a prior hearing under Article 20, para 2 of the Constitution, as a right enjoyed by the interested party in respect of any administrative action or measure taken at the expense of its own other rights or interests. Prior hearing is directly related to the right to legal protection, so that a failure to grant prior hearing may be examined *ex officio* by the court and lead to the nullification of the act for contravening a substantive element of the formal procedure (procedural *ultra vires*). It includes the right of the person to deploy their views before the administrative authority against any individual administrative act unfavourable to their interests is issued and before any measure is taken or action against him or her, as well as the right to be called to present their case, with the corresponding obligations on the part of the administration. The right to a prior hearing is guaranteed in accordance with the case law of the Council of State, for individual administrative acts issued ex officio by the administrative organ in the exercise of its discretionary power and in relation to the subjective conduct of the individual affected by those acts.[1]

A direct consequence of the principles of legality and the protection of the individual is the need for the legal order to provide for the means of reviewing the conformity of the organs of the public administration with the legal norms governing its organization, operation, and activities in general.

II. Administrative procedure legislation and government guidance: adjudication

The Greek legal order envisages four methods of review: parliamentary, administrative, mediatory, and judicial. However, the first three control methods do not fully ensure the observance of the principle of legality by the administration, even though they afford considerable protection to individuals from their own unlawful acts or omissions. Thus, in modem legal orders, systems of review of the actions of the public administration by the courts exist to protect individuals from violations of the principle of legality by the organs of the state and other public legal persons.

The form and extent of the judicial review depend to a great extent on the law applied to it and the prevailing political and theoretical ideas, as well as upon actual

[1] See Ruling No 2306/1964, 2976/1966, 1811-1831/1969 of the Council of State.

needs that have arisen. In the Greek legal order, judicial review of administrative action falls within the framework of 'administrative justice'.

The following are fundamental norms of administrative court procedure:

(a) The observance of the principles of good faith, good morals, and the duty to abide by the truth, from which stems the obligation that remedies, pleadings, memoranda, and other legal documents submitted should be formulated in a proper manner.
(b) The principle of the initiative of the litigants as to the commencement of proceedings, according to which it belongs to the will of the person who is in need of judicial protection to set in motion the relevant procedure at all levels of jurisdiction by seeking the remedy prescribed by the relevant provisions. Related to this is the principle of voluntary dismissal of the action, that is, the ability of the person who seeks the remedy to waive it wholly or in part, if not stipulated otherwise by special provisions.
(c) The principle of the initiative of the court as to the progress of the trial, by which, provided that there are no special provisions prescribing a different regulation, and after the proceedings have begun, the court concerns itself with ordering the initiation of any procedural act required by law or other action, with a view to the earliest possible pronouncement of the judgment.
(d) The failure to appear (absence) of litigants who have been duly summoned to a hearing has no effect on the progress of the proceeding if there is no express provision to the contrary.
(e) The inquisitorial system: the court, if there are no norms to the contrary, examines *proprio motu* the case submitted to it within the limits of the relief sought by the litigants (*intra petita*) and regardless of the pleadings or the facts alleged or established by the litigants, applying the legal norms that govern the case according to the principle *curie novit legem*. Furthermore, the court, in its search for the objective truth, freely makes use of the means of evidence prescribed by the relevant provisions and assesses it freely, unless there is an express regulation to the contrary. It has been ruled that the failure of the Administration to send the file of the case to the court, despite a relevant interlocutory judgment having been issued, creates the presumption of admission of the allegations put forward by the applicant.
(f) The principle of the equality of the litigants, according to which the litigants are equal before the court and have the same rights and obligations so that all the litigants must be provided with the same means of defending their position.
(g) The principle of litigation (*audi alteram partem*), which requires litigants to be summoned in good time, to be represented at every hearing or with regard to any procedural act, and that they should be able to take cognizance of the data of the case, and more particularly of the allegations of their opponent and of the evidence, so that they can present their own arguments.
(h) The public hearing.
(i) The oral nature of the proceedings.
(j) The special reasoning of the judgment.
(k) The pronouncement of the decisions in a public session.

The norms of administrative procedure are codified in the following texts: (i) Decree No 18/1989, which contains special procedural provisions regarding proceedings before the Council of State; (ii) Law 2717/1999, regarding proceedings before the administrative courts (Administrative Court Procedure Code); (iii) Law 4700/2020, regarding proceedings before the Court of Audit.

III. Administrative procedure legislation and government guidance: rule-making

The procedure on public consultation is mainly established by Law 4622/2019 ('Executive State: organization, operation and transparency of the Government, government bodies and the central public administration'), which, among other provisions, lays down an obligation for all ministries to apply the principles of better regulation to all administrative functions. Better implementation of the requirements stemming from the duties of fairness and transparency or in respect of public authorities further simplifies the administrative procedures, especially in the area of impact assessment and stakeholder engagement.

The Presidency of the Government is responsible for initiating the consultation process in cooperation with the competent Service of the Ministry that has the legislative initiative. Requests for consultation on draft laws and regulations are, in principle, sent by e-mail to the Office of Good Legislation of the General Secretariat for Legal and Parliamentary Affairs in the Presidency of the Government.

The National Centre for Public Administration and Local Government, in accordance with its relevant organizational provisions (Article 9, para 4 of Decree No 105/2018), ensures the proper operation and management of the website for the submission of draft laws and regulations put to public consultation.[2]

The OpenGov.gr website has been designed to serve the principles of transparency, deliberation, collaboration, and accountability. It includes three initiatives:

(a) Open calls for the recruitment of public administration officials. Top-level and mid-level openings in the public sector are available on the Internet. Applications are submitted online using a platform available on the OpenGov.gr website.
(b) Electronic deliberation. Almost every piece of draft legislation or even policy initiative by the government is posted on a blog-like platform prior to submission to parliament. Citizens, private entities, and civil organizations can post their comments, suggestions, and criticisms article by article.
(c) Labs OpenGov. An open innovation initiative that gathers ideas and proposals from citizens, the public, and the private sectors. This website[3] attempts to release the power of decentralized knowledge and explore new ways to tackle modern public administration problems.

[2] See www.opengov.gr.
[3] See Labs.OpenGov.gr.

We may now sum up by submitting the following propositions. First and foremost, the Greek legal system lays down both the traditional principle of legality and procedural rights, including the right to be heard, which has a constitutional status. Second, although procedural rights have traditionally been regarded from the perspective of the judicial process, in the last 30 years they have been considered also with regard to administrative procedure. Third, a new generation of procedural rights vis-à-vis administrative authorities concerns consultation and transparency.

7
Italy

*Stefano Vaccari, Nicola Berti, and Mauro Silvestri**

I. General principles

Article 97(II) of the Italian Constitution establishes that public offices are to be organized according to provisions of law to ensure sound and impartial administration. This fundamental provision lays down three fundamental 'pillars' of public administration: the principles of legality, impartiality, and sound administration.

However, according to settled constitutional case law, the rules governing administrative procedure are considered to have constitutional status.[1] Accordingly, the principle of 'due process of law' is not included among the constitutional principles since its rules are subject to the discretion of the lawmaker. However, this does not affect the assurance that the subjective legal situations affected by administrative bodies must be protected before the courts, in compliance with Articles 24 and 113 of the Italian Constitution.

The term 'due process of law' as used in the mentioned case law refers to the principle that administrative procedures must be conducted through joint consultation or with the participation of the affected private citizens or administrations. In other words, when the legislature intends to limit citizens' rights, as a general rule, it is necessary to outline the abstract scenarios and establish an administrative procedure. This procedure allows the competent bodies to effectively impose restrictions while offering private stakeholders an opportunity to present their arguments, protect their interests, and contribute to the public interest as a whole.[2]

Even though the principle of due process of law does not—as yet—have constitutional status, it still qualifies as a general principle of the Italian legal system. Indeed, although 'procedural fairness' as such is not guaranteed in the strict sense by constitutional law, at the very least it constitutes a 'guiding principle' for the legislature and the judiciary.[3]

* The report was prepared, under the supervision of Mauro Renna and Stefano Vaccari, by a working group composed by Stefano Vaccari, Nicola Berti, and Mauro Silvestri. Specifically, Section I was drafted by Stefano Vaccari, Nicola Berti drafted Section III, and Mauro Silvestri drafted Section II.

[1] See, among the many, Constitutional Court, Judgment No 103, 19 March 1993; Constitutional Court, Judgment No 143, 21 March 1989; Constitutional Court, Judgment No 503, 10 December 1987; Constitutional Court, Judgment No 23, 20 March 1978; Constitutional Court, Judgment No 13, 2 March 1962.

[2] Constitutional Court, Judgment No 13, 2 March 1962.

[3] Constitutional Court, Judgment No 210, 13 May 1995; Constitutional Court, Judgment No 57, 24 February 1995.

Stefano Vaccari, Nicola Berti, and Mauro Silvestri, *Italy* In: *General Principles and Sector-Specific Rules in European Administrative Laws.* Edited by: Giacinto della Cananea and Jean-Bernard Auby, Oxford University Press.
 DOI: 10.1093/oso/9780198867579.003.0007

However, the principle of due process of law has been explicitly recognized as a right and guarantee protected by Italian Law No 241 of 7 August 1990, as amended by Law No 15 of 11 February 2005. According to these legislative provisions, the recipients of administrative acts must be notified of the commencement of procedures against them, have the right to be heard, receive a reasoned decision, and be able to bring a claim before a court.[4]

More specifically, stakeholder involvement and subsequent participation are an imperative phase of any procedure that could lead to a punitive measure,[5] as the requirement to notify affected persons about the commencement of a fact-finding phase (generally attributable to Article 7(1) of Italian Law 241/1990), and the consequent opportunity for stakeholders to submit statements and documents must be applied universally. In this way, in accordance with Article 97 of the Italian Constitution, an impartial decision is guaranteed, and with it the most appropriate and efficient pursuit of the primary public interest, in compliance with the principle of sound administration laid down in Article 97, mentioned above.

To conclude, due process of law can be understood to be a general principle of non-constitutional standing within the Italian legal system. Thus, if necessary, the state legislator may derogate from it, as there is no requirement to comply with general principles of the legal system when they do not reflect specific constitutional rules or principles.

Lastly, Article 29 of Law No 241/1990, as amended by Law No 69 of 18 June 2009, upholding the theory posited by authoritative legal scholars (Professor Giorgio Pastori in particular) recognizes that the numerous procedural rights it sets out regard essential service levels for the uniform protection of civil and social rights nationwide (Article 117(II)(m) of the Italian Constitution).[6] These provisions are established by the Italian Administrative Procedure Act (APA) in relation to obligations to ensure stakeholder participation in the procedure, identify the person responsible for it, and conclude it within the specified time frame, respecting its maximum duration, measuring the actual time required for its completion, and guaranteeing access to administrative files (para 2-*bis*). Furthermore, the provisions of the general law on administrative procedure concerning the filing of petitions, reports, and communications; the certified notification of business start-ups; 'tacit consent'; and the provision of services (para 2-*ter*) also come under the same constitutional matrix.

This classification of the main procedural rights as guaranteed by the Italian APA places a precise constraint on regional lawmakers. Article 29(2-*quater*) of Law No 241/1990 establishes that, when regulating the administrative procedures within their competence, regional governments and local authorities may not establish a level of protection lower than those available to private citizens under statutory provisions regarding the essential service levels prescribed in paragraphs 2-*bis* and 2-*ter*. They may only establish higher levels of protection.

[4] Constitutional Court, Judgment Nos 103 and 104, 23 March 2007.

[5] On 'procedural reserve' see Constitutional Court, Judgment No 116, 23 June 2002; Constitutional Court, Judgment No 69, 5 April 2018.

[6] See G Pastori, 'The Origins of Law No 241/1990 and Foreign Models' (2010) 2 IJPL 267.

This means that regional legislators are bound to comply with the principles of the Italian legal system, including those effectively reflecting the principle of 'procedural fairness' (or 'due process of law').

II. Administrative procedure legislation and government guidance: adjudication

In 1990, driven by a consolidated legal theory, Italy introduced a general law on administrative procedure known as Law No 241 of 7 August 1990 (or the 'Italian APA').

This legislative measure was the culmination of a reform effort to revise administrative procedure spanning at least 40 years. As early as 1944, the Government had set up a study commission (the Forti Commission, named after its president) to draw up general procedural rules. However, this first attempt came to nothing, and subsequent endeavours, including the notable Lucifredi proposals, failed to materialize.

The current procedure act is based on the proposal drafted by the Commission chaired by Professor Mario Nigro and was brought to fruition, particularly in terms of its conceptual framework and actual drafting, by Professor Giorgio Pastori. Many of the leading scholars of the time (F Benvenuti, M S Giannini, A M Sandulli, U Pototschnig, G Miele, and many others) contributed to the works of the Nigro–Pastori Commission, either as working members or through their intellectual insights and teachings.

The law's original framework is structured around five main sections: general principles (chapter I), the persons responsible for the procedure (chapter II), stakeholder participation (chapter III), administrative simplification (chapter IV), and the right to access administrative documents (chapter V).

The law has been updated several times, with the most significant amendment introduced by Law 15/2005. This amendment introduced a new section—chapter IV-*bis*—specifically addressing the system of invalidating administrative acts and the administration's authority to retract its own, commonly referred to as 'administrative internal review'.

With regard to principles, Article 1 of the law states that the administration '*pursues purposes determined by law*' and that its actions are guided by '*criteria of economy of action, effectiveness, impartiality, publicity and transparency*', as well as '*the principles underpinning the Community's legal order*'.

The explicit reference to principles, including Community principles, has fostered a gradual expansion of the procedural guarantees available to citizens over time. For instance, it was in relation to the revocation of measures favourable to citizens that the protection of legitimate expectations was first established through judicial decisions relying on general principles. Subsequently, these judicial precedents were assimilated by the legislature, amending the relevant articles in the Italian APA.

Regarding the procedural rules themselves, Law 241 explicitly adopts a perspective that promotes equality and service in the relationship between public administration and citizens based on a logic of equality and service, inspired by the best Italian and foreign legal theory.

The administration has a clear and unequivocal obligation to give reasons for its actions, except those of a general or legislative nature, such as administrative regulations. However, this duty encompasses organizational measures and competitive selection procedures. The requirement to give reasons guarantees the accountability of the administration's decision-making process, as it allows stakeholders to examine the reasoning followed by the public decision maker and to challenge its progression and outcome in administrative courts.

Unless otherwise established by law or regulation, the time limit for concluding proceedings is 30 days. Failure to respect this deadline will result in consequences for the official responsible, including potential disciplinary action and performance assessment mechanisms. Additionally, it may lead to awarding citizens compensation and indemnities.

Furthermore, for many authorizations, failure to issue a rejection within the time limit is legally considered equivalent to a favourable decision (tacit consent). Once tacit consent has been obtained, an authority can no longer withhold authorization unless there are specific grounds for annulling or revoking it through a formal process of administrative internal review.

Likewise, many authorizations have been replaced by a statutory declaration mechanism enabling the persons concerned to start working immediately, thanks to a certified notification of business start-up. In this case, a private citizen informs the administration that they are launching a business and that all the legal conditions have been met. If, over the following 60 days, the authority finds that these conditions have not been fulfilled, it can ask for any necessary adjustments, or, as a last resort, it can prevent the business from going ahead. After the 60 days have elapsed, these compliance or prohibition measures can only be implemented if the conditions for internal review are satisfied.

Another cornerstone of the Italian APA is the requirement to designate a person responsible for a procedure: the law mandates that the competent office must assign a specific official to each procedure. Even when the administration fails to act, the law includes an automatic mechanism for identifying the official. This innovation has proven crucial, as citizens now have a clear contact person whom they can ask for information inside the 'administrative machine', someone to whom they can make their own observations and demand explanations in the event of an error.

The person responsible for the procedure primarily conducts the preliminary investigation, which involves assessing the facts, the interests at stake, and any other circumstances of relevance to the final decision. In so doing, they are not obliged to keep to the facts presented by private citizens, but they are required to conduct independent investigations, adhering to the inquisitorial principle.

Lastly, we turn to the matter of participation. All individuals affected by an administrative procedure are entitled to 'participate'. This right implies a number of fundamental procedural rights and obligations.

Firstly, the notice of commencement of proceedings. When the administration initiates a proceeding, the persons directly concerned must be notified so that they can participate. Failure to fulfil this obligation constitutes a defect in the final measure, which can only be rectified in specific cases (Article 21-*octies*(2)); otherwise, it typically renders the measure unlawful.

There is also a protected right to be heard: this is the right to file documents and written statements during the procedure. The administration must take these into account, and if it decides not to endorse them, specific reasons must be provided in the main part of the final measure. Failure to provide reasons, or insufficient reasons, renders a measure unlawful, and it may be challenged by private citizens and annulled by an administrative court.

Furthermore, the right to access a proceeding is also guaranteed. This means the right to examine and obtain copies of all the documents relating to the proceeding without incurring any charge other than the cost of photocopies or the creation of electronic files.

In general terms, the right to access and the principle of administrative transparency are also protected, irrespective of participation, by Law No 241 and the more recent Legislative Decree 33 of 14 March 2013 and subsequent amendments and supplements (loosely inspired by other countries' Freedom of Information Acts). This legislation addresses the matter of transparency and introduces significant obligations regarding the online publication of public information and a broader right to access administrative documents than had previously been recognized under the general law on administrative procedure.

III. Administrative procedure legislation and government guidance: rule-making

The Italian APA expressly excludes the application of the provisions on stakeholder participation to activities carried out by public authorities for the purpose of issuing legislative (administrative regulations), general administrative, planning, and programming acts (Article 13).

In this regard, the legislature intentionally did not uphold the original formulation of the general outline of the law on administrative procedure proposed by the 1984 government commission (the 'Nigro–Pastori Commission'), which had proposed introducing public engagement in so-called 'mass' proceedings or those of great participatory interest. The already mentioned Article 13 of Law 241 does not affect any rules on participation that may be established by sectoral provisions governing the production of acts of this nature.

More specifically, many sectoral laws envisage a 'notice and comment' mechanism consisting in the obligation to publish the outline of a legislative or general act and then collect the observations of stakeholders.

For example, Article 9 of national legislation governing urban planning (Law No 1150 of 17 August 1942) entitles associations, bodies, and institutions (but also individuals, according to case law) to submit observations on the general urban development plan. Many regional town-planning laws provide additional assurances regarding the participation of private citizens in administrative town and territorial planning activities. Under Article 40 of the Public Contracts Code (Legislative Decree No 36 of 31 March 2023), projects concerning large infrastructure works having an impact on the environment, cities, and the territory must be subject to public consultation and prior debate with the stakeholders (a specific annex to the Code regulates the cases in which public debate is mandatory and the modalities of participation and conduct of the public debate). According to the Environmental Code (Legislative Decree No 152 of 3 April 2006), programmes and projects requiring Strategic Environmental Assessment and Environmental Impact Assessment must be subjected to public consultation, and general access must be given to all the environmental information (in accordance with the Aarhus Convention). Furthermore, a series of special laws require mandatory forms of stakeholder consultation on the outlines of sub-legislative regulatory acts adopted by independent administrative authorities in regulation activities. In domestic case law, participation in the regulation procedure constitutes the main factor legitimizing these authorities, as they are characterized by a structural separation from the representative political system.[7]

On a more general level, domestic case law has tended to consider stakeholder participation in administrative proceedings a general principle of the legal system. This means:

(i) that any provision restricting or excluding this right is to be interpreted narrowly to avoid undermining or circumventing the principle, and
(ii) the absence of a general obligation,[8] to consult the addressees of the administrative activity does not prevent the administration from consulting, for reasons of expediency, the categories concerned before issuing a general administrative act (Lazio Regional Administrative Court, Rome, Div III, No 1121, 7 February 2011).

In this context, we refer to a number of recent legislative changes to promote and regulate forms of consultation (including of a non-mandatory nature) with the public and stakeholders in relation to general administrative activity. For instance, in a Prime Ministerial Directive dated 31 May 2017, (non-binding) guidelines were issued 'on public consultation in Italy', based on recommendations and international best practices and addressed to all areas of administrative activity.

On the other hand, with regard to the procedures for adopting government legislative acts impinging significantly on citizens, businesses, and public authorities, Italian Prime Ministerial Decree No 169 of 15 September 2017 introduced forms of stakeholder consultation in the *ex-ante* analysis and *ex-post* assessment of the impact of the regulation.

[7] Lombardy Regional Administrative Court, Milan, Div III, No 1455, 11 May 2010.
[8] Council of State, Div V, No 2823, 22 May 2001; Council of State, Div IV, No 569, 25 September 1998.

8
Romania

Dacian-Cosmin Dragoş

I. General principles

The principles and process rights applicable to administrative proceedings in Romanian law are scattered over different regulations; the lack of an Administrative Procedure Law or Code means they are not unified.

The Romanian Constitution only summarily established a right to judicial review of administrative action (Article 52):

> Any person aggrieved in his/her legitimate rights or interests by a public authority, by means of an administrative act or by the failure of a public authority to solve his/her application within the lawful time limit, is entitled to the acknowledgement of his/her claimed right or legitimate interest, the annulment of the act and reparation for the damage.

The exceptions to this principle are also set out in Article 126 para (6):

> The judicial control of administrative acts of the public authorities, by way of the contentious business falling within the competence of administrative courts, is guaranteed, except for those regarding relations with the Parliament, as well as the military command acts. The administrative courts, judging contentious business, have jurisdiction to solve the applications filed by persons aggrieved by statutory orders or, as the case may be, by provisions in statutory orders declared unconstitutional.

Although it is not framed as a principle per se, these texts are considered the basis for the principle of judicial review—that every action of the administration should be reviewable in court and that only acts with a political/public security dimension are exempted from this control.

II. Administrative procedure legislation and government guidance: adjudication

The detailed rules on the judicial review of administrative action are contained in Law No 554/2004, which established a *contentieux de pleine juridiction*, so that annulment and damages can be requested at the same time. There are special regulations for

Dacian-Cosmin Dragoş, *Romania* In: *General Principles and Sector-Specific Rules in European Administrative Laws.* Edited by: Giacinto della Cananea and Jean-Bernard Auby, Oxford University Press. © Dacian-Cosmin Dragoş 2024.
DOI: 10.1093/oso/9780198867579.003.0008

specific fields, such as remedies for public procurement, detailed in Law No 101/2016, transposing the Remedies Directive 89/665/EEC with subsequent modifications.

Unfortunately, despite the efforts of scholarship, Romania is one of the few remaining European countries without a true Code of Administrative Procedure. Efforts to codify administrative procedure were undertaken between 2006 and 2008, during which a draft code[1] was agreed upon at the government level. However, these attempts ultimately proved unsuccessful due to subsequent political changes in the government.

Only a minimal surrogate law on administrative procedure exists, namely Governmental Ordinance No 27/2002, which regulates the procedure for responding to petitions. It establishes basic rules, such as a 30-day deadline for answering a petition. However, it does not contain the essential features of administrative procedure, ie the right to be heard, the duty to cite full grounds for a decision, the opinions/approvals necessary for an administrative act to be adopted, and any rules regarding communication, or remedies for unlawful acts. Various provisions are also to be found in Law No 554/2004 on Judicial Review, in which the principle of the revocation of administrative acts is drastically limited by a provision that restricts public authorities from revoking their unlawful acts if they enter the civil circuit, in which case the courts hold sole jurisdiction, so annulment and revocation are merged.

Nevertheless, a different form of codification did take place, and currently Romania is the only European country to have an Administrative Code. However, it predominantly focuses on substantive administrative law concerning the structure of central and local administration, public personnel services, public property, and public contracts. The adoption of this code has been blighted by political controversy.[2] It contains some principles mistakenly labelled as 'substantive', but they actually pertain to administrative *procedure* (activity). The principles in question are legality, equality, transparency, proportionality, the priority of the public interest, impartiality, continuity, and adaptability (Articles 6–13 of the 2019 Administrative Code).

Consequently, current administrative procedures are regulated inconsistently through special legislative instruments that are often uncoordinated with other acts regulating related areas of law. In Romania, considering the significant normative inflation (with an average of three laws adopted per day in recent years) and the

[1] Available here: <www.juridice.ro/wp-content/uploads/2012/12/Proiect-COD-procedura-administrativa.pdf> accessed June 2023.

[2] The 2017–2018 illiberal regime in Romania insisted on the notion that an Administrative Code is a prerequisite for a Code of Administrative Procedure, an idea not supported in the field of administrative law. Despite heated protest from legal scholars, an outstandingly complex piece of legislation (containing 687 articles) putting together several existing pieces of regulation with very little reform was adopted in 2018. The Code was used by politicians to introduce highly controversial provisions under the umbrella of 'simplification'. Scholars raised concerns regarding several issues, including the increased politicization of public servants in public administrations, the promotion of the ruling party's 'governing programme' as a source of legality for the entire public administration, alongside laws and secondary legislation, the provision of special pensions for mayors and members of city councils, and the diminished liability of public servants for unlawful administrative acts. In sum, the administrative code was supposed to bring stability, clarity, coherence, and legitimacy by unifying the legislation on public administration. In reality it was abused by political players for illegitimate purposes. Essentially, the administrative code was used to advance a political agenda rather than for its alleged purpose of modernizing the public administration.

instability of regulations, the codification of administrative procedure would be an appropriate measure to address these challenges effectively.

III. Administrative procedure legislation and government guidance: rule-making

Access to public-sector information, together with procedural requirements regarding the drafting and notification of administrative acts and public hearings/consultations are usually placed under the umbrella of transparency mechanisms.[3] In Romania, Law No 52/2003 governs transparency in the decision-making process and applies whenever public institutions adopt administrative acts, conduct public hearings, or open deliberative body sessions to the public.

Law No 52/2003 distinguishes between citizens' participation in drafting local regulations and citizens' participation in the local decision-making process. For each of these dimensions, the law establishes corresponding obligations vis-à-vis the local public authorities:

a. Publicity. Law No 52/2003, requiring local authorities to inform citizens of any local regulations, is currently pending adoption; it should also regulate public meetings to be organized in the community (local council meetings and public debates). The law establishes three required methods of publicity: online posting on the official website of the local authority, posting inside the building in an accessible place, and publication in a local newspaper. In addition, local authorities can use other methods, such as TV broadcasting and announcements, as well as posting in locations besides the local authority building.
b. Receiving recommendations from the public vis-à-vis draft regulation pending adoption. Both individuals and legally established entities have the right to make recommendations, and it is the responsibility of the public authorities to organize this process by receiving input and engaging in discussion of the suggestions put forward.
c. Organizing public meetings is a requirement when a legally established entity or another public authority requests a public discussion regarding pending regulations. Public authorities also have the option to initiate public consultations whenever they consider it necessary, particularly when matters of general interest are being debated. All local council meetings are open to the public, and all interested parties and the media may participate.
d. Drafting the annual self-assessment report on implementing Law No 52/2003. At the very minimum, the report should include certain compulsory elements as specified in the wording of the law, such as the number of public meetings organized, the number of recommendations received, and the complaints regarding non-compliance with the provisions).

[3] For details, see D C Dragoş, B Neamtu, and B V Cobârzan, 'Procedural Transparency in Rural Romania: Linking Implementation with Administrative Capacity?' (2012) 78 IRAS 134.

In conclusion, as observed initially, in the Romanian legal system there is no general legislation on administrative procedure. As a result, there are various possible options for invoking general principles. Three types of case should be disaggregated in this respect. There are, first, the principles established by the Constitution. There are, second, the general principles defined by the body of legislation regulating the relationship between public authorities, including proportionality and transparency; the latter, in particular, has an increasing importance. Finally, there are sector specific norms.

9
Serbia

Marko Milenković

I. General principles

There are several provisions in the Constitution of Serbia (2006)[1] stipulating process rights and regulating the discharge of administrative functions and powers by public authorities/private bodies operating on their behalf. Article 3 defines Rule of Law as a fundamental prerequisite for the Constitution, which is based on inalienable human rights and is exercised through, among other things, the observance of the Constitution and Law by the authorities. Article 36 of the Constitution—the right to equal protection of rights and legal remedy—stipulates that everyone must have the right of appeal or other legal remedies against any decision concerning his rights, obligations, or lawful interests. Furthermore, Article 137—the delegation of public powers and public services—stipulates that 'In the interest of more efficient and rational exercise of citizens' rights and duties and satisfying their needs of vital importance for life and work', the Law may delegate the performance of particular affairs falling within the competence of the Republic of Serbia to autonomous provinces and local self-government units, and states that particular public powers may be delegated to enterprises, institutions, organizations, and individuals. According to the Law, particular public powers may be also delegated to the specific bodies through which they perform regulatory functions in particular fields or affairs.[2] Furthermore, the Constitution provides that constitutional appeals may be lodged against individual general acts or actions performed by state bodies or organizations exercising delegated public powers which violate or deny human or minority rights and freedoms guaranteed by the Constitution if other legal remedies for their protection have already been applied or are not specified (Article 170).

Article 198 of the Constitution—Legality of administration—directly governs the discharge of administrative functions. This Article provides that *individual acts and actions* of state bodies, organizations with delegated public powers, bodies of autonomous provinces, and local self-government units must be based on the Law. The Constitution further guarantees that the *legality* of final individual acts deciding on a right, duty, or legally grounded interest shall be subject to assessment before the court through an administrative proceeding if another form of court protection has not been stipulated by the Law. It is important to note that the Constitution guarantees these

[1] Constitution of the Republic of Serbia, Official Gazette of the RS, No 98/2006 and 115/2021.

[2] This has served as the basis for the widespread 'agencification' of Serbian public administration in the 2000s. See further: M Milenković and M Milenković, 'Administrative Reform and Debates over Public Agencies' Role in Serbia' (2013) 61(3) Belgrade L Rev 135–50.

Marko Milenković, *Serbia* In: *General Principles and Sector-Specific Rules in European Administrative Laws.*
Edited by: Giacinto della Cananea and Jean-Bernard Auby, Oxford University Press. © Marko Milenković 2024.
DOI: 10.1093/oso/9780198867579.003.0009

rights only in regard to individual acts/decisions adopted by administrative bodies and not general acts with *erga omnes* effect. However, this does not exclude protection through the control of the 'constitutionality and legality' of general acts by the Constitutional court (Article 168), which will be referred to in particular cases below.

Process rights are guaranteed in detail by the Law on General Administrative Procedure (LGAP)[3] (see Section II below) and by a number of sectoral laws governing different 'special' procedures, drawing a distinction between general and special procedure widely found in national administrative practice and scholarly works. Yugoslav legal theory developed the distinction between 'general administrative procedure' and 'special administrative procedures' envisaged by sectoral legislation, which normally comprises both substantive and sector-specific procedural norms, and the notion of the subsidiary application of general administrative procedure in the absence of specific rules.[4] The issue was further muddled by the recent LGAP, although the specific provision in LGAP that it must apply in proceedings in all administrative matters, and that individual issues of administrative proceedings

> may be governed by a *lex specialis* only if this is necessary in certain administrative areas, and if in compliance with the basic principles set forth in this Law and does not reduce the level of protection of rights and legal interests of parties guaranteed under that Law (Article 3)

was an attempt to curtail this to some degree. One of the authors of the draft claimed that this provision 'almost raises its (ie the Law's) rank to the level of basic law'.[5] Even though this is an important guarantee in 'general law', it should be noted that, in the Serbian legal system, any other piece of sectoral legislation has the same legal value as the LGAP; thus, maintaining the same level of guarantees as achieved by the LGAP is a matter for the Constitutional Court. This dubious relationship between general and special procedures created by the recent Serbian LGAP was specifically pointed out by Lilić, who argues that the theoretical distinction between general and special procedures should be removed from the LGAP, providing for the general application of its rules unless deviation is necessary in particular matters.[6]

II. Administrative procedure legislation and government guidance: adjudication

Serbia has a long tradition of legislation governing general administrative procedure dating back to the time when it was part of Yugoslavia. The first Law on General Administrative Procedure of the Kingdom of Yugoslavia was adopted in 1930 and

[3] Law on General Administrative Procedure (Official Gazette of the RS, No 18/2016).
[4] S Lilić, *Special Administrative Law* (Beograd 1998)(in Serbian).
[5] Z Tomić, *General Administrative Law* (University of Belgrade—Faculty of Law 2017) 362 (in Serbian).
[6] S Lilić, *Law on General Administrative Procedure—Anatomy of a Legislative Project with the Model for the General Reconstruction of LGAP* (YUKOM, Dosije 2019)(in Serbian).

came into force in 1931.[7] It was among the first in Europe, after those adopted in Austria, Poland, and Czechoslovakia.[8] Following an interim period between 1946 and 1956, during which no relevant law was in force, the Law on General Administrative Procedure of the Federal People's Republic of Yugoslavia was adopted in 1956 and entered into force on 20 April 1957.[9] Even though a new LGAP was adopted in 1997, following the collapse of Socialist Yugoslavia and the transition to capitalism, changes were limited and mostly terminological. This was because Yugoslav administrative procedural legislation presented a largely adequate modus operandi for public administration regardless of the political or economic context.[10]

The adoption of new LGAP was set as one of priorities of public administration reform[11] after the political changes of 2000. However, this was followed by a lengthy and, at times, confusing and opaque drafting process, with several changes of working groups charged with producing the draft Law.[12] It was finally adopted in 2016 and came into force in 2017. It may be argued that the new LGAP has modernized administrative procedure and brought many innovations, such as the 'Administrative one-stop shop', cooperation and exchange of data between different administrative branches, and the facilitation of e-government.[13] This was indeed demonstrated by the rapid development of e-government services[14] and streamlining procedures in some important areas such as the issuance of personal documents or building permits. However, it has also met with broad criticism from leading scholars, who have highlighted numerous flaws in the legislative act, primarily the 'intrusion of theoretical concepts in the legislative text'[15] and the 'framing of new principles in a vague and imprecise manner' (the below described principle of foreseeability).[16]

Under the heading 'Fundamental Principles', the LGAP mixes the following rights and principles: 1) lawfulness and foreseeability (combined in one with foreseeability referring to the legitimate expectations of parties); 2) proportionality; 3) protection or rights of parties and protection of public interest (again combined in one); 4) aid

[7] For detailed analysis of the influence of the Austrian codification on Yugoslav administrative procedure see: S Lilić and M Milenković, 'Administrative Procedure in Former Yugoslavia and the Austrian Administrative Procedure Act' in G Della Cananea, A Ferrari Zumbini, and O Pfersmann (eds), *The Austrian Codification of Administrative Procedure* (OUP 2023).

[8] The 1930 Yugoslav LGAP had 176 paragraphs—twice as many as the Austrian 1925 LGAP, as it included many norms characteristic for dispute resolution procedure. S Lilić, *LGAP & LAD—Commentary of the Law on General Administrative Procedure and the Law on Administrative Disputes with Comparative Legislation* (Savremena administracija 1997) 14 (in Serbian).

[9] B Majstorović, *Commentary on the Law on General Administrative Procedure* (2nd edn, Savremena Administracija 1959) 3 (in Serbian). Interestingly, before the adoption of the new 'socialist' Yugoslav LGAP in 1956, a new Law on Administrative Disputes was adopted in 1952. Law on Administrative Disputes (Official Gazette FNRJ, No 23/1952).

[10] See further: Lilić, *LGAP & LAD* (n 8).

[11] See inter alia: Č Pištan and M Milenković, 'La semplificazione amministrativa nei Balcani occidentali: i casi della Croazia e della Serbia' (2021) 42(2) DPCE online 2061–89 (in Italian).

[12] See further: I Koprić, P Kovač, V Đulabić, J Džinić, *Legal Remedies in Administrative Procedures in the Western Balkans—Comparative Study* (ReSPA—Regional School of Public Administration 2016) 48–49. Lilić, *Law on General Administrative Procedure* (n 6).

[13] Koprić, Kovač, Đulabić, J Džinić (n 12).

[14] See further: eUprava, <https://euprava.gov.rs/> accessed July 2023.

[15] Lilić, *Law on General Administrative Procedure* (n 6).

[16] D Milkov and R Radošević, "Legitimate Expectations in Administrative Procedure' (2020) 1' Zbornik radova Pravnog fakulteta u Novom Sadu 19 (in Serbian).

to parties; 5) efficiency and cost-effectiveness of the proceedings; 6) truth and free assessment of evidence; 7) the right to be heard; 8) the principle of independence; 9) the right of appeal and complaint; and 10) the principle of validity of rulings, access to information, and data protection (Articles 5–16). Among these, principles of foreseeability, proportionality, access to information, data protection, and the right to be heard were introduced when the LGAP was adopted in 2016.[17] Most of the provisions will be addressed in the subsequent analysis of individual cases.

In terms of administrative dispute, the Law on Administrative Disputes[18] specifically provides for a fair trial before the Administrative Court (Article 2) and stipulates that in such cases, the Court is to decide on the basis of the law in a reasonable time, based on facts determined in an oral public hearing.[19] Finally, on a more general note, the cases in this questionnaire are predominantly constructed to discover how the courts would deal with the matter if it came before them. Serbia has a long history of administrative disputes with specialized courts dealing with the matter.[20] However, administrative judges regularly refrain from exercising 'full jurisdiction' in administrative matters, routinely limiting court decisions to 'limited jurisdiction'. The court normally controls the competence of the administrative authority, adherence to procedural rules, the application of relevant legislation to the matter, and, if a breach is found annuls the administrative act, with the administrative authority having a duty to adopt a new one (limited jurisdiction) (Article 42). In this way, the Court normally acts similarly to the Supreme Court of Cassation, which hears cases brought by extraordinary legal remedies. In this latter case of full jurisdiction, if the Court concludes that the disputed act must be annulled, it is allowed to decide the administrative matter by virtue of its decision 'if the nature of the matter allows for it, and the determined facts are reliable foundation', with the Court's judgment completely replacing the disputed act, ie producing all legal effects as an Act of Administration (Article 43). Unfortunately, this is still rarely used in practice.

III. Administrative procedure legislation and government guidance: rule-making

The Serbian legal system is characterized by inconsistent rules on public debate and consultations before the adoption of 1) general acts—Laws, Government Decrees, Rulebooks (adopted by Ministries), or 2) strategic/planning documents.[21] Public

[17] Tomić (n 5).

[18] Law on Administrative Disputes (Official Gazette of the RS, No 111/2009).

[19] Specifically on oral hearings in administrative disputes in Serbia see: R R Bjelica, 'Oral Public Hearing in an Administrative Dispute' (2020) 54(1) Zbornik radova Pravnog fakulteta Novi Sad 487–502.

[20] V Cucić, 'Historical and Contemporary Development of Judicial Control of Administration in Serbia' in *Identitetski preobražaji Srbije* (Pravni fakultet Beograd 2018) 181–202.

[21] The Law on the Planning System (*Zakon o planskom sistemu*), adopted in 2018, does contain extensive rules on public participation in the adoption of so called 'planning documents', namely various government strategies dealing with development and other sectoral issues. Thus, paradoxically, standards of public participation in the adoption of these documents are much higher and under much more stringent regulation than Laws proposed to the Parliament by the Government or Decrees/Rulebooks adopted by the Government and Ministries. See further: Law on the Planning System (Official Gazette of the RS, No 30/2018).

participation and consultation in regard to the first group is governed by the Law on State Administration[22] and Government rules of procedure.[23] The Law on State Administration provides for public participation in the preparation of draft laws, other regulations, and acts (Article 77). Bodies of State administration are obliged to provide conditions for public participation during the preparation of draft laws and other regulations and acts in accordance with this law. Ministries and special organizations are obliged to inform the public through their website and e-government portal on the start of drafting of the law, while also publishing basic information on the planned solutions that will be proposed. In situations where a body is beginning the preparation of a draft law that will significantly change the legal regime in one area or regulate issues of particular public interest, ministries and special organizations must publish a background document through their website and e-government portal, containing problems in a particular area and their causes, setting out the goals and expected effects of passing the law. In addition, the body must state the basic principles for regulating social relations in that area, including the rights and obligations of the subjects to which the law applies (starting points). By virtue of the Law, during the preparation of the draft law, ministries and special organizations are obliged to consult with all relevant entities, including other state bodies, relevant associations, and professional public (ie experts), as well as any other stakeholders 'in a way that ensures openness and effective public participation in the process'. These rules are also applicable to secondary legislation—decrees and rulebooks which elaborate certain provisions or determine the manner of execution of certain provisions of relevant laws. For draft Laws, public debate is obligatory. The Government rules of procedure set out an obligation for the proposer to conduct a public debate in the preparation of a law 'that significantly changes the regulation of an issue or regulates an issue that is of particular interest to the public'.[24] It is further prescribed, in detail, that the decision on conducting a public hearing, its programme, and the deadline within which it is conducted are determined by the competent committee upon the proposal of the proposer. The programme of the public debate must contain the draft or proposed act subject to public debate together with the explanation and annexes set out in the Rules of Procedure, the deadline for conducting the public debate, important information on activities planned within the public debate (round tables, forums, address and time of their maintenance, etc), the manner for submission of proposals, suggestions, initiatives, and comments, as well as other information important for its implementation.

[22] Law on State Administration (Official Gazette of the RS, No 79/2005, 101/2007, 95/2010, 99/2014, 47/2018, 30/2018).

[23] Government rules of procedure (Official Gazette of the RS, No 61/2006, 69/2008, 88/2009, 33/2010, 69/2010, 20/2011, 37/2011, 30/2013, 76/2014, 8/2019).

[24] According to the Rules, the criteria referred to in paragraph 1 of this Article relating to the obligation to conduct a public hearing are considered to be met in the following cases: 1) during the preparation of the new so-called system law; 2) during the preparation of a new law, unless the competent committee decides otherwise on the reasoned proposal of the proposer; 3) during the preparation of a law on amendments to a law if it significantly changes the decisions from the existing law, on which the competent committee, at the reasoned proposal of the proposer, decides in each specific case; 4) during the preparation of a law on the ratification of an international agreement—only if the competent committee decides to conduct a public hearing, at the reasoned proposal of the Ministry of Foreign Affairs or state administration bodies from whose scope the issues are regulated by an international agreement.

The deadline for submitting initiatives, proposals, suggestions, and comments in written or electronic form is at least 15 days from the date of publication of the public call. The public hearing lasts at least 20 days.[25] The proposer must publish the report on the completed public hearing on its website and e-government portal no later than 15 days from its conclusion (Article 41). If a public hearing is not obligatory, the material becomes available to the public when, at the latest, the competent committee adopts a conclusion proposing that the Government adopt an act or determine a draft act (Article 42). In addition, various sectoral laws require public debate before rules of general application, such as spatial plans or environmental impact assessments are adopted, and will be referred to in specific analysis of the cases.

The problem is worsened by the adoption of Laws in expedited/urgent procedure in Parliament, with the Government using this opportunity to avoid public debate and consultations. This was standard practice until 2019, with up to half of all acts being adopted in this manner[26] and was criticized by the European Commission in annual assessments of reforms in the country.[27]

[25] If a public hearing is obligatory, but the proposer does not conduct one, the competent committee, when considering the draft law, determines the programme of the public hearing and the deadline within which it is conducted. A proposer who does not conduct a public hearing according to the programme determined by the competent committee is obliged to conduct one in full.

[26] <https://crta.rs/wp-content/uploads/2018/03/Finalno_02-ucesce-gradjana-NOVO.pdf> accessed June 2023.

[27] In 2016 the urgent procedure was used 65 per cent of the time while in 2017 it decreased to 44 per cent. See further: European Commission, Progress Report Serbia (Brussels 2018) 6. The 2020 assessment found that urgent legislative procedure was used in only 19 per cent of cases, which demonstrates some improvement. See further: European Commission, *Progress Report Serbia* (Brussels 2020) 11.

10
Spain

Isaac Martín Delgado

I. General principles

In the Spanish legal system, assuming a legal–dogmatic perspective, administrative procedure qualifies as a self-governing legal institution with constitutional status and a threefold purpose: (i) to serve the public (general) interest, (ii) ensure the legality of administrative (public authorities') action, and (iii) engage citizens in administrative decision-making and adjudication.

This threefold purpose is stated in the 1978 Spanish Constitution (from now on *Constitución Española*, CE, or 'the Constitution'), giving rise to principles, standards, and rights applicable to administrative procedures. The administrative procedure thus qualifies as an instrument to fulfil the relevant constitutional principles and standards related to administrative or public authorities' action.

First, Article 9(3) CE precludes arbitrariness, ie, it states the principle of prohibition of arbitrariness. Article 31 provides for standards of efficiency and rationality in public spending, and Article 103 is worded as follows:

> Public authorities shall serve the public interest with objectivity and shall act in accordance with the principles of efficiency, hierarchy, devolution and coordination, being fully subject to the law.

The Constitution instructs the legislature to pass legislation with the impartiality requirements and standards applicable to public officials in the discharge of their duties. Administrative procedure is thus the formal means enabling public authorities to (i) fulfil the public needs provided in the Constitution and the relevant statutory provisions (laws or parliamentary statutes) and (ii) secure the legality principle. Along these lines, according to the preamble of Act 39/2015 on General Administrative Procedure (*Ley 39/2015 del Procedimiento Administrativo Común de las Administraciones Públicas*, LPAC)

> the citizens' set of rights and entitlements is protected vis-à-vis public action by preventive mechanisms and instruments (…) relying on administrative procedure, which ultimately expresses and ensures that public authorities remain fully subject to the law.

On top of that, as shown below, the objectivity standard for public action has a specific bearing on the administrative procedure.

Isaac Martín Delgado, *Spain* In: *General Principles and Sector-Specific Rules in European Administrative Laws*.
Edited by: Giacinto della Cananea and Jean-Bernard Auby, Oxford University Press. © Isaac Martín Delgado 2024.
DOI: 10.1093/oso/9780198867579.003.0010

The Constitution does not expressly provide for the general principle of good administration. However, both Spanish legal scholarship and case law have inferred the requirement of good or sound administration, along with public authorities' legal obligation to conduct fair administrative procedures (due process) and the right to fair administrative procedures (due process right), the purpose being to achieve sound administrative decisions. Therefore, administrative procedure is no longer construed as a process to adopt administrative acts (which was the nineteenth-century and early twentieth-century approach). Rather, it is now a means of guaranteeing good or sound administration.[1]

In its case law, the Spanish Supreme Court has consistently drawn an implied principle of good administration from various constitutional provisions, in line with Article 41 of the Charter of Fundamental Rights of the European Union (CFREU). Note that Article 41 CFREU requires administrative action to be conducted or handled with due care or due diligence.[2]

Over the last few years, good administration has been enshrined as a right in various *Estatutos de Autonomía*—broadly, the regional constitutions of Spain's Autonomous Regions—and in other statutory provisions. The case law consistently refers to, and applies the right to, good administration.[3]

Second, Article 24 provides the right to an effective remedy, which has implications on administrative procedures, both generally (it protects any legitimate rights and interests before the adoption of administrative decisions solely within punitive procedures, according to the Spanish Supreme Court)[4] and regarding specific aspects (eg the delivery of administrative notifications or the filing of administrative appeals).

Third, from the perspective of citizen participation, Article 9(2) provides that

> It is incumbent upon public authorities (. . .) to facilitate the participation of all citizens in political, economic, cultural and social life.

[1] See, among others, J Ponce Solé, *Deber de buena administración y derecho al procedimiento administrativo debido. Las bases constitucionales del procedimiento administrativo y del ejercicio de la discrecionalidad* (Lex Nova 2001)and, more recently, *La lucha por el buen gobierno y el derecho a una buena administración mediante el estándar jurídico de diligencia debida*, Cuadernos de la Cátedra de Democracia y Derechos Humanos, No 15 (Universidad de Alcalá de Henares-Defensor del Pueblo 2019).

[2] See an example of this in the Supreme Court Judgment of 15 October 2020:

> The principle of good administration is implied in Articles 9(3), 103 and 106 the Spanish Constitution. It was also codified in Articles 41 and 42 CFREU (. . .) and, according to the prevailing scholarly opinion, it shifted the 21st century legal paradigm bringing a new approach to public action precluding negligent management (. . .). As previously noted by this Court, the principle of good administration is not an empty shell. In fact, it is imposed on public authorities so that the set of rights and entitlements arising therefrom (the right to be heard, timely adjudication, reason-giving requirements, the requirement to conduct the proceedings and adjudicate the cases fairly or the duty of good faith), along with the relevant requirements incumbent upon public authorities, be effectively enforced.

[3] For instance, see the Judgment delivered on 1 October 2020 by the Catalonia Regional High Court regarding art 30 of the Catalonia *Estatuto de Autonomía* providing for the right to good administration.

[4] Constitutional Court Judgment 145/2011, of 26 September.

This general principle is further defined in Article 105, which includes the requirement that lawmakers come up with procedural participation mechanisms. Under Article 105

> The law [ie, statutory provisions] shall regulate:
>
> a) the hearing of citizens directly, or through the organizations and associations recognized by law in the process of drawing up the administrative provisions which affect them;
> b) access of citizens to administrative files and records, except as they may concern the security and defence of the State, the investigation of crimes, and the privacy of individuals:
> c) the procedures for taking administrative action, guaranteeing the hearing of interested parties [ie, the parties concerned or stakeholders] when appropriate.

This provision entails making unilateral administrative decision-making subject to procedures—including rule-making procedures—qualifying as mechanisms that allow citizens whose rights and interests may be affected by the relevant administrative decision or rule to participate and cooperate. Indeed, the scholarly concept of participation in administrative procedures is not only a means to have an impact on public authorities' final decisions and protect the individual rights at stake. It is also a mechanism for sound decision-making. The Constitutional Court too has stated that constitutional participation requirements are a way of achieving more appropriate and better decisions, tied to other constitutional principles and standards, with very fair and effective administrative operational standards.[5]

Furthermore, as stated above, under Article 9(3) CE, '[t]he Constitution guarantees (. . .) the prohibition of arbitrary action' by public authorities. The prohibition of arbitrariness has a twofold dimension: (i) the rationality requirement arising from the principle of good administration, and (ii) the duty to give reasons (supporting arguments or lines of reasoning) for public action. Therefore, the prohibition of arbitrariness provides general guidance for administrative decision-making and adjudication.

II. Administrative procedure legislation and government guidance: adjudication

The general legislation on administrative action draws a distinction between principles or standards and rights related to administrative procedure.

With regard to principles and standards, Act 40/2015 on the Legal Regime applicable to Public Authorities (*Ley 40/2015 del Régimen Jurídico del Sector Público*, LRJSP) has enshrined in Article 3 various general principles and standards governing public authorities' action. It is worth noting the principles of participation, objectivity, and transparency, along with the duty of good faith, the principle of legitimate expectations, and the principle of institutional loyalty. Article 3 LRJSP only mentions these

[5] Constitutional Court Judgment 112/1995, of 26 June.

principles, without further specifying their content. Also, the Supreme Court has drawn from this provision the principle of good or sound administration.[6]

Also, note the provisions of the Act on Transparency, Access to Public Information, and Good Governance (*Ley 19/2013 de Transparencia, Acceso a la Información Pública y Buen Gobierno*, LTBG), addressed to senior government officials and public authorities. Article 26 sets out several good governance principles, including transparency in the handling of public affairs, impartiality, and non-discrimination. Breaching these principles qualifies as an infringement and carries penalties. Authorities have passed different national and regional codes of ethics and codes of conduct to implement these principles. However, there is an uneven enforcement in practice, due to the lack of ethical frameworks, public compliance systems ensuring that the codes are acknowledged, and training and response systems in case of concerns regarding their application or monitoring.

Furthermore, the Act on General Administrative Procedure (LPAC) lays down a series of general legal principles and standards regarding administrative procedure, eg, the requirement that procedures be streamlined or conducted in a non-formalistic manner, and the adversarial principle.

As for rights or entitlements, the LPAC differentiates between the rights of (i) citizens and (ii) stakeholders (or parties concerned), vis-à-vis public authorities as an expression of good administration.[7] Regarding (i) above, under Article 13 LPAC, everyone has the right to access public information, files, and records. Article 13 refers to the LTBG for the implementation and enforcement of this right. The LTBG secures everyone's right to access public information without stating a specific legal interest justifying the request or application.

Although it has an indirect impact, we should keep in mind that citizens are also entitled to be treated respectfully by public authorities and officials, who should facilitate

[6] The Supreme Court Judgment of 19 February 2019 provides the following:

> We have already discussed the principle of good administration implied in Articles 9(3) and 103 of the Constitution, found in many rulings and codified in Article 3(1) LRJSP. This principle requires public authorities to act diligently so as to prevent possible maladministration. It is not enough for public authorities to comply strictly with the relevant procedural requirements. Rather, the principle of good administration i) requires that all statutory and constitutional rights and safeguards be secured and duly made available to taxpayers [ie, citizens]; and ii) instructs tax authorities to act with due care so as to ensure the effectiveness of these rights and safeguards whilst guaranteeing appropriate legal remedies preventing unlawful profits.

[7] The Supreme Court (see Judgment of 3 December 2020, Appeal 7763/2019) found that the principle of good administration

> under Article 41 CFREU, now qualifies as a fundamental right within the Union. Some scholars claim that the principle falls within the new generation of fundamental rights echoed by the Spanish Supreme Court case law, including the Judgment of 30 April 2012 (…) up to the more recent and often cited Judgment 1558/2020 of 19 November 2020 (…). Some argue that the principle of good administration in Spanish law can be inferred from the prohibition of arbitrariness under Art 9(3) of the Constitution. But, above all, the principle of good administration must be deemed implied in Article 103, particularly in the clause requiring public authorities to remain 'fully' subject to the law. Articles 13 and 53 LPAC clearly rely on EU law when governing the rights of citizens vis-à-vis public authorities. However, good administration is more than a fundamental right, although this is its most significant dimension, because the principle's effectiveness entails a duty or an obligation for public authorities, who become subject to sophisticated and stringent legal requirements.

the exercise of rights and the fulfilment of obligations. In this connection, citizens also have the right to assistance when using electronic means. This is important because the LPAC emphasizes the digitalization of administrative procedures.

Article 53 LPAC provides two types of rights for stakeholders affecting formal and substantive aspects of the procedure. Concerning the formal aspects, it establishes a general entitlement to be informed at any time of (i) the status of any ongoing procedures in which the party qualifies as a stakeholder; (ii) the effect of the so-called *silencio administrativo* (ie, failure by public authorities to reply or adjudicate, considering that such 'silence' can be affirmative—upholding the claim or request—or negative); (iii) the competent body processing and deciding on the procedure; (iv) any non-final procedural resolutions (*actos de trámite*), and it also provides (v) the right to receive a copy of all the documents in the case file. All of these entitlements have implications for transparency and participation. Additionally, Article 53 LPAC provides the right to identify public authorities, public officials, and public servants leading and conducting the procedures. This is a significant entitlement from the perspective of the impartiality requirement. Regarding substantive aspects, the LPAC grants the rights to (i) submit comments, (ii) use any legal means of defence, and (iii) produce documents at any stage of the procedure prior to hearing the parties concerned. Regarding (iii), the competent body must take any produced documents into account before preparing the draft final decision. There is also a right to legal counsel if the parties concerned see fit.

Regarding penalty or sanctioning procedures, the LPAC expressly establishes the parties' right to be duly notified of any offences or infringements attributed to them along with the potential penalties, specifying the identity of the investigating public official, the competent authority that may impose the relevant penalty and the provision that grants competency. This notification should add that no one will be held liable in administrative procedures unless proven otherwise.

There are four sets of supplementing safeguards: (i) the need to move forward and expedite the necessary proceedings and investigative acts required to determine, verify, and establish the facts of the case, (ii) the possibility of taking evidence to prove the relevant facts of the case, and (iii) the duty or possibility of requesting any reports required to adjudicate the case. On top of these, (iv) stakeholders or parties concerned are entitled to participate in the hearing—after the investigative stage and before requesting the competent body's legal report—and there may be a public consultation stage (allowing anyone to submit comments, although submitting comments in this stage does not make the participant a stakeholder or party concerned) if the adjudicating body sees fit.

As for the final administrative decision, the LPAC requires (i) administrative acts to be adopted through electronic means (see Articles 26 and 36) and (ii) the file to be conducted or processed electronically (see Article 70). This guarantees integrity and traceability. The LPAC also requires public authorities to give reasons (supporting arguments) for any decisions or acts (i) restricting rights or interests, (ii) departing from the opinion of advisory bodies or from previous acts, and (iii) falling within the scope of the public authority's discretion (see Article 35). Public authorities will fulfil the aforesaid duty to state reasons as long as they outline the factual background and the relevant legal grounds.

Lastly, Articles 112ff LPAC enable stakeholders to bring administrative appeals challenging both (i) final administrative decisions and (ii) specific non-final procedural resolutions or *actos de trámite*, ie, resolutions, directly or indirectly deciding on the merits of the case, preventing the procedure from going on or moving forward, and rendering the party defenceless or having the potential to irreparably undermine the party's rights or interests. In the case of acts that do not exhaust administrative procedural remedies, if the parties subsequently want to seek judicial administrative proceedings,[8] they must file a hierarchical appeal called *recurso de alzada* before the body to which the adjudicating authority reports (ie, the hierarchically superior body). Conversely, with regard to acts that exhaust administrative procedural remedies, the parties may (they are not required to) file an appeal for review called *recurso de reposición* before the adjudicating authority. Exceptionally (in the event of error of fact, new relevant documents, false statements or documents so declared in a final judgment affecting the decision, or administrative decisions qualifying as a criminal offence), the party concerned may bring an extraordinary appeal for review before the adjudicating or decision-making authority.

Articles 23 and 24 of the Act on the Legal Regime applicable to Public Authorities (LRJSP) provide impartiality and objectivity standards and requirements. In particular, they require adjudicating or decision-making bodies to disqualify themselves, or the parties to challenge them, in specific cases, either for (i) having a personal bias, interest, or connection with the parties, or (ii) having acted as an expert or a witness in the procedure.

It is also worth highlighting a general idea discussed above. Article 75 LPAC is worded as follows:

> [A]ny investigative acts required to determine, verify and establish the facts of the case shall be conducted ex officio and electronically by the body or authority conducting the procedure. This is without prejudice to the stakeholders' [concerned parties'] right to request any acts or proceedings i) requiring their participation, or ii) qualifying as statutory or regulatory requirements.

This gives rise to the due process right to a fair procedure, thereby requiring public authorities to act rationally and to make reasonable and sound decisions, as boldly stated by the Supreme Court in its Judgment of 4 April 2018.[9]

[8] These are sometimes designated as 'contentious-administrative proceedings', although this is clearly a literal translation not truly conveying the legal institution at issue.

[9] See Supreme Court Judgment of 14 April 2021 (Appeal 28/2020):

> The due process right to a fair administrative procedure, which is a corollary to the principle of good administration, ensures that administrative decisions (. . .) be adopted duly giving reasons and in line with the procedural steps, without any procedural impropriety, since there must be no inconsistencies between the facts of the case, the legal grounds, and the content of the relevant administrative decision. Under this constitutional good administration requirement (. . .), public authorities must fulfill the reason-giving requirements and the principles of objectivity, transparency and rationality in accordance with Articles 35 and 129 LPAC. Within this context, regarding the public authorities' duty to comply with all the procedural safeguards, we find an infringement of the due process right to a fair procedure. This due process right stems from the Constitution, namely from i) Art 24, ensuring the right to an effective legal remedy and, generally speaking, the

These premises give a better understand of the scope of Article 34 LPAC when it states that

> administrative acts from public authorities (...) must be issued by the competent body in compliance with the applicable requirements and following the established procedure.

The procedure—and any applicable procedural steps, requirements, and safeguards—ultimately enforces the principles of good administration, transparency, and participation provided in the Constitution.

III. Administrative procedure legislation and government guidance: rule-making

As noted earlier, under Spanish law, there is a constitutional requirement for citizens to be involved in rule-making procedures. Such involvement or participation falls under the good regulation (or best regulatory practice) principles set out in Article 129 LPAC, which stem from the principle of good or sound administration. The individual right established in Article 105(a) of the Constitution (CE) is further specified and implemented in two provisions governing citizen participation in rule-making procedures: (i) Article 133 LPAC and (ii) particularly regarding national Government regulations, Article 26 of the Act on Government (*Ley 50/1997, del Gobierno*, LG). These two provisions also require public authorities to prepare and publish a yearly administrative activity plan. Compliance with this requirement is uneven, particularly after Constitutional Court Judgment 55/2018 declared that the requirement did not apply to regional authorities (ie, to the regional government level) based on the constitutional allocation of powers. Indeed, there is specific regional legislation on this matter.

From this perspective, participation must be construed as a mechanism to strike a fair balance between the interests at stake, enhance regulation, and secure the principle of, and the right to, good administration (along these lines, see the Supreme Court Judgment of 15 July 2010) in order to increase the political legitimacy of the said principle.

This is why the LPAC regulates citizen participation in rule-making procedures for statutory and regulatory provisions implementing the good regulation (or best regulatory practice) principles set out in Article 129 LPAC: necessity, effectiveness, proportionality, legal certainty, transparency, and efficiency. A violation of these principles constitutes grounds for invalidating the relevant provision.[10]

In particular, under the principle of transparency, public authorities will enable (i) friendly, universal, and updated access to the applicable provisions and to the supporting documents, and (ii) 'active participation in rulemaking for the potential

right to effective legal protection, and ii) Art 103, providing that all administrative action should be governed by the principle of objectivity.

[10] Supreme Court Judgment of 4 June 2020.

addressees'. Article 7 LTBG requires public authorities to post on their transparency platforms (i) any guidelines, instructions, resolutions, circulars, or responses to consultations submitted by individuals or other bodies if they include legal interpretations or have legal effects, (ii) draft bills and draft legislative decrees to be passed on their motion when reports are requested of the relevant advisory bodies, (iii) draft regulations to be passed on their motion, (iv) any supporting memoranda and reports used for rulemaking, and (v) any documents which, under the applicable sector-specific legislation, must be subjected to a public consultation stage. However, this provision is not consistent with the LPAC, according to which these disclosure and transparency obligations are only required after the Council of State (or the relevant advisory body) has issued its report, ie, at a later stage in the rulemaking procedure.

There are three mechanisms for citizen participation in rule-making: prior public consultation, public consultations, and the hearing for stakeholders or parties concerned. All mechanisms

> should be carried out so as to allow potential addressees and anyone submitting comments on the provision to give their opinion. To this end, authorities must make available to the parties any necessary documents.

The two consultations are mandatory for any draft regulation, even if the applicable sector-specific legislation does not require them. Therefore, failure to carry out these consultations will render the provision invalid. Nevertheless, they can be excluded in certain cases. Under Article 133 LPAC, authorities will not be required to implement any of the three mechanisms for budget or organizational regulations if justified on overriding grounds of public interest. Additionally, there will be no need for a prior public consultation if the draft regulation (i) does not have a significant impact on economic activity, (ii) fails to impose significant obligations on the addresses, or (iii) regulates only partial aspects of a given matter. These exceptions must be narrowly construed and justified (giving reasons) on a case-by-case basis.

So-called prior public consultation or *consulta pública* must be conducted before preparing a draft bill or a draft regulation through the competent authority's website, in order to

> gather the opinions of individuals and the most representative entities or organizations that could be affected by the future provision on: a) the issues to be tackled by the draft; b) whether the draft is necessary and suitable; c) the aims of the draft; d) possible regulatory and non-regulatory alternatives.

Prior public consultation seeks to obtain information on how to approach rulemaking.

Also, if the draft provision may interfere with individual rights or interests, it should be posted on the relevant online platform or website to hear the parties concerned and gather additional comments from other individual citizens and entities. The requirement to hold this subsequent public consultation or *trámite de información pública* arises from the principle of participation and covers a subsequent and more specific draft provision (as opposed to the prior public consultation discussed above).

Although the applicable legislation mentions 'stakeholders' or 'parties concerned', the reference to additional comments and contributions leads us to think that (as in the case of prior public consultation) any person or organization can participate. This participation mechanism seeks to enhance the draft provision.

Lastly, authorities may directly obtain comments from registered or legally acknowledged organizations and associations representing individuals whose rights and interests may be affected by the provision. This is an individual, ad hoc hearing or *trámite de audiencia* available to whoever may be affected by the draft provision specifically. Since the law says that authorities '*may*' use this mechanism, one could argue that it is not mandatory and that it may supplement the two consultations discussed before. However, if the competent authority decides to hold this hearing, it must comply with the aforesaid requirements. This *audiencia* is aimed at receiving proposals from qualified stakeholders.

It is worth adding that some autonomous regions have passed specific pieces of legislation generally governing citizen participation in the making of rules, plans, and programmes, although there is no such legislation on the national level.

11
Switzerland

Alexandre Flückiger

I. General principles

Before the Federal Constitution of 18 April 1999 (Cst) came into force in 2000, the Federal Supreme Court (TF) had deduced—for more than a century—the procedural guarantees in administrative law from the principle of equality (Article 4 of the 1874 Federal Constitution). Since the entry into force of the ECHR in Switzerland on 28 November 1974, the courts have referred directly to Article 6 ECHR to strengthen these rights, which have had a lasting effect on practice. Since 2000, procedural rights are codified in Article 29ff Cst. These are essentially the right to a fair trial, the right to an impartial authority, the right to be heard, the right to consult the file, the prohibition of undue delay, excessive formalism, and refusal to rule, and the right to free legal assistance.

More specifically, Article 29 Cst defines general procedural guarantees as follows:

> Every person has the right to equal and fair treatment in judicial and administrative proceedings and to have their case decided within a reasonable time. (para 1).
>
> Each party to a case has the right to be heard. (para 2).
>
> Any person who does not have sufficient means has the right to free legal advice and assistance unless their case appears to have no prospect of success. If it is necessary in order to safeguard their rights, they also have the right to free legal representation in court. (para 3).[1]

These general procedural guarantees of Article 29 Cst apply not only to public authorities but also to any person assuming a public function under Article 35 para 2 Cst ('Whoever acts on behalf of the state is bound by fundamental rights and is under a duty to contribute to their implementation.')[2]

The cantonal constitutions also enshrine procedural guarantees inspired by the federal model. One example is Article 40 of the Geneva Constitution of 14 October 2012.

In addition to the general procedural guarantees stipulated in Article 29 of the Federal Constitution, we should mention, in order, Article 29a guaranteeing access to the courts, Article 30 on guarantees of judicial procedure, and Article 31 on the principles applicable in cases of deprivation of liberty.

1 Art 29 Cst.
2 Art 35 para 2 Cst.

Alexandre Flückiger, *Switzerland* In: *General Principles and Sector-Specific Rules in European Administrative Laws.*
Edited by: Giacinto della Cananea and Jean-Bernard Auby, Oxford University Press.
DOI: 10.1093/oso/9780198867579.003.0011

Article 29a Cst is worded as follows: 'In a legal dispute, every person has the right to have their case determined by a judicial authority.'[3] By law, the Confederation and the Cantons may preclude the courts' determination of specific exceptional categories of cases.

According to Article 30 Cst,

> [a]ny person whose case falls to be judicially decided has the right to have their case heard by a legally constituted, competent, independent, and impartial court. Ad hoc courts are prohibited. (para 1).
>
> Unless otherwise provided by law, any person against whom civil proceedings have been raised has the right to have their case decided by a court within the jurisdiction in which they reside. (para 2).
>
> Unless the law provides otherwise, court hearings and the delivery of judgments shall be in public. (para 3).[4]

Under Article 31 Cst,

> No person may be deprived of their liberty other than in the circumstances and in the manner provided for by the law. (para 1).
>
> Any person deprived of their liberty has the right to be notified without delay and in a language they can understand of the reasons for their detention and their rights. They must be given the opportunity to exercise their rights, in particular, the right to have their next of kin informed. (para 2).
>
> Any person in pre-trial detention has the right to be brought before a court without delay. The court decides whether the person must remain in detention or be released. Any person in pre-trial detention has the right to have their case decided within a reasonable time. (para 3).
>
> Any person who has been deprived of their liberty by a body other than a court has the right to have recourse to a court at any time. The court shall decide as quickly as possible on the legality of their detention. (para 4).[5]

II. Administrative procedure legislation and government guidance: adjudication

The federal legislator has codified these procedural guarantees in a code of administrative procedure: the Federal Administrative Procedure Act of 20 December 1968 (APA). The same applies to the cantons: eg the Geneva law on administrative procedure of 12 September 1985. These laws have codified essential procedural principles, rules that have become almost customary, and other procedural practices. The

[3] Art 29a Cst.
[4] Art 30 Cst.
[5] Art 31 Cst.

legislators also drew inspiration from the institutions established in civil or criminal proceedings.

In addition, the legislation (federal and cantonal) establishes special rules: eg in tax law, planning and environmental law, or social insurance law. Often, they relate to transparency and public disclosure.

III. Administrative procedure legislation and government guidance: rule-making

The Federal Constitution gives everyone the right to be heard (Article 29 para 2 Cst). The federal and cantonal procedural codifications specify the principle and special provisions of federal and cantonal legislation.

The principle applies to any procedure that leads to an individual and concrete legal act of a public authority (ruling). It does not apply to general and abstract normative acts (ATF 144 I 318, 334) nor to 'material acts'.[6] In cases concerning urban plans, the affected owners have a right to be heard.

[6] See Switzerland, case 10.

12
United Kingdom

Gordon Anthony and Conor McCormick

Preliminary comments

Before turning to the questionnaire, the following, overarching points about administrative procedures, general principles of law, and sector-specific rules in the UK can be made:[1]

1. The general principles of law that are applied by UK courts are common law creations. This means that they are developed by the courts with reference to judicial experience and contemporary legal demands.[2] While this has given rise to debates about judicial activism—notably in the context of judicial review[3]—it is axiomatic that the common law gives shape to the general principles of law. Such development may occur with reference to the common law's own internal reference points, or it may equally occur through the integration of international and human rights norms into domestic standards.[4] EU law has also had an historical influence on the principles, albeit 'Brexit' has largely ended direct linkages between domestic law and EU law (including at the level of general principles).[5]

[1] Two caveats are helpful. First, this report has been written in the light of discussions held at Bocconi University on 24 and 25 October 2019 and the resulting questionnaire prepared by the COCEAL project team. It follows the structure of that questionnaire and, consistent with earlier guidance note from the organizers, tries 'not only to provide answers to the questions raised … but also to shed light on the doctrines and broader sets of beliefs and ideas about the law that the courts or other public agencies would use when dealing with those cases'. Second, the term 'UK law' is here used for ease of reference but also because the same general principles of law apply in each of its main jurisdictions. On the law in England and Wales see, eg, C Donnelly, I Hare, H Woolf, and J Jowell, *De Smith's Judicial Review* (8th edn, Sweet and Maxwell 2020); on Northern Ireland law see G Anthony, *Judicial Review in Northern Ireland* (3rd edn, Hart Publishing 2024); and on Scottish law see, *The Laws of Scotland: Stairs Memorial Encyclopaedia* (LexisNexis 2000 and re-issues).

[2] See generally Sir John Laws, *The Common Law Constitution* (Cambridge UP 2015). See also, eg, *Re Perry's Application* [1997] NI 282, 300, Girvan J: 'It is a feature of the richness of the common law that old concepts and practices in danger of becoming outdated can be dusted down, repolished and reinvigorated in the evolutionary process of case law'; and *Re T's Application* [2000] NI 516, 533, Coghlin J: 'it is important to bear in mind that history is a continuous process and that the vital dynamic of the common law has been an enduring tension between stability and creative development'.

[3] See, eg, *Judicial Power Project* at <https://judicialpowerproject.org.uk/> accessed June 2023.

[4] For different judicial views on how the common law develops see the judgments of Lords Kerr and Reed in *Elgizouli v Secretary of State for the Home Department* [2020] UKSC 10, [2020] 2 WLR 857.

[5] European Union (Withdrawal) Act 2018, §§ 1 and 5. Note that the general principles of EU still apply in Northern Ireland in cases arising under the Ireland-Northern Ireland Protocol (now often referred to as the Windsor Framework): European Union (Withdrawal) Act 2018, § 7A, as read with art 4 of the EU–UK Withdrawal Agreement and arts 12(4) and 13(2)–(4) of the Ireland-Northern Ireland Protocol. On historical influence see, eg, G Anthony, *UK Public Law and European Law: The Dynamics of Legal Integration* (Hart Publishing 2002).

Gordon Anthony and Conor McCormick, *United Kingdom* In: *General Principles and Sector-Specific Rules in European Administrative Laws.* Edited by: Giacinto della Cananea and Jean-Bernard Auby, Oxford University Press.
 DOI: 10.1093/oso/9780198867579.003.0012

2. UK courts apply the general principles of law on the understanding that, '*in law, context is everything*'.[6] The link between 'application of principles' and 'context' is perhaps most pronounced in relation to the rules of fairness/natural justice, where the common law's requirements can vary significantly. In *Lloyd v McMahon*, Lord Bridge said:

> the so-called rules of natural justice are not engraved on tablets of stone. To use the phrase which better expresses the underlying concept, what the requirements of fairness demand when any body, domestic, administrative or judicial, has to make a decision which will affect the rights of individuals depends on the character of the decision-making body, the kind of decision it has to make and the statutory or other framework in which it operates.[7]

This encapsulates the very essence of the common law's approach to procedural protections: they may be at their height when a decision affects an individual's fundamental rights (subject to public interest arguments about, for instance, national security); and they may be considerably less developed if an individual has only a peripheral interest in the matter to be decided.[8]

3. The contextual approach also governs the substantive review of decisions and measures. Here, the courts have long emphasized that the level of scrutiny that is appropriate will depend on factors such as: (i) the decision maker (legislature; executive; or public authority); (ii) whether fundamental rights are affected by a decision and whether those rights are absolute or qualified in nature; and (iii) the extent of discretion enjoyed by a decision maker.[9] This is true whether a decision is challenged at common law (where the standard of 'reasonableness' exists on a sliding scale) or with reference to the proportionality principle that applies under the ECHR/Human Rights Act 1998.[10] In the latter setting, the courts can exercise restraint by recognizing that the decision maker enjoys a '*discretionary area of judgement*'.[11]
4. Legislation in particular fields can impose procedural requirements that are akin to the common law's general principles, where the courts will give priority to statutory requirements whilst supplementing them with common law principle. An example of legislative intervention is in the field of planning law, where the legislative framework imposes consultation requirements, as well as a duty to give reasons for particular decisions.[12] Some of the procedural requirements as

[6] *R (Daly) v Home Secretary* [2001] UKHL 26, [2001] 2 AC 532, 548, Lord Steyn.
[7] [1987] AC 625, 702.
[8] For more general discussion see further *McInnes v Onslow-Fane* [1978] 1 WLR 1520, below; and for national security considerations see, eg, *R (Begum) Special Immigration Appeals Commission* [2021] UKSC 7, [2021] AC 765.
[9] See, eg, *International Transport Roth GmbH v Home Secretary* [2003] QB 728, 765ff, Laws LJ.
[10] *R (Daly) v Home Secretary* [2001] UKHL 26, [2001] 2 AC 532.
[11] *R v DPP, ex p Kebeline* [2000] 2 AC 326, 381, Lord Hope.
[12] See A Sheppard *et al*, *The Essential Guide to Planning Law: Decision-making and Practice in the UK* (Policy Press, 2017); and, eg, *R (PCRE Kent) v Dover District Council* [2017] UKSC 79, [2018] 1 WLR 108.

apply in this area have their origins in EU law, many of which now take the form of 'assimilated law' under the domestic legislation that gave effect to Brexit.[13]

5. Legislation can also impose limitations on procedural rights, for instance by narrowing the scope of the privilege against self-incrimination in certain areas. Its capacity to do so is, however, constrained by two factors. The first is the common law: while the courts accept that the Westminster Parliament can limit rights through legislation, they require Parliament to use express and unambiguous language to achieve that outcome.[14] The second factor is the Human Rights Act 1998: limitations on rights contained in Acts of Parliament must be consistent with guarantees in the ECHR or be subject to a remedy under the Human Rights Act (either a Convention compliant interpretation or, where that is not possible, a declaration of incompatibility).[15]
6. The idea of sector specific rules is to be seen in the light of the above. In short, a sector will be relevant to the context within which the courts will make a decision, but it will not pre-determine the judicial approach. All will depend on a range of related factors, in particular the nature of the decision maker, whether rights are engaged, and the extent of the decision maker's discretion.

I. General principles

The UK famously does not have a written constitution, so there is no formal constitutional clause that grounds and protects process rights. The foremost source of process rights is thus the common law rules of fairness/natural justice, which correspond, at their height, with a common law right of access to justice.[16] The manner in which the rules and the right of access to justice operate is, however, always context dependent, and the common law accepts that even judicial proceedings can be subject to limitation for reasons of public interest (specifically national security).[17] Discrete pieces of legislation can also enhance process rights, as well as limit them. In the latter instance, the courts will require that any limitation on rights is expressly authorized by statute—the so-called 'legality' principle.[18]

II. Administrative procedure legislation and government guidance: adjudication

The UK has neither an administrative procedure act nor a dedicated code of conduct that expressly imposes duties of due process, etc on public decision makers. Procedural

[13] For EU law requirements see, eg, *R (Buckinghamshire CC) v Secretary of State for Transport* [2014] UKSC 3, [2014] 1 WLR 324; and for 'assimilated law' (formerly 'retained EU law') see European Union (Withdrawal) Act 2018, §§ 2–7.

[14] *R v Home Secretary, ex parte Simms* [2000] 2 AC 115. The position in relation to the legislatures in Northern Ireland, Scotland, and Wales is less clear, as it is arguable that they cannot limit common law rights: see *Axa v HM Advocate* [2011] UKSC 46, [2012] 1 AC 868.

[15] On the Act see M Amos, *Human Rights Law* (3rd edn, Hart Publishing 2021).

[16] *R v Lord Chancellor, ex p Witham* [1998] QB 575.

[17] *R (Begum) Special Immigration Appeals Commission* [2021] UKSC 7, [2021] AC 765.

[18] *R (UNISON) v Lord Chancellor* [2017] UKSC 51, [2020] AC 869.

requirements will therefore be found (sometimes *ex post facto*) in the common law or in discrete pieces of legislation, as in the example of planning law, above. All public bodies are subject to the common law, where government Ministers are also bound by a code of conduct which includes duties to act fairly and transparently. Such codes are not typically enforceable in law, meaning that any consequence for breach of the code lies in the political realm.[19] Codes are also in place in relation to local government decision makers and these codes can typically be enforced against local councillors who act in breach of their obligations.[20]

III. Administrative procedure legislation and government guidance: rule-making

Again, there is no administrative procedure act or code of conduct that imposes a blanket duty to consult stakeholders, and the duty to consult will arise either from the common law (where there may be a procedural legitimate expectation of consultation given past practice)[21] or from a requirement in legislation (which may give a decision maker a discretion as to whom to consult)[22]. Where there is a duty to consult, the consultation must accord with the so-called '*Gunning*' criteria: (1) Did the consultation occur at a time when proposals were still at a formative stage? (2) Was the consultee given adequate information on which to respond? (3) Was the consultee given adequate time in which to respond? (4) And did the decision maker consider conscientiously the response to consultation?[23] In the important cases of *Reilly* and *Mosley*, the Supreme Court identified such requirements with a higher quality of decision-making and ideas of justice, participation, and democracy.[24]

Public authorities have since issued guidance that reflects the above requirements, as well as a number of others. Such guidance is in the form of 'principles' and a 'checklist' that, if followed, should allow the decision maker to meet the standards that are required by the courts (though each case will always stand on its own facts).[25]

[19] For the Code as it applies to UK government Ministers see <https://www.gov.uk/government/publications/ministerial-code> accessed June 2023; for Wales see <https://gov.wales/ministerial-code> accessed June 2023; for Scotland see <https://www.gov.scot/publications/scottish-ministerial-code-2018-edition/ > accessed June 2023. An exception applies in Northern Ireland where the Ministerial Code is judicially enforceable: see <https://www.northernireland.gov.uk/topics/your-executive/ministerial-code> accessed June 2023 and, eg, *Re Solinas' Application* [2009] NIQB 43.

[20] See, eg, *Re Bunting's Application* [2023] NIKB 50.

[21] See, most famously, *Council of Civil Service Unions v Minister for the Civil Service* [1985] AC 374.

[22] See, eg, *Agricultural, Horticultural & Forestry Industry Training Board v Aylesbury Mushrooms Ltd* [1972] 1 All ER 280.

[23] *R v Brent London Borough Council ex p Gunning* [1986] 84 LGR 168, 189.

[24] *Re Reilly's Application* [2013] UKSC 61, [2014] AC 1115; and *R (Moseley) v Haringey LBC* [2014] UKSC 56, [2014] 1 WLR 3947.

[25] See UK government guidance at <https://assets.publishing.service.gov.uk/government/uploads/system/uploads/attachment_data/file/691383/Consultation_Principles__1_.pdf > accessed June 2023, and local government guidance at <https://www.local.gov.uk/consultation-check-list> accessed June 2023.

13
Venezuela

Flavia Pesci-Feltri

I. General principles

The current Constitution (1999) enshrines due process in Article 49 as a fundamental right whose respect and materialization are mandatory for each of the public authorities that make up the Venezuelan State.

The provision mentioned above includes principles derived from the constitutional values of the constitutional state that are, in turn, established as inherent rights of the people. These rights are the following: defence, appeal, and the presumption of innocence, the right to be heard with all due protection in a reasonable time, the right to a fair trial, and lastly, the right not to testify against oneself.[1]

Each of these principles must underpin every judgment regarding the public authorities of the state and are, in addition to the principles that shape the action by the state, genuine fundamental rights protected in the Constitution, as well as in the international treaties on human rights the state has entered into.

The 1999 constituent aimed to collect Venezuelan legal scholarship and the case law of previous decades and established unequivocally that the protections under Article 49 of the Constitution and, especially, the right to defence should be honoured not only in judicial proceedings but also in administrative proceedings.

In fact, Article 49 of the Constitution lays down a fundamental principle by establishing that the rights contained in the provision must underpin all judicial and administrative proceedings.

In short, due process is a part of the Venezuelan legal system, together with the right of access to justice, one of the primary constitutional provisions protecting the freedom and rights of the people before the action of the public power. This protection materializes through the prior regulation of a process that sets the limits of action of the public authorities, such as establishing the rights and duties that all citizens must be granted.

In Venezuela, administrative procedure is an essential formal means of determining the administrative will and is based on the following constitutional foundations, namely the principle of legality, due process, and citizen participation.

[1] Art 49 of the Constitution.

Flavia Pesci-Feltri, *Venezuela* In: *General Principles and Sector-Specific Rules in European Administrative Laws*. Edited by: Giacinto della Cananea and Jean-Bernard Auby, Oxford University Press. © Flavia Pesci-Feltri 2024.
DOI: 10.1093/oso/9780198867579.003.0013

II. Administrative procedure legislation and government guidance: adjudication

Venezuelan legislation imposes on the public administration the duty to guarantee due process and respect the rights of the citizens.

In Venezuela, there are three general provisions that aim to regulate administrative action, its organization, and operation in order to guarantee, on the one hand, the rights of citizens in their relationships with the public administration and, on the other, to ensure that it carries out its tasks efficiently, effectively, and transparently. These are the Organic Law of Administrative Procedures (1982), the Law of Simplification of Administrative Procedures (2014), and the Organic Law of Public Administration (2014).

The Organic Law of Administrative Procedures seeks principally to materialize the content of the principle of administrative legality. Under the premise that the entire exercise of the administrative function must be subject to a previous rule that limits and establishes it, this Law generally regulates the behaviour of the public administration in the broadest sense of the term.

The Organic Law of Administrative Procedure is called to control the exercise of power to ensure that the rights of the citizens are respected in the performance of administrative action. In this sense, it provides the principles ruling the legal relationship between the people and the public administration, the limits of its performance, and the rights to be protected. All of this is conceived within the requirement for the administration to act rationally and effectively in pursuing the goals attributed to it, satisfying the requests of the administrators.

This law regulates four fundamental points:

1) The administrative powers and duties of public officers in the exercise of the administrative function, as well as the rights of individuals that must be guaranteed when they are linked to the public administration.
2) The administrative act is a unilateral manifestation of will emanating from the public administration after the previous development of an administrative procedure; requirements are the validity and effectiveness of the administrative act, as well as its effects and methods of appeal. It also regulates administrative silence.
3) The provision of ordinary and extraordinary administrative procedures, including challenging administrative acts by administrative agencies.

The Law of Simplification of Administrative Procedures, first passed in 1999 and then amended in 2008 and 2014, seeks to rationalize administrative action and, in this regard, requires the public administration, in the execution of administrative procedures, to avoid endless proceedings that prevent its execution from being effective and efficient. It also enshrines, in parallel, its duty to inform citizens about the purposes, powers, and behaviour of the various administrative agencies.

On the other hand, the Organic Law of Public Administration that entered into force in 2000, later amended in 2008 and 2014, regulates the administration—understood as a set of organs—so that it can adequately fulfil the aims of the state.

Understanding the administration as an organization, the object of the Organic Law of Public Administration, is the regulation of the fundamental principles that govern it, as well as those that underpin their activity, organization, and operation. Thus, in accordance with Article 1, the regulation concerns:

1) The establishment of the principles and foundations that govern the organization and operation of the Public Administration.
2) Provision of the principles and guidelines of the organization and operation of the National Public Administration and the Functionally Decentralized Administration.
3) The regulation of management commitments.
4) The creation of mechanisms to promote participation and control over public policies and results.
5) To establish the basic rules for public records and archives.

III. Administrative procedure legislation and government guidance: rule-making

Under the Venezuelan legal system, the public administration is compelled to consult the interested parties and the people when issuing general administrative norms or acts.

From what has been said so far, it can easily be concluded that under the Venezuelan constitutional system, the operations of the public administration must be developed following and materializing a series of principles that all ensure that: (i) administrative action is efficient and rational in achieving its tasks, and (ii) the rights of citizens are guaranteed when they are affected by it.

Following these premises, Article 141 of the Constitution states that Public Administration is based on

> the principles of honesty, participation, expeditiousness, efficacy, efficiency, transparency, accountability and responsibility in the performance of public functions, being fully subject to the law.[2]

These principles are confirmed in Article 10 of the Organic Law of Public Administration insofar as it provides that the actions of the administration must be based on

> principles of economy, speed, simplicity, accountability, effectiveness, proportionality, opportunity, objectivity, impartiality, participation, honesty, accessibility, uniformity, modernity, transparency, good faith, parallelism of form and responsibility in exercising it, full submission to the law, and eliminating non-essential formalities.[3]

[2] Art 141 of the Constitution.
[3] Art 10 of the Organic Law of Public Administration.

Similarly, Article 5 of the Law of Simplification of Administrative Procedures establishes the principles according to which simplification plans must be drawn up bearing in mind the presumption of good faith on the part of the citizens, simplicity, transparency, the speed and efficiency of the Public Administration in its work, and the Public Administration must be at the service of the citizens, who must participate in the governing bodies' decision-making.

Lastly, Article 30 of the Organic Law of Administrative Procedures provides that the principles of the administrative procedure are those of 'economy, efficiency, speed and impartiality'.[4]

In addition, and in accordance with the Venezuelan Constitution, the people have the right to participate freely in public affairs (Article 62), to make requests, and to obtain a timely and adequate response (Article 51), in addition to having their representatives render public, transparent, and regular accounts of their management (Article 66).

Likewise, under Article 143 of the Constitution, people have the right to be expeditiously and truthfully informed of situations in which they have a direct interest, be apprised of any final decisions adopted in the matter, and have access to the relevant administrative files and records without prejudice to the right of equality before the law (Article 21 CRBV) and due process (Article 49 CRBV).

Under the state's legal order, there is no doubt that the public administration has to consult the public before issuing regulations.

Thus, Article 62 of the Constitution provides that 'all citizens have the right to participate freely in public affairs, either directly or through their elected representatives',[5] so that the participation of the people in forming, carrying out, and controlling the management of public affairs is the necessary way of achieving the involvement to ensure their complete development, both individual and collective [. . .].[6]

Consequently, 'It is the obligation of the State and the duty of society to facilitate the generation of optimum conditions for putting this into practice.'[7]

The 2001 Organic Law of Public Administration developed the contents of this provision and added sectoral regulations to public consultation so that the public bodies and entities were required to send the drafts to organized communities and public organizations, as well as to non-state entities enrolled in the registry created for that purpose. They were also compelled to submit those drafts to the general population so as to obtain feedback from the people. The observations resulting from public consultation were not binding; however, failure to consult resulted in the absolute nullity of the regulation.

The 2008 Organic Law of Public Administration and the current one (2014) both envisage and maintain the duty of the Public Administration to publicly consult the preliminary draft of regulatory norms, as provided in Articles 140 and 141. The latter, together with Articles 139 (promotion of citizen participation), 142 (duty to inform the population of its actions), and 143 (duty to make the scheme of their organization

[4] Art 30 of the Organic Law of Administrative Procedures.
[5] Art 62 of the Constitution.
[6] ibid.
[7] ibid.

available to the people as well as informative guides on administrative procedures, services, and benefits) define and regulate all that pertains to so-called 'social participation in public management'.

In short, and following the standards mentioned above, the conclusion is that before issuing any sectoral regulation, the competent body or entity must carry out a public consultation process that implies:

a) referral of the preliminary project to the organized community;
b) informing the community through the administration's web portal and any other means of communication so that interested parties can present their considerations or observations, which are not binding.

The absence of this consultation procedure will make the approved regulation null and void.

On the other hand, the Law of Simplification of Administrative Procedures requires citizen participation by establishing that 'promoting public participation through organized communities, especially communal councils'[8] is a mechanism for improving and simplifying administrative procedures.

[8] Art 6.2.f of the Law of Simplification of Administrative Procedures.

PART III
CASES

14
Cases

Several Authors

I. Questionnaire

A. Case 1—The rejection of an asylum application

Fatima is a Sudanese national who fled her country to save her life. She illegally entered a country that has signed several international treaties committing them to provide assistance and asylum for those fleeing war, civil war, and revolution. When she applies for asylum, her request is rejected by a Board consisting of three members, presided over by a man who often gives interviews to newspapers alleging that the Board's role is to stop the invasion of African migrants, whatever their reasons for seeking asylum.

Fatima contests the rejection of her request before the competent court, claiming that the President of the Board was clearly biased, that he unduly influenced the whole procedure, and that the final decision should, therefore, be overturned. The Board objects that there is no provision in the legislative framework that established it or the asylum procedure that obliges its members to refrain from expressing their thoughts outside official proceedings. Nor is there any provision requiring them to abstain from taking part in any decision after so doing.

Would the court endorse Fatima's argument? Or would it uphold the literal argument put forward by the Board?

B. Case 2—Establishing the 'rules of the game' in advance

Parliamentary legislation allows public grants of up to €100,000 (or its equivalent in local currency) within an overall budget of 1 million euros to individual toy

Several Authors, *Cases* In: *General Principles and Sector-Specific Rules in European Administrative Laws*.
Edited by: Giacinto della Cananea and Jean-Bernard Auby, Oxford University Press. © Several Authors 2024.
DOI: 10.1093/oso/9780198867579.003.0014

manufacturers that promote greater environmental awareness in children under the age of 10. According to this legislation, which gives the executive branch no power to draw up regulations, the Department of the Environment (DE) can award grants for 'new games'. The DE establishes some rules of practice, including one whereby no game costing more than €50 will be eligible for a grant. Toys World (TW) applies for a grant for a new game, but its application is rejected because the price of the game for the public would be €55, thus exceeding €50.

TW thus brings a claim before the competent court, claiming that the DE was not entitled to reject the application for a grant simply because each new game would cost more than €50. It argues that: (i) this would not be an exercise of discretion but would eliminate it altogether. In its reading of the Act, each application should be considered on its merits, and (ii) before defining its rules of practice or standards, the DE should have consulted the stakeholders instead of acting unilaterally. The DE objects that discretion was not eliminated since it retains the power to decide on all individual applications concerning new games whose price does not exceed €50. Additionally, it observes that no legislative provision requires it to consult stakeholders before adopting any rule or policy.

Assuming that this case does not conflict with EU legislation on state aid or any equivalent regulations outside the EU, would the competent court endorse the argument that once Parliament endows a public authority with discretionary powers it must exercise them in all cases? Or would it accept the idea that administrative discretion should be limited and structured in such a way as to facilitate decisions in individual cases? Furthermore, would it give any weight to the application based on the fact that stakeholders had not been consulted? In either case, would it strike down the disputed rejection of TW's application?

C. Case 3—A local authority withdraws a licence *inaudita altera parte*

The Municipality of Belleville decides to withdraw some existing licences authorizing the sale of certain products in the city centre. It does so without previously providing the licensees with any opportunity to be heard. It proceeds but without publishing in advance the criteria or justification for the withdrawal of individual licences. It merely states that it is 'in the public interest'.

One licensee, Ms Trompier, challenges the withdrawal of her licence before the competent court. She argues that the withdrawal breached the general principles of due process and sound administration. The Municipality replies that (i) neither its statute and regulations nor national legislation governing local authorities lay down such principles, (ii) it follows on from this that the principles of due process do not bind it, and (iii) hearing all those licensees before taking a final decision would waste too much time and resources.

Would the competent court find for the applicants, and if so, would it order against the disputed withdrawal? Or would it endorse the respondent's arguments?

D. Case 4—The unfair dismissal of a civil servant

A disciplinary board (DB) dismisses Alvin, a civil servant working for a national agency, after he has been acquitted of several serious offences (corruption) during criminal proceedings. The DB asserts that Alvin had failed to give other employees professional and moral leadership. Before reaching this decision, it neither informed Alvin of the grounds on which it intended to proceed, nor did it give him a reasonable opportunity to present his defence.

Alvin contests his dismissal before the competent court because, under the general principles of administrative procedure, he should have been given a fair opportunity to be heard beforehand, including legal assistance and the right to cross-examine witnesses. He adds that, had he been able to exercise these rights, a disciplinary measure other than dismissal would have been taken against him. The employer replies that the specific rules on disciplinary procedure state no such requirements.

Would the court accept the defendant's argument that the specific rules governing the case did not mention the procedural requirements referred to by Alvin? Or would it endorse the argument based on general principles according to some current doctrine? If so, would it rule against the disputed measure?

E. Case 5—A regulator requesting information concerning market abuse

Bud is a young stockbroker with a top-ranking financial firm. During a casual conversation with an old friend, he obtains some inside information about the likely increase in value of a corporation's share in the near future. He reveals this information to his boss, who places an order to buy the corporation's shares, making a considerable profit. Sometime later, officers from the Financial Market Authority (FMA) request Bud to reveal what he knows about this circumstance, warning him that if he refuses to do so, his licence is unlikely to be renewed.

Although Bud is ready to collaborate with the FMA officers, he affirms that he is unwilling to reveal everything he knows about the situation as he fears incriminating himself. FMA officers inform him that there is no rule within the sector-specific legislation that allows him to keep silent. They also warn him that if he fails to speak his licence may not be renewed.

Bud challenges the order before the competent court. Would it endorse his argument based on the right of defence? If so, would it affirm a general principle, such as a sort of privilege against self-incrimination or *nemo tenetur se detegere*, and the like? Or would it affirm that there is no such thing and dismiss Bud's case?

F. Case 6—A taxpayer who disputes the tax authority's statements

Based on the information it collected on its own initiative, the tax authority (TA) applies some specific provisions of tax legislation that are financially less favourable than the general provisions to a certain taxpayer, Mr Paine. He objects to the tax administration's action and, in order to defend himself, he makes a formal application to be given access to the personal data concerning him that is held by the tax authority.

The tax administration refuses access as the rules governing its action state no duty to make its dossiers available. Mr Paine asserts that the principles of due process and fairness should apply without exception, and that he should be permitted to understand the points of fact that led to the TA's decision.

Mr Paine challenges the denial of access to the competent court. Would the court hold that, whatever the content of the sector-specific rules, some form of access to the documentation held by the administration is required, or would it side with the TA? If the court endorses Mr Paine's argument, would it order the TA to disclose its documents?

G. Case 7—The unjustified denial of a licence

The national legislation governing electronic communications endows the Communications Regulatory Authority (CRA) with two related but distinct powers: first, to set out a plan for the use of radio frequencies and, second, to issue private operators with licences on the basis of objective criteria. According to the plan, due to technical limitations, the maximum number of terrestrial channels available for private operators is ten. A public tender procedure is then set up to award national television broadcasting rights on terrestrial frequencies. Totally Unnecessary Productions (TUP) participates in the tender procedure, but its application is rejected.

TUP requests a statement of reasons based on the records of the tender procedure, holding that they are necessary to check whether the right to operate has been awarded on the basis of objective criteria. Otherwise, they argue, private operators are left with no explanation for their rejection. The CRA challenges this line of argument, holding that sector-specific legislation requires it to determine and respect objective criteria, but it does not set out a specific duty to provide reasons based on findings that emerge during administrative proceedings.

TUP brings an action challenging the refusal to provide reasons based on the records before the competent national court. Would the court endorse TUP's claim, and if so, would it rule to overturn the rejection of TUP's application due to a lack of reasons based on its records? Or would it side with the CRA and dismiss the action?

H. Case 8—Failure to consult a stakeholder before setting new tariffs

In a country that has long had only two railway companies, a third one—High-Speed Rail (HSR)—has now entered the market. Before establishing new tariffs, the

Department of Transport (DT) decides to consult with stakeholders, although it is under no obligation to do so. However, it consults only the two incumbents without engaging with the newcomer, HSR.

HSR then disputes the new tariffs, arguing that it should have been consulted on the grounds that (i) the conduct of the DT infringes the principles of procedural fairness and (ii) its conduct prevents the regulator from obtaining information from all relevant sources. It thus argues that the new tariffs are unlawful or, at least, not binding on it. The DT responds that under the sector-specific legislation that governs its actions there is no obligation to consult all stakeholders.

Would the competent court uphold the respondent's argument, or would it endorse the newcomer's claim that if the regulator consults some stakeholders, it is legally bound to hear them all?

I. Case 9—Failure to consult the affected community before building a new gas pipeline

The legislation of Terranova provides that, before the Department of Infrastructure (DI) takes any decision concerning the construction of new electricity plants by private companies, the affected community must be consulted, and the documentation for the new plant must be made publicly accessible on its website for reasons of transparency. No such provision exists for new gas pipelines. When the DI receives a proposal for a private company to build a structure for a new gas pipeline bringing gas from abroad, it decides not to consult the affected community.

Two environmental associations of citizens living in the area likely to be affected by the new gas pipeline challenge the decision before the competent court, arguing that the DI erred in narrowly interpreting the legislation because it should have tried to achieve transparency. In their view, a narrow interpretation frustrates the legislator's explicit intent to maximize transparency. The DI points out that existing legislation only requires the assessment for electricity plants but not for other structures, and that had the legislator intended to make it compulsory, it would have specified to this effect.

Would the competent court decide the case based on the sector-specific legislation and endorse the literal interpretation followed by the DI, or would it reach a different conclusion, either based on existing general principles or as a matter of prudence?

J. Case 10—Refusal to give access to an algorithm

A unit of soldiers from the Town of Two Rivers played a crucial role in several battles during the Second World War. Seventy-five years later, the Municipality of Two Rivers decides to erect a funeral plaque in the town's central square in honour of all those who 'contributed most to their nation', engraving their names on the plaque. The selection of 'those who contributed most' is based on all the information that can be gathered from civil and military archives. An algorithm specially developed by a private company handles this information and selects the names to appear on the plaque.

Although more than one member of Hector's family fought in the Two Rivers Unit during the Second World War, his family is not selected. Hector asks the Mayor of Two Rivers about the reasons for this exclusion. But the answer he receives is simply that the choice was the result of the data as the algorithm processed them and that, in any case, the Municipality had the greater margin of discretion.

Hector challenges the decision of the Municipality before the competent court. Does it make any difference whether a local authority, as distinct from a national authority, makes the decision? And, more importantly for our purposes here, does it make any difference whether the decision is based on an algorithm?

II. Case 1—The rejection of an asylum application

A. Austria

Stefan Storr

The court will probably replace the board's decision with its own ruling.

No law explicitly obliges board members to refrain from expressing their thoughts outside an official procedure, as Article 10 ECHR permits such freedom of expression. However, there could be a conflict of interest in this case. § 7 (1) AVG states that administrative officers must abstain from exercising their duties and appoint a substitute:

1. in cases where they are involved or which involve one of their relatives or a person entitled to protection represented by them;
2. in cases where they were or are appointed as a representative of a party;
3. if any other important elements raise doubts concerning the bias of officers in charge;
4. in an appeal proceeding, if they were involved in issuing the administrative decision appealed against or the preliminary decision on appeal.

Only in the event of imminent danger and if there is no possibility of appointing a substitute immediately, a biased administrative officer is entitled to perform the necessary official acts himself.[1]

In Fatima's case, the president of the board would be in breach of § 7 (1) nr 3 rather than § 7 (1) nr 1, 2, or 4 AVG. His statement that the body aims to stop 'the invasion of African migrants' raises doubts about his being unbiased. It is simply sufficient that there is reasonable suspicion of his bias, even if the decision maker is actually impartial. From the subjective point of view, a member of a tribunal is presumed to be biased if, for example, he or she indicates before the proceedings that he or she has already determined a decision on the merits. In this context, the concrete position of the party concerned (Fatima) is important but not decisive.[2]

The board has to guarantee that it will act unbiasedly *ex officio*. No party has a right to refuse a body or organ's authority on the grounds of partiality; however, a party may either notify the organ itself or a higher body of his or her concerns that the board is biased. Hence, the involvement of a biased body may indeed lead to an unlawful procedure. However, this failure can be remedied by the party taking legal action.[3]

Nevertheless, it is important to emphasize here that shortcomings in the administrative procedure caused by an authority can also be corrected by the administrative court deciding on the merits.

[1] § 7 (2) AVG.

[2] *VwGH* 11.07.2019, Ro 2019/03/0015.

[3] G Wielinger, *Einführung in das österreichische Verwaltungsverfahrensrecht und in das Recht der österreichischen Verwaltungsgerichtsbarkeit* (2nd edn, Leykam 2019) 32 and 33.

Lastly, it should be noted that a decision taken by a board with no semblance of impartiality does not necessarily violate the constitutional principle of a fair trial[4] nor the right to a judge (Article 83 (2) B-VG).[5]

B. China

Xiaowei Sun

The court cannot endorse Fatima's argument.

Indeed, the Administrative Litigation Law provides in its Article 13 that the court does not accept lawsuits against 'administrative acts for which the law provides that an administrative organ has the final judgment'.[6]

As such, Article 36 of the Exit and Entry Administration Law provides:

> Decisions made by the exit/entry administration of public security organ on rejecting applications for visa extension or reissuance, or on not issuing foreigners' stay or residence permits or not extending the duration of residence shall be final.[7]

The board's decision cannot be challenged before a court.

However, the judge would act differently if the plaintiff's request falls within the competence of administrative litigation jurisdiction.

The Civil Servant Law provides that a civil servant should recuse him- or herself if he or she 'may not perform his or her duties fairly'.[8] The absent of the recusal may be considered as a 'breach of legal procedure'[9] within the meaning of Article 70 of Administrative Litigation Law. In this sense, the High People's Court of Zhejiang annulled a decision of a local education agency for non-recusal.[10] But for the moment, there is no case law concerning bias towards foreigners.

C. France

Sébastien Saunier

The asylum application procedure is governed by the 'Code for the entry and residence of foreigners and the right to asylum' (CESEDA), a dedicated text. The legislative and regulatory rules on the right to asylum have been contained in it since 2005.

An application for asylum in France, as is the case here when the responsibility of France is involved, falls within the competence of the Ofpra (*Office français de*

[4] VwGH 17.12.1999, 98/02/0078.

[5] E Schulev-Steindl, *Verwaltungsverfahrensrecht* (6th edn, Verlag Österreich 2018) 70.

[6] 法律规定由行政机关最终裁决的行政行为.

[7] 公安机关出入境管理机构作出的不予办理普通签证延期、换发、补发，不予办理外国人停留居留证件、不予延长居留期限的决定为最终决定.

[8] 可能影响公正执行公务.

[9] 违反法定程序.

[10] High People's Court of Zhejiang, 2018, No 539 (2018浙行终539号).

protection des réfugiés et apatrides—'Office for the protection of refugees and stateless persons'), an administrative body created under the now codified law of 25 July 1952 (CESEDA, Article L. 531-1). The Ofpra is a public administrative establishment associated with the Minister in charge of asylum (CESEDA, Article L. 121-7). It recognizes the status of refugee or stateless person. An appeal against the dismissal of an application is examined by the *Cour nationale du droit d'asile*, a special administrative jurisdiction (CESEDA, Article L. 532-1) that rules in first and last resort on appeals lodged against the decisions of the Director General of the Ofpra under the control of the *Conseil d'Etat*, which functions as a court of cassation.

Impartiality in the processing of cases is a requirement stated in Article L. 121-7 of the CESEDA, although the obligation is established as regards the general functioning of the Ofpra and its relations with the ministerial supervisors ('The office exercises the aforementioned missions with complete impartiality and, in their accomplishment, receives no instruction').

Independently of this provision, the impartiality of the authority's action has long been monitored by the administrative court, which does so indirectly (eg inquiring as to the proper use of power, respect of the principle of equality, and the neutrality of the public authorities) but also directly. The principle of impartiality constitutes a principle of the law of general administrative procedure. It was erected as a general legal principle by the *Conseil d'Etat*'s ruling in *Bourdeaux*, 29 April 1949.[11] According to the formula used in case law, the general obligation of impartiality 'is incumbent on all administrative bodies' holding decision-making or consultative power, whether it consists of one or several persons. Personal and/or institutional partiality is prohibited. Article L. 100-2 of the CRPA now states that

> The authority acts in the public interest and respects the principle of legality. (. . .) It conforms with the principle of equality and guarantees impartial treatment for every person.

The matter of application to the Ofpra of the general rule of impartiality is hardly in doubt. On the organic level, as a public administrative establishment, it is one of the '*administrations*' subject to the CRPA (Article L. 100-3). Since the entry into effect of the CRPA, administrative judges have often had to rule on the question of the juncture of the rules prescribed by the CESEDA and the CRPA, respectively. One will recall that the CRPA applies only in the absence of applicable special provisions: it is of a suppletive nature and forms a subsidiary regime to be applied in the absence of specific provisions. The primacy of the CESEDA or the CRPA has been stated several times in case law (eg in the area of administrative diligence, the application of CRPA Article L. 114-5 with regard to an application for a temporary residence permit as an 'employee' governed by CESEDA Article L. 313-10, 1°).[12]

[11] *Rec* p 188, a case regarding the purge of administrative bodies: the Council considers that Sieur Sporry cannot rule on facts that he himself had denounced; CE, 7 July 1965, *Fédération nationale des transporteurs routiers*, *Rec* p 413.

[12] TA Paris, 20 September 2018, *Mme Eka N.*

The prohibition of publicly taking a position on matters which the body must consider is sometimes stated in the texts (eg concerning the regulatory authorities, such as the *Conseil supérieur de l'audiovisuel*, which vitiates the resolution adopted).[13] Case law also deduces from the principle of impartiality the obligation to refrain from any public assumption of a position that would be prejudicial to the proper functioning of an independent administrative authority.[14] However, assumptions of position are not systematically deemed incompatible with compliance with this principle.[15]

On the other hand, an allegation of procedural irregularity is unlikely to obtain a positive decision. Indeed, asylum litigation is litigation of unlimited jurisdiction.[16] Thus, the formal and procedural defects of the decision of the Director of the Office are not actionable.[17] According to the formula used in case law, it does not fall to the Court to appreciate the legality of the decision but to rule on the interested parties' right to refugee status. Only those instances restrictively mentioned by the code, like absence of an '*individual examination of the application*' or of '*personal interview*', could entail annulment by reason of the essential character and the guarantee in question.[18]

D. Germany

Dian Schefold

In Germany, the situation could not arise, because according to German law (*Asylverfahrensgesetz* in the version of 2-9-2008 with modifications, § 5), asylum requests have to be decided by civil servants from a Federal authority (*Bundesamt für Migration und Flüchtlinge*), and no board is involved.

For these civil servants, the problems of exclusion and the suspicion of partiality are very similar. Interviews with newspapers cannot justify exclusion (§ 20 VwVfG) but they do give rise to the suspicion of partiality (§ 21 VwVfG). This presupposes facts based on suspicion. Although the interviews were not directly linked to the case of a particular refugee, the often-repeated manifestation of a specific understanding of the function of the procedure may justify suspicion. On the other hand, freedom of speech and scientific activities are also guaranteed to civil servants. In our case, understanding the role of the asylum procedure contradicts international treaties, and the interviews do not express scientific arguments but political opinions. Founding the decision on these aspects would be unlawful. Therefore, the suspicion may be justified.

[13] CE, 11 July 2012, No 351159, *SARL Média Place Partners c/CSA*; see CE, sect, 30 December 2010, No 338197, *Sté Métropole Télévision c/ADLC, Rec* p 544.

[14] CE, 1re et 4e ch Réunies, 18 July 2018, No 411345, *Féd des médecins de France*, regarding the Haute Autorité de Santé.

[15] CE, 16 December 2019, No 422672.

[16] CE, 8 January 1982, No 24948, *Aldana Barrena, Lebon* p 9; CESEDA, Art L. 532-2.

[17] CE, 10 December 1990, No 93296, *Mufwaya Abaa*, alleged illegality of a delegation. CE, 11 October 1991, No 95105, *Moustapha Bangoura*, alleged illegality of a ground. CE, 9 November 2005, No 254882, *Altun*: the ground drawn from the irregularity of the procedure followed before *Ofpra* is inoperative; CNDA, 20 March 2014, req No 130118009, *Rec* CNDA 25; CE, 27 February 2015, req No 380489, 2015, req No 380489.

[18] CESEDA, Art 532-3; CE, 10 Oct 2013, No 362798, *OFPRA c/Yarici, Lebon*.

According to § 21 VwVfG, the civil servant has to inform the head of the authority and, according to his decision, abstain from deciding on the asylum request.

Because this procedure has not been followed, the procedure and the decision on asylum requests breaches § 21 VwVfG and are thus unlawful. Therefore, this decision would, upon recourse, be annulled by the administrative court unless unequivocally justified (§ 46 VwVfG). According to the facts, there is no reason to suppose this. The recourse will, therefore, be successful.

There are decision-making boards on matters other than asylum procedures in Germany. If there is a suspicion of partiality on the part of the president or a member, the person concerned has to inform the board, which, excluding the person concerned, will decide on the question of partiality (§ 21.2 referring to § 20.4 VwVfG). Here too, the omission of this procedure would not comply with the board's decision.

E. Greece

Theodore Fortsakis

According to Article 7 of the Greek Administrative Process Code (hereinafter referred to as the Administrative Process Code), the persons who make up the administrative organs, whether single-member or collective, must guarantee impartial judgment in order to inspire confidence in the unimpeachability of the acts issued (rule of impartiality).

Impartiality is synonymous with justice, straightforwardness, and objectivity, not being influenced by opinions, judgments, or subjective considerations. Thus, the rule of impartiality constitutes a general principle of law, as a more specific manifestation of the rule of law principle, which expresses in modern liberal and democratic regimes the value that an organ exercising legitimate power over any interested party must, on the one hand, be—and appear to be—free from any internal or external influence that may distort its judgment in the exercise of its power to the detriment or benefit of the person concerned, and, on the other hand, to inspire confidence that its judgment will be based on objective facts and evaluations. In the Constitution, this is explicitly recognized by the use of the term 'transparency' as a guarantee of the observance of the principle of legality, according to Articles 14 para 9, 29 para 2, 102 para 5, and 103 para 7. In its positive version, impartiality equates to a judgment free of subjectivism, while in the negative, it refers to the idea of non-intervention of a specific person, and their abstention or neutrality.

Consequently, the persons who make up the administrative organs must refrain from any act or proceeding that constitutes participation in taking a decision, or the formulation of an opinion or proposal, and more particularly, in the case of collective organs, the members must not take part in the meeting, if—among things—they have a particular bond or relationship with, or hostility towards, the interested parties. This is because there would be an assumption of bias, which undermines the conviction of the individual that the judgment of the organ is unimpeachable. These norms are applied regardless of whether the provisions dealing with the collective organ provide for reasons of impediment or incompatibility in the acquisition of the capacity of a member.

Specifically, Fatima, a Sudanese national, fled her country and entered another, requesting asylum of the national authorities to save her life from the grave danger of war. Her asylum petition was rejected by a three-member administrative body, presided over by a person who has continuously and publicly declared that the main purpose of the aforementioned authority is the containment of the 'invasion by African migrants'.

The fact that the president of the collective organ has already publicly expressed their view on matters relating to the performance of their duties as a member of the committee enhances the estimation that a severe danger of bias arises, which is sufficient enough for their abstention from this committee. In other words, there is no need for a finding as to whether the act of the collective organ was actually partial, as the hostility and prejudice of a member have already been established. Of course, according to a general principle of administrative law, the formal irregularities of the composition of the administrative body, including the lack of impartiality, invalidate its decision only if it appears that the participation of the member in question has an impact on its content, as in this case.

Moreover, regarding the argument of the board, the fact that the president is not prohibited from expressing their views publicly and freely on a matter, even if it is directly related to the performance of their duties, does not mean that he is not legally subject to the duty of impartiality, which, according to the laws, requires him to abstain from any action related to the decision on the matter.

Therefore, given that the board reached a decision on the basis of its discretionary power, the Court must endorse Fatima's argument on the grounds that applications have to be examined and decisions taken individually, objectively, and impartially. On the contrary, if the board had binding competence to reject Fatima's application, the Court would not endorse her appeal, on the grounds that the factual or legal prerequisites for the aforementioned application, as prescribed in the law, are not fulfilled and therefore the discriminatory judgment of one of the members (even as president) did not affect the decision to reject the application, relying on ascertaining compliance with the formal requirements rather than a substantive judgment.

F. Italy

Mauro Silvestri

Fatima's appeal would most likely be upheld. Rejection of the application for asylum could indeed be considered unlawful, primarily due to the direct breach of international treaties, Community rules, and domestic constitutional and legislative provisions on the right to asylum. The rejection would also run counter to the general principles of administrative action and, in particular, the principle of impartiality, as specified by the Italian Administrative Procedure Act (APA) and other laws, as well as in case law.

It is firstly necessary to remark that, even though this aspect has not been highlighted in Fatima's appeal, the rejection would be unlawful due to breach of Article 33 of the Geneva Convention of 1951, to which Italy is a signatory, as well as Council Directive 2004/83/EC of 29 April 2004 and Article 10(III) of the Italian Constitution.

All these laws recognize the right to asylum and lay down the principle of 'non-refoulement' whenever the refugee's life is endangered in their country of origin.

These treaty, Community, and constitutional provisions were implemented in Italy with Legislative Decree No 251 of 19 November 2007, whose Article 2 recognizes the right to international protection in cases such as Fatima's.

Firstly, the refusal of asylum would therefore be unconstitutional and would breach the domestic rules implementing the aforementioned international treaties and Community rules.

But let us assume that these rules do not exist or that Fatima did not invoke them in her appeal. As we have observed, rejection could still be unlawful on grounds of breaching the general principles of administrative action.

In Italy, the action of the public administration is not only underpinned by sectoral laws but also and above all by the applicable constitutional principles and certain general laws.

More specifically, Article 97 of the Italian Constitution requires the administration to be guided by principles of impartiality and sound administration, while Article 98 requires public officers to '*exclusively serve the Nation*', therefore ruling out the possibility that they can lawfully pursue interests other than the public interests laid down in the laws under which their powers are assigned.

It follows from these higher principles that administrative activity is not only subject to compliance with the rules expressly laid down in individual laws. Instead, it should also comply with a set of additional principles and obligations arising from the application to the specific case of the general principles of the legal system, and specifically those on administrative action.

A number of these principles have also been set down in law. For example, Article 1 of the general law on administrative procedure (Law No 241 of 7 August 1990) lists, among others, the principles of impartiality, publicity, and transparency, as well as those laid down by Community law.

Similarly, Law No 190 of 6 November 2012 (the 'anti-corruption law') lays down detailed rules for the direct implementation of the principle of impartiality in the public administration.

Lastly, in the Italian legal system, there is actually an explicit, albeit general, provision intended to prevent malfunctions of the kind described in the case under review. It is contained in Article 6-*bis* of Law No 241/1990, dedicated to the prevention of 'conflicts of interest'. Public officers called upon in any capacity to decide on a given matter with regard to which they have a real or potential conflict of interest—even if only opinions or participating in a panel—are legally required to abstain and to report the circumstance to the competent bodies.

Furthermore, the code of conduct for public employees (issued by Presidential Decree No 62 of 16 April 2013) clarifies the scope of the concept of conflict of interest, stating that the conflict may concern interests of any kind, including non-material and therefore even ideal interests, and that the obligation to abstain may also exist for '*serious reasons of convenience*'.

However, even before these explicit provisions were introduced, and regardless of their existence, there is no doubt that these rules applied. Administrative case law applied the rules on the impartiality of courts (Articles 36 f of the Italian Code of Civil Procedure and Article 51 of the Italian Code of Criminal Procedure) by analogy and directly applied the constitutional principle of the impartiality of the public authorities.

Even if we were to disregard the specific obligation to abstain arising from the law, an act adopted by a public official who has publicly expressed his or her ideological position on the matter forming the subject of the decision in such a way as to cast doubt on their impartiality, could be deemed by an administrative court to be unlawful due to 'abuse of discretion' ('*excès de pouvoir*').

Abuse of discretion is one of the three defects of administrative acts currently set out under Article 21-*octies* of Law No 241/1990 but in force in Italy since the administrative court was instituted (the Fourth Division of the Council of State) in 1889.

Excess of discretion encompasses all defects not attributable to the breach of a specific law but consists in the pursuit of purposes other than those laid down by the law (misuse of power or *détournement de pouvoir*) or a breach of the general principles of administrative action.

As the expression is a general one, its meaning has been consolidated and made increasingly specific over the years in administrative case law.

To facilitate the assessment of the existence of a breach of principles, the administrative court has drawn up a number of recurrent factors regarded as 'symptomatic' of excess discretion. Of these, the most relevant for our purposes are unequal treatment and serious and manifest injustice.

In the case at issue, it is likely that the board's decision would be annulled due to abuse of discretion in the form of misuse of power (for having used their power to pursue their own political aims rather than those laid down by the law), unequal treatment (for having unlawfully treated very different asylum applications in exactly the same way), serious and manifest injustice, and, lastly, due to breach of the legal obligation for public officers to abstain in the event of conflict of interest.

However, it must be stated that not every idea voiced by officials, publicly or otherwise, on matters involving administrative procedures constitutes a breach of impartiality requirements.

For example, criticisms or observations made in a scientific context (articles or reports in conferences) do not constitute a conflict of interest. Likewise, voicing opinions, publicly or otherwise (eg on social media platforms) regarding the subject of the procedure is not in itself sufficient to constitute a breach of impartiality requirements. The actual contents of these statements and the way they are expressed must be verified. For example, statements that are fully in keeping with constitutional values are generally lawful.[19]

G. Romania

Dacian-Cosmin Dragoş

In the Romanian legal system, the facts of the case described above would be evaluated according to the specific rules governing the asylum request procedure as outlined

[19] See Council of State, Div III, Order No 7508, 27 November 2020 for opinions expressed on environmental issues by an administrative judge.

in Law No 122/2006. Article 13 of the law lays down rules for addressing asylum requests, including the principle of impartiality:

> Examination of the asylum application: 1. The decision on the settlement of the asylum application shall be taken after a proper examination of the applicant's situation by the designated officials qualified in the field of asylum. This means: a) the individual examination of each asylum application and the taking of an objective and impartial decision; and b) consultation of information from the country of origin, obtained from different sources, necessary for the assessment of the personal situation of the asylum seeker.

Furthermore, when addressing the issue of bias, the Administrative Code[20] is also relevant, as it includes in Article 11 the principle of impartiality, applicable to all administrative activities. However, the Code does not specify the main features of this principle.

Based on these two legal references to the principle of impartiality, the courts would have a sufficient legal basis to evaluate the decision concerning the principle of impartiality and to consider whether the prior expression of an opinion by a member of the deciding committee has influenced the final decision, and, if so, to annul the decision.

H. Serbia

Marko Milenković

In line with international obligations and ratified treaties, the Constitution of Serbia provides for the right to asylum for any foreign national with reasonable fear of persecution based on race, gender, language, religion, national origin, or association with some other group or political opinions (Article 57). Procedures related to asylum are contained in the Law on Asylum and Temporary Protection.[21] Decisions regarding asylum seekers' status rights at the first instance are made by the Office on Asylum, which is part of the Ministry of the Interior (Article 20). Appeals are decided at second instance by the Asylum Commission (Article 22), whose decisions are final (in administrative procedure) and can be disputed before the Administrative Court. In the case examined, the biased member of the deciding body would be the president of the Asylum Commission. As laid down in the Law on Migration, the regulations governing general administrative procedure should apply to any issues related to the asylum procedure that are not directly regulated by this Law (Article 3). As there are no provisions pertaining to bias in this sectoral legislation (which is the literal argument put forward by the committee in this hypothetical case), the rule from Article 40 LGAP applies. It stipulates that 'the authorised officer must be exempt: . . . if there are other facts which raise doubts as to his/her impartiality'. Bearing in mind that a Commission president in this case has demonstrated clear bias, Fatima would

[20] <http://legislatie.just.ro/Public/DetaliiDocumentAfis/215925> accessed June 2023.

[21] Law on Asylum and Temporary Protection (Official Gazette of the Republic of Serbia, No 24/2018).

be able to seek annulment of the decision on the basis of Article 23 of the Law on Administrative Disputes which enumerates reasons to initiate a dispute, including non-compliance with procedural rules during administrative adjudication. It is very likely that the Court would accept this argument, annul the decision, and return it to the administrative body for new deliberation.

I. Spain

Isaac Martín Delgado

In the Spanish legal system, the right to asylum is governed by (i) Act 12/2009 on the right to asylum and subsidiary protection, and (ii) Royal Decree 203/1995. Neither piece of legislation contains provisions specifically applicable to the case, since it involves a general issue directly related to administrative procedure and the operations of the public authorities. Consequently, although the 1st additional provision of the LPAC provides that any actions and procedures regarding foreign nationals and asylum are subject to their sector-specific provisions, we will rely on general legislation to solve the case at hand.

Article 103 CE requires public authorities to serve the public interest objectively and thus to apply the law impartially. The impartiality standard precludes single-case decisions being swayed by personal or partisan interests and requires the absence of bias or prejudice vis-à-vis a party. The impartiality standard has a twofold dimension: first, decision makers must voluntarily disqualify themselves from the procedure or be instructed to do so by their superior (it also allows the parties to challenge them if they had to disqualify themselves and failed to do so) if there is a connection between the decision maker and the case that prevents him or her from being objective. In this regard, see Article 23 LRJSP.[22] Secondly, the impartiality standard also prohibits compromising the appearance of impartiality in order not to undermine the public authorities' image and standing, as stated in the case law.

The objectivity principle also requires public authorities to ensure the equal application of the law, as established by Article 14 of the Constitution. Under this provision,

> Spanish nationals are equal before the law and may not in any way be discriminated against on grounds of birth, race, sex, religion, opinion or any other personal or social condition or circumstance.

Obviously, Article 14 covers everyone and not only 'Spanish nationals' since equality is a general principle of law. According to the Spanish Constitutional Court,

[22] This provision is worded as follows:

> Acts, decisions or adjudications by public authorities, officials and public servants there being grounds for disqualification shall not necessarily render their acts, decisions or adjudications invalid automatically.

So, failing to disqualify oneself does not entail, in itself, that the acts, decisions or adjudications be invalid. This will have to be examined on a case-by-case basis.

authorities must avoid any kind of discrimination when applying the law. In a nutshell, the case law has established a link between objectivity, equality, and authorities being fully subject to the law, so that discrimination regarding the exercise and enforcement of individual rights, including the right to asylum, is precluded on any grounds.

An apparent bias or connection with the case is not sufficient grounds for disqualification or a challenge. Any such bias or connection should also have an actual impact on the decision. In Fatima's case, the president's remarks about how the board should stop the invasion of African migrants does not entail, in itself, the invalidity of the adopted decision. It is significant that we are dealing with a three-member board (ie that the allegedly biased president is not the only one making the decision), and we must also consider how the other two members voted. A unanimous decision would be evidence that there was no decisive influence in the case at hand, despite the inappropriate remarks coming from the board president and even if we consider that such remarks should prevent him from holding that office. Also, we should bear in mind that the controversial remarks are general statements that do not specifically refer to Fatima's case.

In sum—and without entering into the president's potential disciplinary liability – given the facts of the case, it would be unlikely that a court could invalidate or annul the board's decision rejecting Fatima's application on the sole grounds that the president had made general remarks clearly unrelated to the specific case at hand. It should be noted that the biased person's intervention in the case should have a decisive influence.[23]

J. Switzerland

Alexandre Flückiger

The court would endorse Fatima's argument.

According to Article 6 of the Federal Asylum Act of 26 June 1998 (AsylA), Asylum procedures are governed in particular by the Administrative Procedure Act of 20 December 1968 (APA) and the Federal Administrative Court Act of 17 June 2005, which contain specific rules on recusal.

However, let us admit that the Swiss legislation on the asylum procedure would not explicitly contain such a rule, as the question states. In this case, since the opinions publicly expressed by the president in his interviews with newspapers call into question his impartiality, Fatima can directly invoke Article 29 para 1 Cst ('Every person has the right to equal and fair treatment in judicial and administrative proceedings'). Accordingly, an obligation to recuse oneself is inferred when persons responsible for preparing or issuing a ruling give the impression of having a preconceived opinion. Within its scope, it is also possible to refer to Article 6 ECHR.

[23] Castilla-La Mancha Regional High Court Judgment of 24 February 2003.

K. United Kingdom

Gordon Anthony and Conor McCormick

This scenario can be addressed in short order as it is almost inevitable, on the given facts, that the reviewing court would endorse Fatima's argument. There are two reasons why. The first is that the test for 'apparent bias' in UK law requires the reviewing court to ask whether a fair-minded and informed observer, having considered the relevant facts, would conclude that there existed a real possibility that the panel member was biased by reason of his public pronouncements.[24] It is difficult to see how a perception of bias would not arise here: the panel member has clearly attributed to the panel a role that does not accord with immigration and asylum law and which suggests that he would be exercising his powers for racially motivated reasons. Indeed, were Fatima able to adduce sufficient proof about such motives, she might even be able to argue that his decision was vitiated by 'actual', rather than 'apparent', bias. (Actual bias is said to exist where the decision maker is 'either (1) influenced by partiality or prejudice in reaching the decision, or (2) actually prejudiced in favour of or against a party'[25]—a claim that there has been such bias will succeed only 'when supported by the clearest evidence'.[26])

The second reason concerns the likely judicial approach to the proposed, literal reading of the statute. While it is theoretically possible for the Westminster Parliament (the competent legislature in the field of immigration and asylum) to legislate in a way that can displace common law principle, the reality is that it rarely does so and, moreover, that it is required to use express words where it wishes to do so.[27] In the absence of express words to that effect in this scenario, the courts would presume that the legislature has intended to legislate in a way that is consistent with common law principle (here, the rule against bias).[28] An argument based upon literalism would be most unlikely to prevail.

A further point that can be made concerns the fact that the panel has three sitting members, only one of whom has made objectionable comments. Might it be said that the neutrality of the two would outweigh the bias of the one? The answer here would likely be 'no'. While the common law can allow certain decisions to stand where the underlying reasoning is predominantly lawful,[29] the current scenario would not lend itself to that approach. The President's public pronouncements are such that his apparent or actual bias would taint and discredit the entire decision-making process; indeed, it is difficult to see how he could remain in post moving forward.[30]

[24] *Porter v Magill* [2001] UKHL 67, [2002] 2 AC 357 and, eg, *Helow v Advocate General for Scotland* [2008] UKHL 62, [2008] 1 WLR 2416.

[25] *Re Medicaments and Related Classes of Goods (No 2)* [2001] 1 WLR 700, 711, para 38, Lord Phillips MR.

[26] *Re Foster's Application* [2004] NI 248, 265, para 66, Kerr J.

[27] *R (UNISON) v Lord Chancellor* [2017] UKSC 51, [2020] AC 869. For an instance of the legislation displacing a finding at common law see Terrorist Asset-Freezing Act (Temporary Provisions) Act 2010 and Terrorist Asset-Freezing Act 2010, enacted in the light of *Ahmed v HM Treasury* [2010] UKSC 2 and 5, [2010] 2 AC 534. See now also the Sanctions and Anti-Money Laundering Act 2018.

[28] *Unison*, ibid.

[29] *Hanks v Minister of Housing and Local Government* [1963] 1 QB 999, 1020, Megaw J.

[30] See, by analogy, *Re Duffy* [2008] UKHL 4, [2008] NI 152.

L. Venezuela

Flavia Pesci-Feltri

Article 21 of the Venezuelan Constitution provides the right to equality before the law, which is why it expressly prohibits

> discrimination based on race, sex, creed or social standing ... nor, in general, any discrimination with the intent or effect of nullifying or encroaching upon the recognition, enjoyment or exercise, on equal terms, of the rights and liberties of every individual.

Article 26 of the Constitution regulates the right of access to justice and requires that

> The State shall guarantee justice that is free of charge, accessible, impartial, suitable, transparent, autonomous, independent, responsible, equitable and expeditious, without undue delays, superfluous formalities or useless reinstating.

In addition, Article 49 of the Constitution requires that due process—the mechanism for accessing justice—be observed in all administrative procedures.

For its part, Article 141 of the Constitution requires that, in the exercise of its functions, the Public Administration must submit to the provisions of the Constitution and the laws; therefore, respect for the right to equality before the law is mandatory for public officials.

In our legal system, impartiality and, therefore, the requirement of objectivity in the exercise of administrative action constitutes an essential principle that must govern any administrative procedure.

To be genuine, impartiality must therefore respect several elements. It must be *objective* in so far as the public official has to resolve the matters submitted for consideration, taking into account only the satisfaction of the general interest pursued by the norm applicable to the specific case, thus excluding all personal, political, religious, economic, or any other considerations.

This principle also requires the *subjective* impartiality of the public official, meaning that they must not have a preconceived position as to what they are called to decide. If not, they would be obliged to refrain from deciding the matter submitted for their consideration, after which the procedure provided by the legislator in Articles 37 to 40 of the Organic Law of Administrative Procedures must necessarily be applied when the official is involved in any of the causes of inhibition outlined in Article 36 of the same law, all of this precisely to guarantee impartiality.

In this sense, Article 49.3 of the Constitution that regulates due process states that:

> Every person has the right to be heard in proceedings of any kind, with all due guarantees and within such reasonable time limit as may be legally detained, by a competent, independent and impartial court established in advance. Anyone who does not speak Spanish or is unable to communicate verbally is entitled to an interpreter.

Likewise, Article 145 of the same regulation requires that 'Public officials are at the service of the State and are impartial.'

Articles 30 and 10, respectively, of the Organic Law of Administrative Procedures and the Decree with the Rank and Value of Organic Law of Public Administration establish the principle of impartiality among those that must govern the activity of the Public Administration, impartiality being a general principle of law applicable in all proceedings, and one which supposes that the decision-making official is not bound by any link with the parties involved in the procedure; nor, on the contrary, that they have a manifest enmity with them.

In Venezuela, asylum has been defined in the 1999 Constitution as a political right, stating that 'the Bolivarian Republic of Venezuela recognizes and guarantees the right of asylum and refuge.' (Article 69).

The Organic Law on Refugees and Asylees was enacted in 2001, providing that

> the status of asylum will be granted to foreigners if the State determines that they have been persecuted for their beliefs, opinions or political affinities, or due to acts that could be considered political crimes, or common crimes committed with political intent. (Article 38)

According to Article 2 of the Organic Law on Refugees and Asylees, the right to asylum is based, among other things, on the following principles: the prohibition of discrimination based on race, sex, creed, political opinions, social standing, country of origin, or having the intent or effect of nullifying or undermining the recognition, enjoyment, or exercise in situations of equality, of the status of refugee or asylee of any person who so requests.

From the foregoing, it can be concluded that the corresponding court of contentious-administrative jurisdiction in Venezuela would surely support the first of Fátima's arguments based on the inadequate protection of her due process rights and would completely annul the challenged decision upon demonstrating that the President of the Board is accustomed to publicly stating that the Board's purpose is to stop the 'invasion of African migrants'. This public demonstration is undoubtedly discriminatory and highlights the bias of the person who chairs the Board, violating, on the one hand, the human right to equality before the law on grounds of race and, on the other, Fatima's constitutional right to have her case resolved by an impartial Board.

Regarding the Board's arguments regarding the non-existence of a legal provision preventing Board members from giving voice to their ideas outside the official procedure and establishing that, if they do express them, they must refrain from participating in the corresponding decision, it should be noted that the competent judge would reject the argument since Article 36 of the Organic Law of Administrative Procedures lists the grounds for recusal of an official, including an official's obligation when they have prejudiced the decision on the matter (Article 36. 3), a situation which arose when the President of the Board publicly expressed that the role of the Board is to stop the invasion of African migrants, whatever their reasons for requesting asylum.

To guarantee the recusal of officials on the grounds specified in the law, the regulation establishes a particular recusal procedure that obliges them to withdraw from the proceeding if they consider themselves affected by any of the grounds stipulated in Article 36; and, if they fail to do so of their own free will, their hierarchical superior may order them, *ex officio*, or at the request of the interested party, to recuse themselves.

On the other hand, the fact that the regulations established by the Board do not prohibit members from expressing their thoughts outside the special proceeding is not a ground since the regulatory framework established by the Board, being a standard of sub-legal rank, cannot breach an existing law.

III. Case 2—Establishing the 'rules of the game' in advance

A. Austria

SS

This case concerns some particularities of Austrian subsidy law. Authorities generally grant subsidies by means of private law instruments, such as a contract between an authority and a beneficiary, rather than by public law instruments. The administration may use private law instruments ('*Privatwirtschaftsverwaltung*'), but it is then not generally bound to public procedural law like the AVG.

Basically, if the law does not specify whether granting subsidies must follow private law or public law regulation, the legislator is free to choose between these two legal orders.[31] If the law is unclear, it may be necessary to examine the circumstances of individual cases to determine whether an authority needs to act based on private or public law. In particular, the Parliaments Act, which provides the legal framework for granting subsidies, can stipulate that they must be granted through public law instruments. If it does so, the rules for an authority's discretionary in the sense of Article 130 (3) B-VG apply.

If the authority grants subsidies based on private law, it may define the requirements for granting them as long as it complies with the given legal framework. In this context, the principle of equality, especially important for an authority granting subsidies on a private law basis, is of particular significance. In such cases, it will be one of the main tasks of the authority to issue funding guidelines to ensure that its funding is handled following the principle of equality. Potential beneficiaries can refer to the guidelines in conjunction with the said principle.

If an authority grants subsidies based on public law, it can exercise discretionary power if the law permits the authority to do so. Any such authority exercising its discretion is limited to acting within the legal framework established by the relevant law.[32] In exercising discretion, an authority can specify the conditions for funding and has the power to issue guidelines as long as these do not violate the principle of objectivity. In this respect, though, it must be noted that such guidelines only have internal effects and do not apply to claimants directly, and any discrepancy must be objective and reasonable.[33]

An administrative court is only competent to decide about an authority granting subsidies on the basis of public law. In cases where the award is deemed unlawful, the administrative court cannot annul the authority's decision until a consultation has been undertaken. If the relevant facts have been clearly established, the administrative court will decide on the merits of the case.[34] This means that the court can consult directly with the stakeholders in such cases.

[31] C Fuchs and P Thalmann, 'Förderungs- und Beihilfenrecht' in B Raschauer, D Ennöckl, and N Raschauer (eds), *Grundriss des österreichischen Wirtschaftsrechts* (4th edn, Manz 2021) 627, 698.
[32] Art 130 (3) B-VG.
[33] C Fuchs and P Thalmann (n 31) 699.
[34] § 28 (2) *VwGVG*.

B. China
XS

The court may accept the idea that administrative discretion should be limited and structured in order to facilitate the taking of decisions in individual cases. But if the Parliament did not delegate any power to set out regulations to the executive branch, the court may strike down the rejection of TW's application, without considering the claim based on the lack of consultation of stakeholders.

Indeed, the court will consider the rules defined by the DE as regulatory acts. According to Article 53 of Administrative Litigation Law:

> Citizens, legal persons or other organizations who believe that a regulatory act formulated by the State Council or local people's government on which the administrative act is based are illegal, may request the review of the regulatory act when a lawsuit is filed against the administrative act.[35]

According to Article 64 of the same law:

> During the administrative suit, if the judge determines that the regulatory act is not lawful as provided for in article 53 of this Law, this regulatory act will not be considered as a legal basis for the contested administrative act, and a regularization recommendation will be issued to the administrative authority.[36]

More precisely, the Supreme People's Court determined in its Judicial Interpretation of 13 November 2017 relating to the application of the Administrative Litigation Law[37] (Article 148), that when the court reviews a regulatory act, it may consider whether the administrative organ has exceeded its competence or violated a legal procedures article.[38] The Supreme Court specifies four unlawful situations:

1. The administrative authority exceeds its statutory competence or the scope delimited by law and regulations;
2. The regulatory act is not in compliance with the law or superior regulations;
3. The regulatory act has no legal basis and illegally increases obligations or restricts rights of citizens, legal persons or other organizations;
4. The administrative authority failed to comply with legal approval procedures and publication procedure or carried out serious procedural violations.[39]

[35] 公民、法人或者其他组织认为行政行为所依据的国务院部门和地方人民政府及其部门制定的规范性文件不合法，在对行政行为提起诉讼时，可以一并请求对该规范性文件进行审查。

[36] 人民法院在审理行政案件中，经审查认为本法第五十三条规定的规范性文件不合法的，不作为认定行政行为合法的依据，并向制定机关提出处理建议。

[37] 关于适用《中华人民共和国行政诉讼法》的解释.

[38] 人民法院对规范性文件进行一并审查时，可以从规范性文件制定机关是否超越权限或者违反法定程序、作出行政行为所依据的条款以及相关条款等方面进行。

[39] （一）超越制定机关的法定职权或者超越法律、法规、规章的授权范围的；（二）与法律、法规、规章等上位法的规定相抵触的；（三）没有法律、法规、规章依据，违法增加公民、法人和其他组织义务或者减损公民、法人和其他组织合法权益的；（四）未履行法定批准程序、公开发布程序，严重违反制定程序的.

Considering that the Parliament did not delegate any power to set out regulations to the executive branch, the DE's act may be considered as exceeding its 'statutory competence or the scope delimited by law and regulations'.

In 2018, the Supreme People's Court published a guiding case[40] concerning a rejection of medical payment by the Social Insurance Office.[41] In this case, the local Social Insurance Office made a rule relating to reimbursement of medical care. According to this rule, to be repaid, local citizens must choose public hospitals when seeking medical care outside their city. The court considers this rule as a restriction of citizens' rights and that it's not compliant with the superior regulation. The regulatory act made by the local Social Insurance Office is declared unlawful, and the administrative authority has to make a new decision about the plaintiff's demand.

If we apply this case law, the DE's act, which imposes a general limit on obtaining the grant can be considered a restriction of rights. Without considering the claim based on the lack of consultation of stakeholders, the court may quash the contested act.

C. France

Jean-Bernard Auby

This case raises some issues within the French legal system. It does so, first, because both the national tradition and the Constitution shape the executive's rule-making powers very broadly. While Article 34 of the Constitution defines the ambit or scope of application of parliamentary legislation ('*le domaine de la loi*'), Article 37 defines the area within which the executive may adopt its decrees; that is, all the sectors which are not reserved to parliamentary legislation. This area is very broad because it includes not only the decrees which are necessary to implement legislation, but also the sectors which are not included within the domain of parliamentary legislation.[42] The second issue concerns stakeholders' participation. While the individual right of defence is protected by both the settled case law of the administrative judge and general legislation, there is no such thing as a generalized 'notice and comment' procedure.

That said, the solution of the case must be based on the following ideas. First, as observed earlier, in the French legal system, the government's power to define rules does

[40] Supreme People's Court, 30 October 2018, Guiding Case No 1. 'Guiding cases' refer to cases with judgments that have taken legal effect and which have gained wide public attention, deal with basic principles of law and are representative, complicated or novel, or any other cases having a guiding function. Guiding cases play a significant role in unifying the application of legal standards, providing guidance in the judicial work of lower courts. Guiding cases are not the jurisprudence of the Supreme People's Court. They are chosen by the Court for pedagogical purposes. Judgments are public documents published by the courts. They can be viewed via the website of the Supreme People's court: https://wenshu.court.gov.cn. But only Guiding cases, commented by the Supreme Court, have a special juridical value attributed by the Organic Law of the People's Courts (Art 18).

[41] Intermediate People's Court of Rizhao, Shandong province, 28 December 2016, No 2016-11-9 (日照市中级人民法院，（2016）鲁11行终9号行政判决).

[42] For further remarks, see F Luchaire, 'Le Conseil d'Etat et la Constitution' [1979] Revue administrative 141 (discussing the government's autonomous power to adopt regulations); C Gueydan, *Le Conseil d'Etat, garant du domaine de la loi et du règlement* (Editions universitaires européennes 2013).

not need to be delegated by Parliament. It simply has to remain within the limits of the division of powers between the legislature and the regulatory authority. In this case, setting a financial threshold is certainly within the remit of the regulatory authority. However, the government would have exceeded its power if, for example, its regulation had excluded all non-digital toys.

Second, in this case, it is questionable whether setting a financial threshold is consistent with the objective of the law. This could be contested before administrative courts. Moreover, French administrative law established a rule of 'particular examination of the circumstances' (particular examination of individual cases) but this only applies when the decision to be taken is conditioned by circumstances specific to the addressee. This does not appear to be the case in our hypothetical scenario, because the standard to be applied (the 50 euros) is perfectly objective and not associated with the circumstances. It would also be conceivable to challenge the 50 euros on grounds of 'manifest error of assessment', which is the usual way of contesting choices made in the context of discretionary powers.

Thirdly, as observed initially, in the French legal system, the drafting of a government regulation must be preceded by a consultation of interested parties only when a particular rule so provides.

D. Germany

DS

The case raises the question of public grants. The core of the problem is the necessity for a legal basis. It is clear that all state expenses need a basis in the budget, but if this exists, it is controversial whether the conditions have to be regulated by law. While a liberal–democratic position insists on the reserve of the law or delegated legislation, administrative practice and the prevailing legal scholarship envisage discretionary administrative powers, to be concretized through administrative rules and enacted by the heads of administration without the need for delegation. Even so, legal regulation may be necessary if the grants are of primary importance (such as the scholarship system for students) or if they involve third parties (eg in the case of economic competition).

In the present case, there is a norm precisely defining the aim and the conditions of the grants, the total amount, and the maximum amount of a single grant. Therefore, a legal basis exists. Nevertheless, the rules of practice have to be concretized. It does not seem problematic to allow this step in the case of the Department involved by means of administrative rules. Thus, what characterizes our case is the fact that these rules, without legal delegation, establish an additional condition for the grants, ruling that toys costing over 50 euros cannot be promoted. This additional rule, perhaps acceptable if the regulation of the grants were left to administrative rules, alters the legal regulation without a delegated statutory instrument empowering the administration to do so. It is incompatible with the law and is, therefore, unlawful, not on account of the principle of the reserve of the law but because of its pre-eminence. This is even more relevant because the additional rule affects competition between the potential grant winners.

Indeed, one may argue that, in light of the legal regulation, the administration has a broad margin of discretion. An argument in favour of preferring producers offering moderate prices is that a higher number of enterprises would be able to receive the grant; therefore, a clause in this sense could be qualified as an administrative rule on exercising discretionary power and structuring the application of the law. Nevertheless, seen in this way, precise limitation to a certain sum is not a manifestation of discretionary power; instead, it establishes a condition exceeding and thus breaching the legal rules.

As stated earlier,[43] German administrative law does not envisage consultations with stakeholders before implementing administrative rules. The present case clearly illustrates that, in a free-market economy, the circle of stakeholders interested in grants is not defined *ex ante* but only when they apply for a grant. There is no right to be consulted before administrative rules are implemented.

For these reasons, TW's objections appear founded. The competent court would oblige the Department to decide on TW's petition without applying the 50 euro limit.

E. Greece

TF

According to Article 50 of the Constitution, the President of the Republic, as the Head of State, and therefore head of the public administration, has no powers other than those explicitly conferred upon him or her by the Constitution and the laws concurrent with it. This means that the principle of legality stems from the principles of popular sovereignty and the representative system and, consequently, of the presumption of competence of the legislative organ, which is made up of representatives of the electorate. The subordination of executive power to the legal norms established by the acts of the legislative organ ensures the indirect subordination of the public administration to the electoral body, ie to the agent of popular sovereignty.

Thus, the principle of legality requires the actions of the administrative organs to be in accordance, or in harmony, with the legal norms established by acts of the legislative organ and those of a formal force superior or equal to them or to be in harmony with them. In other words, the administration has no autonomous regulatory power, a competence that is either granted directly by the Constitution or through a legislative act.

On the other hand, certain rules of administrative practice are considered necessary for the definition and interpretation of laws and the regulation of the administrative decision-making process in general, the so-called interpretative circulars. Therefore, when circulars are issued during the exercise of a prior hierarchical control by the competent administrative organs, in order to repeat, comment upon, and explain the provisions of legislative and regulatory acts, in addition to providing instructions on their manner of implementation, they are not classified as administrative acts.

[43] D Schefold, 'Germany' in this book, III in the end.

In this direction, the case law accepts as a generally applicable principle of administrative law[44] that the administration is allowed to set its own interpretative criteria when the law does not contain a relevant provision, in order to ensure uniform and equal treatment in each individual case. However, these criteria must be lawful, insofar as they have been established to serve the objective purposes of the law which the public administration is called upon to apply. On the other hand, the so-called 'regulatory circulars', which impose obligations or grant rights to individuals, have the nature of the regulatory administrative act.

Nevertheless, the interpretation of the provisions that the administrative organ applies by issuing an administrative act should not be confused with discretionary power. Interpretation consists in establishing, by means of various methods of interpretation, what competence the legal norm actually gives to the administrative authority and leads to the adoption of only one view; more particularly, in connection with the character of the competence, it is established to what extent there is binding competence or discretion, and what the limits of the latter are. If the interpretation by the administrative authority is challenged, it will ultimately be given by the competent court.

Therefore, the criterion for distinguishing between interpretative and regulatory circulars, on which their different procedural treatment is based, is that the former, constituting, proposing, or defining conduct that follows directly from the interpreted provision, do not affect the legal order or contain a new regulation that can oppose the interested party, so they cannot be challenged through a request for annulment. On the contrary, regulatory circulars, insofar as they contain legal rules, also produce legal effects in the external world, either by granting rights or guarantees or by imposing obligations beyond those provided by the law related to the relevant circulars. Therefore, they can be challenged via a request for annulment, as they are assimilated to regulatory administrative acts.

The ambiguities and fluidity of the above criterion regarding the changing external legal world—inferred from the regulatory nature of the circular in question—have created serious problems of application, resulting in an expansive approach to the notion of normativity. Initially, recognition of the regulatory nature of the circular and, consequently, the admissibility of its application for annulment on grounds of its internal legality, depended on its compatibility with the legal rule it interpreted. In other words, the court examined whether the circular complied with the laws and regulations to which it was attached and, in the event of an affirmative answer, described it as interpretative in the case of a non-enforceable act: hence, the lawful nature of the circular made it interpretive. On the other hand, in the event of a negative answer, that is to say, a deviation in the interpretation of the circular from the rule of law which it was supposed to interpret, the case law classified it as regulatory and considered the application for annulment admissible. In any case, what matters for the classification of the circular as an executor of an act is not its object but its function, ie the obligation it imposes on its recipient.

[44] See Ruling No 614/2008, 3345, 3650/2005, 4447/2014, and 276/2016 of the Council of State.

Therefore, the fact that the circular ignores the meaning and content of the legal provisions it is intended to interpret, such as general principles of law, in particular the principle of fair and equal treatment, constitutes a ground for its annulment. In this sense, we should not neglect to mention that equality in the sense in which it is enshrined in Article 4 para 1 of the Constitution is substantive and proportional, not formal or arithmetical. In other words, similar cases require similar treatment, and different cases different treatment.

In this case, the applicable legislative statute makes no provision for the executive branch to introduce rules of law (regulatory competence). This is the reason for the annulment of the 'regulatory circular' since an administrative act is grounded on the lack of competence of the authority issuing the challenged act, insofar as no administrative authority is competent to do so. The case law has ruled in similar cases that there is a general principle of administrative law (stemming from the principle of legality), which provides that each administrative authority must issue administrative acts only when, in accordance with the legislation in force, they have been brought within its *ratione materiae* jurisdiction.[45]

Therefore, the Court will annul the aforementioned act on grounds of incompetence due to the fact that the Department of the Environment imposed obligations beyond those provided by the law, thus violating, among others, the principle of equality and fair treatment under the law.

F. Italy

Stefano Vaccari

In the case at issue, the Italian administrative court would dismiss Toys World's application, firstly because the Italian APA requires public authorities to self-limit their discretionary powers regarding the award of grants and contributions, and, secondly, because the said law expressly precludes participation in the activities involved in issuing general administrative acts (Article 13).

More specifically, Article 12(1) of the Italian APA establishes that before awarding grants, contributions, subsidies, financial aid and, more generally, before assigning economic benefits of any kind to public and private persons and entities, the competent administrations must determine the criteria and procedures with which they must comply.

Administrative case law[46] has consistently held that pre-establishing criteria for assessing applications for public benefits constitutes a general rule, which not only guarantees equal treatment of the possible recipients of the grants but also protects the expectations of those applying for the contributions, and that it is therefore necessary to apply the pre-determined rules to the applications filed within the established time

45 See Ruling No 1350/2002 and 2780/2012 of the Council of State.

46 See, among the many, Council of State, Div VI, No 5319, 29 July 2019; Council of State, Div V, No 2914, 14 June 2017.

limit. Furthermore, it has been clarified[47] that Article 12 of Italian Law 241/1990 constitutes a general principle of the legal system, and—in particular—of the provisions governing all public contributions, the allocation of which must at least be regulated by planning rules defining a minimum level of activities to be financed, so as to provide a benchmark for the possible comparison of applications that exceed the allocated funds. In other words, the purpose of the aforesaid Article 12 is to oblige public authorities to 'self-limit' their discretionary powers,[48] so that benefits are only disbursed on the basis of pre-determined objective criteria that also serve to strengthen the subsequent judicial review. Indeed, pre-establishing the criteria and arrangements for allocating economic benefits is in itself an early exercise of discretionary powers based on a separate act that can be challenged independently of the final measure disbursing the grants (or together with it).

Again, regarding the matter of giving reasons, the rules on public grants set out in Article 12 of Law No 241/1990 are also regarded as fundamental tools for ensuring transparency of administrative acts. Thus, administrations must publish the criteria regarding the existence and the amount involved in their action before commencing comparative or selective procedures, giving potential applicants the opportunity to know of the existence and scope of the criteria to be used in assessing the candidates before (and not after) their applications are filed.[49] In case law,[50] it has in fact been reiterated that the allocation of economic benefits requires particular transparency to ensure the lawfulness of administrative action and that the allocation of individual grants complies with the principles of impartiality and formal and substantive equality enshrined in Article 3 of the Italian Constitution.

Furthermore, from a more general point of view, pre-establishing the criteria also allows the political and social (or political and economic as the case may be) objectives pursued by the public authorities to be stated in administrative terms.[51] In this respect, using a contribution for a purpose that is not consistent with the one pursued on the basis of the criteria pre-determined by the authority will not only conflict with the principle of legality but could even constitute a possible case of 'abuse of discretion' ('*excès de pouvoir*'), due to 'misuse' of the individual public measure.

Lastly, tender invitations and notices regarding the allocation of grants or economic contributions are traditionally classified in case law as general administrative acts.[52] This means that they are subject to the general rule of exclusion from participation laid down in Article 13 of Law No 241/1990, according to which the relevant provisions do not apply to the actions of public bodies geared to issuing legislative (administrative regulations) and general administrative, planning, and programming acts, for which the special rules governing their formation apply.

47 Council of State, Div V, No 1552, 23 March 2015.
48 Council of State, Div III, No 4864, 30 September 2014.
49 Puglia Regional Administrative Court, Bari, Div III, No 1591, 21 October 2011.
50 Lazio Regional Administrative Court, Rome, Div II, No 622, 13 January 2017.
51 Lombardy Regional Administrative Court, Milan, Div III, No 11425, May 2014.
52 See, among the many, Puglia Regional Administrative Court, Bari, Div II, No 615, 22 April 2013.

G. Romania

D-C D

Different rules of administrative law apply to rule-making and adjudication processes.[53] Under Romanian law, the terms 'normative acts' and 'individual acts' are used to describe different types of administrative acts. The former is usually called a *general* act in comparative administrative law, so we will use this term. A general act governs general situations affecting an unspecified number of cases and individuals and is issued upon legal authorization. On the other hand, an individual act is specific to a particular case based on the law and affects identified or identifiable persons.

Romanian legislation allows both general and individual decisions (acts) to be challenged by any person with the standing to sue in court. Before the new law came into effect in 2004, there had been debates concerning the right to directly challenge a general decision,[54] considering that such decisions are usually followed by the implementation of individual decisions. However, the current legislation clarifies the issue: even general acts can have legal effects, so they should be directly challengeable in court.

The legality of general acts is assessed in the light of acts with greater legal force, and provisions in this regard are contained in special Law No 24/2000 on drafting general regulatory acts.[55] Article 7 of the law provides that every draft normative act should be based on a Regulatory Impact Assessment; however, this is not consistently adhered to in practice.

> (1) The preliminary assessment of the impact of draft laws, legislative proposals, and other draft normative acts represents a set of activities and procedures carried out in order to ensure an adequate substantiation of legislative initiatives. Preliminary impact assessment involves identifying and analysing the economic, social, environmental, legislative, and budgetary effects of the proposed regulations. (2) The preliminary assessment of the impact of the draft normative acts is considered the substantiation method for the proposed legislative solutions and must be carried out before adopting the normative acts.

Moreover, Law 24/2000 has special rules for normative acts adopted by central public authorities (Article 77):

> Normative orders, instructions, and other such acts of the heads of ministries and other bodies of the specialised central public administration or of the autonomous administrative authorities shall be issued only on the basis of and in the execution of the government's laws, decisions and ordinances. The introductory formula of these normative acts will include all legal grounds provided in Article 42(4).

[53] This section is an adaptation from D C Dragoş, B Neamtu, and R Veliscu, 'Judicial Review in Romania between Tradition and dialogue' in R Caranta and A Gerbrandy (eds), *Traditions and Change in European Administrative Law* (Europa Law Publishing 2011).

[54] ibid.

[55] High Court of Cassation and Justice, Administrative and Fiscal Law Section, Decision No 688/2007, <www.rolii.ro> accessed June 2023.

Therefore, the hierarchy of the normative acts is clearly defined: normative acts adopted by the central administration (which, in the case described, would be competent to implement the application law adopted by Parliament) should have a basis in the law. Furthermore, Article 78 goes further, stating that:

> Orders, instructions, and other such acts must be strictly limited to the framework established by the acts on the basis of and in the execution of which they were issued and may not contain solutions that contravene their provisions.

In conclusion, the central administration possesses discretionary power when implementing the law, but this power should not contradict the provisions of the law.

The relationship between *bound competence* and *discretion* was discussed above in Case 1. Coming back to the case at hand, the aggrieved applicants have the right to challenge the manner in which the central authority responsible for implementing the law enacted by parliament has exercised its discretion and supplemented the law with new conditions. I believe the courts would consider this a case of bound competence and that no discretion was granted in this instance. The limitations imposed by the administrative acts exceeded the competence of the administrative authority to organize the practical implementation of the law.

As for the obligation to consult interested parties before enacting regulatory acts, this duty arises from the Constitution, which, in Article 31 para (2) states that: 'The public authorities, according to their competence, shall be bound to provide correct information to the citizens in public affairs and matters of personal interest', but it also stems from Law No 52/2003 on transparency in decision-making, referred to above, which requires public consultations on drafts of normative acts:

> Article 2—The principles underlying this law are the following:
>
> a) informing in advance, *ex officio*, persons on the issues of public interest to be debated by the central and local public administration authorities, as well as the draft normative acts;
> b) the consultation of the citizens and the legally constituted associations, at the initiative of the public authorities, in the process of elaboration of the drafts of normative acts;
> c) the active participation of the citizens in the taking of administrative decisions and the process of elaboration of the drafts of normative acts, with the observance of the following rules: 1. the meetings and debates of the public authorities and institutions that are the object of the present law are public, in accordance with the law; 2. the debates will be recorded and made public; 3. the minutes of these meetings will be recorded, archived and made public, in accordance with the law.

Therefore, it can be argued that the interested parties should have been duly informed about the intended limitations to be included in the implementing act and consulted regarding their practical impact. Consequently, this serves as another argument supporting the unlawfulness of the executive order that implements the law, which the reviewing court may consider.

H. Serbia

MM

In the Serbian system, the Government, or in this case the Ministry in charge, has powers to set detailed rules if empowered to do so by a hierarchically higher act—in this case a legislative act (Law) adopted by Parliament. In adopting the Decree (Government) or Rulebook (Ministry), it is bound by the limitations set in the relevant Law delegating the power to adopt the secondary act. In the given case, two issues would arise. The first is limits of discretion when setting general rules, which would be addressed by the Constitutional Court in the procedure for control of the constitutionality and legality of acts. The second is discretionary decision-making in terms of which the applicant receives aid under the scheme described.

The first issue—to what extent the relevant department overstepped the powers/limitations stipulated by the Law in setting the 'rules of the game'—would have to be challenged before the Constitutional Court of Serbia, which is competent to decide on the compliance of other general acts with the Law (ie the law providing the adoption of the general act) (Article 167). In the given case, Toys World would be successful if they managed to prove that setting the price threshold which resulted in their elimination from the game had been such an overstepping. A related question is an issue of holding public consultations when setting the rules. As pointed out in the general part of the analysis on Serbia, public participation and consultation in regard to the legislative acts (including decrees) is mainly governed by the Law on State Administration and the Government rules of procedure. Even though there are some rules on transparency, public debate is envisaged for draft laws but not for other acts, such as the one setting the rules of the call for applications in the case concerned. Furthermore, the act in the case in question would not meet the criterion that it 'significantly changes the legal regime in one area or regulates issues of particular interest to the public'. Therefore, the Constitutional Court is not expected to declare the Decree in breach of the principle of constitutionality and legality based on the absence of public participation.

As for the other issue—that of discretionary decision-making—the authority in charge of applications is bound by the principles set by the LGAP. According to Article 5 (Principle of lawfulness and foreseeability), any authority must proceed in accordance with the law, other regulations, and statutory instruments. Furthermore, *when authorized by law to make discretionary decisions, an authority must render a decision within the scope of its statutory power and the purpose for which this power has been granted.* Under the Law on Administrative Disputes,[56] the administrative act may be challenged if: 1) the Law, other regulation, or general act is not applied at all or is not properly applied in the disputed individual act/decision; 2) the decision was made by an incompetent body; 3) the procedural rules for making the decision were not followed; 4) the factual situation is incompletely or incorrectly established or if an incorrect conclusion has been drawn from the established facts regarding the factual situation; 5) or in an act adopted at its own discretion, the body/authority has exceeded the limits of legal authority or if such an act has not been in accordance with

[56] Law on Administrative Disputes (Official Gazette of the RS, No 111/2009).

the purpose for which the authorization was given (Article 24). In the given case, the application was rejected on the basis of not meeting the limits set by the Decree—the €50 threshold—thus the applicant could not claim before the Administrative Court that the body/authority had exceeded the limits of legal authority, or that such an act had not been in accordance with the purpose for which the authorization was given. In this case, the body had not even reached the phase of a discretionary decision whereby the applicants should receive grant support. In conclusion, it is expected that the administrative court would reject the applicant's claim and find the disputed individual rejection decision lawful. However, Toys World would have a chance in the Constitutional Court if they managed to prove that the authority had overstepped the power delegated when adopting the Decree.

I. Spain

IMD

The applicable provisions are (i) Act 38/2003 on Subsidies and Grants (*Ley General de Subvenciones*, LGS), and (ii) its implementing regulation, Royal Decree 887/2006 (RDLGS). Both provisions focus on streamlining subsidy spending and making it more effective and efficient.

From the applicant's perspective, the framework for granting subsidies is as follows. First, the applicant has a right to participate in the award procedure. Any eligible applicants (ie those who have fulfilled the eligibility requirements laid down in the call) are entitled to this 'right to participate'. Second, as soon as the eligible applicant qualifies as a beneficiary or subsidy recipient, it holds a credit claim. The very definition of subsidy under Article 1 LGS revolves around how subsidy recipients have a right to receive payment. However, receipt of payment is subject to the completion of a specific target, project, activity, or action, which should make it possible to promote public objectives or public interests. This whole process is governed by the conditions established by public authorities.

Regardless of which branch of Government decides to allocate funds to a given activity (the legislature or the executive), the public spending decision must be implemented through the so-called ground rules or *bases reguladoras* (in the question above, 'rules of practice'). This is a regulatory binding instrument defining the subsidy's—or grant's—subject-matter and scope, along with any eligibility requirements, the award procedure, the ways of justifying the award, and related details and requirements. Although public authorities are free to specify lines of action and overall amounts, (i) the principles of legality and budgetary stability narrow their scope for decision-making, particularly regarding resource availability (ie there may be caps on the use of resources), and (ii) the principles of effectiveness and efficiency limit their decisions on the allocation of resources to lines of action and beneficiaries.

However, within the aforesaid boundaries, authorities do enjoy discretion in specifying the various grant/subsidy schemes, not only regarding the subject matter and the public aim pursued but also concerning the amounts and the award criteria. Although the award decision is often rule-based (ie not discretionary, based on determining conformity with a fixed standard), authorities may exercise technical or knowledge-based discretion when assessing applications. This has been stated by the Supreme Court, finding that providing for the subsidy falls within the public authorities' scope of discretion, but after the subsidy has been regulated by an applicable provision, there is no longer room for discretion, and authorities only make rule-based decisions.[57] In any case, the award of subsidies must be subject to the requirements laid down in the applicable provisions. Otherwise, the award would be arbitrary and contrary to legal certainty.[58]

Article 8(3) LGS expressly provides that subsidies must be subject to the following principles and standards: publicity or disclosure of information, transparency, objectivity, equality and non-discrimination, effective fulfilment of the awarding authority's objectives, and efficient use of public resources. The objectivity standard, stemming from the principle of good administration, requires that the decision to award a subsidy be based on objective criteria appropriately and reasonably considering and weighing all relevant factors. Accordingly, Article 22 LGS provides that the standard subsidy award procedure will be a competitive tender process

> comparing the submitted applications in order to subsequently rank them all subject to the assessment criteria established in the ground rules and the call.

Article 22 adds that

> without exceeding the cap provided in the call and having regard to budgetary availability, the top-ranked applications according to the said criteria will be awarded the subsidy or grant.

Calls for subsidies or grants must be in line with the previously drafted ground rules, which must conform to the subsidy strategic plan. Therefore, subsidy awards require a prior rule-making procedure—draft these ground rules—making it possible to specifically regulate (albeit in the abstract) the administrative activity needed before conducting the award procedure, by determining (i) the subject matter of the relevant subsidy or grant, (ii) eligibility requirements, (iii) the award procedure, (iv) the award criteria and their weight, (v) the competent bodies to conduct the procedure, assess the applications, and decide, (vi) the applicable time limits and forms of award, (vii) whether the relevant subsidy is compatible with other subsidies or grants, and (viii) remedies and criteria in case of non-compliance (Article 17 LGS). Consequently, the room for decision-making during the procedure is limited to enforcing, applying, and specifying the abstract provisions of the ground rules.

The purpose of the procedure is (i) to assess the submitted applications in order to verify whether they meet the formal requirements to participate in the call, and (ii) subsequently rank the applications based on the objectively established criteria (including both formal and substantive criteria and the priorities or weight thereof established in the call). This ranking must be performed by a multi-member board whose composition should be previously specified. The board submits a report stating the result of the assessment to the authority conducting the proceedings. The

[57] See the Judgments of 7 April 2003, RJ\2003\3541, or the Judgment of 22 October 2010, RJ\2010\7537.

[58] Supreme Court Judgment of 20 May 2008, RJ\2008\2767.

assessment can be based on an automatic application of fixed standards or parameters or otherwise leave some room for technical discretion. In any case, the board must state reasons (supporting arguments) in its report, justifying the assessment included therein and the proposal for the subsidy award.

Subsidy ground rules must include the '*objective*' award criteria and, if appropriate, their weight (see Article 17(3)(e) LGS). Award criteria can be substantive and formal. From a formal perspective, a general rule for subsidies is that the rights to receive payment (ie the credit claims) be granted to the applicants by distributing the financial resources available in each call based on common parameters. From a substantive perspective, the decision is based on a twofold parameter: the applicants' specific characteristics and their project proposing how to use the resources to which they apply. As for the specific award criteria, Article 24 LGS points out that the early stages of the procedure include an 'assessment of the applications subject to the criteria, processes and priorities established in the call'.

The administrative act awarding the subsidy results from an individualized and careful assessment of the applications that were accepted, based on the criteria laid down in the call. The award decision considers the ranking proposed by the body or authority first conducting the procedure, which previously relied on the proposal of the multimember board that first assessed the applications. Thus, the administrative act awarding the subsidy entails selecting some of the applicants and excluding all the others.

In sum, regarding the case at hand, ever since the competent Department of the Environment (DE) exercised its discretion specifying the eligibility requirements (including, eg, that the game must not exceed €50), all applicants must abide by them. The specification of these criteria, applicable to all applicants, ensures objectivity and equality. It is a formal requirement that must be met. Otherwise, the applicant would be excluded. Thus, a Spanish court would uphold the DE's decision.

As for whether there should have been a public consultation with stakeholders before specifying the potential recipients of the subsidy scheme (grant), a twofold premise must be taken into account. Subsidy ground rules have been considered by the case law as regulatory provisions, and therefore the participation principles and standards discussed above would apply. However, in practice, authorities rarely hold prior public consultations or public consultations with stakeholders regarding subsidy ground rules or *bases reguladoras* precisely because it is not a common regulation. In conclusion, it is unlikely that not holding a public consultation would invalidate the (i) administrative decision excluding TW or (ii) the call altogether. Therefore, the Spanish court would dismiss TW's claim.

J. Switzerland

AF

Such rules of practice are called 'administrative ordinances' in Swiss law. They are not binding on the judge. In principle, if we assume that the legislator wanted to give the executive discretionary power, it must exercise it.

However, such ordinances can limit and structure administrative discretion to unify and streamline the practice. In this way, administrative ordinances ensure equal treatment, the proper functioning of the administration and legal certainty, more specifically, administrative predictability.[59] However, the administration is not exempt from considering all the circumstances of the case. The authority must not apply an administrative ordinance mechanically as a pretext for not exercising—in concrete cases—the freedom of discretion conferred on it by the legislation: to do so would be tantamount to eliminating the possibility of adapting to the particular circumstances of the various cases, an option which constitutes a power that must be exercised.[60]

The right to be heard must be exercised prior to the decision to refuse the grant. There is no general obligation to consult with stakeholders before adopting an administrative ordinance.

K. United Kingdom

GA and CM

This scenario touches upon two aspects of administrative law in the UK: 'policies' and the 'fettering of discretion'; and 'procedural legitimate expectations' and the 'duty to consult'. It is arguable that there has been a breach of the 'fettering' principle in relation to TW, but not that there has been an *ex ante* failure to consult with stakeholders.

The starting point in relation to 'policies' and the 'fettering of discretion' is that a public authority must retain for itself the option of exercising on a case-by-case basis any discretion that has been entrusted to it. While public authorities are allowed to formulate policies that are 'legally relevant to the exercise of (their) powers, consistent with the purpose of the enabling legislation, and not arbitrary, capricious or unjust',[61] they must remain free to depart from their policies, or make exceptions to them, as the circumstances of individual cases require.[62] In terms, this means that a public authority cannot adopt a policy that (a) is so rigid that it in effect becomes a rule to be applied in any given case or (b) establishes an unacceptably high threshold for individual applicants to cross. Should such a policy be adopted, the decisions of the authority may be challenged either on the ground that they are *ultra vires* the empowering statute (where appropriate)[63] or, depending on circumstance, that the individual has not been given a fair hearing on the matter. In the event that an individual has been given a hearing, the decision maker is then free to apply its policy, subject to three possible challenges: to the legality of the policy itself; to the reasonableness of the authority's decision; and/or to the authority's failure to have meaningful regard for the individual's representations.[64]

[59] Swiss Federal Court Decisions [ATF] 130 V 163, 172.

[60] ATF 133 V 346, 352, 394, and 398.

[61] *Re Herdman's Application* [2003] NIQB 46, para 19, quoting Halsbury's Laws of England, Vol 1 (1), para 32.

[62] *British Oxygen Co Ltd v Ministry of Technology* [1971] AC 610.

[63] UK government ministers can also formulate policies on the basis of the Royal prerogative, when the fettering doctrine does not apply: see, eg, *R (Sandiford) v Foreign Secretary* [2014] UKSC 44, [2014] 1 WLR 2697.

[64] On the scope for challenging the legality of policies see *R (A) v Home Secretary* [2021] UKSC 37; on reasonableness etc see, eg, *Re Bogues' Application* [1985] NI 218.

TW could plainly argue that the policy that had been adopted in this case was in the form of a rule (it is described as such in the scenario) and that it had been applied rigidly to its application for a grant. While the DE may wish to defend the €50 threshold as significant in some way, it appears to be an arbitrary figure that has not been linked to some specific point in the statutory scheme. Moreover, even if there were such a link, that should not automatically preclude an application by an entity whose proposed costings are 10 per cent beyond the notional upper threshold. Consideration should at the very least have been given to TW's rationale for its costing and whether they could be accommodated within the statutory scheme.[65]

On the question of whether there ought to have been consultation with stakeholders before the rule/policy was adopted, the answer here is more likely to be in the negative. This is because, in the absence of any statutory requirement to consult, a common law duty would arise only if the DE had either expressly promised that it would engage with specific stakeholders or if it had a previous practice of engaging with those stakeholders.[66] Such a promise or practice would ground a so-called 'procedural legitimate expectation' of consultation, which would, subject to any countervailing argument of public interest, require the DE to satisfy the so-called 'Gunning' criteria: (1) Did the consultation occur at a time when proposals were still at a formative stage? (2) Was the consultee given adequate information on which to respond? (3) Was the consultee given adequate time in which to respond? (4) And did the decision maker consider conscientiously the response to consultation?[67] On the facts as given, there does not appear to have been any prior promise or practice, and a finding that there should have been consultation in this case would potentially create an unworkable imbalance in public administration (ie if public authorities were required to consult with an uncertain number of stakeholders when adopting any measure, rule, or policy).

To repeat: TW may have grounds to argue breach of the 'fettering of discretion' principle; but there would appear to be only weak grounds for arguing that there should have been consultation before the scheme was adopted.

L. Venezuela

FP-F

Article 2 of the 1999 Constitution proclaims the social nature of the state in Venezuela, which implies that its authorities are obliged to perform a set of actions geared towards achieving the citizens' material, cultural, and educational well-being.

The development policy of the Venezuelan State runs throughout its Constitution, which obliges the Legislative Power to enact laws to develop specific areas that require greater attention, also imposing on the Executive the obligation to carry out public policies apt to implement the will of the legislator.

One of the techniques that the Venezuelan regulatory system puts in place to promote the interest of individuals in specific areas linked to the public interest, and that

65 *British Oxygen Co Ltd v Ministry of Technology* [1971] AC 610, 624–25, Lord Reid.
66 See, most famously, *Council of Civil Service Unions v Minister for the Civil Service* [1985] AC 374.
67 *R v Brent London Borough Council ex p Gunning* [1986] 84 LGR 168, 189.

the administration deems must be satisfied, is *subsidy*, understood to be a credit, advance, fiscal, or tax incentive exemption to encourage individuals to develop their businesses in areas requiring special attention.

Although there is no general rule in Venezuela regulating techniques fostering development, the laws that provide for subsidies of this kind limit the administration's margins of discretion by setting out in detail the assumptions or parameters for eligibility in addition to a procedure for potential beneficiaries, who must meet a series of previously established requisites. In other words, the norms that promote development must set parameters within which the administration has a margin of discretion that allows it to rationally and proportionately grant or not grant the subsidy.

However, if the regulation, as in this case, fails to specify these requisites, the administration must, in applying the regulation, act in accordance with the principles of rationality, equality, equity, proportionality, and the suitability of the means.

In this sense, Article 12 of the Organic Law of Administrative Procedures of 1982 regulates the limits of administrative discretion, stating that

> Even when a legal or regulatory provision leaves certain measures or decisions to the judgment of the competent authority, the measure or decision must conform to due proportionality and appropriateness to the situation and the purposes of the regulation, and accord with the procedures, requirements, and formalities necessary for its validity and effectiveness.

From this norm, it follows that the discretion of the administration is circumscribed insofar as it must be adapted to the circumstances from which it arises, and its purpose must coincide with that of the norm, observing the corresponding forms and procedures so that the decision is reasonable, timely, fair, and applied equally to all involved.

All these elements allow the contentious-administrative court to rule on the discretionary action of the public administration, bearing in mind the principles of manifest injustice, irrationality, good faith, the proportionality of means to ends, and equality.

The contentious-administrative court can determine whether the discretionary action is unreasonable in the choice of timing (being manifestly inappropriate) or the choice of election methods (use of disproportionate means), or in the form of action (unequal or discriminatory), all of which allow it to recognize whether the discretionary act is proportional or not, ie if the means or measures used are consistent with the intent of the law and if the measures are appropriate to the circumstances.

In addition to proportionality, the discretionary action must be reasonable, ie it should not constitute a manifest injustice, since the principle of equity is one of the principles that must inspire administrative action. This will make it possible to choose, from the several options or solutions available, one that respects both the interests of the administration and those of the administered parties.

It should be remembered that administrative activity is not 100 per cent discretionary or 100 per cent regulated, so there is always a little of each; hence the constraints that the Department of the Environment must consider, not only when issuing the rules for granting the subsidy but also when deciding to award funding.

On the other hand, the Venezuelan legal system requires the Public Administration to publicly consult with citizens and civil societies on draft regulations or any other general rule that impinges on any group of people in accordance with the provisions of Articles 62 and 143 of the Constitution, as well as those of Articles 139ff. of the Organic Law of Public Administration, which regulate social participation in public management and lay down the mandatory consultation procedure that must be activated in these cases.

From the above considerations, it can be concluded that the DE should have consulted the games sector before issuing the rules for granting the subsidy under the legislation promoting environmental awareness among children under 10 years old. If it had done so, it would probably have understood that 50 euros for the production of each toy was insufficient or excessive; otherwise, it would have established price limits.

Given the foregoing, the contentious-administrative court would first analyse TW's argument regarding the need to conduct public consultations with the toy sectors in order to establish price ranges adjusted to the reality of the market and the parameters to be taken into account when granting the benefit. Upon verifying that no such consultation had been conducted, the tribunal would annul the rule whereby the subsidy cannot be granted for toys costing more than 50 euros.

In addition, the purpose of discretion is not to avoid public consultation but rather, once it has taken place—and the administration has sufficient elements to allow it to issue general rules—to establish criteria for selecting the beneficiaries in accordance with the opinions provided by the sector.

Discretion would not only be a factor in assessing the value of the toy but also the nature of the toy itself: the quality of the game and the quality of the message, ease of handling, and the qualities or merits of the companies that produce toys, etc. The administration would thus have to analyse individually and within the designated parameters the offers of those who wish to benefit from the legally-provided subsidy.

IV. Case 3—A local authority withdraws a licence *inaudita altera parte*

A. Austria

SS

The administrative court will conduct the hearing itself and, in this case, it is safe to assume that the action by the municipality is not intended to target a particular vendor operating at an event taking place in a local area (marketplace, market hall), on certain market days, and at certain market times. If that were the case, the Regional Chamber of Commerce, the Chamber of Labour, and the Chamber of Agriculture would have to be heard, with the chance to submit a statement.[68]

Moreover, the case is problematic because the municipality has no competence to prohibit the sale of certain products through a licensing procedure.

Nevertheless, the AVG applies to municipal authorities,[69] and § 37 S 1 AVG obliges the authority to enable affected parties to make claims regarding their rights and legal interests. Furthermore, § 45 (3) AVG gives the parties the right to be made aware of the result of any evidence taken and to comment on it. The right to be heard is considered a fundamental procedural right,[70] and the Supreme Administrative High Court takes it very seriously.[71] However, the parties' right to be heard under § 37 and § 45 (3) of the AVG only regards establishing the relevant facts following an authority's investigation procedure but not to the legal assessment of these facts.[72]

The administrative court will convene a hearing.[73] It will conduct a procedure in order to catch up on the administrative authority's failures. This also applies to proceedings on legal matters concerning issues falling within a municipality's sphere of competence.[74]

B. China

XS

The court would endorse the plaintiff's arguments and quash the contested decision for violation of 'Due process'.

In the event of lack of legal precision on the consultation procedure, in practice, the courts often use the concept of 'Due process'. As to the content of this concept, the Supreme People's Court explained in its Judicial Interpretation of 2017, referring to

[68] §§ 286, 290 GewO.

[69] § 1 (2) Z 1 und § 2 (1) *Einführungsgesetz zu den Verwaltungsverfahrensgesetzen—EGVG* (Introductory Act to the Administrative Procedure Acts), Orig Vers: BGBl I No 87/2008.

[70] Wielinger (n 3) 64.

[71] § 1 (2) Z 1 und § 2 (1) *EGVG*.

[72] VwGH 05.12.1961, 0839/61.

[73] § 17 VwGVG in connection with § 37 and 45 AVG.

[74] § 36 VwGVG.

'fundamental procedural rights, such as the right to be heard, the right to make observations and the right to defend oneself'.[75]

Since the year 2000, many administrative decisions have been annulled because the interested person was not sufficiently heard by the administration and could not state all his or her arguments before the decision was made. As such, an Intermediate court declared that when a decision is likely to exert an influence on the rights and duties of the interested person, the participation of that person in the proceedings is a fundamental element in ensuring the fairness of administrative procedure. Being heard is an essential condition of the participation of the interested person.[76]

Under the supervision of the Supreme People's Court, the Intermediate People's Court of Beijing has developed the concept of 'Due process' in a case concerning an administrative sanction.[77] Two principles emerge from its judgment.

Firstly, the substance of the 'Due process' principle resides in the necessity of hearing the arguments of the interested person before a decision that could undermine his or her rights is taken. 'Due process' is a minimum requirement for procedural fairness. Even if there is no legally defined procedure, the activities of the administration are not without procedural limitations. The Administration has no discretion. It must take appropriate measures in accordance with the principle of 'Due process'.[78]

Secondly, the participation of the interested person in the administrative procedure is how the principle of 'Due process' guarantees the fairness of the procedure and even the result. The interested person may not usefully participate in the procedure unless he or she has an adequate and fair understanding of the facts and interests, can make observations, and invoke his or her arguments. Participation should not be reduced to a mere formality.[79]

C. France

SS

The case described raises the essential question of the juncture between the general law of administrative procedure and the law of public properties, and within this, the law of public domain. Administrative property law is a special law, forged well before that of relations between the authorities and the citizens, one that possesses its traditions, its own concepts, and specific dynamics. Within it, the asymmetry between

[75] Supreme People's Court, Judicial Interpretation on 13 November 2017 relating to the application of the Administrative Litigation Law, art 96.

[76] Intermediate People's Court of Nantong, Jiangsu, 23 July 2015, No TZXZ00169 (通中行终字第00169号).

[77] Intermediate People's Court of Beijing, 6 June 2017, No J01XZ277 (京01行终277号).

[78] 正当程序原则的要义在于，作出任何使他人遭受不利影响的行使权力的决定前，应当听取当事人的意见。正当程序原则是裁决争端的基本原则及最低的公正标准. 即使法律中没有明确的程序规定，行政机关也不能认为自己不受程序限制. 对于正当程序原则的适用，行政机关没有自由裁量权。只是在法律未对正当程序原则设定具体的程序性规定时，行政机关可以就履行正当程序的具体方式作出选择.

[79] 正当程序原则通过保障相对人的程序参与权，来确保程序与结果的公正。而相对人只有在充分了解案件事实、法律规定以及可能面临的不利后果的情形下，才能够有针对性地进行陈述与申辩, 发表有价值的意见, 从而保证其真正地参与执法程序, 而不是流于形式.

authorities and citizens is probably even more marked than in the general relations between the authorities and the public, and the sources of administrative property law have undergone some deep transformations. The law on public properties was the subject of significant codification in 2006 following the order of 21 April 2006 regarding the legislative part of the *Code général de la propriété des personnes publiques* ('general code of property of public persons'—CGPPP) enabling the entry into effect of the said code regarding property that had entered the domain after 1 July 2006. The written law was fragmented and piecemeal. Furthermore, most of the law applicable was derived from case law. We might also stress, as a preliminary point, that the public properties of the state, local authorities, and public establishments are divided under French law into two categories of property, and thus there are two legal regimes: one for property within the 'public domain' and another for that of public entities in the 'private domain'. This distinction is also the result of a historical construction maintained by the CGPPP.

The case evoked concerns the purpose of authorizing the private occupation of property in the public domain. In cases of private use of space in the public domain (street, square, public thoroughfare etc) the space is withdrawn from collective use (ie use by all) for the benefit of an individual, a citizen, an association, a trader, or an undertaking. In these cases, it will permit the exercise of an economic activity (eg the sale of newspapers in the public domain). The most typical examples include café and restaurant terraces, shop stalls, taxi rank positions, the installation of water, gas, or electricity grids, street furniture, and newspaper kiosks etc.

The legal regime for private use differs greatly from that for use by all. It rests on a written, unilateral, or contractual authorization (CGPPP, Article L. 2122-1) and calls for payment of a licence fee (CGPPP, Article L. 2125-1). The laws and regulations on the occupation of the public domain juxtapose the occupier and his rights with the prerogatives of the authorities. However, the law as it stands accords rather broad powers to the authorities both at the time of granting the authorization and at the end. It is precisely the absence of a general law of administrative procedure that has allowed the emergence of special administrative procedures, which is quite diverse but also strongly characterized, as is the case of public property.

The laws and regulations on the private occupation of public property are governed by the principle of precariousness. Occupation is temporary, precarious, and revocable (CGPPP, Article L. 2122-2 and L. 2122-3). This is generally justified as being a consequence of the principle of the inalienability of the public domain. The state may put an end to any such occupation at any time.

The procedural regime differs, however, depending on whether an authorization has been terminated on grounds of fault or in the absence of one (on grounds of public interest).

The procedure for withdrawing authorization to occupy the public domain is subject to respecting the rights of the defence when a fault has been committed. Here, withdrawal is considered to be a sanction. The case law from *Dame Veuve Trompier-Gravier* settled the question of the application of the defence's rights regarding decisions on withdrawal of this kind,[80] the issue even affording the occasion to see the

[80] CE, sect, 5 May 1944, *Dame Veuve Trompier-Gravier*, *Rec* 133, RDP 1944, p 256, concl Chenot, note Jèze: withdrawal of authorization to occupy a kiosk.

making of a 'major ruling' on administrative procedure whose import went beyond the law on public domain. After stating that the reason was a fault for which the applicant was allegedly liable, the *Conseil d'Etat* considered that

> having regard to the character which, in the aforementioned circumstances, the withdrawal of authorisation presented and the gravity of this sanction, such a measure could not legally be taken without the widowed Mrs Trompier-Gravier's being enabled to discuss the grievances expressed against her.

But withdrawals without fault need not be grounded and are exempt from any adversarial procedure, a fact that encourages false qualifications.[81] According to the case law formula,

> no principle binds the authority managing the public domain to apply an adversarial procedure, when, as in the present case, it takes, in the interest thereof, a measure not having the character of a sanction.[82]

The absence of an adversarial procedure is also standard in refusals of renewal decided '*in the interest of the public domain*'.[83] Hence one can easily understand the choice that may be made by the authorities not to sanction a private occupant who has breached his obligations and to favour the simple refusal of renewal on grounds of public interest, not formally grounded and without adversarial procedure. The decision is irregular.

Thus, the obligation to apply an adversarial procedure is in no way a general rule. Other situations exist which are not mentioned here (the absence of adversarial procedure in applications for authorization to occupy the public domain). This complex regime's reasons for being lie principally in the protection of the interests of the public domain, its owner, and the public interest.

D. Germany

DS

Assuming that the licences concern the sale of products on public land, because otherwise no licence would be required, withdrawal raises two problems.

Firstly, the municipality of Belleville has not heard Ms Trompier. Withdrawal of the licence is an administrative act revoking a right. As there is no special regulation on the matter, § 28 *VwVfG* must be respected. It provides, as a principle, for the prior hearing of the persons concerned as an element of due process. There are exceptions, mentioned in § 28.2. One of them is nr. 4, which excepts the general acts (*Allgemeinverfügung*, § 35.2) and similar acts concerning numerous persons. The fact

[81] eg CAA Paris, 18 Nov 2010, No 09PA07023, *SARL Sominord.*

[82] CAA Nantes, 17 January 2014, *Sté Finist'Mer Cie Maritime*, No 12NT01618, unpublished.

[83] CE, 20 March 1996, *Veber*, No 121601, unpublished; CE, 6 October 1997, No 172278, *EURL JPC Loisirs*, unpublished.

that many people are involved could, as a principle, justify the exception. However, the acts remain individual, and the number of 'some' concerned persons is limited. Each case may raise individual problems, and the choice of the subjects affected by the withdrawal needs individual and special justification. Therefore, the conditions for an exception are not given; the right to be heard, as an element of due process, must be respected, but, in this case, it has been infringed.

The law provides for the redress of this infringement, allowing a hearing during the procedure before the court judging the facts (§ 45.1 No 3, 45.2 VwVfG). So, Ms Trompier's opinion may be examined and judged either by the administration or in court proceedings. Furthermore, infringement of the right to be heard would not be enough to overturn the withdrawal if the fault 'clearly' did not affect a substantially correct decision (§ 46 VwVfG)—which was not the case here, because the arguments of the licensees and the criteria for selecting those whose licences were to be withdrawn were not considered.

Secondly, no reasons for withdrawal have been provided. As the act of withdrawal weakens the legal position of the licensees, this act needs to be explicitly grounded (§ 39.1 VwVfG). Here too, there are exceptions for numerous administrative acts with the same content where the motivation is evident (§ 39.2 No 3, parallel to § 28.2 No 4 VwVfG). As the choice of the licences to be withdrawn and the arguments in the single cases raise individual problems, the conditions for an exception of this kind are not given. Nevertheless, in this situation too, the grounds can be stated during the administrative court proceedings (§ 45.1 No 2, 45.2 VwVfG). Also in the case of the absence of reasons, irrelevance for the reasoning of an obviously correct result (§ 46 VwVfG) cannot be maintained.

Therefore, the court would annul the withdrawal on both grounds unless the administration presented convincing reasons upon examining Ms Trompier's arguments.

E. Greece

TF

As far as the applicant's arguments are concerned, the norms regulating the revocation of individual administrative acts are essentially prescribed by general principles of administrative law. These norms seek to ensure the stability of legal and factual situations created by administrative acts in the interests of normal and reasonable administration, the protection of individuals, and the public interest.

In principle, the revocation of a lawfully favourable administrative act such as the applicant's licence is permitted for reasons of public interest, regardless of whether a long period of time has elapsed since they were issued. However, an ascertainment that its content is contrary to the public interest must be based on factors subsequent to those existing at the time the act was issued. Opposition to the public interest must be supported by a special statement of reasons, given that it is an onerous measure for the individual, and the Municipality's decision that there are reasons of public interest will be reviewed by the courts.

Therefore, according to a general principle of administrative law, as recognized by the Greek Council of State, an administrative act that revokes a previous act favourable to the applicant, therefore creating a new and unfavourable situation, must, by its very nature, be accompanied by specially argued reasoning. It is obvious that if an administrative act produces legal effects favourable to the interested party, as a result of which a favourable situation is created for it, and, for a long period of time, the Administration must include a detailed reasoning in the revocation administrative act, clearly stating both the specific irregularity of the act and the other conditions under which the revocation of the act is permitted. In this event, failure to state the reasoning in the body of the act is a defect and constitutes the grounds for an annulment due to 'procedural *ultra vires*'.

On the other hand, the right to a prior hearing, asserted by the applicant, consists in the possibility of the individual, prior to the issuance of an administrative act unfavourable to her, to express her views, following a summons to do so on the part of the administrative authority. This right is established by a general principle of administrative law. It is already provided for in Article 20 para 2 of the Constitution and further regulated in Article 6 of the Administrative Process Code and must be granted to the individual at all stages of the administrative process.

The range of implementation of the general provision of Article 20 para 2 of the Constitution is delineated by the case law of the Council of State.[84] Thus it is ruled out that a prior hearing of the individual is necessary in the case of individual administrative acts issued *proprio motu* containing a regulation connected with the subjective behaviour of the interested party and causes positive prejudice to their rights or lawful interests; a prior hearing is not required when the judgment of the administrative authority as to the fulfilment of the legal conditions for issuing the unfavourable administrative act (by virtue of binding competence) is based on objective data.

In particular, it is not clear whether the Municipality had binding competence or the discretion to issue the act revoking the licence. Therefore, in accordance with the general principle of administrative law, there is a presumption in favour of discretion; that is to say, where it is not clear from the relevant provisions that there is a binding obligation on the administrative authority to issue an act with specific content, it must be accepted in case of doubt that its competence has the nature of discretion, such as in this particular case.

A further condition for the exercise of the right to a prior hearing is that it should be possible for the individual concerned to be informed of the facts that may lead to the issue of an administrative act unfavourable to him. In this case, it must emerge from its reasoning that the individual was summoned to exercise the right of a prior hearing and that the competent authority took into account their views. For the reasoning to be complete, some comment on the substantive arguments of the individual is required. In particular, the Municipality has not previously published the criteria it used to identify the licences to be revoked. As a result, the interested parties did not exercise their right to produce relevant counter-evidence.

As far as the Municipality of Belleville's arguments are concerned, the Court would not endorse them on the following grounds. Firstly, the principle of legality requires the activity of the Public Administration to be governed by the legal norms as a whole,

[84] See Ruling No 2078/1976, 2152/2000, and 2370/2007 of the Council of State.

ie the Constitution and legislative acts, and any norm of formal effect superior or equal to that of these norms, which constitute the framework of legality. Conversely, it entails the obligation of the Public Administration, ie of the state and other public legal persons and their organs, such as local government agencies, to observe the above norms.

Consequently, the acts of the organs of local government agencies (ie the Municipality) should be in accordance or in harmony with the above norms. More specifically, in the Greek legal order, Articles 26 paras 2, 43, 50, 82, 83, and 95 para 1 of the Constitution establish the principle of legality in this sense, without exception, and thus the Public Administration cannot carry out legal acts, so it cannot issue administrative acts or implement material actions, except on the basis of the competence granted to it by the law.

Furthermore, besides the fact that local government agencies enjoy both administrative and financial independence (Article 102 para 2 of the Constitution), the Constitution does not allow them full independence in the sense of the power to introduce their own legal rules. On the contrary, according to Article 102 para 4 of the Constitution, they are subjected to state supervision, which consists in reviewing the legality of their action.

Therefore, the Municipality of Belleville, as a local government agency, has not only to take any action that is not prohibited by the norms or is not contrary to them but has to engage solely in acts that are prescribed, imposed, or permitted by the aforementioned norms.

On the other hand, regarding the arguments referring to the waste of time and resources that may be caused by the prior hearing of the licensees, it should be mentioned that the administration is not obliged to comply with the law simply because of its formal binding nature and power but mainly because it is not self-evident and independent in the regulation of social life. The rule of law principle is not a formal and value-neutral principle but contains a fundamental ethical claim to the primacy of the principle of legality. Therefore, the indisputable need to ensure the efficiency of administrative action cannot enjoy absolute and general priority over legality. Efficiency and legality, in this case, are in a relationship of marginal equivalence, which solely allows the legislator to settle—on the basis of its own judgements of expediency—the balance between the two opposing principles in each particular case. In other words, the requirement of a speedy and less costly administrative procedure, as a manifestation of efficiency, cannot be undermined by the observance of procedural guarantees of legality.

Therefore, on the grounds mentioned above, the Court would endorse the claimant's arguments and order against the disputed withdrawal on the grounds of violation of the principle of legality, as a specific manifestation of the constitutional principle of the rule of law, the right to a prior hearing, and the obligation of the Municipality to state-specific reasons.

F. Italy

Nicola Berti

The withdrawal of Ms Trompier's licence would be annulled by the competent court (administrative court), as it took place in breach of certain fundamental guarantees established in domestic law to protect the recipients of this type of measure, especially when they concern the withdrawal of an act with beneficial effects, such as a licence.

In the Italian legal system, the act adopted, in this case, by the municipality is classified as a 'withdrawal' ('*revoca*') and is governed by Article 21-*quinquies* of the APA (Law No 241 of 7 August 1990, as supplemented by Law No 15 of 11 February 2005). This provision allows an authority to withdraw a lawful administrative measure due to a change of factual circumstances or in order to better pursue the public interest.

According to domestic case law, in accordance with Article 7 of Law No 241/1990 and the general principles of due process of law, before a pre-existing administrative act can be withdrawn, the person concerned must first be notified of the initiation of the relevant procedure, unless there are duly justified grounds of urgency.[85] The notice of commencement is a fundamental institution as it allows addressees to defend themselves since they are able to access the proceeding file and submit documents and statements of defence, which must be taken into due account by the administration when giving its reasons (if pertinent).

Furthermore, domestic case law holds that stakeholder participation in the administrative procedure constitutes a general principle of the legal system and that exclusions must be expressly established by law.[86] Failure to provide notice of the initiation of the proceeding and the consequent breach of the right to be heard render the final measure unlawful unless the court finds that the final content of the measure could not have been different (eg because of the fettered nature of the administrative measure) or because in practice the right to defence had not been violated (eg because the recipient had still participated in the procedure). This provision, currently laid down in Article 21-*octies*(2) of the APA, is consistent with established case law, holding that the extension of the general principle of procedural fairness, by obliging public administrations to allow procedural participation, must be limited by rationality and sound administration, effectiveness, speed and economy of action, and therefore by the practical utility of such participation in order to avoid pointless or pretextual procedural delays.[87] On the contrary, whenever the recipient's participation can influence the outcome of the procedure, the right to a fair procedure cannot be sacrificed for the sake of the speed and economy of the administrative act (so that, in our case, the authority cannot defend its action by stating that hearing all the licensees would have wasted too much time and energy).

The fact that the acting administration is a municipality makes no difference to this framework, as Law No 241/1990 also applies to proceedings conducted by local authorities, and the assurances required from them cannot be waived as the private citizens' right to participate pertains to essential levels of public services.[88]

The measure taken by the municipality of Belleville also appears unlawful in the light of the vagueness of the reasons stated, as the withdrawal of a measure requires a thorough statement of reasons specifying the actual and substantive reasons of public interest that make it necessary (and it is not sufficient to simply say that it 'is in the

[85] Council of State, Div IV, No 6603, 30 December 2008.

[86] Council of State, Div V, No 2823, 22 May 2001; see, in greater detail, S Vaccari, N Berti, and M Silvestri, 'Italy' in this book, para 1.

[87] Lazio Regional Administrative Court, Rome, Div I, No 6399, 2 July 2009.

[88] Art 29 Italian Law 241/1990, see Vaccari, Berti, and Silvestri (n 86).

public interest'). Furthermore, under Italian law, when the withdrawal of a measure injures the recipient, the administration must pay compensation.

In this context, failure to pre-establish the criteria for selecting the licences and the conditions for exercising authority is irrelevant to the lawfulness of the withdrawal, given that specific reasons should be provided for each individual withdrawal measure, regardless of whether the criteria were pre-established. Furthermore, when exercising the power of withdrawal, the administrative body has broad discretionary powers which do not require *ex-ante* limitations other than those already legally established in abstract terms (eg prohibition of the withdrawal of measures 'granting authorisations or allocating economic benefits' on the mere grounds that the authority has had second thoughts ('*ius poenitendi*').

G. Romania

D-C D

This case accurately highlights one of the significant shortcomings of Romanian legislation: the lack of comprehensive and detailed rules for administrative procedures. Without a code of administrative procedure in place, when analysing a case like this, the courts are compelled to rely on fragmented regulations and dispersed principles to assess the legality of a measure like the one in question.

There is no general right to be heard in Romanian administrative procedure. Some isolated normative texts provide for such a right—for instance, the Administrative Code contains a provision regarding penalties for civil servants (Article 493),[89] and the Code of Fiscal Procedure (Article 9)[90] envisions procedural rights during fiscal investigations.

However, some arguments support the possibility for the courts to gather sufficient legal grounds to scrutinize the exercise of discretion in this particular case. I begin with the scholarly literature, which indicates that procedural fairness or due process should include the obligation of transparency in decision-making, the duty to provide reasons for decisions, and guaranteed access to judicial protection and remedies.[91]

[89] Art 493 (1). The disciplinary sanctions outlined in Art 492(3) (b) to (f) may only be applied after the preliminary investigation into the alleged misconduct and after the civil servant has been heard. The civil servant's hearing must be recorded in writing, under pain of nullity. If the civil servant refuses to attend the hearings or sign a statement regarding the alleged disciplinary offences against him or her, it must be recorded in a report. However, such refusal does not prevent the completion of the preliminary investigation or the imposition of the penalty.

[90] Art 9—The right to be heard: (1) Prior to reaching a final decision, the fiscal organ shall give the tax payer the possibility to express an opinion on the facts and other aspects relevant for the decision; (2) The previous paragraph is not mandatory when: a) delay in reaching a final decision shall compromise the assessment of the real fiscal situation regarding execution of fiscal obligations or other measures provided by law; b) the facts to be presented will have little effect on the tax debt; c) the tax payer has given a written declaration or other document that serves this purpose and it is accepted as such by the tax authority; d) enforcement of the fiscal decision is at issue.

[91] See, for instance, G della Cananea, 'Equivalent Standards under Domestic Administrative Law: A Comparative Perspective', Paper for the BIICL conference on 'Fair and equitable treatment in investment treaty law', London, 9 September 2005, available here: <https://www.biicl.org/eventpaper/30> accessed June 2023.

According to Law No 554/2004, Romanian courts can review administrative acts issued with excess discretionary power. This provides a general competence for the courts to examine the procedural aspects and consider general principles of law, such as proportionality, impartiality, equality, and transparency (as specified in the Administrative Code, Articles 6 to 13). As a result, there is access to judicial review, which can be used to assess the obligation to hear or consult the interested parties in this case.

As set out in Law 52/2003[92] referred to above, the principle of transparency establishes clear rules regarding the participation of individuals interested in administrative proceedings and decision-making processes. However, this law only pertains to general (normative) administrative acts adopted by the administration, leaving aside individual acts such as the one described in the case study.

In conclusion, there is no requirement to hear the interested party in the general administrative law regarding individual acts, such as a licence to sell products in the city centre.

In the absence of such an obligation in general administrative law, one should refer to the special legislation governing the authorization of commercial activities, particularly licensing. Government Ordinance 99/2000 on selling products and services (Article 5 para 1)[93] and Government Decision No 384/2004 on market activities in public spaces[94] grant local authorities the power to license these activities within the territory of their municipalities. These two central government regulations do not include procedural safeguards for the authorization process. Each municipality has implemented its own local regulations for licensing businesses. Regrettably, from a review of several of these,[95] it emerges that they include no provisions regarding the right to a hearing either during the authorization stage or in the event of revocation.

In conclusion, the proceeding for withdrawing the licence in Romania described above would be exactly like the one in the example, ie without hearing the interested party. The local authority may bring the same arguments before the courts, which do not typically apply principles of good administration without a legal basis, so there is slim chance of a counter-argument holding. However, the court can assess on its own motion whether the decision is lawful or issued in an excess of discretionary power. If this is held to be the case, the general principles of proportionality, equality, and impartiality may be considered, potentially leading to the measure being annulled.

Due to the absence of a general administrative procedure law, the duty to give reasons (or 'justification') for administrative decisions is not a general requirement in Romanian administrative proceedings. However, some particular legislation does

[92] Law No 52/2003 on transparency in decision-making, republished in the Official Monitor No 749/3 December 2013.

[93] Republished in the Official Monitor No 603/2007.

[94] Published in the Official Monitor No 269/2004.

[95] Cluj Napoca: <https://primariaclujnapoca.ro/informatii-publice/regulament-local/regulament-privind-activitatea-de-comert-stradal-pe-raza-municipiului-cluj-napoca/> accessed June 2023; Suceava: <http://www.primariasv.ro/portal/suceava/stiri.nsf/0/0530CB21ACE3F0CAC2257B910033129F/$FILE/DOCREGULAMENT.pdf> accessed June 2023; Municipality of Sector 3, Bucharest <https://www.primarie3.ro/index.php/informatii_publice/detaliu_act/emiterea-acordului-de-functionare-pentru-activitate-comercial-comer-produse-alimentare-nealimentare-servicii-de-pia/ > accessed June 2023.

contain provisions in this regard. For instance, administrative acts issued in response to a petition brought by a person[96] must include legal grounds. In other cases, the authority must provide factual reasons in addition to legal grounds. Law No 544/2001 on free access to public information states an obligation to 'justify' a refusal to provide public information. However, in practice, public bodies usually get away with stating only the legal grounds for their negative decisions. Some provisions contained in specific legislation impose a more robust obligation to give reasons, such as the Code of Fiscal Procedure, which sets forth quite detailed rules on justification.[97]

Legal doctrine has always stressed the importance of justification as a principle of administrative procedure, and the courts have upheld this principle even in the absence of a written law. For instance, the High Court of Cassation and Justice[98] stated in 2008 that

> a detailed description of the reasons for issuing administrative acts is necessary even when the administration has ample discretionary power for reasons to provide administrative transparency and allow private persons to verify whether the act is well founded, also allowing the courts to judicially review them.

The court has based its decision on

> (. . .) the principles of EU law, inter alia, transparency, and therefore interpreting the duty to give reasons as mandatory is the only way to make these principles effective.

As a consequence, the Supreme Court declared the duty to give reasons

> a general obligation of the administration which has a dual role: transparency for the beneficiary of the act, and permitting courts to verify the factual and legal elements considered when the act was issued.

In this context, there are enough legal sources to consider the duty to give reasons an essential element in proceedings and that the lack of sufficient reasons renders a decision unlawful. Furthermore, applying the principle of proportionality, enshrined in Article 9 of the Administrative Code, should require the measure to be proportionate to the purpose pursued. The fact that the administration has withdrawn the licence without previously publishing the criteria it used to identify the licensees or justify withdrawal in a particular case breaches the principle of proportionality. Moreover,

[96] Government Ordinance No 27/2002, Art 13.

[97] Art 43—The content and reasoning of the administrative-fiscal act: (1) The administrative-fiscal act is issued only in written form; (2) The administrative fiscal act consists of the following elements: a) the title of the issuing authority; b) the date of issuance and the date from which it enters into force; c) the data of the tax payer and its representative, if there is one; d) the purpose of the administrative fiscal act; e) the factual reasoning; f) the legal reasoning; g) the name and signature of the representatives of the public authority; h) the stamp of the issuing organ; i) a statement about eligibility for appeal, the deadline and the authority competent to hear it; j) information on hearing the tax payer.

[98] The High Court of Cassation and Justice, Decision 1580/2008, available here: <https://legeaz.net/spete-contencios-inalta-curte-iccj-2008/decizia-1580-2008> accessed June 2023.

the mere statement that this is 'in the public interest' does not satisfy the duty to give reasons and may be reviewed in court.

Lastly, with regard to the likelihood of successfully annulling a decision like the one described in the case study, the courts would also need to assess whether the procedural error had a decisive impact on the outcome of the decision. If, after hearing the interested parties, the courts determine that the decision remains valid and that the failure to hear the parties during administrative proceedings was not a significant procedural error, the prospects of annulment solely on procedural grounds are slim. The court can therefore rule on the merits and still dismiss the claim, regardless of procedural deficiencies. Courts do not typically censure procedural deficiencies per se if they have no bearing on the substance of the case.

H. Serbia

MM

In the case of the withdrawal of Ms Trompier's licence, several constitutional guarantees would be applicable in addition to the procedural rights set by the Law on General Administrative Procedure (LGAP). In accordance with the Constitution, all are equal before the Constitution and Law, and everyone shall have the right to equal legal protection without discrimination (Article 21). As already outlined in the general section, the right to equal protection of rights and legal remedy is guaranteed to everyone, and everyone has the right to an appeal or other legal remedy against *any decision on his rights, obligations, or lawful interests.* The Law on Local Self-government[99] stipulates that local self-government bodies manage public affairs of *direct, common, and general interest to the local population.* It also envisages the right and obligation of such bodies to plan, regulate, and manage public affairs in their jurisdiction and of interest to the local population (Article 2). According to the Law, the municipality, through its bodies and in accordance with the Constitution and the Law, has the competence to develop and improve tourism, crafts, catering, and trade (Article 20). Therefore, the authority would claim these articles as the basis of their decision. However, the local authority must adhere to all the principles and rights set by the LGAP on administrative proceedings when acting upon so-called administrative matters. The Law defines an administrative matter as the individual situation in which an authority directly applying laws, other regulations, and statutory instruments legally or factually affects the position of a party by *adopting administrative acts*, passing letters of guarantee, concluding administrative agreements, undertaking administrative actions, and providing public services (Article 2). In this particular case, this would be the adoption of an administrative act with the effect of revoking Ms Trompier's licence. As already stated, the LGAP stipulates that a party to administrative proceedings must be allowed to plead on the facts of relevance for issuing a decision on the administrative matter, and that the decision may be rendered without prior pleading of a party only when this is prescribed by law (Article 11). Therefore, the relevant legislation would have to

[99] Law on Local Self-government (Official Gazette of RS, No 129/2007, 83/2014—other law, 101/2016—other law, 47/2018 and 111/2021).

exclude the right to be heard (in collision with general principles) in order for the local authority to claim that it was not obliged to allow Ms Trompier to exercise her right to be heard in this case. This kind of exclusion is not envisaged by the relevant legislation governing local self-government. In the case of Ms Trompier, the Administrative Court would therefore annul the decision of the municipality on the basis that it is in the breach of the rules of procedure set in the LGAP. In addition, should her claim be unsuccessful before the Administrative Court, Ms Trompier would be able to resort to constitutional appeal as her rights (or lawful interests) were breached.

I. Spain

IMD

Within the Spanish legal system, scholars consider withdrawals to be a way of reversing administrative acts on the grounds of timeliness or expediency. If the act to be reversed or withdrawn is detrimental to the party concerned, Article 109 LPAC allows for withdrawing it

> as long as such withdrawal not i) qualify as an unlawful exemption, waiver, dispensation or privilege, or ii) be contrary to the principle of equality, public interest (public policy) or the applicable law.

However, the LPAC does not regulate the reversal or withdrawal of favourable acts.

According to the Supreme Court, the principle of effectiveness of administrative action set out in Article 103 CE requires public authorities to be free to overturn or withdraw their acts, but the principle of legal certainty of Article 9(3) CE protects the situations arising from acts that declare or provide for rights. This is why the reversal or withdrawal of administrative acts that declare rights qualifies as an exceptional prerogative to be exercised only in specific cases and following the relevant administrative procedure.

From the perspective of sector-specific regulation, Article 16 of the Service Regulations for Local Governments states that

> 1. The validity of licences shall be subject to certain conditions. Non-compliance with these conditions will render licences ineffective. Licences shall be withdrawn i) in the absence of the circumstances justifying the granting thereof; or ii) if new circumstances occurred that could have constituted grounds for denial or could constitute such grounds if the applicable criteria were modified.

This is a non-discretionary rule-based act that requires a procedure to be followed. Therefore, as repeatedly declared in the case law, the two formal requirements arising from the concerned party's right of defence apply: (i) the duty to give reasons (ie supporting arguments) and (ii) that the party be heard.

The required reasoning or supporting arguments must be short. However, solely mentioning public interest grounds will not suffice to fulfil the duty to state reasons since the party concerned would be deprived of his or her right (the licence was granted lawfully), and such a deprivation of rights must be grounded on (i) non-compliance with the applicable conditions or (ii) new circumstances. Although specific public interest grounds could suffice to withdraw the licence, they would have to be specified. According to the Supreme Court, 'unclear, non-transparent, standardised wordings that depart from the [legal] requirements' would not be good enough.[100]

Accordingly, the reasons and arguments supporting withdrawal of the licence do not suffice, thus providing grounds for annulment. Spanish courts should declare the withdrawal 'voidable', ie subject to annulment if requested by the parties concerned.

Let us examine the requirement for the party concerned to be heard. According to Supreme Court case law, regardless of whether the withdrawal qualifies as a penalty or not (ie punitive or not) it is subject to the safeguards and standards governing penalty or sanctioning procedures.[101] Thus, relying on this case law, hearing the party is an indispensable (non-derogable) procedural step for allowing the party to be aware of the grounds for withdrawal and submit any objections. As a result, since hearing the parties concerned is an indispensable and essential due process requirement, withdrawing a lawfully granted licence or permit—like Ms Trompier's—without allowing the parties concerned to object or submit comments would constitute grounds for annulling the administrative act. Failing to hear the parties would be equivalent to not conducting the legally required procedure altogether. A Spanish court would uphold Ms Trompier's claim and invalidate the withdrawal.

J. Switzerland

AF

Article 29 para 2 of the Federal Constitution, according to which '[e]ach party to a case has the right to be heard', applies to administrative procedures. According to the Swiss Federal Court, the right to be heard is of a formal nature, so it is independent of the outcome and the merits of the case.

It follows that the competent court would therefore side with the claimants and would, in principle, annul the contested withdrawal. Exceptionally, the defect could be 'cured' if the claimant brings the case before an appeal body that gives her the opportunity to be heard, provided that this authority has the same power of review as the first and that the violation of the right to be heard is not too serious.[102]

K. United Kingdom

GA and CM

This type of scenario is very familiar to the common law, where licences are often used to illustrate how the principles of fairness apply in a context dependent way. A leading

[100] Supreme Court Judgment of 20 April 2021 (Appeal 7137/2018).
[101] Supreme Court Judgment of 13 May 2021 (Appeal 5011/2021).
[102] ATF 142 II 218, 226.

authority on the point is *McIness v Onslow Fane*,[103] which was a case about the denial of a licence to an aspiring boxing manager. In his judgment, Megarry V-C made a distinction between three categories of cases: (i) those in which a licensee would forfeit an existing licence (where common law protections would be high); (ii) those in which an individual was applying for a licence to be renewed (where common law protections would be less high); and (iii) those in which an individual is merely applying for a licence for the first time (where the demands of the common law would be less high again). On the facts that have been given here, Ms Trompier (and presumably all of the other claimants) would fall into the first category of cases.

What does this mean for the points that were put forward by the municipality? In the first instance, the fact that there is no statutory framework that sets down procedural guarantees is irrelevant: fairness is a common law construct and, unless legislation expressly provides that aspects of the common law should not apply, the courts will give effect to the requirements of fairness in accordance with context. This, in turn, disposes of the municipality's second point, as the fact that this is a forfeiture case means that many of the common law's procedural protections would apply (among them, advance notification of the proposed decision; an opportunity to make oral and written submissions before the decision is taken; and reasons for the subsequent decision). Nor would the municipality's third point be persuasive in the given context. While the courts are mindful of the need not to overburden administrative decision makers,[104] the different categories of cases recognized by Megarry V-C are intended to enable the courts to strike a balance between an individual's interests and those of the administration as the facts of discrete cases require. In Ms Trompier's case, the idea of balance (and legality) would be lost were the administration not to be tied to heightened requirements of fairness (which in turn support the idea of good administration).

Two further observations should be made.

The first concerns the municipality's reliance on the idea of 'the public interest' in seeking to justify its decision. As noted in the 'preliminary comments' section that accompanies this chapter, the common law rules of fairness can be subject to countervailing matters of public interest, where 'national security' is the ground that is most often used to limit procedural entitlements. While it cannot be gainsaid that the court would not accept that there is a matter of public interest that would justify the withdrawal of the licences in this case, there is nothing on the facts as given to indicate what that matter is. In the absence of that information, it could be expected that the court would be sceptical about the municipality's position and that it would require evidence to be placed before it (in camera, if needs be).

The second point concerns a potential overlap with the common law and human rights principles in this case. In short, if it could be argued that a licence for an economic activity is a property right for the purposes of Article 1 of Protocol 1 ECHR, this would mean that it would be a 'civil right' within the meaning of Article 6 ECHR. If so, many of the procedural protections that would be guaranteed by the common law

[103] [1978] 1 WLR 1520.

[104] See G Anthony, 'Transparency, Public Administration, and the Common Law' in A Pottakis (ed), *Transparency and Reform of Administrative Procedures* (Esperia Publications 2010) 187.

would be paralleled under the Human Rights Act 1998 (section 6 of that Act requires that public authorities act in a way that is compatible with the Convention rights that have effect under the Act).

To summarize: Ms Trompier and the other licence holders would have strong grounds for challenging the municipality's decision as having been taken in breach of common law (and human rights) principles. It could be expected that the reviewing court would quash the municipality's decision and require that it be taken again, in a procedurally fair manner.

L. Venezuela

FP-F

The Venezuelan Constitution of 1999 (Article 49) declares that all judicial and administrative procedures must respect due process and, therefore, among other things, all interested parties have the right to be heard in any type of proceeding, with all due guarantees, by a court or competent, independent, impartial administrative authority established in advance and that they must have legal assistance and defence, which are inviolable rights at all stages and levels during the investigation and the procedure.

Regarding administrative procedures, the Venezuelan Law of Administrative Procedure guarantees the interested party the right to be heard, to be assisted by a lawyer, and to prove and plead (*audire alteram parte*) in all administrative procedures that conclude with the issuance of an administrative act that could affect in some way their rights, interests, and legal position.

For this reason, the contentious-administrative tribunal would annul the decision because, in addition to the fact that the Municipality of Belleville violates the constitutional right to due process and, therefore, the right to be heard, with its decision, it also violates the economic right to freedom of business provided for in Article 112 of the Venezuelan Constitution, so the reasons put forward by the Municipality would be dismissed in their entirety because the right to be heard is a fundamental constitutional right that the public administration must respect in all the procedures that it develops, more so if they are procedures that lead to an administrative act that eliminates rights acquired by individuals.

In addition to the foregoing, it must be remembered that before any general provision enters into force, it must be published, and this principle must have been violated since the Municipality's criteria were not made public; therefore, it sought to apply a legal consequence without the individual knowing the requisites assumption, leaving her in a situation of defencelessness and legal uncertainty. Subsequent publication would not be possible either, as it would be an attempt to apply the disposition retroactively, violating the law's principle of non-retroactivity.

V. Case 4—The unfair dismissal of a civil servant

A. Austria

SS

This case would not go to court immediately, as prior to any judicial proceeding, the civil servant can object to the decision taken by the disciplinary board through a special fast-track procedure. This objection is then presented to the Federal Disciplinary Board, which must decide on any further proceedings.

In principle, disciplinary proceedings are governed by the *AVG*; however, the Federal Act for Civil Servants ('*BDG*') also provides for a fast-track procedure. The authority for civil servants may issue a disciplinary decision (which can include the termination of employment) in writing with no further proceedings if the civil servant has confessed to wrongdoing, if a breach of official duty has been concretely proven because of conclusive evidence, or if the civil servant has been punished by a criminal or administrative court as a result of breaching his or her official duties. In all three scenarios, the facts must be sufficiently established to justify the imposition of sanctions for failure to comply with official duties.

In this case, the decisive point is that the validity of the facts is not relevant in the further proceeding. This is because an official (and also a disciplinary lawyer) has up to two weeks to object ('*Einspruch*') to the disciplinary decision.[105] In such situations, the objection defers the disciplinary decision, and the Federal Disciplinary Board has to decide whether it will initiate another proceeding or not.

The Federal Disciplinary Board cannot decide this by a fast-track procedure as it has to respect the right to be heard. If it skips this procedural requirement, the administrative court, which reviews the decision of the Federal Disciplinary Board in the case of a remedy, will hold the hearing itself.

B. China

XS

Under Chinese law, a court cannot be seized of such a challenge.

According to Article 13 of the Administrative Litigation Law, 'decisions of an administrative organ on awards or punishments for its personnel or on the appointment of its personnel'[106] are excluded from the scope of an administrative suit. In its Judicial Interpretation of 2017, the Supreme People's Court clarifies that the exclusion made by this legislative provision concerns all acts relating to the rights and obligations of civil servants.[107]

105 § 132 *BDG*.
106 行政机关对行政机关工作人员的奖惩、任免等决定.
107 Supreme People's Court, Judicial Interpretation on 13 November 2017 relating to the application of the Administrative Litigation Law, art 2.

This exclusion can be explained on practical grounds: the will of the legislator not to overburden the courts. But this would not suffice on its own. There is another, ideological, and more important reason for this exclusion.

Ideologically, the Chinese Lawmaker does not consider civil servants as normal subjects of Law. The status of civil servant, intrinsically linked to the public interest, puts the employees of public services in a particular situation. They are part of the public administration, and not common subjects of the administrative order.[108] Furthermore, judicial authority and administrative authority are equally subject to Parliament. The courts have no power to rule on conflicts within the administration.

According to the Civil Servant Law,[109] civil servants can only challenge acts relating to their rights and obligations before the competent administrative authorities, by way of administrative remedies.[110]

C. France

SS

The procedure for applying penalties against a state employee is regulated by the statutory provisions regarding public services (Law No 83-634 of 13 July 1983 on the rights and obligations of state employees, Article 24; Law No 84-16 of 11 January 1984 on statutory provisions regarding the national public services, particularly articles 66 and 67; and Decree No 84-961 of 25 October 1984 regarding disciplinary procedure for state employees). These rules are largely uniform and often apply in the same manner, regardless of belonging to such-and-such a public service (national or local authority, public hospital, etc).

Dismissal constitutes a penalty of the 4th group in the scale of sanctions (Article 66, Law No 84-16 of 11 January 1984, bearing statutory provisions regarding the national public services). It is the severest sanction, imposed in cases of grave professional wrongdoing, often compared to a dismissal for misconduct in labour law.

Decree No 84-961 of 25 October 1984 regarding the disciplinary procedure for civil servants states the rules in detail. In addition, Article L. 121-1 of the CRPA, applicable to relations between the public authorities and their employees, requires a prior adversarial procedure.

The textual establishment of the right to have access to a case file against one is old; moreover, the rule was established first by the legislator before being taken up again in case law and then being developed in the legislative and regulatory texts regarding disciplinary proceedings. It was article 65 of the budget law of 22 April 1905 that, for the first time, consolidated the right of public employees to obtain 'access' to the 'documents making up their case file (…) before being subjected to disciplinary

[108] They can be considered common subjects of administration orders as citizens, but not as civil servants in their service.

[109] 公务员法.

[110] Arts 95 to 99 of the Civil Servant Law.

proceedings'. The *Conseil d'Etat* extended this rule to non-tenured state employees and then erected it as a general legal principle with its famous decision in *Aramu*:

> It results from the general principles of law, applicable even in the absence of a text, that a penalty as such cannot be decided legally without the interested party's having been enabled to present his defence properly; that he must, consequently, be made aware beforehand if not of the actual text of the report established or of the complaint lodged against him, then at least of the essential substance of the grievances contained therein, so as to be able to formulate all observations regarding the same which he deems necessary.[111]

As may be seen, in the *Aramu* case law, the logic of the right to know the contents of a case file against one is extended by its effects to the ability to present observations, written or oral, prior to any penalty.[112]

The administrative courts have thus forged general principles of administrative law and criminal law which the disciplining authority must not ignore. They have drawn general principles of disciplinary procedure,[113] amongst which is the right to present one's defence adequately.[114]

Constitutional case law is also protective. The principle of respect for the rights of the defence constitutes a fundamental principle recognized by the laws of the Republic. It was erected in PRFLRL by decision No 77-83 DC of the *Conseil constitutionnel* of 20 July 1977, which now attaches it to article 16 of the DDHC of 26 August 1789. No penalty may be imposed without the interested party's having been able 'to have access to the case file concerning him' or without his 'having been enabled (…) to present his observations on the facts of which he is accused.[115]

This has led to a significant degree of formalism, bringing with it the risk of invalidating the procedure. A measure to remove a public employee, whether tenured or on a contract, can be annulled on grounds of *ultra vires* if it rests on an external or internal legal defect (despite the shift, begun in 2009, from the litigation of sanctions to litigation of the unlimited jurisdiction, the *ultra vires* appeal remains the judicial recourse available against disciplinary measures imposed on public employees).

The regulation of the sanctioning procedure for public employees has been modified to take into account the requirements of case law. It sometimes goes beyond what the general legal principle or the PFRLR (eg on the possibility of calling witnesses) demands. It is not always easy to say whether the rule of procedure is purely textual or derives from a general legal principle (applicable even in the absence of a text) or from a constitutional principle. Applications in case law do not systematically specify what rule is violated by the breach observed.

[111] CE, 26 October 1945, *Aramu*, *Rec* p 213; S 1946.III.1, concl Odent.

[112] See also CE, Sect, 19 April 1968, *Conseil départemental de l'ordre des médecins du Puy-De-Dome*, *Rec*, p 254.

[113] CE, Sect, 23 March 1962, *Mast*, *Rec*, p 203.

[114] CE, 5 July 2000, *Mermet*, req no 200.622, Rec Lebon, p 292: concerning the sanctioning of a prefect.

[115] Cons Const, Decision No 88-248 DC of 17 January 1989, CSA, cons No 29.

In view of the facts mentioned in the case, several irregularities appear that would probably be sanctioned by the administrative court. It may be helpful to study the different stages of the disciplinary procedure later on.

Among the steps prior to the handing down of the sanction is that when the authority decides to bring proceedings against one of its employees, it must draw up a report (D No 84-961 prev, Article 2) clearly specifying the facts alleged and the circumstances of their occurrence. This constitutes the 'act of pursuit'. The authority may, in preparing this report, institute an inquiry and rely on testimony.[116] However, no general legal principle obliges it to do so.[117] During the internal inquiry stage, the general principle of the rights of the defence does not require it to be conducted in an adversarial manner.[118] The employee must be able to know the contents of this report by consulting the case file. It is recalled that by virtue of the Aramu case law, the general principle of the rights of the defence entails the right to receive knowledge, if not of the actual text of the report established or of the complaint lodged against one, then at least of the essential substance of the grievances contained therein (CE, 26 October 1945, *Aramu*, prev).

Mr Alvin's lack of cognizance of the facts of the accusation brought against him constitutes the first breach of this principle.

The right to know that case file exists is essential: the employee must be informed that disciplinary proceedings have been brought against him and what the nature of the alleged grievances is. He must also be informed of the possibility of knowing the contents of the case file and that he can be assisted by one or more defenders of his choice.[119] The disciplinary procedure therefore begins when the employee is sent a letter informing him of his rights. This obligation known as 'communication of the case file' is inscribed in case law in the extension of the general legal principle, established by the *Conseil d'Etat*, according to which a sanction of a public employee cannot legally be pronounced without the employee having been allowed to present a proper defence.[120] It is therefore a matter of a substantive irregularity. The *Conseil d'Etat* has specified that informing a party of the existence of a case file is a protection in line with the Danthony precedent,[121] the irregularity of which cannot be neutralized. Besides, the right to be assisted by a defender exists insofar as the file has been made known to the interested party.[122] This formality is obligatory, even when the penalties envisaged or pronounced consist of a warning or reprimand.[123]

The failure to inform Mr Alvin of his case file thus constitutes a new breach of the general legal principles and the legislative and regulatory rules.

[116] CE, 10 July 1963, *Hôpital-hospice Georges-Renon*, *Rec*, p 422.

[117] CE 31 March 2017, No 393627.

[118] CAA Bordeaux, 11 December 2007, *Yannick X*:

> that no legislative or regulatory provision, nor any general legal principle requires that the internal inquiry instituted by the authority within the context of a disciplinary procedure be conducted in an adversarial manner by questioning the interested parties.

[119] Law No 83-634 of 13 July 1983 prev, Art 19; Decree No 84-961 of 25 October 1984 prev, Art 1.

[120] CE, 26 October 1945, *Aramu*, prev.

[121] CE 31 January 2014, req No 369718, Lebon T.

[122] CE 30 October 1959, *Marcoulet*, No 47171, *Rec* p 568.

[123] CE 17 June 1988, *Labrosse*, No 81815, *Rec* p 244.

The interested party must be granted sufficient time to consult his case file in order to prepare a defence, even though no text specifies the duration of this period,[124] also in the case of a mere reprimand. The question of the period for response assumes greater or lesser importance with regard to the circumstances and complexity of the matter. The case file must include all the items useful for the employee's defence, including the written testimonies provided by the authority, the minutes, and any documentation gathered during the preliminary administrative inquiry.[125]

The disciplinary board must be convened in the event of a penalty of this type, as prescribed in the written law.[126] It will be noted, however, that no general legal principle requires the authority to refer systematically to such a committee.[127] The intervention of a body of this type is therefore not systematic in the disciplinary procedure.

The procedure before the disciplinary board requires the chair to summon the employee at least fifteen days prior to the date fixed for the meeting via registered post with receipt of delivery.[128] This is a point of substantial guarantee, the omission of which constitutes a defect of external legality.[129]

The board will proceed as follows: at the start of the session, the chair explains to the members the conditions under which the employee is subjected to the procedure and, as the case may be, whether his defender or defenders have exercised their right to gain access to the complete personal file and appended documents. The report, and any written observations submitted by the employee, are read aloud.[130] It has recently been specified that reading the report before the board is not in itself a guarantee which, if disregarded, may jeopardize the legality of the final decision, as long as the report has been conveyed to the interested party prior to the session and the latter has been enabled to respond to all the grievances stated.[131]

At any time during the hearing, the employee and, as the case may be, his defender of defenders may apply to the chair for authorization to intervene in order to submit oral observations.[132] He or they must also be invited to submit final observations before the board begins to deliberate (Article 5 prev). It has been ruled that disregard of this formality subjects the procedure to substantive irregularity. Whilst several precedents relate this obligation to textual provisions,[133] the *Conseil d'Etat* has recently specified that

[124] CE, 27 March 1963, No 54178, *Corbin, Rec* p 215.

[125] CE, 5 February 2020, No 433130, *M Decottignies*.

[126] Law No 83-634 of 13 July 1983 prev, Art 19.

[127] CE, 30 March 1990, *Fédération générale des fonctionnaires FO*:

> considering (…) that no general principle nor any legislative provision requires the consultation of a joint body prior to imposition of a disciplinary sanction.

[128] D No 84-961 of 25 October 1984 prev, Art 4.

[129] CE 1 March 1996, *Reynes*, No 146854: Lebon T 988: NB, the *Conseil d'Etat* cites an obligation resulting from 'the aforesaid provision' and not from the general legal principle.

[130] D No 84-961 of 25 Oct 1984 prev, Art 5.

[131] In application of the Danthony precedent: CE 12 Feb 2014, *M B*, req No 352878, Lebon T.

[132] D No 84-961 of 25 October 1984 prev, Art 5.

[133] CAA Paris, 28 Oct 2005, *M Breton*, No 03PA01839; CAA Bordeaux, 28 June 2013, No 12BX01333, *Durieu*.

> the general principles of disciplinary law imply that, during the hearing, the person subjected to the procedure should be enabled to take the floor last.[134]

There is thus another breach of the general principles of disciplinary law sustained by Mr Alvin.

On the question of witnesses, by virtue of the texts, both the employee subjected to proceedings and the disciplinary authority dispose of the capacity to bring witnesses.[135] The *Conseil d'Etat*, however, in the absence of texts refuses to infer a general legal principle giving the employee a right to have persons heard who are able to inform discussions before disciplinary boards.[136] Does the constitutional principle offer more protections here? It is not certain. With regard to penalties imposed on detainees, the *Conseil d'Etat* has ruled that

> it emerges from the principle of the constitutional value of the respect for the rights of defence that in the absence of legislative or regulatory provisions, the chair of the disciplinary committee always has the possibility, if he or she deems it useful for the good conduct of the procedure and for the manifestation of the truth, to have witnesses heard by the committee.[137]

However, 'the appropriateness of such a decision remains reserved to the sole discretion of the chairman of the disciplinary committee'. Besides, the simple fact that the person detained may request to have witnesses heard leads one to exclude any disregard of the principle of constitutional value of the respect for the defence's rights.

On the other hand, the employee subjected to proceedings must have been allowed to attend the hearing of witnesses before the disciplinary board. If not, there is 'disregard for the rights of the defence and the procedure's adversarial character'. The contents of the testimony are irrelevant, even if it amounts only to a reminder of elements already mentioned in the inquiry report.[138] Therefore, there is once again, in this case, a breach of the general principle of the rights of the defence sustained by Mr Alvin.

D. Germany

DS

The Disciplinary Board (DB) wants to dismiss Alvin even after his acquittal by the criminal court. This would, in principle, be possible according to German law. The fundamental law on the civil service (*Beamtenstatusgesetz* of 17-6-2008—*BeamtStG*, § 21 nr. 3) mentions dismissal under the disciplinary laws as one of the reasons for terminating the employment of a civil servant. For the Federal civil service, there is

[134] CE 7 Dec 2015, No 376387.
[135] D No 84-961 of 25 October 1984 prev, Art 5.
[136] See already, CE, 21 October 1931, *Lota, Rec*, p 886: in the absence of texts the hearing of witnesses presented by the employee is not obligatory; CE, 2 December 1954, *Lettré, Rec* p 806; then, CE, 2 March 1984, *Fédérations des affaires sociales CGT, Rec* p 658.
[137] CE, 11 July 2012, No 347146.
[138] CE, 7 March 2005, No 251137, *Zanardo*.

a *Bundesdisziplinargesetz* of 9-7-2001 (*BDiszG*), which, while referring to the *VwGO* and the *VwVfG* (§ 3 *BDiszG*), contains nearly complete regulation on this matter.

According to § 17 *BDiszG*, in the event of the suspicion of disciplinary malpractice, a procedure is initiated *ex officio*. Although heads of administration have disciplinary power in relation to petty violations of duties, in cases of greater severity, especially if dismissal appears possible, the DB must refer to the administrative court (§ 34 *BDiszG*). The civil servant concerned must be informed and can present his arguments and points of view. A civil servant can be dismissed only if so decided by an administrative court.

Therefore, the dismissal pronounced by the DB is unlawful, especially if the civil servant has not been heard. It would be annulled by the court, which could even qualify it as void (§ 44 *VwVfG*).

Nevertheless, according to § 38 *BDiszG*, in severe cases, there is the possibility of provisional dismissal, which can be imposed by the DB when it seizes the administrative court or during the proceedings, but not before. The right of the civil servant to be heard is always guaranteed.

E. Greece

TF

The rules governing the special legal relationship between a civil servant and the state provide for a system of specific sanctions and the procedure for enforcing them in order to ensure that the special rules governing the restrictions and duties of the official are complied with. The provisions relating to sanctions and the procedure for enforcing them, usually referred to as disciplinary law, do not enjoy systematic autonomy in relation to the other rules of civil service law. On the contrary, they are directly related to these rules.

According to Article 108 para 1 of the Greek Code of Civil Servants (from now on the 'Code of Civil Servants'), the principles and rules of criminal law and criminal procedure apply *mutatis mutandis* to disciplinary law, provided that they are not incompatible with the provisions of the Code and are consistent with the nature and purpose of the disciplinary proceedings. The main means of this protection are: 1) the process of verifying that disciplinary misconduct has occurred, 2) giving accused employees the opportunity to defend themselves, and 3) the impartial judgment of the disciplinary bodies.

However, disciplinary proceedings are independent of criminal proceedings. The disciplinary organ is bound by the judgment contained in an irrevocable decision of a criminal court or in an irrevocable acquittal, but only with regard to the existence or non-existence of facts that substantiate the objective existence of disciplinary misconduct. Therefore, the disciplinary procedure will be repeated if, after a disciplinary decision imposing a sentence, an irrevocable acquittal is issued for the act or omission for which the employee was disciplined.

In this case, according to Article 124 para 2, exceptionally, a disciplinary investigation is not compulsory since the investigation has been carried out for a criminal offence, which is also a disciplinary offence according to the provisions of the Code of Criminal Procedure. However, if a disciplinary inquiry is carried out, accused civil servants must be summoned for questioning in accordance with Article 132, while they should not be deprived of their right to be present with their lawyer.

Subsequently, the summons to respond, according to the Article 134 of the Code of Civil Servants, constitutes a basic means of protecting the respondent and must set out clear and detailed facts, which form the objective substance of the disciplinary offence attributed to the respondent, as well its legal characterization. Therefore, no disciplinary action may be legally imposed unless the employee has previously been summoned to speak before the competent disciplinary body. Moreover, questioning the respondent during the oral proceeding does not replace the call for a response. To this end, an overdue response must be considered in each case, provided it is submitted before the time limit is issued.

The response must be submitted in writing, and the respondent is also allowed to make an additional oral defence. For these reasons, it must be explicitly mentioned in the disciplinary decision whether or not the respondent has submitted a defence in order to ascertain compliance with the essential procedural conditions.

When the proceeding is linked to the purpose of the act, which has the nature of a sanction and makes it possible for the individual to defend his or her rights, issuing an act which has the same consequences through a different procedure that precludes defence ('misuse of procedure') also constitutes procedural *ultra vires*.

As explained, the norms of administrative procedure determine the actions of the administrative authorities or individuals necessary for the issuing of an administrative act. The ground of annulment consists precisely in the violation of the procedural norms, which occurs upon the omission or defective performance of the actions prescribed.

In particular, the right to a prior hearing entails the possibility of the individual, prior to the issuance of an unfavourable administrative act such as a disciplinary decision to express his or her views, after a relevant summons to do so by the competent authority. This right stems from a general principle of administrative law, already enshrined in Article 20 para 2 of the Constitution and further regulated by the Administrative Process Code. Thus, it must be available to the individual at all stages of the disciplinary proceedings.

Moreover, in accordance with Article 103 para 4 of the Constitution, the competent court of civil servants' claims is the Council of State. The provision for a special judicial remedy in respect of the substance is connected with the institution of the permanent status of these servants and constitutes a uniquely Greek feature originating in Greek history. Namely, decisions of service councils are subject to this special remedy when they relate to decisions of disciplinary councils where the penalty of final dismissal is imposed.

Specifically, when the Council of State hears a civil servant's claim, it re-examines the case as a whole, from the point of view of law and facts. Here lies the most important difference between the civil servants' proceedings and the two other remedies before the Council of State: the application for annulment and the final appeal, where the Council of State assesses the facts only in certain exceptional cases. In other words, the case is adjudicated again from the beginning in a new proceeding, while the applicant can invoke legal arguments and challenge the verification and assessment of the factual prerequisites for the application of the relevant provisions by the authority whose act is being challenged.

In this case, the civil servant has been deprived of their fundamental constitutional right to be heard prior to the issuance of the final act of dismissal.

Therefore, the court would accept the defendant's argument and annul the disciplinary decision in question on the grounds of procedural *ultra vires*, due to the lack of a prior hearing of the defendant.

F. Italy

MS

Firstly, it must be said that under Italian law, all public employees are fully entitled to the procedural rights demanded by Alvin.

The consolidated law on public service employment, Legislative Decree No 165 of 30 March 2001, provides that disciplinary procedures must be underpinned by numerous guarantees, which include written notice of the charges, the right to be assisted by an attorney or by a trade union representative, the right to submit written statements and to be heard, as well as access to the case files (Article 55-*bis*). Similar rules have also been laid down in various special laws for certain categories of public employees ('non-privatised public employment': magistrates, state legal advisors, servicemen, policemen, university professors, and so on).

So, in our case, Alvin's dismissal would certainly have been unlawful, and the court could annul it and reinstate the employee in his position, also awarding him compensation.

Public employees actually enjoy greater protection as, in the event of their unlawful dismissal, they must always be reinstated to their former position, while in private employment relationships, reinstatement is, in some cases, ruled out (eg where small companies are involved).

Furthermore, the relationship between disciplinary procedures and criminal proceedings is strictly regulated (Article 55-*ter*). More specifically, the outcome of criminal proceedings can influence a disciplinary procedure, even if this was concluded earlier. If the criminal judgment contains factual findings (that the actions of which the employee is accused were or were not committed) that differ from the outcome of the disciplinary procedure, the Disciplinary Board will have to reopen the procedure to conform to these new results.

So, in our case, if Alvin were acquitted at the criminal trial and found not to have committed the acts with which he was charged at the disciplinary procedure, the court would have to annul the dismissal.

However, if we were to assume that these rules were not explicitly laid down by the laws on public service employment, the same rules should still apply in accordance with the general principles of the legal system but with certain differences between the two macro-categories of public employees.

In Italy, employment by public authorities is divided into two macro-segments: 'privatized' and 'non-privatized' public employment. The latter group includes a number of specific categories: magistrates, state legal advisors, servicemen, policemen, and university professors. Related disputes fall within the jurisdiction of the administrative court. The former group encompasses all other public employees. Related disputes fall within the jurisdiction of a specialist court of first instance: the employment tribunal.

However, as the case at issue concerns the application of very general principles, similar considerations can be made regarding both groups.

Non-privatized public employment is subject to a series of special rules governing the different categories. These special rules are supplemented by the application of the constitutional principles of legality, impartiality, and sound administration, as well as the general principles contained in the Italian APA. Furthermore, application of the defect of abuse of discretion ('*excès de pouvoir*') allows the court to review the actions of the administration in relation to all the principles of the legal system.

The general law on administrative procedure also applies to disciplinary administrative procedures, because it mainly lays down standards and minimum guarantees that cannot be completely disregarded by sector rules.

Whenever its application is not expressly precluded by specific special provisions, the Italian APA applies and completes the rules governing all administrative procedures. This was clarified by the Plenary Meeting of the Council of State in Judgment No 14 of 15 September 1999 and then consistently confirmed in case law.[139]

As the principles laid down by the Italian Constitution and Law No 241/1990 must be applied, Alvin's appeal would most likely be upheld. Notice of the charges, the right to be heard and, more generally, participation in the administrative procedure, are fundamental rights of the Italian administrative system. Their breach could therefore render the dismissal unlawful, and the court could order Alvin to be reinstated and award him compensation.

Instead, with regard to privatized public employment, the case law holds that dismissal does not constitute an expression of administrative powers but of the employer's powers, which are exactly the same as those of a private employer. Hence, Law No 241/1990 does not wholly apply to the dismissal.

The only part of the Italian APA that would definitely apply to the dismissal of a 'privatised' public employee is the right of access. This applies to all administrative documents '*regardless of the public or private nature of their substantive rules*', as the wording now reads, and as the Plenary Meeting of the Council of State had already acknowledged in its Judgment No 5 of 22 April 1999 on the subject of dismissals.

In this case, the dismissal is subject to the constitutional principles of legality, impartiality, and sound administration, as well as the general principles of employment law contained in the Italian Civil Code, the Workers' Statute (Law No 30 of 20 May 1970) and in the law on individual dismissals (Law No 604 of 15 July 1966).

Under employment law, disciplinary dismissals are subject to almost identical rules to those of administrative procedures: notice of the accusations, the requirement to give reasons, and the possibility of being assisted by a lawyer or a trade union representative.

[139] Most recently, Council of State, Div VI, No 2254, 6 April 2020.

It should also be noted that in Italy employment tribunal decisions are shaped by a legal culture that tends to grant greater safeguards to the worker, as the weaker party to the contract.

All this means that also in the case of privatized public employment, assuming that there were no specific rules on the matter, the court would most likely annul Alvin's dismissal, applying the constitutional principles of legality, impartiality, and sound administration, as well as the general principles of employment law.

G. Romania

D-C D

In the Romanian legal system, the facts described in Case 4 would be evaluated by considering the rules governing the disciplinary liability of public servants, as established in a procedure regulated by the 2019 Administrative Code, Title VI, Chapter VIII.

First, looking at the case at hand, the relevant provision is the one in Article 492 (2) (g) of the Administrative Code, which penalizes 'attitudes or behaviours that affect the service's or the public body's prestige'. The disciplinary penalties for civil servants' misconduct (Article 492(3) of the Administrative Code) are: (i) a written warning; (ii) a 5 to 30 per cent decrease in salary for up to three months; (iii) suspension of the right to promotion for a period from one to three years; (iv) demotion for a period of up to one year; and (v) dismissal.

The investigation must be conducted by the disciplinary commission. The procedural fault invoked by the applicant is the lack of a proper hearing before taking the decision. Among the rules provided by the Administrative Code for such a proceeding, a prominent role is played by the hearing of the interested party, which is stated in clear terms in the Code (Article 493):

> The disciplinary sanctions specified in Article 492(3), letters b) to f) can only be applied following the preliminary investigation of the alleged offence and after hearing the civil servant. The hearing must be recorded in writing, under pain of nullity. If a civil servant refuses to attend hearings or sign a statement concerning the disciplinary offences attributed to him or her, such refusal shall be recorded in the report. However, it shall not prevent the completion of the preliminary investigation and imposition of the sanction.

Thus, the court's analysis is twofold, based on procedural grounds and the merits.

On procedural grounds, it is evident that the absence of a hearing constitutes a procedural error that renders the proceedings null and void. There is little to discuss here. The courts have relied on the right to be heard as enshrined in Article 6 of the ECHR to invalidate unlawful disciplinary investigations against civil servants.[140]

[140] Bacau Court of Appeal, Decision No 126/2010, available with comments in Romanian language here <https://www.juridice.ro/223328/articolul-6-cedo-si-dreptul-intimatului-la-introducerea-contestatiei-in-anulare-speciala.html> accessed June 2023.

However, the court can also proceed to examine the merits of the case and determine whether the public servant has been acquitted of the criminal charges. In doing so, the court would consider the clear rules governing the relationship between criminal proceedings and disciplinary proceedings (Article 493 para 9 of the Administrative Code):

> If the civil servant's action is reported as both a disciplinary offence and a crime, the procedure for initiating disciplinary liability is suspended until a dismissal order or waiver of criminal prosecution is issued, or until the court renders a verdict of acquittal, withdrawal of punishment, postponement of the punishment, or termination of the criminal trial. Once these situations are met, the procedure for engaging disciplinary liability is resumed, and the disciplinary sanction is applied within a maximum of one year from the date of resumption.

In the case described above, the disciplinary proceedings occurred after the criminal proceedings were dismissed with the offender acquitted (1), and they regard the same offences that were dismissed by the criminal courts (2). The question is whether the fact that a criminal court has considered that the offences do not pertain to criminal law prevents the administrative authority from concluding that they are still disciplinary. Based on the provisions cited above, it can be concluded that this is not the case, and an independent disciplinary procedure is legally permissible.

In this case, the court could dismiss the case entirely, not only on procedural grounds, which could entail beginning the disciplinary procedure from scratch if it considers the penalty without merit.

On the other hand, the court might consider that, setting criminal liability aside, there are grounds for disciplinary liability and would confirm or reduce the penalty. As stated in Article 492(6) of the Administrative Code, there are legal grounds for penalties to be proportionate. Hence, the sanctioning authority can decide whether dismissal is appropriate for the offences attributed to Alvin, and the court can review the severity of the sanction. The courts rely on the proportionality principle when ruling on the legality of disciplinary sanctions and have sometimes substituted the penalty with a lesser one.[141] Thus, there are sufficient grounds to believe that the wrongful termination of Alvin's employment would, in this case, be annulled in court on procedural grounds.

H. Serbia

MM

The provisions regulating proceedings before the disciplinary boards in labour relations in Serbia are found in general labour legislation—the Labour Law[142]—as well as legislation related to local administration, labour relations in the state services, and the Law on Civil Servants. The Labour Law (Article 179) stipulates that an employer may cancel an employee's employment contract for a just cause that relates to the

[141] Ploiesti Court of Appeal, Decision No 1059/2010, available at <www.rolii.ro> accessed June 2023.

[142] Labour Law (Official Gazette of RS, No 24/2005, 61/2005, 54/2009, 32/2013, 75/2014, 13/2017—decision of the Constitutional Court, 113/2017 i 95/2018—authentic interpretation).

employee's work ability and conduct, such as if 'he has been sentenced by a final judgment for a crime in the workplace or related to the workplace'. No other provision of the Law may be connected to the case observed to provide grounds for dismissal based on 'not giving professional and moral leadership to other employees'.

However, Alvin's status would also be governed by the specific provisions of the Law on Civil Servants,[143] 'liability for a criminal offence or petty offence does not exclude disciplinary liability' (Article 107). Procedural provisions relevant to this case (Articles 112 to 117) provide that a disciplinary proceeding must be initiated by the manager, at his or her own initiative, or at the proposal of a person superior in rank to the civil servant. However, it is explicitly provided that a disciplinary proceeding must be initiated by a written conclusion (type of administrative act), 'which is served to the civil servant' (Article 112). In the given case, the employer failed to fulfil this obligation. It is further provided (Article 114) that in disciplinary proceedings, a hearing shall be held 'in which the civil servant has the right to present his defence'. Civil servants may mount their own defence or go through a representative,[144] and they may also present a written defence. A hearing may be held in the absence of the civil servant, if there are important reasons for doing so, and if the civil servant has been duly summoned. It may be concluded that *Alvin's right to be heard has been violated*, and even if the agency can prove that important reasons for his exclusion from the hearing existed (which would be hard to prove in the case of corruption charges), failure to serve him a written notice of the procedure would be a sufficient ground to annul the decision. Finally, Article 114 provides that other issues concerning the conduct of disciplinary proceedings will be governed by the provisions of the law regulating general administrative procedure. The LGAP envisages the right to plead the facts relevant for issuing a decision on the administrative matter (Article 11).

Bearing in mind the aforementioned facts, particularly the superiority of criminal proceedings over disciplinary board processes, the decision to dismiss Alvin was not delivered in accordance with the law of Serbia. Therefore, the competent court would annul the decision.

I. Spain

IMD

In Spain, the disciplinary rules for public servants can be found in the so-called Public Employment Act or *Estatuto Básico del Empleo Público* (Legislative Decree 5/2015, EBEP). The EBEP (i) provides that public servants will be held liable for any infringements committed in the discharge of their duties, and (ii) requires public authorities to impose penalties for these offences. Article 94 EBEP also provides that any disciplinary proceedings (ie the relevant enforcement authorities' punitive power) are subject to the following principles and standards:

[143] Law on Civil Servants (Official Gazette of RS, No 79/2005, 81/2005—ispr., 83/2005—ispr., 64/2007, 67/2007—ispr., 116/2008, 104/2009, 99/2014, 94/2017, 95/2018, 157/2020 i 142/2022). The analysis is based on the Law applicable at the time of writing in 2020.

[144] The right to legal assistance is primarily guaranteed by the Constitution (art 67).

a) The legality principle and the *lex certa* requirement for any infringements and penalties based on (i) pre-established provisions or (ii) regarding public employees with employment contracts (ie not public servants in the strict sense), on collective agreements.
b) The requirement of non-retroactivity of detrimental penalty provisions and the principle of retroactivity of the more lenient or favourable provisions for the alleged offender.
c) The proportionality principle, applicable to both the categorization and enforcement of offences and penalties.
d) The principle of guilt, ie, that there be a subjective or mental element (awareness, knowledge, a guilty mind) allowing to find that the offender was at mental fault when committing the offence.
e) The presumption of innocence.

Dismissal is envisaged as a possible penalty, although only for very serious offences. Article 95 EBEP does not include any disciplinary offences where the punishable behaviour is similar to Alvin's, ie 'not giving professional and moral leadership to other employees.' In any case, assuming that such behaviour was defined as an offence and thus Alvin could be lawfully dismissed, such dismissal must 'follow the previously established administrative procedure' as expressly required under Article 98 EBEP. This provision adds that such administrative procedure must comply with a set of minimum requirements: (i) abiding by the principle of effectiveness, (ii) being expeditious, and (iii) respecting the alleged offender's rights of defence.

On the national level, disciplinary proceedings are subject to the Disciplinary Regime for National Civil Servants (adopted through Royal Decree 33/1986, RD 33/1986). Under this provision, disciplinary proceedings can run parallel to any judicial proceedings for public servants' civil or criminal liability. Thus, Alvin's acquittal in a criminal trial does not prevent disciplinary proceedings being instituted.

For institution and processing, RD 33/1986 refers to the LPAC. As for the investigative stage, Article 34 RD 33/1986 provides as follows:

1. The official leading the investigative stage will take any actions or procedural steps that may be necessary to determine and verify the facts of the case, and, in particular, the leading official will take and allow for the production of any evidence that may clarify the facts and any punishable offences.
2. The official leading the investigative stage will first take (i) a statement from the alleged offender and (ii) any actions or procedural steps that may be necessary having regard to the complaint giving rise to the proceedings and to the alleged offender's statement.

Therefore, the requirement that the party concerned must be heard is indispensable, both under the sector-specific regulations and the general provisions. As discussed above, failing to hear the party invalidates the disciplinary proceedings.

Moreover, Articles 35ff lay down several safeguards for this investigative stage. In a nutshell, the official leading this stage, based on its inquiries, must prepare and send the party a statement of objections indicating the charges or alleged offences and any potential penalties. This statement should be clear and precise. These requirements result from the general entitlement provided in Article 53(2) LPAC, under which the parties to penalty procedures (disciplinary proceedings in the case at hand) have the right to be duly notified of any offences or infringements attributed thereto along with the potential penalties, identifying the leading public official, the competent authority potentially imposing the relevant penalty, and the provision empowering the competent authority.

As for Alvin's claim regarding evidence-taking and cross-examination, Article 36 RD 33/1986 requires the statement of objections be submitted to the alleged offender, who may submit (i) comments objecting to the statement and (ii) any documents that he or she may see fit in their defence. If deemed convenient, at this procedural stage, the alleged offender may request to have evidence taken. Although only the leading official may decide whether to take evidence, rejecting (i) evidence brought by the party or (ii) an evidence-taking stage requires a duly justified decision, giving reasons or supporting arguments. As for Alvin's legal assistance, it should be noted that Article 53 LPAC establishes the parties' right to legal counsel, if they see fit. There is no sector-specific provision in this regard, but the right to legal counsel must be deemed applicable in disciplinary proceedings involving public servants. The notion of legal counsel must be broadly construed and not limited to the strictly legal domain (ie including economic, technical, or other experts or advisors deemed necessary by the party).

The omission of an evidence-taking stage and legal counsel does not automatically invalidate the dismissal. According to the Constitutional Court, no procedural infringement, fault, or impropriety entails a violation of constitutional rights. It does so only if the party is prevented from exercising his or her rights of defence, with all the relevant safeguards and guarantees, thus rendering the party defenceless due to the challenged public authorities' actions and decisions.[145] Also according to this line of case law, the rights of defence can be raised as fundamental rights in penalty procedures (or disciplinary proceedings), and if they are violated, any breach will render the unlawful administrative act invalid in the event of an actual lack of defence.

In the case at hand, (i) the acquittal (if Alvin had been found guilty, there would be objective evidence of a very serious offence) and (ii) the absence of a hearing, an evidence-taking stage and legal counsel would lead us to think that a Spanish court would uphold Alvin's argument and invalidate the dismissal on the grounds of the violation of Alvin's fundamental rights of defence.

J. Switzerland

AF

The right to be heard guaranteed under Article 29 para 2 of the Federal Constitution includes the right to be informed of the procedure, in particular about the initiation, purpose, object, stakes, stages, and other modalities of a proceeding.[146] It also includes

[145] Constitutional Court Order 320/1986 of 9 April.
[146] ATF 136 V 117, c 4.2.

the right to consult the case file, ie all the means of proof, the parties' writings, exchanges of correspondence, summonses, etc.

It also includes the right to allege facts, to propose evidence, including from witnesses, to participate in the administration of evidence, and to determine the result of this administration.[147] According to the courts, the exclusion of a party from the hearing of witnesses constitutes a serious infringement of procedural rights, in particular the rule of 'equality of arms' in the trial. The right to be confronted personally with witnesses and to ask them questions does not only apply in criminal trials but also in administrative proceedings, as part of the general procedural guarantees offered by the right to be heard of Article 29 para 2 Cst.[148] The right to have contact with witnesses and to question them is not absolute. It can be restricted if the party concerned can benefit from procedural compensation that puts him in a position to fully exercise his right.[149]

Lastly, the right to be heard under Article 29 para 2 Cst includes the right to be assisted in administrative or judicial proceedings.[150]

Thus, Swiss courts would not accept the defendant's argument that the particular rules governing the case did not establish the procedural requirements referred to by Alvin. They would endorse the argument based on Article 29 para 2 Cst (the right to be heard), thus leading them, in principle, to annul the contested measure.

K. United Kingdom

GA and CM

This scenario is redolent of one of the most famous cases on common law fairness: *Ridge v Baldwin*.[151] That case concerned Charles Ridge, the Chief Constable of Brighton Police, who had been charged with conspiracy to obstruct the course of justice. Although Ridge was acquitted at trial, the judge made a number of critical comments about him and, as a result of that criticism, the police oversight body dismissed him the day after his trial ended, without notice and without a hearing. The House of Lords held that the dismissal was unlawful, not just because legislation in the field required that *Ridge* ought to have been given notice of any disciplinary charges against him, but also because common law fairness required that he ought to have been given a hearing so that he could have commented on the charges against him. *Ridge v Baldwin* was thus one of the most important cases on a recurring theme on the common law: the more serious a decision's consequences for an individual, the more the common law will demand by way of procedural protections.

What does this mean for Alvin? In the first instance, it is clear that common law protections would apply and would require not just that he should have been

[147] ATF 142 II 218, c 2.3.

[148] ATF 129 I 151, 153f.

[149] Court of administrative and public law of Canton of Vaud, X. vs Département de la santé et de l'action sociale, 1 February 2016, c 1 e.

[150] ATF 132 V 443, c 3.3; see also art 29 para 3 Cst.

[151] [1964] AC 40.

given notification and a hearing, but potentially also that he should have been entitled to legal assistance and the right to cross-examine witnesses. Although the common law does not always require legal assistance etc, it will favour representation where a matter is serious and complex and where the individual would not be able to present his or her case effectively without such representation.[152] The point is true irrespective of the absence of sector-specific legislative requirements to that effect: the common law supplements legislative schemes and will imply 'so much and no more . . . by way of additional procedural safeguards as will ensure the attainment of fairness'.[153]

One further point concerns Alvin's statement that, had he been able to exercise his process rights, a disciplinary measure other than dismissal would have been preferred. While this is speculation on his part—there may ultimately be substance to the allegations against him—his statement goes to the heart of the common law's rationale for hearings. In short, the common law accepts that what is written on paper may not have the same import once oral submissions have been made by the affected individual. As Megarry LJ expressed the point in *John v Rees*:

> As everybody who has anything to do with the law well knows, the path of the law is strewn with examples of open and shut cases which, somehow, were not; of unanswerable charges which, in the event, were completely answered; of inexplicable conduct which was fully explained; of fixed and unalterable determinations that, by discussion suffered a change.[154]

To conclude: the absence of sector-specific rules would be irrelevant, as the common law would fill any procedural void to ensure fairness towards Alvin. The disciplinary decision would likely be quashed and the matter have to be heard by a differently constituted DB.

L. Venezuela

FP-F

We have already indicated that the Venezuelan Constitution of 1999 (Article 49) declares that all judicial and administrative procedures must respect due process and, therefore, among other things, all interested parties have the right to be heard in any kind of procedure, with all due guarantees, by a court or competent, independent, and impartial authority established in advance and that they must receive legal assistance and defence, which are inviolable rights at all stages and levels during the investigation and the proceedings.

In this sense, everyone has the right to be notified of the charges for which they are being investigated, to access the evidence, and have the time and means necessary to

[152] On legal representation, etc see *R v Home Secretary, ex parte Tarrant* [1985] QB 251.
[153] *Lloyd v McMahon* [1987] AC 625, 702, Lord Bridge.
[154] [1970] Ch 345, 402.

carry out their defence. In addition, anyone who does not speak Spanish or cannot communicate verbally is entitled to an interpreter.

Therefore, this principle applies to procedures that may lead to the Administration imposing sanctions on a person and, of course, in the event of disciplinary procedures against public servants, regardless of their status.

Alvin, who was subjected to a procedure with no official hearing, was entitled to be heard, to request legal representation, and to be accompanied by a lawyer to exercise his right to defence.

Furthermore, the sanction imposed, based on testimony from third parties without Alvin being able to defend himself or control such evidence, is excessively disproportionate since the reasons given by the Disciplinary Board to sanction Alvin should have led to a written warning and not his dismissal.

The Venezuelan contentious-administrative tribunal would, therefore, declare the administrative act null and void for having violated Article 49 of the Constitution on due process, by not having allowed the official to exercise his right to defence and be heard. It would also declare it absolutely null under Article 19.4 of the Organic Law of Administrative Procedures insofar as it declares that those administrative acts that have been issued with total and absolute disregard for the legally-established procedure are subject to such nullity. If the case had been raised in Venezuela, it would be concluded that the Disciplinary Board had failed to initiate the corresponding disciplinary procedure provided for in the Civil Service Statute.

Moreover, as it had decided to dismiss Alvin, the Disciplinary Board would be violating the principle of proportionality of administrative sanctions that governs the administrative sanctioning procedure and applies to the quantitative and qualitative determination of the sanction to be imposed once it has been verified that an employee has breached a rule of administrative law.

The sanction fulfils a double purpose: a) to repress the violating conduct and b) prevent its repetition in such a way that the principle of proportionality derives from the need, in the quantitative determination of the sanction, for the seriousness of the facts and the characteristics of the offender to be weighed with careful balance so that the purpose of the sanction be fulfilled, in other words, that it does not become so extreme as to excessively limit the rights of the offender, nor that it be so slight that it does not fulfil its preventive function.

Lastly, in Venezuela, dismissal as a disciplinary measure is subject to specific grounds if Alvin was a career civil servant, which is not specified. If he were freely appointed and removed, the reason for dismissal would matter little.

VI. Case 5—A regulator requesting information concerning market abuse

A. Austria

SS

Basically, the rule that applies here is that the investigation procedure must be carried out by the authority. The authority will proceed *ex officio* and determine the specifics of the investigation procedure in accordance with the existing rules and regulations.[155]

However, the parties must cooperate in the investigation proceedings to a certain extent.[156] In particular, they should exercise their legal rights, and if they fail to do so, they cannot subsequently accuse the authority of not having investigated the facts correctly.

A party has to support the authority in investigating the facts of a case, especially if his or her contribution is necessary for the investigation.[157]

In this regard, however, there is a restriction regarding self-incrimination. The Austrian constitution guarantees that no one need incriminate himself or herself. This right is an integral part of Article 90 (2) B-VG which reads: 'In criminal proceedings the procedure is by indictment.' Though the wording of this guarantee refers to criminal proceedings, the Constitutional Court extended this right to administrative penalty proceedings.[158] If an authority intends to find the party guilty of a punishable act, the Court has ruled that the obligation to communicate all the facts to the authority may include a confession to being the (hitherto unknown) perpetrator of the act. However, the person concerned is not obliged to cooperate in this manner.

B. China

XS

The court will not endorse Bud's argument based on the right of defence. It will affirm that there is no principle amounting to a sort of privilege against self-incrimination or *nemo tenetur se detegere* in the administrative investigation and thus dismiss Bud's action.

Under Chinese law, the privilege against self-incrimination only exists in criminal investigation.[159] Despite the strong suggestion in the legal literature, such a principle does not exist in the administrative investigation. On the contrary, most administrative procedures require the cooperation of the citizens during the administrative investigation, such as the Administrative Penalty Law.[160] This same law offers the

155 § 39 (1) AVG.
156 Wielinger (n 3) 64.
157 Schulev-Steindl (n 5) 202.
158 VfSlg 9950/1984.
159 Art 52 of the Criminal Procedure Law (刑事诉讼法).
160 Art 55 of the Administrative Penalty Law provides that

> persons subject to an administrative investigation should answer the questions truthfully, co-operate with investigation or inspection, and must not refuse or obstruct (当事人或者有关人员应当如实回答询问，并协助调查或者检查，不得拒绝或者阻挠).

possibility to reduce the administrative penalty if the person subject to an administrative sanction 'confesses on his own initiative illegal facts of which the administration was not aware'.[161]

Chinese administrative legislation is still largely based on the efficiency of administrative actions. Administrative investigation is supposed to ensure that administrative authorities can collect necessary information, prevent and correct illegal situations in a timely manner, and protect public interests. Citizens must provide administrative authorities with all information even against themselves.

C. France

SS

Under French law, stock market-related offences and breaches can be the subject of dual penalties: they are sanctioned by criminal law and the financial markets authority (*Autorité des marchés financiers—AMF*) created by Law No 2003-706 of 1 August 2003. These penalties can refer to insider offences and breaches and, more generally, the breach of regulations applicable to privileged information. Inside information is defined as information of a precise nature that has not been made public and which may have a significant influence on the price of financial instruments.[162] This definition is used by European stock market regulators in their oversight procedure.

Powers of inquiry are particularly strengthened in markets subjected to strong industrial and technical legislation, such as healthcare, banking, and insurance, the audio-visual sector, and the financial markets.

The administrative sanctions prescribed by the monetary and financial code are in fact incurred in cases of breach of the obligations under European regulations, legislative or regulatory provisions, or professional rules designed to protect investors from insider transactions, market manipulation, and the unlawful disclosure of privileged information, or any other breach able to impair investor protection or the proper functioning of the market when such actions concern specific financial instruments (Article L. 621-14, II on referral from Article L 621-15, II c, 4 and d, 4). The AMF's sanctions commission may sanction any person who, in the context of an inquiry or a check, refuses to give access to a document or to convey information (Article L. 621-15 II f of the monetary and financial code).

The question invites us to analyse the importance of the right to remain silent in administrative proceedings, particularly during those prior to the handing down of an administrative sanction, as is the case here. The adage *nemo tenetur se ipsum accusare* enshrines the right against self-incrimination.

If, in criminal law, the right of defence implies the right to silence, this is not the case in the law of criminal administrative procedure. The existence of a right to silence in general administrative procedural law is uncertain. It has never been consolidated by the administrative courts. Nevertheless, in a good number of cases, this

161 主动供述行政机关尚未掌握的违法行为 (art 32 of the Administrative Penalty Law).

162 Regulation No 596/2014 of 16 April 2014 on abuses of the market (MAR).

is not materially possible. For example, the burden of proof often falls on the person subjected to the procedure. Indeed, the burden of proof in punitive administrative law, which is not favourable to the person placed under investigation, is an important question. The situation is the opposite of the criminal law scenario since it will most often be incumbent on the person subjected to the procedure to prove his innocence.[163] Progress has been made in the acknowledgement of the importance of the presumption of innocence. The *Conseil constitutionnel* at first limited its application (Article 9, DDHC of 26 August 1789) to criminal matters and fiscal sanctions.[164] Its position has evolved in favour of extension,[165] noting that 'the principles resulting from articles 8 and 9 of the DDHC (...) apply (...) to penalties and sanctions of a punitive nature'.[166]

The *Conseil d'Etat* has raised it to the rank of a fundamental freedom that can be invoked in interlocutory proceedings.[167] The presumption of innocence is also an integral part of the concept of fair trial pursuant to Article 6 of the European Convention for the Protection of Human Rights. The same is true of the right to silence.[168] However, the majority of administrative sanctions fall outside the scope of Article 6 of the Convention inasmuch as the sanctioning authorities are not 'tribunals'. Since its *Didier* ruling of 1999, however, the *Conseil d'Etat* has granted numerous independent authorities the status of a court. Such is the case with the penalties procedure adopted by the AMF.[169] It will be noted that the AMF has adopted a 'control charter'—a soft law instrument—which specifies the rules applicable during its inquiries for information purposes. The paragraph entitled 'not to obstruct the investigations conducted' does not mention the right to silence of the persons concerned. It states that the fact of obstructing the investigations carried out by AMF officials can give rise to an administrative and/or penal sanction.

In addition, the right to silence runs counter to the right that the authority has in certain cases to demand information that citizens must provide it. In this respect Article L. 642-2 of the monetary and financial code prescribes, for example, a penalty of two years' imprisonment and a fine of €300,000 for any person guilty of obstructing an AMF fact-finding activity or inquiry, as per Articles L. 621-9 to L. 621-9-2, or of providing inaccurate information. Several penalties have been imposed by the AMF since 2018 for refusal to provide information.

The status of punitive law is therefore uncertain. This ambiguity is also present in constitutional case law. In a decision of 8 July 2016,[170] the *Conseil constitutionnel* specified that article L. 450-3 of the commercial code regarding the simplified inquiry of the competition authority did not infringe the right against self-incrimination insofar

[163] CE, 30 January 1951, *Jacquesson*, *Rec* p 39.

[164] Cons Const, 19 and 20 January 1981, dec No 80-127 DC, *Sécurité et Liberté*.

[165] See initially, Cons Const, 10 June 2009, No 2009-580 DC, *Hadopi*).

[166] Cons Const, 21 January 2011, No 2011-90 QPC, *M. Jean-Claude C.*

[167] CE, 14 March 2005, No 278435 *Gollnisch*.

[168] *Funke v France* App no 10828/84 (ECtHR 25 February 1993); *John Murray v United Kingdom* App no 18731/91 (ECtHR, 8 February 1996) § 45; eg *J B v Switzerland* App no 31827/96 (ECtHR 3 May 2001).

[169] CE sect 27 October 2006, *Parent et autres*, *Lebon* 454.

[170] Cons Const, 8 July 2016, No 2016-552 QPC, *Sté Brentag*.

as its purpose was not to obtain a confession from the person concerned but 'simply to obtain the documents necessary for the conduct of the inquiry'.

The surest argument now comes from the case law of the Court of Justice of the European Union (CJEU). In a recent and noted judgment, it ruled that

> Natural persons who are subject to an administrative investigation for insider dealing have the right to remain silent when their answers might establish their liability for an offence that is punishable by administrative sanctions of a criminal nature, or their criminal liability.[171]

As the CJEU points out,

> Since protection of the right to silence is intended to ensure that, in criminal proceedings, the prosecution establishes its case without resorting to evidence obtained through methods of coercion or oppression in defiance of the will of the accused (see, to that effect, ECtHR, 17 December 1996, Saunders v. the United Kingdom, CE:ECHR:1996:1217JUD001918791, § 68), this right is infringed, inter alia, where a suspect is obliged to testify under threat of sanctions and either testifies in consequence or is sanctioned for refusing to testify (see, to that effect, ECtHR, 13 September 2016, Ibrahim and Others v. the United Kingdom, CE:ECHR:2016:0913JUD005054108, § 267).

Persons subjected to an administrative inquiry thus possesses the right not to respond to the questions put.

Given the proximity of Italian and French law, this solution applies to administrative inquiries conducted by the AMF. However, the Court specifies that

> the right to silence cannot justify every failure to cooperate with the competent authorities, such as a refusal to appear at a hearing scheduled by those authorities or delaying tactics designed to postpone it (§ 41).

There exists therefore an obligation of cooperation with the administration concerned, an obligation with which it is difficult to see how to reconcile the right to remain silent at present.

D. Germany

DS

Bud contests the order obliging him to give complete information concerning the acquisition of the corporation's shares. In relation to the FMA's request, he may bring a claim before the administrative court to annul the order or, if the order is considered a

[171] Case C-481/19 *DB v Commissione Nazionale per le Società et la Borsa (Consob)* (CJEU, gd ch, 2 February 2021).

merely procedural act, to annul the measures taken against him because of his refusal to give complete information (§ 44a VwGO).

In general, according to the law on administrative procedure, the involved persons 'must' contribute to the ascertainment of the facts, but the general law does not establish any obligation on the persons involved to reveal these facts (§ 26.2, § 26.3 *VwVfG*). Only the specific sectoral legislation has established these duties. Therefore, there is no doubt under the general law as to the protection of a right to refuse to give evidence like in the codes of civil or criminal procedure (*§§ 383–390 ZPO*, according to *§ 98 VwGO* also important for administrative procedure, *§§ 52–56 StPO*).

By way of contrast, the law on the stock exchange (*Börsengesetz*) of 16 July 2007 essentially regulates FMA controls and its right to demand information and examine the functioning of the stock exchange (see the detailed rules in § 3, esp § 3.4). The FMA is empowered to ask participants in the stock exchange about their activities, and, in the event of an unsatisfactory state of affairs, it may ask anyone for the specific information they need to fulfil their tasks. This information concerns the stock exchange activities mentioned in the law. There is no legal right to refuse any information.

On the other hand, the law requires all stockbrokers to hold a licence to be admitted to the stock exchange. The licence presupposes reliability and a professional qualification (§ 19.5 *Börsengesetz*); it does not expire. However, in the event that the conditions for admission have not been fulfilled or no longer exist, the stock exchange management may suspend the admission of a stockbroker for up to six months and, in serious cases, revoke the licence (§ 19.8 *Börsengesetz*).

Therefore, if the Authority applies the law and does not recognize Bud's right to refuse to divulge certain information, he may be suspended for up to six months or lose his licence. Only after such a decision, and if Bud takes action, will the administrative court be called upon to make a decision.

Three argumentations appear possible. First, the court may consider whether this sanction is justified because, notwithstanding the law, Bud's procedural rights, such as a fair trial, his analogous situation to that of the accused in a criminal trial, the right to refuse to give evidence in the different procedural codes, or the principles of Article 6 ECHR, justify Bud's silence. Second, the court may consider the sanction, perhaps balancing the interest of a strict application of the law with the mentioned arguments, to be disproportionate and, therefore, partly annul the sanction. Nevertheless, thirdly, the court could, upholding the purpose of the law and the interest of correct stock exchange trade, prioritize the duties of the stockbrokers and reject the appeal.

The structure of the regulation of administrative procedure would appear to favour this third solution, in my opinion. As there is no general duty to cooperate and no general limitation to this duty, the question of duty and limits has to be regulated by sector-specific law. There is no general rule to guarantee limits of cooperation, and if an essential sphere has to be respected, such as the right to refuse to give evidence, this differs for the different procedures and processes; the rules for the accused in criminal procedures with the risk of criminal sanctions must not be the same as in administrative procedure, where there the only risk is that of revocation of a licence. On the other hand, the interest in ensuring correct trade in the stock exchange, with its enormous financial consequences, is evident. A stockbroker neglecting the duties resulting from this situation may be deemed untrustworthy and thus unsuited to work at the stock exchange.

E. Greece
TF

In the context of the Greek legal order, the right to remain silent and the right to non-self-incrimination (*nemo tenetur se detegere*), as an extension of the right to personality find sufficient basis in Article 5 para 1 and Article 2 para 1 of the Constitution, as well as in the provision of Article 6 of the European Convention of Human Rights. The latter, by virtue of Article 28 para 2 of the Constitution, has greater formal force and therefore prevails over any contrary regulation of the common legislator.

In particular, the person called to give explanations in the context of an administrative procedure, due to which a criminal prosecution may be initiated, must enjoy protection similar to those relating to criminal proceedings. Therefore, according to Article 20 of the Penal Code, the intrinsically unfair nature of the refusal to provide information by the respondent is removed on the grounds that refusal by silence constitutes the exercise of a legal right.

However, even more crucial in this case is the question of whether the holders of the right can, in addition to being the legal representatives, also be employees of the liable companies. The answer to this question must be in the affirmative. The invocation of the right is in any case reasonable if the recipient of the request in question, also in their capacity as an employee, would, in answering, lead to their own prosecution. In addition, even if the defendant is forced to confess, the confession cannot be used to substantiate any accusation against him or a third party as this confession constitutes illegally acquired evidence.

According to Article 19 para 3 of the Constitution, the use of illegally obtained evidence is expressly prohibited. This constitutional provision is absolute and without reservation, except when it is necessary to protect human dignity and human life. It is always subject to the principle of proportionality. In this sense, under Article 177 para 2 of the Code of Criminal Procedure, evidence cannot be admitted if it has been acquired through illegal acts unless it is to be used in support of the accused.

On the other hand, in the context of the legal order of the European Union, the CJEU has considered that the 'right to remain silent' in the field of competition law does not cover the answers to questions concerning facts, unless the questions are intended to compel the undertaking concerned to admit the infringement under investigation by the Commission. In other words, the protection of that right implies that it must be ascertained whether the answer of the undertaking to whom these questions are addressed is in essence equivalent to the admission of an infringement.

In this particular case, the Financial Market Authority (FMA) has requested Mr Bud to reveal everything he knows about a market abuse case regarding the corporation he works for. For this purpose, the FMA repeatedly warned him that if he refuses to provide further details about what he knows, his licence is unlikely to be renewed.

On the one hand, the FMA thus violates the right of the defendant to remain silent and not incriminate himself, while on the other, it threatens to impose severe administrative measures, ie the non-renewal of a licence, violating the law, and abusing its power in order to force the defendant to confess.

Therefore, the Court would endorse Bud's argument based on grounds of abuse of his right to remain silent and his right to non-self-incrimination (*nemo tenetur se detegere*).

F. Italy

NB

In the case at issue, Bud could rightfully refuse to answer to the request for information put by regulatory authority, claiming he would risk incriminating himself (although he could not decline to cooperate with the officers in additional respects). The competent authority (in Italy, *Commissione nazionale per le società e la borsa*—Consob) incorrectly warns Bud that his reticence could constitute an unlawful obstruction of its supervisory activities, punishable under Article 187-*quinquiesdecies* of Legislative Decree No 58 of 24 February 1998 (consolidated law on financial intermediation) by a fine and a supplementary sanction of temporary suspension or permanent loss of licence.

Italian legislation on the prevention and combating of market abuse is the result of the adjustment of domestic legislation to European law. More specifically, Law No 62 of 18 April 2005 assimilated the contents of Directive 6/2003/EC of the European Parliament and of the Council (Market Abuse Directive) and the Commission Implementing Directives 124/2003/EC, 125/2003/EC, and 72/2004/EC. This required a radical amendment of Italian Legislative Decree No 58/1998, with the introduction of new rules on insider trading and market manipulation. The matter was the subject of additional legislative measures taken at Community level in 2014, with Regulation 596/2014/EU of the European Parliament and of the Council (Market Abuse Regulation), directly applicable to the Italian legal system, and Directive 2014/57/EU of the European Parliament and of the Council (Criminal Sanctions Market Abuse Directive).

The new rules contained in Legislative Decree No 58/1998 establish a 'two-track sanction' approach to the offence of abuse or unlawful disclosure of inside information, setting out the premises for both a criminal offence (Article 184) and an administrative offence (Article 187-*bis*). The sector regulator (Consob) is responsible for imposing administrative sanctions and thus has effective investigation and fact-finding powers, the results of which can potentially be used in parallel criminal proceedings.

In this context, and in accordance with Article 14(3) of Directive 2003/6/EC of the European Parliament and of the Council, Article 187-*quinquiesdecies* of Italian Legislative Decree 58/1998 imposes a specific obligation to cooperate with the regulatory authority, also by the alleged perpetrator of the offence. The article envisages penalties for those who fail to respond promptly to Consob's requests and/or hinder its inspection procedures. The relevant penalties consist of fines and disqualifications and could even lead to uncooperative persons being prevented from carrying on their business.

However, this provision may not conflict with certain constitutional guarantees concerning the right to defence in procedures to determine penalties of an essentially 'punitive' nature.

Accordingly, following a ruling by the CJEU,[172] the Italian Constitutional Court (No 84, 30 April 2021) declared unconstitutional the aforementioned Article 187-*quinquiesdecies*, insofar as it also applies to a person who refuses to provide the supervisory authority with answers that may bring to light his responsibility for offenses of a (formally or substantially) criminal nature.

However, the Constitutional Court has also clarified that the recognition of the aforementioned guarantee does not imply the legitimacy of conduct of an obstructive nature with respect to supervisory activities, such as the refusal to attend the hearing or its systematic request for postponement for merely dilatory purposes; nor does it mandate conduct of an omissive nature with respect to the delivery of data, documents, and records pursuant to Article 187-*octies* of Legislative Decree No 58 of 24 February 1998.

The declaration of unconstitutionality was based on the parameter of Article 117 of the Italian Constitution, which requires the lawmaker to comply with the constraints arising from Community law and international obligations. First and foremost, these include due compliance with the protection consisting of a fair trial provided by Article 6 of the European Convention on Human Rights and, as this is an area where EU law is implemented, and by Articles 47 and 48 of the Charter of Fundamental Rights of the European Union, which clearly also apply to administrative procedures of an essentially 'criminal' nature.

Article 14(3)(g) of the International Covenant on Civil and Political Rights is also relevant as it states—even more explicitly—that accused persons have the right not to be forced to testify against themselves or to confess to being guilty (known as the 'right to silence'). The right to remain silent in criminal proceedings (*nemo tenetur se detegere*) is also established in the Italian constitutional tradition and therefore forms part of the safeguards of due process referred to in Article 111 of the Italian Constitution.

To conclude, Bud could assert his right to remain silent in response to the regulatory authority's requests, in accordance with the Italian Constitutional Court's judgment on the point.

G. Romania

D-CD

In addition to EU legislation, the legislative framework[173] for the financial markets consists of Law No 297/2004 on capital markets, Law No 24/2017 regarding the

[172] Case C-481/19 *DB v Commissione Nazionale per le Società et la Borsa (Consob)* (CJEU, gd ch, 2 February 2021).

[173] R Stoicescu, O Stan, 'Equity capital markets in Romania: Regulatory overview', available here: <https://uk.practicallaw.thomsonreuters.com/w-023-8817?originationContext=document&transitionType=DocumentItem&contextData=(sc.Default)&firstPage=true> accessed June 2023.

issuers of financial instruments and market operations, Law No 126/2018 regarding securities markets, and Financial Supervisory Authority (FSA) Regulations. The Financial Supervisory Authority (*Autoritatea de Supraveghere Financiara*) (Financial Supervisory Authority (FSA)) serves as the primary regulatory body overseeing the Romanian equity capital markets.

Market abuse and insider dealing are principally regulated by the Market Abuse Regulation[174] and Directive 2014/57/EU on market abuse (MAD II),[175] transposed into Romanian national legislation by Law 24/2017. The scenario where an individual possesses inside information and uses it to acquire or dispose of financial instruments, either for their own account or on behalf of a third party, is prohibited under Articles 114 to 116 of Law 24/2017. Penalties for market abuse/insider dealing include an administrative fine of up to RON 22,000,000 for individuals who violate the provisions on market abuse/insider dealing, provided that the violation does not constitute a criminal offence.

When investigating offences under this law, the FSA applies Regulation 596/2014 along with the accompanying safeguards. Additionally, according to national legislation (Article 98 of Law No 24/2017), the FSA has the right to request any information deemed useful to the investigation. There is no express provision regarding the possibility of refusing disclosure of information on the ground of self-incrimination in the national transposing law either. However, in general, the person under investigation may refuse to *sign* documents drafted by FSA during the inspection (Article b125(10) of Law No 24/2017), which may contain information not recognized by the person being investigated.

In this context, the court would not accept the defendant's argument as there is no rule or principle on self-incrimination in administrative procedural law.

H. Serbia

MM

The competences of the Serbian Securities Commission include, inter alia, the licensing of brokers.[176] According to the Law (Article 153) and Rulebook on Licensing Brokers, classes and examinations for investment advisers and portfolio managers,[177] and the licensing of brokers are organized by the Commission. After successfully completing an examination and obtaining the title of broker, those who wish to perform these activities must file an application with the Commission for a broker's licence

[174] Regulation (EU) No 596/2014 of the European Parliament and of the Council of 16 April 2014 on market abuse (market abuse regulation) and repealing Directive 2003/6/EC of the European Parliament and of the Council and Commission Directives 2003/124/EC, 2003/125/EC, and 2004/72/EC ELI: <http://data.europa.eu/eli/reg/2014/596/oj> accessed June 2023.

[175] Directive 2014/57/EU of the European Parliament and of the Council of 16 April 2014 on criminal sanctions for market abuse (market abuse directive), ELI: <http://data.europa.eu/eli/dir/2014/57/oj> accessed June 2023.

[176] Law on the capital market (Official Gazette of RS, No 31/2011, 112/2015, 108/2016, 9/2020, 153/2020, and 62/2023), art 262. The analysis is done on the basis of law applicable at the time of writing in 2020.

[177] Official Gazette of RS, No 10/2012, 68/2012, 3/2016, and 13/2018.

(Article 50). The Commission must grant a licence if the applicant meets the following requirements: 1. the person has obtained the title of broker; 2. the person is not subject to statutory disqualifications (Article 51).

Neither the Law nor the Rulebook provide for a time limit on the validity of the licences once issued; therefore, in the Serbian context and in this particular case, the Serbian Commission could resort to the revocation of the licence in the absence of Bud's cooperation. As stipulated by the Rulebook, the Commission will revoke a licence from a broker, investment adviser, or portfolio manager if it establishes that: 1. the decision on granting a licence was made on the basis of false or incomplete information; 2. the person is subject to statutory disqualifications; 3. the person has *committed a violation of the relevant regulations* and the *Commission considers the violation sufficiently serious* and *systemic to cause the person to no longer be deemed fit and proper to carry out the licensed activities*; lastly, and most pertinently to this case, 4. the *person has not acted as instructed and within the time period stipulated by the Commission decision imposing measures* (Article 54). In administrative matters, therefore in this case as well, the Commission shall apply the provisions of the law governing general administrative procedure. The decisions the Commission adopts are final but may be disputed in Court (Article 242 of the Law). Therefore, in the event of a request for information and Bud's refusal to provide it, the Commission could revoke his licence, a decision which Bud would have the option of challenging in court.

Privilege against self-incrimination is guaranteed in Serbian Law. The Constitution provides that any person charged with or prosecuted for a criminal offence shall not be obliged to provide self-incriminating evidence or evidence to the prejudice of persons related to him, nor shall he be obliged to confess guilt. Furthermore, it is guaranteed that a person prosecuted for other offences punishable by law will have all the rights of a person charged with a criminal offence pursuant to the law and in accordance with it (Article 33). In addition, The LGAP guarantees the right to refuse to testify and provides that a witness is entitled to refuse to testify on certain issues if his/her reply would expose him/her[178] to *serious disgrace, considerable material damage, or criminal prosecution* (Article 125).

Thus, it could be argued that Bud would be able to refuse to testify/provide information insofar as it would constitute self-incrimination and expose him to considerable material damage. As underlined above, in the Serbian case, Bud could resort to court proceedings to invoke this right and ask for the annulment of the Commission's decision if the licence were revoked.

I. Spain

IMD

Article 24(2) CE provides for the fundamental right not to testify against oneself and not to incriminate oneself. Article 24(2) is worded as follows:

[178] In addition to his/her lineal antecedent or descendant, or collateral blood relative within the third degree of consanguinity, spouse, common-law spouse, or in-law up to the second degree, even after the termination of marriage, guardian or protégé, adoptive parent or adoptive child.

> [A]ll persons have the right not to make self-incriminating statements; not to declare themselves guilty; and to be presumed innocent.

In this connection, regarding detainees' rights, Article 17(3) CE states that

> [a]ny person arrested must be informed immediately, and in a manner understandable to him or her, of his or her rights and of the grounds for his or her arrest and may not be compelled to make a statement.

According to the Constitutional Court's settled case law, criminal justice principles also apply to penalty or sanctioning procedures (including the right not to testify against oneself) but not as strictly, because penalty procedures carry more lenient punishments. Thus, not all procedural infringements entail a breach of the said constitutional right. They only do so if there has been a violation of the applicable constitutional safeguards.

The right not to incriminate oneself (or 'to not declare [oneself] guilty' in terms of the Spanish Constitution) is considered a passive dimension of the constitutional right of defence, ie that authorities be precluded from requiring parties to (i) make self-incriminating statements or (ii) produce self-incriminating documents or evidence. According to constitutional case law, the right not to testify against or incriminate oneself qualify as safeguards or entitlements that are ancillary to the general right of defence. These ancillary entitlements or safeguards supplement the passive (or non-active) dimension of the right of defence, where the accused takes no action, being entitled to defend him or herself as he or she sees fit, but in any case not being forced or otherwise compelled or coerced to incriminate him or herself.[179] The Spanish Constitutional Court has been strongly influenced by the case law of the European Court of Human Rights (ECtHR) and, as a result, it advocates that the right not to incriminate oneself requires the public authorities to prove their case without relying on evidence obtained through methods of coercion or oppression in defiance of the accused party's will.[180]

This right preventing self-incrimination by no means entitles the accused to openly refuse to cooperate with enforcement authorities. However, the case law has been extending the right's scope of application and courts now consider that threatening a witness to get a statement violates the right not to incriminate oneself. Still, this right has to be reconciled with the duty to cooperate with public authorities provided in Article 18 LPAC:

> 1. Everyone shall cooperate with public authorities as required by the applicable legal provisions. Absent an express provision, everyone shall submit to the authorities any reports, inspections and other investigative acts required thereby, unless disclosing the requested information could entail i) a violation of the right to honour or privacy; or ii) the unlawful disclosure of confidential third party data arising from the provision of legal counsel, advice or defence services, without prejudice to any applicable money laundering and terrorist-financing regulations.

[179] Constitutional Court Judgment 197/1995, of 21 December, legal basis 6.
[180] Constitutional Court Judgment 21/2021, of 15 February.

So, the right not to incriminate oneself is not provided as a restriction on the duty to cooperate with public authorities.

Neither the legislation on the general administrative procedure nor sector-specific rules on the authorities' power to punish stock market violations specifically regulate the right against self-incrimination. However, this right applies as a general principle or standard any time authorities exercise their punitive power, so that, alongside the due process right to a fair procedure, it entitles the parties not to make statements on facts that can be subsequently relied on by the authorities to impose a penalty. In other words, a penalty cannot be based on a statement made by a party who has been forced, compelled, or coerced into testifying. Therefore, the case law claims that this right sets an indispensable limit on authorities' punitive power arising from the right of defence applicable to any penalty or sanctioning procedures. Moreover, regarding the relationship between the duty to cooperate and the right not to incriminate one-self, the Spanish Constitutional Court has found that parties should not be required to produce a statement disclosing certain aspects, admitting their guilt, but to accept being subject to a specific type of expert evidence.

In sum, according to the case law, the right not to incriminate oneself within penalty procedures prevents authorities from forcing a statement from the party or compelling the party to submit new documents threatening further penalties. Under this perspective, the degree of coercion is relevant. Indeed, the core safe-guards underlying Article 24(2) of the Constitution would be undermined if public authorities were allowed to compel or force the accused to confess to any offence or to produce an otherwise self-incriminating statement. In fact, this safeguard not only serves as a protection against being forced to produce self-incriminating evi-dence within criminal proceedings or administrative penalty procedures but also prevents public authorities from using coercively obtained material as inculpa-tory evidence in any other proceedings or procedures. Even failing or refusing to produce evidence on the facts of the case cannot reverse the burden of proof and qualify as a presumption that the offence attributed to the party be true. However, the right's material scope of protection only covers the production of incriminating evidence and any cases where the degree of coercion by public authority wipes out the safeguard's essence.

Finally, it should be borne in mind that the right not to incriminate oneself, con-sidered an ancillary safeguard to the right of defence, applies to future penalty pro-cedures that may be conducted. Accordingly, it applies to merely investigative procedures aimed at clarifying the factual background, and can be raised as a 'pre-emptive defence' where the duty to disclose information or produce a statement is self-incriminating.

Thus, the FMA's requirement urging Bud to divulge what he knows about the shares, under threat of not renewing his licence, could affect Bud's rights of defence. If the FMA actually failed to renew his licence, Bud's right not to incriminate him-self, and thus his right of defence, would be breached. However, Bud's right to avoid self-incrimination would also allow him to challenge the request itself (exercising some sort of 'pre-emptive defence'), avoiding being forced to produce incriminating evidence under the threat of penalties on the grounds that the mere request violates Bud's fundamental right of defence. In any case, both the act of non-renewal of Bud's licence—if there was proof that the cause for non-renewal is Bud's refusal to produce a statement—and the act requiring the information under pain of a penalty, would be null and void for entailing a fundamental right's violation.

Also, failing to renew the licence on grounds other than public interest as required by the specific regulations, ie coercing Bud into producing a statement, could constitute abuse of power, thereby rendering the act of non-renewal voidable (ie subject to annulment if requested to do so by the parties concerned).

J. Switzerland

AF

The right not to incriminate oneself in criminal law (*nemo tenetur*) is opposed to the obligation to collaborate found in administrative law.[181] This leads to tensions between the two principles when an administrative procedure is related to a criminal one. In this case, the protection of *nemo tenetur* applies in administrative proceedings as soon as they have a sufficient connection to criminal proceedings: eg if the administrative authority is obliged to give the criminal authority legal and administrative assistance, if the criminal authority is investigating at least partially the same facts as the administrative authority or if a truthful statement by the person concerned could, in itself, trigger the criminal investigation. More specifically, in supervisory proceedings for violation of the supervisory prohibition of market manipulation under Article 143 of the Federal Act on Financial Market Infrastructures and Market Conduct in Securities and Derivatives Trading of 19 June 2015 (FinfraG), the prohibition of self-incrimination must therefore be observed. Not only because the proceedings themselves constitute a criminal charge within the meaning of Article 6 para 1 ECHR, but also because they are sufficiently related to possible criminal proceedings for price manipulation under Article 155 FinfraG due to FINMA's duty to provide legal and administrative assistance under Article 38 FINMASA.[182]

In conclusion, to the extent that the administrative proceeding against Bud had a sufficient connection to a criminal proceeding, the privilege against self-incrimination applies; otherwise, it will not.

K. United Kingdom

GA and CM

This scenario touches upon the same issues as the famous case of *Saunders v UK*, albeit the legislation in *Saunders* compelled the interviewee to answer questions or face criminal sanctions.[183] That case also arose in the financial sector, where Mr Saunders

[181] ATF 132 II 113 and 115.

[182] See M Hanslin, *Markt- und Kursmanipulation, Article 143 and Article 155 FinfraG sowie Article 122 ff. FinfraV* (Dike 2017) 282ff; Swiss Federal Court, Decision 6B_90/2019 07.08.2019 c 5.4.

[183] (1997) 23 EHRR 313.

had been required by section 434 of the Companies Act 1985 to answer questions from inspectors about a take-over, in circumstances where his answers could be admitted into evidence in any future criminal proceedings. Mr Saunders was subsequently convicted of a number of offences at a trial in which the prosecution relied in significant part on the answers that he had given under section 434. In the domestic courts, it was held that such use of the interview material did not render the criminal proceedings unfair, as Parliament had expressly and unambiguously provided that answers could be admitted into evidence, even though this might override the common law's privilege against self-incrimination (this is thus one example of how statute law can override common law rights—see point 5 in the 'preliminary comments' section that accompanies this chapter). In contrast, the European Court of Human Rights (ECtHR) considered that there had been a breach of Article 6 ECHR: the Court considered that the right to silence was central to Article 6 ECHR and that the prosecution in a criminal trial must be able to prove its case without resorting to evidence obtained under compulsion.

What, then, of Bud, who is told that there is no rule within the sector specific legislation allowing him to remain silent and that, if he does remain silent, his licence may not be renewed? There are two points that might be made.

The first is that the absence of a rule in the legislation which safeguards the right to silence is immaterial and that Bud ought to be able to assert the right. While it is possible for legislation in the UK expressly to limit in part the right to silence in certain areas, it does not follow that legislation must expressly guarantee the right to silence for it to be enforceable in a matter. This is because the right to silence exists at common law and, unless Parliament expressly legislates to override the right, it will remain unabridged.[184] Bud should thus be able to rely upon the common law; and he could equally rely upon his fair trial guarantees under Article 6 ECHR, as has effect under the Human Rights Act 1998.

The second point concerns the threat not to renew Bud's licence in the event that he exercises his right to silence. While it can be expected (as a matter of reality) that Bud would encounter difficulties when seeking to renew his licence, the threat that is being made by the officers may well be unlawful, notably if it does not have a basis in the underlying legislative scheme. The point here is simply that officers could not use their more general powers to punish a person who is exercising a lawful right, as that would be to go beyond what is permitted by the relevant statute. Were the threat to materialize, Bud might therefore be able to challenge the officers' actions as, among other things, motivated by an improper purpose (even bad faith), as an abuse of power, and/or as irrational.[185]

To summarize: it could be expected that Bud would be able to rely upon the right to silence and that any attempt by officers to dissuade him from doing so may well breach a number of well-established public law principles.

[184] *R v Home Secretary, ex parte Simms* [2000] 2 AC 115.

[185] For such concepts at common law see *R (Lumba) v Home Secretary* [2011] UKSC 12, [2012] 1 AC 245.

L. Venezuela

FP-F

The Financial Market Authority (FMA) cannot force Bud to testify against himself, because this is contrary to the due process rule established in Article 49 of the Venezuelan Constitution, paragraph 5 of which expressly establishes that

> No person shall be required to confess guilt or testify against himself or herself or his or her spouse or partner, or any other relative within the fourth degree of consanguinity or the second degree of affinity,

which is why 'a confession shall be valid only if given without coercion of any kind'.

Hence, the contentious-administrative tribunal would support Bud's argument, not only because he does not have the right not to testify against himself but because, if he did, and he confessed, he would be doing so under duress due to the FMA officials' threat not to renew his licence.

VII. Case 6—A taxpayer who disputes the tax authority's statements

A. Austria

SS

The administrative court itself may grant access to the file as soon as it becomes responsible for conducting the proceedings. According to § 13 (4) S 1 of the Federal Act on Proceedings of Administrative Courts ('*VwGVG*'), the administrative authority must submit the files to the administrative court when the court proceeding starts.

More specifically, § 90 (1) 1 of the Tax Proceedings Act ('*BAO*') rules that the tax authority must allow the parties to inspect and copy the files or parts of files, knowledge of which is necessary to assert or defend their tax law interests or fulfil their tax law obligations. A similar right to inspect the files is guaranteed by § 17 AVG for administrative proceedings in general.

If there is no specific legal provisions on the right to inspect files, such as § 90 *BAO* or § 17 AVG, it can be safely assumed that the competent court would deduce such a right from the right to be heard and the principle of a fair trial. The right to access files requires a party's rights and legal interests to be respected, a right closely related to the right to be heard.[186] The right of access to files enables a party to form his or her own opinion by directly inspecting the results of an investigation procedure and can thus gain precise knowledge of the course of a procedure and the basis for an authority's decision.[187] This right to inspect files has its constitutional roots in the '*Rechtsstaatsprinzip*' and ensures 'equality of power'[188] between the authority and the party involved in administrative court proceedings.[189]

However, the right of the parties to inspect files conflicts with the obligation of the administrative bodies to maintain confidentiality under Article 20 (3) B-VG and to keep personal data confidential under Article 1 (1) of the Federal Data Protection Act.

B. China

XS

Under Chinese law, the court will rule in favour of Mr Paine, not on grounds of the 'principles of the due process and fairness', but under the Regulation on Open Government Information. It will order the TA to disclose its documents.

The Regulation on Open Government Information were first issued in 2007, newly revised by the State Council on 3 April 2019. Its Article 13 provides that 'all government information must be disclosed, except the information specified by articles 14,

[186] VwGH 19 March 2003, 2000/12/0110.
[187] VwGH 22 October 2013, 2012/10/0002.
[188] VwGH 7 October 2010, 2006/17/0123; VfGH 23 June 2020, E 706-707/2020-11.
[189] J Hengstschläger and D Leeb, '§ 17' in Hengstschläger and Leeb (eds), [Commentary on the] AVG (Manz status 1 January 2014, rdb at) rec 1.

15, and 16 of this Regulation.[190] According to these provisions, the information that may be withheld from disclosure includes:

- 'state secrets';[191]
- 'information prohibited by laws and regulations from being disclosed';[192]
- 'information whose disclosure may endanger national security, public security, economic security, or social stability';[193]
- 'information whose disclosure may infringe the lawful rights and interests of a third party, such as commercial secrets and personal privacy';[194]
- 'Internal administrative information, including personnel management, logistics management, internal processes, and information in other such areas';[195]
- 'in-process information such as deliberation records, draft documents, consultation letters, requests for instruction, and other such in-process information';[196]
- 'administrative law enforcement files.'[197]

The question would be whether the personal data concerning Mr Paine could be considered as 'in-process information' within the meaning of the Regulation on Open Government Information. As such, the Supreme People's Court published a guiding case judged by the Intermediate People's Court of Fuzhou about in-process information.[198] According to the commentary of the Supreme Court, 'in-process information should not be an absolute exception from disclosure. Once the decision is made, the information that was under investigation, discussion, and processing is no longer in-process information. If the need for disclosure is greater than the need for non-disclosure, it should be disclosed.'[199] In the commented case, the administrative act was already in the implementation stage. However, the administrative authority did not disclose the information on the grounds that the information was in-process information, which constituted an 'improper obstruction to the plaintiff from exercising his right to access information.'[200] This case can be analysed as an application of the principle of due process in terms of Open Government Information.

In the application of the solution resulting from this guiding case, the personal data concerning Mr Paine would no longer be considered in-process information and would have to be disclosed.

190 除本条例第十四条、第十五条、第十六条规定的政府信息外，政府信息应当公开。

191 国家秘密.

192 法律、行政法规禁止公开的政府信息.

193 公开后可能危及国家安全、公共安全、经济安全、社会稳定的政府信息.

194 涉及商业秘密、个人隐私等公开会对第三方合法权益造成损害的政府信息.

195 行政机关的内部事务信息，包括人事管理、后勤管理、内部工作流程等方面的信息.

196 行政机关在履行行政管理职能过程中形成的讨论记录、过程稿、磋商信函、请示报告等过程性信息.

197 行政执法案卷信息.

198 Supreme People's Court, guiding cases relating to Open Government Information (最高人民法院公政府信息公开十大案例) on 13 September 2014, No 5.

199 过程性信息不应是绝对的例外，当决策、决定完成后，此前处于调查、讨论、处理中的信息即不再是过程性信息，如果公开的需要大于不公开的需要，就应当公开。

200 对当事人行使知情权构成不当阻却.

C. France

SS

Can the French tax authority rely on the absence of a provision requiring access to documents and items in a tax dossier, in order to refuse access? How does the right of access to administrative documents combine with the particularities of the taxation procedure? That is the question posed in this case.

A citizen may have access to all administrative and, therefore, tax documents concerning him. Articles L. 311-1ff of the CRPA enable any person to request the authorities to share the contents of the administrative documents they hold, whatever their form. The right of access to documents held by the authorities has been established since Law No 78-753 of 17 July 1978, which constitutes the first general regulation in the area. Until then, the texts recognizing the right to information were only specific provisions, derogating from the rule of secrecy. There existed no obligation to convey documents without text, except in application of the principle of the rights of defence. Since 1978, the perspective has been reversed. The rule is communication; secrecy the exception. The provisions of the law of 17 July 1978 regarding the right of access to administrative documents, which have been modified several times, have been codified in book III of the CRPA, whose articles L. 311-5 to L. 311-8 list the documents excluded from the right of communication.

Freedom of access to administrative documents constitutes one of the 'fundamental guarantees accorded to citizens for the exercise of public freedoms' pursuant to Article 34 of the Constitution.[201] After recognizing a constitutional right of access to public records,[202] the *Conseil constitutionnel* has recently acknowledged that the right of access to administrative documents is a constitutional requirement.[203]

The administrative courts have on several occasions specified that the old law of 1978 applied to tax authority documents[204] concerning reports on the tax situation of a taxpayer, drawn up after audit operations, whatever the actions following up on such operations; see also, on the communicability to a taxpayer of 'items from the tax file'.[205]

Numerous specifications have since been provided by the tax authority on the application of the major concepts, on the rules and exceptions pertaining to the area.[206]

There are, however, special regulations on access to administrative documents, some of which also enable the *Commission d'accès aux documents administratifs* ('commission for access to administrative documents'—CADA) to make rulings before referral to the court. All the situations exist in the taxation area (eg Article L. 104, L. 105, L. 106, and L. 111 of the *Livre des procédures fiscales*) ('book of taxation procedures'—LPF).

[201] CE 29 April 2002, *Ullmann*, req No 228830, *Rec* p 156.

[202] Cons Const, 15 September 2017, No 2017-655 QPC, *M François Graner*.

[203] Cons Const, 3 April 2020, No 2020-834 QPC, *Union nationale des étudiants de France*.

[204] CE, sect, 1 December 1989, No 58277, *Blanc* and No 58.896, *S.A.R.L. Sté nouvelle d'édition et de diffusion (S.N.D.E.D.)*.

[205] CE, 9th and 8th ss-sect., 30 November 1994, No 136625, *Cambrune*.

[206] BOFIP, BOI 12 September 2012, DJC-CADA-10: *Dispositions Juridiques Communes—Accès aux documents administratifs—Règles générales* ('common legal provisions—access to administrative documents—general rules'.

There is a first solution to the juncture between the *lex generalis* (the CRPA) and the special regulations in the supplementary character of the CRPA.[207] However, the status of the law is more complex. The general right to communication provided by the CRPA applies regardless of the specific communication rights prescribed for the area of taxation, particularly the right to communication for the benefit of taxpayers (a document that is not communicable pursuant to the CRPA may be communicable according to the book of taxation procedures). Conversely, the fact that the rules of taxation procedure do not oblige the authority to convey a given document does not exclude the taxpayer's right to obtain access to them on grounds of the general right of access prescribed by the CRPA.[208]

Mr Paine may therefore challenge the decision to refuse to provide documentation.

However, the juncture between the general law and the special law rests, in reality, essentially on the judge's interpretation. Since 2015, the administrative courts have had the occasion to decide on a conflict of rules between the CRPA and the LPF (Article L. 256 and R. 256-1 and 2 of the LPF). The *SAS BT Zimat* case[209] concerned the request made by a building company entitled to financial support under article 1724-*quater* of the general tax code regarding concealed employment by one of its subcontractors. It wished to obtain access to the documents relating to the taxation procedure followed with respect to the legally taxable subject. The *Conseil constitutionnel* and the *Conseil d'Etat* had ruled that the documents be made available.[210] On the other hand, the question of the mode of communication had not been resolved. The *Conseil d'Etat* deemed that communication of taxation procedure documents was within the scope not of the *lex generalis* but of a regime of *lex specialis*. The solution here, however, is favourable to the taxpayer, for it follows that, conversely to what the authority claimed, it must convey the requested documents free of charge (application of the CRPA would in this case have led to charging a fee).

D. Germany

DS

The court deciding on Mr Paine's application finds itself in a particular situation since, in tax cases, access to personal data in an administrative procedure is regulated differently from procedural acts in other fields. While the general laws on administrative procedure at Federation and Länder levels (§ 29 VwVfG) and the law on administrative procedure in social security matters (*Sozialgesetzbuch* book X—*Verwaltungsverfahren—SGB X*, § 25) provide, in principle, a right of access to personal data during an administrative procedure, the procedural code for cases concerning taxation (*Abgabenordnung—AO*) does not contain a correspondent right.

207 Art L. 100-1: 'this code governs the relations between the public and the authorities in the absence of applicable special provisions'.

208 BOI, 12 September 2012, prev, §170.

209 CE, opinion, 6 June 2018, No 418863, *SAS BT Zimat*.

210 Cons Const, 31 July 2015, No 2015-479 QPC, *Sté Gecop*; CE, 22 February 2017, No 386430, *Sté Gecop*.

This difference can be interpreted in two opposite ways: first, the right of access to documents may be seen as a general principle of administrative procedure and thus be extended to the taxation procedure as well; secondly, the rules in the code covering taxation matters may be qualified as an intentionally different regulation.

The practice moves in the second direction. The administrative ruling on the execution of the taxation code (*Anwendungserlass zur Abgabenordnung, AE AO*) of 31 January 2014, commenting on § 91 *AO* and binding in terms of practice, denies a general right of access to documents in the taxation procedure and permits access only in accordance with the discretionary power of the tax administration; it refers to a letter of the Federal Minister of Finance of 17 December 2008 (*BStBl* I 2009, p 6). Access may be allowed, but only in relation to the interests of third persons and administrative goals; there is no legal right.

As a matter of fact, the right of access, according to the other laws on administrative procedure, is limited in different ways. Federal law (§ 29 VwVfG) states that the right is strictly limited to administrative procedure (§ 9) until an administrative act is implemented. It does not include the drafts or preparatory works of the act, and it must not infringe the rights of third persons. The other laws establish further and partly different exceptions; the law of Schleswig-Holstein even recognizes the discretionary power of the administration if particular rules do not establish an absolute right of access.

One may conclude from these different regulations—augmented by other regulations concerning environmental acts and by a general right of access to documents without limitation on administrative procedure, but with other limits—that there is a tendency to permit access to documents, but without general implications and with sector-specific limits. Nevertheless, the problem remains whether the Constitution guarantees the core of the right and, especially, whether it excludes or limits the discretionary power of the administration.

Thus, from this point of view, the constitutional situation is unclear. There is no explicit right to gain access to documents. The right to seize a court (Article 19.4 *GG*)[211] concerns courts, not administrative procedure, and the same applies to the right to be heard (Article 103.1 *GG*). Nevertheless, one may conclude from these protections regarding the principle of the fair trial that it should also be extended to administrative procedure. This may exclude the general discretionary power of the administration to give or refuse access to documents. However, for the taxation procedure—a classical mass procedure—one may object that there are problems of complexity and that there is the possibility of correcting the decision during the court proceedings. Thus, upon being seized by Mr Paine, the court would disclose the documents during its proceedings (see § 78 *Finanzgerichtsordnung—FGO*).

E. Greece

TF

According to Article 10 para 3 of the Constitution, the competent service or authority is obliged to reply to requests for information and to supply documents within a set

[211] See above Schefold, 'Germany' (n 43) I.

deadline not exceeding sixty days, as specified by law. If this deadline elapses without an action being taken or in the event of unlawful refusal, in addition to any other sanctions and legal consequences, the applicant will also receive monetary compensation.

The aforementioned right is further defined and specified under Article 5 of the Administrative Procedural Code and Presidential Decree 28/2015, which codifies the provisions on access to public documents and data. Specifically, individuals have the right to take cognizance of administrative documents, which are considered to be those drawn up by the service units of the state, local government agencies, and public law legal persons. Thus, they may, provided that they have a reasonable interest, seek, through petition to the competent administrative authority, either to study the document on the premises of the service unit or to obtain a copy (unless reproduction of the document might damage the original). It is a matter of indifference whether the documents concern the petitioner or third parties.

Furthermore, individuals also have the right to take cognizance of private documents held by public authorities relating to a pending case or one that has already been decided against them. A private document, as distinct from an administrative one, is deemed to be any document drawn up by any person who is not an authority of the state or a local government agency or public law legal persons. Such documents include notarial documents, reports of court bailiffs, agreements, declarations, and letters, etc, of private individuals. A special interest is the pursuit of the satisfaction of a specific right by the administration, or the pursuit of judicial protection. Of course, in order for public administration compliance to provide access to the information requested, the application must specify the documents required either individually or on the basis of a specific criterion capable of classifying them into a particular category or group.

In this case, the tax authority refuses Mr Paine access to his personal data and information to defend himself, rejecting his relevant formal request. Therefore, in light of the above, the refusal of the authorities to divulge the contents of the above-mentioned documents is an administrative act, which means that it will be challenged in order to obtain an annulment, and the Court will order the tax authority to disclose the requested documents.

F. Italy

SV

In the case at issue, the Italian administrative court would recognize Mr Paine's right to view and obtain copies of the documentation held by the tax administration and would consequently order the Tax Authority to produce them. This decision would be justified on the basis of the prevailing (and almost unanimous) interpretation of the protective nature of Article 24 of the Italian APA (Law No 241 of 7 August 1990).

More specifically, it should be noted that the Italian APA expressly states that tax procedures are not covered by the rules on access to administrative documents, and therefore reference is made to the special rules governing these proceedings (Article 24(1)(b)).

Nevertheless, there is no legislative provision establishing a general taxpayer's right to access to administrative files regarding these procedures within the realm of tax-related regulations. It is worth noting, however, that legal theory and case law have suggested the potential for progress in this area by expanding upon the principles outlined in the Taxpayer's Bill of Rights—Law No 212 of 27 July 2000—particularly Article 6, which focuses on 'knowing the content of files'.

Nonetheless, administrative case law has gradually adopted a constitutionally oriented interpretation of Article 24 of Law No 241/1990,[212] asserting that tax proceedings are exempt from an obligation to disclose the contents of file solely during the 'pending' stage. Once this stage has concluded, no grounds of secrecy can reasonably justify a denial of access to the requested documents. It should be specified that, in relation to tax matters, 'conclusion of the procedure' means the moment when the 'tax assessment notice' is issued based on the investigative evidence gathered by the authority that ultimately determines the precise calculation of the amount of tax due.

This now well-established interpretative approach[213] is also based on specific emphasis given to Article 24(7) of the Italian APA. The provision stipulates that the right of access to administrative documents, essential for safeguarding and defending legal interests, must be consistently ensured.

This means that every taxpayer has an actual and substantive interest in accessing all documentation relating to the tax assessment, collection, and payment stages, as knowledge of these documents can reveal substantial or procedural defects highlighting the total or partial unlawfulness of the tax claim.[214]

Lastly, in procedural terms, administrative decisions regarding access to administrative documents can be appealed before administrative courts (Regional Administrative Court and Council of State) by bringing a specific action within a thirty-day limit and following a 'special' procedure governed by Article 116 of the Code of Administrative Procedure (Italian Legislative Decree No 104 of 2 July 2010). If the administrative court holds that the appellant's claim is founded, it issues a judgment ordering disclosure of the requested documents within a time limit that usually does not exceed thirty days and, if necessary, establishes the procedures to be followed.

G. Romania

D-CD

Access to administrative records is a significant legal issue that has been widely and heatedly debated in relation to tax and fiscal procedures in Romania. The tax authorities have consistently denied access to records and imposed penalties based on information that was not available for review by the taxpayer. Most courts have upheld this approach, citing the absence of a national rule allowing access to files for taxpayers and emphasizing that taxpayers can exercise their rights before the court.

212 See, specifically, Council of State, Div IV, No 5588, 13 November 2014.

213 See, among the many, Council of State, Div IV, No 5565, 24 September 2020; Council of State, Div IV No 908, 6 February 2019; Council of State, Div IV, No 3847, 22 June 2018; Sicily Regional Administrative Court, Catania, Div III, No 1983, 31 July 2017; Lombardy Regional Administrative Court, Brescia, Div II, No 573, 2 May 2017; Lazio Regional Administrative Court, Rome, Div II No 3250, 8 March 2017; Council of State, Div IV, No 5588, 13 November 2014.

214 Council of State, Div IV, No 317, 28 January 2016.

Case C-298/16, Ispas[215] has arisen due to this reluctance to ensure defence rights for taxpayers during administrative investigations. In national judicial proceedings, Ispas raised the question of access to administrative records containing information used by the tax authorities to determine supplementary tax obligations.[216] The claimants argued that lack of access to their files affected their ability to challenge the information. Another aspect was the finding that the information was collected illegally before formal tax inspections were initiated. The national court ordered the tax administration to provide the files, which led to suspending the proceedings and the referral of the following question for a preliminary ruling:

> Is an administrative practice that involves imposing obligations on an individual without allowing them access to all the information and documents considered by the public authority when it adopted the decision, including the information and documents contained in the administrative file (not a public file) created by the public authority, compatible with the principle of respect for the rights of the defence?

The CJEU rightfully stated that

> The general principle with EU law of respect for the rights of the defence must be interpreted as a requirement that, in national administrative procedures of inspection and establishment of the basis for the assessment of value-added tax, an individual is to have the opportunity to have communicated to him, at his request, the information and documents in the administrative file and considered by the public authority when it adopted its decision unless objectives of public interest warrant restricting access to that information and those documents.

However, the Court stopped short of imposing a *general obligation of tax authorities to provide ex officio access to the administrative file*:

> (32) To that end, as the Advocate General observed in points 121 and 122 of his opinion, national tax authorities are not under a general obligation to provide full access to the file or to communicate on their own motion documents and information that support the intended decision.

In his conclusions, the Advocate General evaluated the national legislation and found that it provides the right of the taxpayer to express a view on the relevant facts before the decision is taken, the right to be informed and to receive the draft of the fiscal inspection report setting out the results of the findings (Code of Fiscal Procedure, Article 9, Article 109). However, even if these provisions align with the

[215] Case C-298/16 *Ispas v Direcția Generală a Finanțelor Publice Cluj* ECLI:EU:C:2017:843 (Judgment of the Court (Third Chamber) of 9 November 2017).

[216] C F Costaş, 'Access to File: Right(s) of the Defence or Defence of the Right(s)?' (2018) 5 Cluj Tax Forum Journal 21.

effectiveness principle and do not make hearing the party excessively difficult or impossible, the national court will assess the effectiveness in each specific case.[217]

Later, in C-430/19, SC C.F. SRL,[218] which also arose in the context of a national procedure involving the application of the Romanian fiscal procedure and the right to defence, the Court stated that

> The general EU law principle of observance of the rights of defence must be interpreted as meaning that where, in the context of national administrative procedures for inspection and for determining the taxable amount for value-added tax purposes, a taxable person has not been allowed access to the information in the administrative file that was taken into consideration when an administrative decision imposing additional tax liabilities on that taxable person was adopted, and where the court hearing the case finds that, in the absence of that irregularity, the outcome of the procedure might have been different, that principle requires that that decision be annulled.

The case pertained to the fiscal authorities' denial of providing a taxpayer with essential information, which was requested within a reasonable time frame. The authorities provided no objective justification for their refusal.

Following the Ispas judgment, the courts' inaction[219] concerning the right to defence changed when the High Court of Cassation and Justice set a precedent of annulling tax decisions without allowing the taxpayer to be heard beforehand.[220] Furthermore, the highest court even referred to Article 41 of the Fundamental Charter and the relevant case law of the Court of Justice to assert that tax authorities cannot consider their obligation to hear the taxpayer to have been fulfilled if he/she only responds to questions during the tax inspection, receives the findings of the tax inspection, and is provided with a copy of the tax report. The national court stated that the taxpayer should be genuinely heard, in accordance with the principle of the right to defence.[221] The first definitive ruling to mandate the National Fiscal Authority (ANAF) to allow full access to administrative files came in 2019.[222]

In this context, Mr Paine's claim in the case study that the principles of due process and fairness should be applied, in full, thus allowing him to understand the factual elements that influenced the TA's decision, has a fair chance of finding acceptance in

[217] C-298/16 *Ispas v Direcția Generală a Finanțelor Publice Cluj* ECLI:EU:C:2017:843, Opinion of AG Michal Bobek paras 123–124.

[218] C-430/19 *SC C.F. SRL v A.J.F.P.M. and D.G.R.F.P.C.* ECLI:EU:C:2020:429 (Judgment of the Court (Sixth Chamber) of 4 June 2020).

[219] For the trials and tribulations of taxpayers in Romania, see C F Costaş, 'Towards a Magna Carta of Taxpayers' Rights in the Times of the Hunger Games?' in M Tofan, I Bilan, and A-M Bercu (eds), *EUFIRE 2018* (Editura Universității 'Alexandru Ioan Cuza' 2018) 427.

[220] High Court of Cassation and Justice, Administrative and Tax Section, decision No 2615 of 21 May 2009; decision No 4759 of 29 March 2013; decision No 4008 of 28 October 2014. See for more details C F Costaş, *Codul de procedură fiscală. Comentariu pe articole* (Ed Solomon 2016) 30–33.

[221] Decision No 2323 of 4 June 2018, in Costaş, 'Access to File' (n 216) 21.

[222] Tribunalul Bucureşti Decision No 436 of 29 January 2019, confirmed in appeal by the Bucharest Court of Appeal see <https://costas-negru.ro/acces-dosar-administrativ-prima-hotarare-definitiva-de-obligare-a-anaf-la-predarea-dosarului-administrativ/> accessed June 2023.

Romanian courts. A court ruling is likely to order the tax authority to provide the information necessary for the claimant's right to defence.

H. Serbia

MM

In the Serbian legal system, Mr Paine would have a set of due process guarantees for access to his tax documents. The Constitution stipulates that the protection of personal data is to be ensured and that all have the right to be informed about personal data collected regarding them, in accordance with the law, and the right to court protection if such data are abused (Article 42). Furthermore, the LGAP sets out in detail the right to examine the case files. According to the Law, the right to examine the case files entails the right of a party to examine them in the presence of an official, to have a copy made at their own expense and for that copy to be delivered to them via post or in another suitable manner, again at their own expense. Case files shall be examined on the premises of the authority that keeps them. If documents are kept in electronic form, the authority will enable the examination and reproduction of documents in electronic or printed form (Article 64). In addition, parties to the proceeding may request to examine case files and have the right to be notified on the course of the proceedings: within eight days of receiving the request, an authority must notify the party or the interested person on how they can examine and/or reproduce the case files and receive a copy of them, or rule to dismiss the request. If the authority fails to act within the set time limit or dismisses or rejects the request through a ruling, the requester may file an appeal with the second instance authority within eight days (Article 65). As already underlined, a decision by the second instance authority may be challenged before the Administrative Court.

The sectoral Law on Tax Procedure and Tax Administration envisages the principle allowing a Review of Facts (Article 6) stipulating that prior to passing an act determining the rights and obligations of the taxpayer, the Tax Administration will, at the taxpayer's request, allow them to review the legal and factual basis for passing the act. Therefore, the Court would accept Mr Paine's request and grant access.

In addition, it should also be noted that the Law on Tax Procedure and Tax Administration provides (Article 182) that Responsible Officers in the Tax Administration who deny a taxpayer access to data on tax assessment and collection regarding them held by the Tax Administration or, at a taxpayer's request, fail to modify incomplete or inaccurate data on the taxpayer, commits a misdemeanour and faces paying a fine.

I. Spain

IMD

In Spanish law, the right to access public information is governed by the Act on Transparency, Access to Public Information, and Good Governance (*Ley 19/2013 de Transparencia, Acceso a la Información Pública y Buen Gobierno*, LTBG). This right of access implements the constitutional right to access public files and records provided in Article 105(b) CE. This right is granted to everyone, does not require justifying or giving reasons for access requests or applications, and is subject to an exhaustive list of limitations provided in the LTBG to protect additional rights or interests, whether public or private.

The LTBG is generally applicable, although it refers to specific implementing regulations in two cases: (i) within ongoing administrative procedures, if the access request is submitted by the party concerned, the legislation on the general administrative procedure applies, and (ii) if there is a sector-specific provision laying down a special regime governing access to public information, it will supersede the general provision (regardless of whether the more specific provision is a statute or a regulation and whether it is more or less lenient) and the LTBG will apply by default.

According to the Supreme Court's case law, the specific tax regulations do not include a comprehensive, self-governing framework for access to public information within tax procedures. Thus, the LTBG applies to the case at hand.[223] Although everyone is entitled to the right of access with no need to supply a reason, the requesting party must be the one concerned, and a request must be made to learn the legal bases of a decision affecting such a party. Prior decisions by the national and regional Transparency and Good Governance Councils and the case law do not unanimously agree on which legal framework applies to requests or applications submitted by the party concerned regarding documents within the administrative file, regardless of whether the procedure is ongoing or already concluded.

In any event, if the LTBG framework is applied, the request or application can only be denied on two types of grounds: (i) the grounds for rejection specifically provided in Article 18 LTBG, or (ii) if some of the limits set out in Articles 14 and 15 are applicable. In Mr Paine's case, the applicable grounds could be either the formal limit related to the ancillary nature of public information or the restrictions arising from the confidentiality of deliberations.

Under Article 18(a), any requests or applications regarding ancillary information, such as that included in notes, drafts, opinions, summaries, communications, and internal reports must be rejected outright without granting leave to proceed, duly stating reasons. However, both the national Transparency and Good Governance Council (an independent body responsible for securing the right of access) and the case law of judicial administrative courts deem this ground for denial inapplicable if the request or application refers to information on which administrative decisions are based.[224] Also, Article 14(k) provides that the right of access must be limited by confidentiality or secrecy requirements in decision-making processes. However, this limit does not apply automatically. Rather, it is necessary to strike a fair balance between the risk for the right of access and the public interest involved in the disclosure of public information. This limit would not be applicable since access to the data kept by the tax administration (TA) is essential for the parties to be able to enforce their rights or be informed of public action.

[223] Supreme Court Judgment of 24 February 2021 (Appeal 2162/2020).
[224] National High Court Judgment of 25 July 2017 (Appeal 46/2017).

In the case at hand, Mr Paine qualifies as a party concerned, seeking to understand the grounds for an administrative decision in order to subsequently challenge it. Unreasonably denying access to that information could interfere with Mr Paine's right of defence, but it would also violate the right of access provided as a generally applicable individual right in the LTBG. It should be borne in mind that Article 53 LPAC grants any parties concerned the right to access the file:

> The parties concerned in administrative procedures shall be entitled to access and obtain a copy of the documents kept within the procedures.

It is also worth noting that the right of access allows the parties concerned to verify whether public authorities have information on the party, as well as the origin and the purpose for storage, according to Act 3/2018 on Personal Data Protection and Digital Rights (*Ley Orgánica 3/2018, de 5 de diciembre, de Protección de Datos Personales y garantía de los derechos digitales*).

Under this threefold entitlement, the information specifically included in the file and any other information that could constitute grounds for the relevant decision must be accessible. Therefore, a Spanish court would order the TA to make the information available. The court could only uphold the TA's arguments for denial if the information specifically qualified as privileged or confidential, *quod non*.

J. Switzerland

AF

The principle of self-determination over personal data stipulated in Article 13 para 2 of the Federal Constitution ('Every person has the right to be protected against the misuse of their personal data') establishes the right to access one's personal data. Exceptions are possible if there are overriding public or private interests.

Henceforth, access to the personal data concerning Mr Paine held by the tax administration should be granted to him, provided that there are no overriding public or private interests.

K. United Kingdom

GA and CM

This is a relatively straightforward scenario from the perspective of UK law, where two main points can be made. The first concerns the workings of data protection legislation (primarily the Data Protection Act 2018); and the second concerns the rules of disclosure that apply when legal proceedings have been initiated. A further, ancillary point concerns the relationship between the data protection regime and legal proceedings.

In terms of the Data Protection Act 2018—which is based upon, and gives effect, to the GDPR (now called the 'UK GDPR', post-Brexit)—this would be read across the relevant tax provisions to guarantee Mr Paine's right of access to the data, unless his request falls within one of the exemptions under the Act. As things stand, it appears that the tax authority claims only that the relevant tax law does not require disclosure, so it can be assumed that it is not relying upon one or more of the exemptions in the Act. In those circumstances, it is difficult to see how it could lawfully refuse to disclose the information.

In terms of the rules of disclosure in legal proceedings, these can be described in very short order. Public bodies are under a 'duty of candour' by which they must disclose all information that is relevant to the issues before the court, save where they apply for, and are granted, 'public interest immunity'.[225] It is difficult to see what feature of public interest immunity would be engaged here, so Mr Paine should be able to gain access to his records by means of legal proceedings. Should the tax authority not disclose the information pursuant to its duty of candour, Mr Paine would be able to make an application for discovery under the relevant rules of court and he might expect that application to be granted.

The ancillary point concerns the means by which Mr Paine would challenge the tax authority's determination. In the first instance, he would be required to raise the issue with the Information Commissioner, as that office has powers in relation to data protection and could order disclosure. Any dispute between the parties would thereafter be heard by specialist Tribunals and, on appeal, the Court of Appeal.[226] All proceedings in the Tribunal system and on appeal would fasten upon the interpretation of the Data Protection Act 2018 and the application of common law principles.

In sum: Mr Paine should be able to obtain access to his requested material as a matter of right under the Data Protection Act 2018 and/or under the relevant rules of procedure if bringing legal proceedings.

L. Venezuela

FP-F

One of the constituent elements of the right to defence in the administrative forum is *access to the file*, which means that the Public Administration is duty-bound to guarantee the administered party, throughout the procedure, access to the documented content of the administrative actions, documents, and procedures, as well as to obtain a copy of same, so that they can adequately support their arguments and defence.

According to Article 143 of the Venezuelan Constitution, all persons have the constitutional right to administrative information and access to official documents. If a sectoral norm prohibits this right, the rule in question is unconstitutional, and the public administration is therefore obliged not to apply it.

In the case in question, the tax administration prevented Mr Paine from accessing certain essential documents and applied less favourable tax regulations to him without giving him access to the dossier or informing him of the reasoning applied by the tax

[225] On the duty of candour see, eg, *R (Bancoult) v Secretary of State for Foreign and Commonwealth Affairs* [2016] UKSC 35, [2017] AC 300; and on public interest immunity see *Conway v Rimmer* [1968] 2 WLR 1535 (then called 'Crown privilege').

[226] Data Protection Act 2018, Part 5; and Tribunals, Courts and Enforcement Act 2007, § 13.

administration. This is a violation of due process whereby, in order to properly defend themselves, all persons have the right to access the corresponding evidence, which constitutes one of the constituent elements of the right to defence in the administrative forum.

However, Mr Paine also requested access to the personal data information concerning him on which the prosecutor based the decision.

In this sense, given the refusal of the tax administration to provide information on Mr Paine's personal data, he could file the *habeas data* appeal provided in Article 28 of the Venezuelan Constitution as a procedural protection of the citizens' constitutional right to access personal information.

Habeas data is a writ in any law suit against a public authority that prevents or denies, ignores, or evades the guarantee of access to information and personal data, and from this point of view, those who seize a court to obtain the update, rectification, or destruction of information or data if they are erroneous, incomplete, false, and/or unlawfully affect their rights.

VIII. Case 7—The unjustified denial of a licence

A. Austria

SS

In Austria, the planning, construction, and operation of terrestrial multiplex platforms are put out for tender.[227] Because the AVG applies, the authority's decision to reject an application has to be explained whenever the party's point of view is not fully shared, or decisions are taken on the objections or submissions of the persons involved.[228] If the authority's reasoning is faulty, the administrative court may provide a statement regarding the reasons by itself.[229] The Constitutional Court ruled that a decision by an authority will be deemed arbitrary if sound reasoning is lacking.[230] If the administrative court cannot decide on the merits, it may, in principle, annul the authority's decision.

B. China

XS

The court will endorse the claim brought by TUP, and annul the rejection of TUP's application.

The Regulation on Open Government Information provides, in Article 13, that 'all government information must be disclosed, except the information specified in articles 14, 15, and 16 of this Regulation'.[231]

According to Article 16 of this regulation:

> Internal administrative information, including personnel management, logistics management, internal processes, and information in other such areas, may be not disclosed.
>
> In-process information such as deliberation records, draft documents, consultation letters, requests for instruction, and other such in-process information, as well as administrative law enforcement case files, may be not disclosed. Particular laws or regulations provide that the information above shall be disclosed.[232]

The record of the tender procedure could be considered to be 'in-process information'. However, we have shown, in Case 6, that the Supreme People's Court does not

[227] § 23 und § 25a *Bundesgesetz über audiovisuelle Mediendienste—Audiovisuelle Mediendienste-Gesetz—* AMD-G (Audiovision Media Act), Orig Vers: BGBl I No 84/2001.

[228] § 58 (2) AVG.

[229] Schulev-Steindl (n 5) 261.

[230] VfSlg 16.333/2001.

[231] 除本条例第十四条、第十五条、第十六条规定的政府信息外，政府信息应当公开。

[232] 行政机关的内部事务信息，包括人事管理、后勤管理、内部工作流程等方面的信息，可以不予公开。
行政机关在履行行政管理职能过程中形成的讨论记录、过程稿、磋商信函、请示报告等过程性信息以及行政执法案卷信息，可以不予公开。法律、法规、规章规定上述信息应当公开的，从其规定。

consider in-process information as an absolute exception from disclosure.[233] More precisely, once the decision is made, the information that was under investigation, discussion, and processing is no longer in-process information. The rejection of TUP's application will be considered as an improper obstruction to the plaintiff exercising his or her right to access information.

Another question is whether the record of the tender procedure could be considered as 'internal administrative information'. As such, the Supreme People's Court made a definition of internal administrative information in its commentary on another guiding case relating to Open Government Information.[234] According to the Supreme Court, internal administrative information refers to 'general policies which have no direct effect outside of the administration'[235] or to 'non-final opinions on individual cases'.[236] The purpose of not disclosing internal administrative information is to 'ensure the communication within the administration or between different administrative organs, so that administrative employees can speak freely and express their true thoughts without misgiving'.[237] If the information could 'have an impact on the rights and obligations of the interested person',[238] it is not a piece of internal administrative information.

In application of this case law, the record of the tender procedure, which can have an impact on TUP's rights and obligations, will not be considered internal administrative information and should be disclosed.

C. France

SS

The regulation of the audio-visual sector is another example of a juncture between the general and the special laws of administrative procedure. French audio-visual law was long grounded exclusively in the area of the terrestrial frequencies necessary for the transmission of radio and television programmes. Since the 2000s and the technical development linked to digital technology, the balance of the sector has been profoundly modified. The transmission of audio-visual programmes is no longer the concern of terrestrial media alone.

Bearing this in mind, it can be noted that in France the distribution of frequencies for broadcasting via terrestrial, mobile, or satellite media is carried out by a number of institutions: the Prime Minister's office, the 'national frequencies agency', the *Conseil supérieur de l'audiovisuel* ('high audio-visual council'—CSA, for audio-visual communication services), and the 'regulatory authority for electronic communications and

[233] Supreme People's Court, guiding cases relating to Open Government Information (最高人民法院公政府信息公开十大案例) on 13 September 2014, No 5.

[234] Supreme People's Court, guiding cases relating to Open Government Information (最高人民法院公政府信息公开十大案例) on 13 September 2014, No 6.

[235] 对外部不产生直接约束力的普遍政.

[236] 对个案的非终极性意见.

[237] 保护机构内部或不同机构之间的交流，从而使官员能够畅所欲言，毫无顾忌地表达自己的真实想法.

[238] 对行政相对人的权利义务产生影响.

posts' (mobile telephony). We shall focus here on the laws and regulations regarding refusals to allocate frequencies by the CSA.

For private audio-visual undertakings, the conduct of business requires authorization to use frequencies. After a long battle in the courts, the frequencies were placed within the public domain of the state (CGPPP, Article L. 211-17). Authorizations are contemplated by Law No 86-1067 of 30 September 1986 on freedom of communication (for radio, Articles 29 and 29-1; for television, Articles 30 and 30-1). These authorizations are for private use of the public domain (CGPPP, Article L. 2124-26).[239] They are, however, subject to a different legal regime from that of traditional authorizations. Since 1986, awards have been made following a procedure of publication and competitive selection managed by the CSA. The 1986 law requires the latter to state the reasons for an adverse decision (Article 32). The law thus constitutes a specific text imposing such a requirement. The obligation, therefore, results neither from the general law constituted by the CRPA, which prescribes the cases of obligatory grounding of the decision outside specific legislation (CRPA, Article L. 211-1 to L. 211-8), nor from the rule, still valid in French law, whereby the author of an administrative decision is not bound to inform those concerned of the grounds.[240]

The law of 30 September 1986 fully governs the question of the statement of grounds for decisions to refuse a licence. It states that refusals are to be grounded and notified to the applicants within one month following the publication of the authorizations. The grounds may be conveyed in a summary report explaining the regulatory authority's decisions (Article 32 above).

The *Conseil d'Etat* has handed down several rulings showing how grounding is monitored. In a first decision in *Association Radio-Panoramas*, it deemed insufficient the regulatory authority's statement that it had examined all the authorization requests for the Paris region, its reminder of the points focused on in the overall examination, its affirmation that by reason of the number and characteristics of the project in competition, and the very limited number of available frequencies, it was not possible, in view of the criteria, to grant the authorization. For the administrative court, the ground

> does not specify the factual elements that the commission considered in order to deem that, in view of this criterion, the application should be rejected.[241]

Several annulments have been decided for lack of a statement of grounds.[242]

One result of the obligation to state grounds is the illegality of an implicit refusal, by nature ungrounded; another is the impossibility for the authority to proceed to rectify

[239] For the definition, *supra* France, Case No 3.

[240] Already seen in CE, 30 April 1880, *Harouel et Morin c/min Guerre, Rec* p 419; Cons Const, 27 November 2001, dec No 2001-451 DC, consid 40.

[241] CE, 18 May 1990, No 105061, *Assoc Radio-Panoramas*, annulment of the refusal; *Rec* p 127; same day, CE, 18 May 1990, No 105293, *Association arménienne d'aide sociale*, annulment for the same reasons.

[242] eg CE, 12 July 1993, *Entreprise unipersonnelle à responsabilité limitée Thot Communication, Rec* p 217.

this defect with an express justified decision.[243] Notification of the rejection must be given within the one-month period mentioned in the law.[244]

On the juncture between general law and special law, the *Conseil d'Etat* has also specified that the decision granting authorization for the use of frequencies is not within the field of application of the CRPA (it is not an unfavourable decision as understood in the provisions of the law of 11 July 1979, so reasons need not be given in virtue of this law).[245]

Thus, under French law, TTU may invoke an infringement of Article 32 of the law of 30 September 30 1986, which prescribes the obligation to give reasons in order to obtain, with marked success, the annulment of the rejection.

D. Germany

DS

The decision on the result of the free frequencies tender is an administrative act of the competent regulatory authority, the *Landesmedienanstalt*, based on the law of the Land, within the legal framework of the broadcasting treaty between all the German Länder (*Rundfunkstaatsvertrag*) and determined by the legal criteria. Taking the example of the law of Bremen (*Landesmediengesetz* of 17 July 2012), firstly, there is a licence from the broadcasting programme (§ 6), with conditions and a procedure primarily regulated by the law. If a licence is refused, there is no doubt that this decision has to be motivated and that, if challenged, it must be reviewed by an administrative court.

If there are free frequencies, the second step is a tender procedure between the licensed public law broadcasting institutes and the Land's institute of media (*Landesmedienanstalt*) for private broadcasting enterprises—like TUP—with programme licences (§ 25 of the law). The potential institutes will be informed by the government chancellery (*Senatskanzlei*) and can present their programmes. If there is only one application, the frequency is attributed to this; if there are more applications than available frequencies, the chancellery strives to find an arrangement. If successful, the frequency is attributed according to the arrangement. If there is no arrangement, an arbitration committee is set up, half of which is made up of the public law broadcasting institutes concerned and half by the Land's institute of media, with an additional president chosen by the other members by a qualified majority; a representative of the chancellery also participates with a consulting vote. The arbitration committee decides, basing its actions on legal rules. The chancellery can make objections and ask for changes to the decision. The arbitration committee then has to decide again. If there is no arrangement, the decision has to be motivated (§ 39 VwVfG) and may be challenged.

[243] CE, 25 March 1994, No 124765 142516.

[244] CE, 18 November 2011, No 321410: in this case, five months after publication in the *Journal Officiel* of the list of authorizations granted.

[245] CE, 12 May 2003, *Sté TF1*, Nos 247353 and 248337.

Lastly, in a third step, the Land's institute of media has to assign the free frequencies to the private broadcasting enterprises with licensed programmes asking for assignment. For this step again, there is a procedure regulated in § 29 of the law with criteria for the decision set out in § 30. Therefore, if there is a conflict between different candidates, the administrative act of assignment has to be motivated and may be reviewed by the administrative court.

Thus, in German law, TUP's standpoint would be founded because the general administrative procedure act binds the sector-specific legislation, and the court would endorse the claim, obliging the media institute to present a motivated decision.

E. Greece

TF

The reasoning generally consists of a statement of the rules regulating the issuance of the administrative act and their interpretation, the factual and legal conditions in view of which the issuance of the act is imposed or permitted in the application of these norms, the assessment of the relevant facts, and the considerations of the administrative organ that have led to the issuance of the administrative act or omission to issue it. Consequently, the contents of the reasoning may concern either the lawfulness or the merits and advisability of the act when this is discretionary. Related to the reasoning is the burden of proof of the existence of the facts, which are a prerequisite for issuing the administrative act.

The purpose of the reasoning is to enable both the individual and the court to examine to what extent the administrative act has been issued to serve the public interest or to safeguard the individual and how far it is in accord or in harmony with the legal norms determining the framework of the principle of legality.

In principle, according to Article 17 of the Administrative Process Code, a statement of reasons is required in relation to all individual administrative acts. Of course, not every infringement of these norms of administrative process constitutes a ground for annulment but only the omission of actions characterized as substantive, which is a matter for the judgment of the competent administrative court.

Thus, it has been ruled that the following serve as criteria for shaping this kind of judgment: (a) the significance of the norm, (i) the protection of the individual, since it enables him to enlighten the administration regarding the case concerning him or to exercise the right to a prior hearing, also guaranteeing impartial judgment of his case, (ii) for the proper operation of the Administration with a view to serving the public interest, (iii) for the judicial review of the act, and (b) for the normative content of the act.

In this case, the Communications Regulatory Authority (CRA) refused to provide the participant, ie Totally Unnecessary Productions, with a statement of reasons for rejecting his application. As a result, the participant filed a petition asking for the annulment of this act before the competent administrative court on the grounds of the failure to state reasons.

Consequently, in light of the above, the competent court would endorse the participant's demand and order the annulment of the act. That is, the CRA will have to issue the same act anew, this time in accordance with lawful process.

F. Italy

MS

In Italy, the issue at hand would be addressed on the basis of the principles and rules on the statement of reasons for administrative measures, under which the Italian court could annul the TUP's exclusion.

The requirement to state reasons is one of the cornerstones of the Italian APA (Law No 241 of 7 August 1990). Article 3 establishes this obligation for every measure issued (excluding regulatory or general measures), and that, with regard to the outcome of the investigation, this statement must specify the factual basis and legal grounds for the decision.

Administrative bodies must state the reasoning they follow in reaching their decision as a means of showing that it has closely complied with the law and the principles and rules for conducting the procedure as laid down in its own acts and regulations.

The complete absence of reasons—or giving only insufficient ones ('inadequate statement of reasons')—render administrative measures unlawful, as they are vitiated by a breach of law and abuse of discretion ('*excès de pouvoir*') under Article 21-*octies* of Law No 241/1990, and will lead to annulment by the administrative court.

This general rule has been specified even more explicitly in case law with regard to tendering procedures, namely any administrative procedure involving the use of competitive mechanisms. For example, competitive exams for public employment, public procurement, or procedures such as the one found in our case.

In all these examples, the law usually sets the general criteria by which the winner or winners are to be selected. However, the actual specification of these criteria is left to the administration, which acts through invitations to tender, calls for competition, or similar acts.

These acts must contain binding specifications from which the administration may not subsequently deviate. As their aim is to define the administration's discretionary powers, they can be regarded as self-imposed constraints or limits for public administration. Hence, their purpose is to make the actions of administrations more predictable and ensure effective competition among those participating in the procedures.

Obviously, even in these cases, in its final decision on the procedure, the administration is required to state the reasons for applying the criteria to the various competitors and cannot simply cite the criteria without providing any explanation. These considerations should evidently emerge from the procedure reports, especially when the decisions are made by an assessment panel specifically appointed for the purpose.

According to case law, the extent of the obligation to provide reasons is inversely proportional to the level of precision, clarity, and specification of the criteria and sub-criteria.[246]

In other words, if there are few criteria, worded in general terms and leaving ample discretion, the administration will be required to provide explicit and detailed reasons for awarding each competitor a higher or lower score for each criterion in its final decision.

[246] See, among the many, Council of State, Div VI, No 2221, 2 April 2020; Council of State, Div V, No 6103, 5 September 2019; Council of State, Div IV, No 5091, 9 November 2015, Council of State, Div V, No 2430, 13 May 2014; Council of State, Div V, No 2214, 19 April 2013.

Instead, if there are numerous criteria, appropriately broken down into analytical sub-criteria and clearly and unequivocally worded, the requirement to give reasons can be reduced so as to allow numerical reasoning to be considered sufficient. Numerical reasoning consists in simply declaring a score within the range established for each of the criteria named in the tender with no need for any further verbal explanation.[247]

In summary, in most cases, it is obligatory to give reasons for a measure, with only a few explicit exceptions established by law or identified through case law. Also, in the case of tendering procedures, administrative bodies must first specify the criteria for selecting a possible winner. Then, in the final decision, authorities must explain how these criteria were applied to each of the bids received. If the criteria are extremely precise and detailed, the reasons may merely consist of the score in relation to points allocated for each of the sub-criteria.

On these grounds, as we mentioned, the Italian court would uphold the TUP's appeal and annul its exclusion from the tender due to the failure to provide adequate reasons.

G. Romania

D-C D

This case raises two questions: a) is there a general duty to provide reasons for administrative decisions? and (b) is there such a duty according to the special rules on licensing radio frequencies?

As to the first question, the answer is 'no'. There is no general duty to give reasons in Romanian administrative law, mainly due to the lack of an Administrative Procedure Law (or Code). There are scattered provisions regarding the duty to justify administrative decisions: for instance, administrative acts issued following a petition[248] need to provide legal but not factual grounds.

However, the doctrine has always stressed the importance of justification as a principle of administrative procedure, and the courts have embodied this principle even in the absence of written legislation.[249] In this context, there are enough legal sources to consider that the duty to give reasons is essential to due process and that the lack of a sufficient reason renders the decision unlawful. In addition, applying the principle of proportionality enshrined in Article 9 of the Administrative Code would require the measure to be proportionate to the purpose pursued.

As to the second question, we should first of all note that radio frequencies represent an interesting example of limited rights, as in this case, the scarcity arises from both natural limitations and technological factors. Some limitations are inherent to the level of technological development that exists at a certain moment. Moreover, the regulatory regime for the use of the radio spectrum is soundly developed under the EU law. In addition, the legal regime includes both EU and national rules concerning

[247] On the sufficiency of numerical reasoning in these cases, see Council of State, Div III, No 4871, 10 July 2019.

[248] Government Ordinance No 27/2002, Art 13.

[249] See the comment of Romania, Case 3.

electronic communications: Directive 2002/21/CE and Directive 2009/140/CE, Law No 504/2002 on the audio-visual field, GEO No 111/2011 on electronic communications, as well as secondary legislation issued by ANCOM (national regulatory agency).

According to Law No 504/2002, ANCOM awards radio broadcasting licences through a tendering procedure (Article 60).

Radio frequencies can be used only after a licence is issued by ANCOM under conditions to ensure efficient use of the limited resource. These include preventing interference that could harm networks operated by others who use the radio spectrum under legal conditions, ensuring technical quality, and fulfilling other objectives of general interest. ANCOM grants the right to use the radio frequencies on a case-by-case basis, either through allocation or assignment, also monitoring the status of licence usage.

In the wording of Article 7 of Emergency Government Ordinance 22/2009 on the functioning of ANCOM,

> (2) in carrying out its attributions, ANCOM pursues the objectives set out in Articles 4–6. It shall take reasonable measures, respecting the principles of proportionality, non-discrimination, transparency, and full objectivity.

Additionally, ANCOM published a code of good practices at the start of its regulatory activity in 2003.[250] It contains a set of principles with practical applicability, designed to ensure the efficient implementation of the regulatory framework. Some of these principles were already present in the existing laws,[251] while others were derived from good practice and regulatory expertise at the international level (transparency, proportionality, opportunity, predictability, and stability). A more recent programmatic document,[252] the ANCOM Strategy 2020, mentioned the principles of objectivity, transparency, non-discrimination, and proportionality in its *regulatory* activities. It is unclear whether these principles are also applicable when *adjudicating*, namely, when awarding licences, so there is no express mention of the duty to give reasons in ANCOM licensing decisions.

That these principles are applicable when awarding licences is reaffirmed in Article 26ff of the OUG 111/2011 on electronic communications. Licences for the use of radio frequencies are awarded through an *open, objective, transparent, non-discriminatory, and proportional procedure* (Article 26). When the number of licences to be awarded is limited, allocation is decided via a competitive or comparative selection based on an objective, transparent, non-discriminatory, and proportional procedure, which should not limit, hinder, or distort competition. Competitive selection is a procedure for awarding a licence to use radio frequencies whereby the right to use these frequencies is awarded to the bidder offering the largest amount of money for the licence.

[250] ANCOM, 'Document de poziție privind strategia de reglementare a sectorului comunicațiilor electronice din România pentru perioada 2007–2010 [Position document regarding the regulatory strategy for the electronic communication sector, Romania, 2007–2010], 49–51, online at <http://www.ancom.org.ro/uploads/links_files/strategie_2007-2010.pdf> accessed June 2023.

[251] Law No 504/2002 (on audio-visual activities), GEO No 111/2011 on electronic communications.

[252] ANCOM, 'Strategia ANCOM 2020 (ANCOM Strategy 2020)' online at <https://www.ancom.ro/uploads/forms_files/Strategia_de_Reglementare_20201469688911.pdf> accessed June 2023.

The government sets the minimum price through an official decision. Additionally, the winner must meet some technical, administrative, or financial requirements as prequalification criteria. On the other hand, comparative selection is a procedure to award the licence for using radio frequencies to the applicant who ranks first based on the bid. The evaluation is conducted using a set of pre-established technical, administrative, or financial criteria.

There is no express provision on the duty to give reasons for rejecting licence applications. However, the review procedure established by ANCOM for competitive/comparative procedures is quite simple: aggrieved economic entities can lodge a complaint with ANCOM, which acts as a review body (OUG 111/2011). Members of the award commission may not sit on the review commission. In its administrative appeal decisions, ANCOM must state the legal and factual reasoning for its decision (Article 116(9) of the OUG 111/2011). The highest court of appeal is the Administrative Law Court, under the 2004 Law on Judicial Review.[253]

Returning to the case study at hand, in the absence of an express duty to justify the decision to grant or deny a licence, the general principles of transparency and proportionality apply, so the court can invoke these principles to annul a decision when no reasoning has been provided.

Awarding a licence without previously publishing the criteria used to identify the best offers would infringe the principle of proportionality and transparency.

H. Serbia

MM

In Serbia, *Totally Unnecessary Productions* (TUP) would apply for a licence to the Regulatory Authority for Electronic Media under the conditions set by the Law on Electronic Media,[254] whose work is governed by that Law. The principles set by the LGAP are also applicable to this procedure. The LGAP states that reasons must be provided in a separate part of the administrative act, the rationale. According to Article 141, the rationale must be intelligible and contain a brief outline of the party's claim, the facts and evidence of the basis on which the facts have been established, the decisive reasons in the assessment of individual pieces of evidence, regulations, and reasons which, in view of the established facts, refer to the decision in the wording and the reasons why a request or proposal has been rejected. It is further prescribed that the rationale must also indicate why the authority has deviated from the rulings previously issued regarding the same or similar administrative matters. Concerning this case in particular there are relevant rules for discretionary decision-making. In these cases, the rationale must indicate the legislation granting the authority the power to do

[253] D C Dragoş, B Neamtu, and Raluca Suciu, 'The Allocation of Gambling Licences, Radio Frequencies and CO2 Emission Permits in Romania' in P Adriaanse, F van Ommeren, W den Ouden, and J Wolswinkel (eds), *Scarcity and the State II. Member State Reports on Gambling Licences, Radio Frequencies and CO2 Emission Permits* (Intersentia 2016) 203–41.

[254] The analysis is based on the Law applicable at the time of writing in 2020. Law on Electronic Media, Official Gazette No 83/2014, 6/2016.

so, the reasons taken into account in the decision-making, and the scope and purpose of exercising the power to make discretionary decisions.

The Law on Electronic Media sets detailed rules for granting licences on the basis of a public tender (Articles 92–96). The licence granting the right to provide television broadcasting services, as well as radio media services via terrestrial analogue and digital transmission, is issued on the basis of a public tender announced by the Regulator in accordance with the Law (based on the availability of radio frequencies for terrestrial analogue transmission). The regulator adopts more detailed rules which determine the minimum technical, organizational and other conditions related to the programme that must be met by the applicants for the public competition, ie the holders of the licence for the provision of media services. According to the Law, the Regulator issues a (general) act determining non-discriminatory, objective, and measurable criteria for decision-making, which correspond to the activities for which a permit is issued and prescribes the application form for the competition. The conditions and criteria determined by the act may not be changed during the procedure according to the announced public competition. It is further envisaged that, within fifteen days from the day the deadline for submission of applications expires, the regulator must publish, in the manner in which the announcement for the public competition was published, a list of all applicants whose applications are complete and submitted within the stipulated deadline. The regulator makes a decision on issuing a licence in accordance with the established criteria and prescribed conditions. If several entities who meet the prescribed conditions for the provision of media services have applied for the same coverage area, the Regulator gives priority to the one that, it has reasonably concluded, based on the submitted documentation, will achieve higher quality and diversity of content. If the applicant has already provided a media service, the Regulator, when deciding, will also take into account their practice in fulfilling the obligations of the prescribed laws and respecting the conditions contained in the licence. The regulator publishes the list of persons who have acquired the right to provide media services in the manner in which the announcement for the public competition was published, without delay and no later than fifteen days from the day the decision was made (Article 96). According to this Law, in the event of an administrative dispute initiated upon a lawsuit filed against a decision made in the procedure for issuing a licence concerning the provision of media services, imposing measures or revoking a licence, the court may not resolve the administrative matter by a judgment (full jurisdiction dispute) (Article 42). Therefore, TUP would be able to challenge the decision on the ground of lack of reasons, which would constitute a serious breach of procedural norms, and it is expected that the Administrative Court would annul the decision and order the Regulator to adopt a new decision clearly stating the reasons.

I. Spain

IMD

Tenders to award audio-visual licences are governed by Act 7/2010 on Audiovisual Communications (*Ley 7/2010, de 31 de marzo, General de la Comunicación Audiovisual*), requiring calls to include specific objective criteria to be considered in the award procedure, eg the participants' experience, professional standing, and their available means to operate under the licence. Although the licence must be granted by the competent audio-visual authority, it is up to the National Audio-visual Board to submit a report on both the terms and conditions of the tender and the proposals submitted by the participants.

Generally, the duty to provide supporting arguments and reasons for an administrative decision has a twofold dimension: first, the actual duty to give reasons, and second, the duty to disclose the documents kept on record and used to make the decision.

As discussed above, the obligation to state reasons for any detrimental decision that may limit an individual's right or legitimate interest is a general requirement under Article 35 LPAC. According to Article 35 LPAC, the required reasoning, including the facts and supporting arguments, must be brief, ie an outline. Ultimately, it is the act itself that must include its supporting arguments and reasons. Referring to the report that must be issued by the National Audio-visual Board would suffice to fulfil this requirement (the so-called reasoning by proxy or *in aliunde*).[255] Also, paragraph 2 of Article 35 is worded as follows:

> The reasoning for any acts terminating or deciding on competitive procedures and tenders must be in line with the provisions governing the calls. In any case, the supporting arguments and reasons for any decisions must be clearly established in the procedure.

This is a more stringent duty to state reasons since it requires the CRA to explain how it has applied the criteria to TUP's proposal and, more broadly, how it has assessed the remaining proposals.

Thus, there must be a logical and rational link between the content of the records, the final decision, and its supporting arguments and reasons. This obligation stems from the principle of—and the right to—good or sound administration, as stated in the aforesaid Supreme Court Judgment of 4 April 2021.

In addition, the right to access the record and, more generally, the right to access public information (or, even more so, its actual enforcement by duly stating reasons for the decision on TUP's comments),[256] could also support TUP's claim

[255] In legal English, this Latin expression is more often rendered as *aliunde*: eg 'evidence *aliunde*', meaning extrinsic or external evidence.

[256] Supreme Court Judgment of 22 July 2015, legal basis 1:

> The appellant public body claims that the public consultation (*información pública*) was duly conducted during the rule-making procedure for the Territorial Plan [...]. However, the appellant disregards the substance of the public consultation mechanism under Art 4(e) of the Land Use Act (*Real Decreto Legislativo 2/2008*) and the actual scope of public consultations according to the case law [...]. It does not suffice to formally request the parties to submit comments. Rather, public bodies must give a duly reasoned response, with supporting arguments, which they did not in the case at hand, thereby violating Art 4(e) of the Land Use Act.

Supreme Court Judgment of 6 October 2015:

> Ultimately, as previously declared by this Supreme Court Chamber in various rulings, including the Judgments of 25 February 2003 (appeal 6876/1999), 16 February 2009 (appeal 9414/2004)

to know how the bodies involved in the call acted and, in particular, how they established and applied the objective criteria to award the licence. The absence of a sector-specific provision does not preclude the application of the general administrative procedure rules and the right to access public information. In this case, the court would examine whether: (i) the decision's supporting arguments are sufficient and (ii) the denial to disclose information about the decision-making process violates the LPAC or the LTBG. If the court found a violation, it would consider, regarding (i) that the decision is voidable on grounds of an insufficient reasoning and (ii) that the CRA should allow access to the requested information. However, it would not invalidate or annul CRA's decision. The court would simply declare the right to access public information, ordering the CRA to disclose the relevant information. Only if there were a direct connection between the lack of access to the information and TUP's inability to find a legal basis for challenging the award would there be a violation of TUP's rights of defence, and the claim would thus be upheld.

Focusing on this approach, it should be borne in mind that the Constitutional Court has found that a party is without defence if deprived of its right to submit comments or objections, produce evidence and, if appropriate, contest the decision-making body's arguments, actually and effectively undermining the party's interests. In other words, there will be a violation of a party's rights of defence if there is actual and substantial defencelessness. This can occur if the administrative act is ill-founded or if the party does not know the reasons for a given administrative decision. However, it would be necessary to verify whether the party is unaware of the reasons for the relevant administrative decision and if, as a result, the party concerned has been rendered defenceless. The Supreme Court's case law also takes this approach. Accordingly, Articles 105(b) CE and 53(a) LPAC would support TUP's claim (i) to access any information within the records, including, where appropriate, the information on the assessments of other participants' proposals; and (ii) that the decision-making body issue the relevant copies unless otherwise provided for by the applicable legislation. If this was not the case, there would be no reason to prevent TUP gaining access to the information, so CRA's decision would be unjustified and unlawful. However, in order to invalidate CRA's decision, it would be necessary to prove, having regard to the facts and circumstances of the case, that TUP has been rendered substantially defenceless. If so, CRA's decision would be considered voidable, ie subject to annulment if so requested by the parties concerned. Otherwise, TUP's claim would be dismissed.

and 15 March 2012 (appeal 6335/2008), failing to respond to the comments submitted during the public consultation stage entails a violation of the right to be heard and thus qualifies as an omission of an essential procedural mechanism. In fact, the strict fulfilment of this procedural requirement does not only rely on the mere submission and receipt of stakeholders' comments. Also, public authorities must carefully read and specifically respond, duly giving reasons, explaining why the comments are accepted or rejected. This is the only way the public consultation requirement, aimed at enabling citizen participation, will be deemed fully complied with.

J. Switzerland

AF

The right to be heard under Article 29 para 2 of the Federal Constitution implies the right to a statement of reasons for both administrative and judicial decisions.[257] The purpose of this right is to allow the party to verify that the authority was not guided by unjustifiable or unwarranted arguments or facts. The requirement to state reasons relates to both the facts and the reasoning of the decision.[258] It applies in all legal fields, including those, and especially those that leave a wide margin of appreciation to the authorities.

Thereupon, the competent national court would endorse the claim brought by TUP and annul the rejection of TUP's application due to the lack of reasons based on the record.

K. United Kingdom

GA and CM

This scenario raises the question of when (and why) the courts will impose a common law duty to give reasons in the absence of a statutory duty to do so. The historical position has been that the courts have not imposed any general common law duty *in lieu* of a statutory requirement, largely because of the burden that it was thought this might place upon decision makers (ie it could 'demand an appearance of unanimity where there can be diversity; call for the articulation of sometimes inexpressible value judgments; and offer an invitation to the captious to comb the reasons for previously unsuspected grounds of challenge').[259] However, while it is true that there still is no general duty to give reasons, the common law now regularly imposes duties in a wide range of circumstances in the interests of 'fairness'.[260] While the courts acknowledge that there is uncertainty about the factors that will trigger the common law duty, they have explained that all depends on context and the nature of the statutory scheme that co-exists with the common law. Conceptually, the concern has been for 'good administration' and 'transparency' in decision-making, where it has been said that

> a principal justification for imposing the duty was seen as the need to reveal any such error as would entitle the court to intervene, and so make effective the right to challenge the decision by judicial review.[261]

257 ATF 138 I 232, c 5.1.

258 ATF 142 II 154, c 4.2; 138 I 171, c 3.3.

259 *R v Higher Education Funding Council, ex p Institute of Dental Surgery* [1994] 1 All ER 651, 665, Sedley J.

260 *R v Home Secretary, ex parte Doody* [1994] 1 AC 531.

261 *R (CPRE Kent) v Dover District Council* [2017] UKSC 79, [2018] 1 WLR 108.

It has also been said that, where there is a common law duty to give reasons, the reasons that are given must be '*adequate and intelligible*'[262] so that an individual might understand them (the same threshold applies in relation to a duty under statute law).

Set against this background, TUP makes for an interesting case, and arguments might be made either way. Certainly, the fact that this is a licence case might be said to bring it within the statements of principle in *McInnes v Onslow Fane*, as discussed under scenario 3 above. It will be recalled that Megarry V-C there made a distinction between three categories of cases and noted that the common law would be less demanding when an individual is merely applying for a licence for the first time. On one reading, that is precisely what has happened here, and *McInnes* might therefore mean that TUP could expect no more than that its application would be processed in the light of the criteria that were adopted by the CRA. As against that, the fact that the CRA is making decisions in an area of undoubted public interest might mean that the court would be more inclined to demand transparency in its processes. The point here is that, to the extent that *McInnes* sought to shield public bodies from overly burdensome procedural obligations across all types of cases, this is a standalone decision-making process that governs the award of national radio frequencies. In those circumstances, a court may well hold that reasons should be given not just because of fairness towards TUP but also because of the public interest that is engaged by the decision. Judicial oversight would in that way be possible.

To recap: there is no general common law duty that could automatically be pleaded by TUP, but it could arguably rely upon the demands of fairness and the particular context of this case to be given such reasons. This is notably true given the engagement of a point of very real public interest.

L. Venezuela

FP-F

For an administrative act to be considered valid, it must have been decided on the basis of certain factual and legal criteria that the Administration has to take into account and which must necessarily be expressed in the text of the administrative act so grounds must be provided. These must be made known to the interested party.

Venezuela's Law of Administrative Procedure obliges the Public Administration to justify its decisions, ie to explain and set forth the reasons in fact and law that support the administrative act; consequently, the factual and legal basis of the administrative resolution must be reasonably explained in the same text.

Giving reasons for administrative acts guarantees the right of legitimate defence, with all unreasoned acts being deemed a violation of this right and a ground for its annulment by the courts.

Indeed, according to Article 18 para 5 of the Law of Administrative Procedure, an administrative act must contain a 'succinct expression of the facts, the reasons that have been posited and the pertinent legal bases'.

[262] *R v Mental Health Tribunal, ex p Pickering* [1986] 1 All ER 99, 102, Forbes J.

Giving reasons is, therefore, the formal expression of the reasons for the act, and it is mandatory for all administrative acts, except those of procedure, except in cases where the procedural act is relevant for the proper exercise of the individual's right to defence.

That said, we believe that in the case in hand, the contentious-administrative tribunal would annul the decision of the Communications Regulatory Authority (CRC) for not stating reasons and, therefore, the lack of justification, which prevents the company from knowing the reasons for the rejection of its offer, violating both the principles of legal certainty and legality, as well as that of the transparency of administrative action—one of the essential principles governing its execution, especially with regard to bidding processes for awarding contracts, concessions, etc.

The CRC's argument concerning the objective nature of the reason for the refusal would be rejected because it provides no exemption from justification. Hence, as we understand it, the contentious-administrative court could annul the administrative act, revoke it, and roll back the bidding procedure to the moment prior to the rejection of the award.

IX. Case 8—Failure to consult a stakeholder before setting new tariffs

A. Austria

SS

The competent national authority in Austria is Schienen-Control GmbH, a company organized under private law and entrusted with state authority. According to § 78 (1) Railroad Act (‘*Eisenbahngesetz*’—EisbG), Schienen-Control GmbH has to apply the AVG in its official procedures. While train operators may levy tariffs on passengers for the use of railway services, they are also obliged to pay tariffs for the use of railway infrastructure.

Tariffs for the use of passenger services are set by the railway companies themselves and are only reviewed by the regulatory authority to ensure they are lawful. In this procedure, there is generally no right for other railway companies to be heard.

As tariffs for the use of railway infrastructure are set, a railway company that wants to use the railway infrastructure and the railway company that authorizes its use of the railway infrastructure have to negotiate the tariffs. Schienen-Control GmbH simply supervizes these negotiations and therefore has no authority to set tariffs.

However, if the authority has to decide on setting tariffs—which, as mentioned, is not the case here—and the amount of the tariffs is to be set in a specific procedure according to specific conditions (eg cost principles of effort, economic efficiency, etc), the authority must first carry out an investigation. If the railway companies are parties to this procedure, they have the right to be heard.

However, if no administrative procedure is carried out because the tariffs are to be set by way of existing regulation (as explained administrative procedures are generally concluded with the issuing of a ruling (*Bescheid*) then the railway companies would not be parties in an administrative procedure.

In such cases, the obligation of equal treatment can be derived from the constitutional principle of equal treatment according to Article 7 B-VG and even more so from Article 20 FRC.[263] Therefore, if Schienen-Control GmbH consults with one railway company, it must also do so with all the other railway companies.

B. China

XS

The court may endorse HSR’s argument and declare the DT’s act unlawful in the light of Provisional Regulation on 20 April 2019 on Major Administrative Decision Making Procedures.

In China, rail transport is not open to private providers. The service is provided by China Railway[264] which is a state-owned company. There are still no rules relating

[263] Charter of Fundamental Rights of the European Union, OJ C 326, 26 October 2012, 391.
[264] 中国国家铁路集团有限公司.

to rail infrastructure charges. However, the Government has very recently declared its intention to open up the rail transport market.[265] As in the telecommunications market there will be rules in this area. We can cite as an example the Regulation on Telecommunications.[266]

This regulation provides, in Article 27, that the infrastructure charges be decided by the Information Industry Department in conjunction with the Financial Department and the Authority for Prices, and be approved by the State Council. Such an act may constitute a 'major administrative decision' within the meaning of Provisional Regulation on Major Administrative Decision Making Procedures.

According to Article 6 of this text:

> Major administrative decisions shall be made under the principle of democratic decision-making, opinions shall be fully solicited from all parties, and it shall be guaranteed that the people participate in decision-making through various channels and forms.[267]

Article 12 of the same text states:

> The decision-making authority shall prepare draft decisions with extensive and in-depth investigation and research, comprehensive and accurate information, and full consultation and coordination.[268]

According to the Judicial Interpretation of the Supreme People's Court relating to the application of the Administrative Litigation Law, the courts can check the compliance of an administrative act with a superior regulatory administrative act.[269] The court can review the DT's act in light of these provisions. If the court considers that opinions were not 'fully solicited from all parties' and DT did not prepare its draft decision with 'full consultation and coordination', the new tariffs decision may be judged unlawful.

C. France

SS

French law in procedures of the 'notice and comment' type remains patchy.

It will be recalled that in the field of railways, a regulatory authority, the *Autorité de régulation des activités ferroviaires* ('regulatory authority for railway activities') was created in 2009 (Law No 2009-1503 of 8 December 2009 on the organization and regulation of rail transport); its competence was broadened to cover urban bus

265 State Council, Notice on Railway Construction Planning (关于进一步做好铁路规划建设工作的意见), 15 March 2021.

266 中华人民共和国电信条例.

267 作出重大行政决策应当遵循民主决策原则，充分听取各方面意见，保障人民群众通过多种途径和形式参与决策。

268 决策承办单位应当在广泛深入开展调查研究、全面准确掌握有关信息、充分协商协调的基础上，拟订决策草案。

269 Art 148 of the Judicial Interpretation.

transport and motorways under concession (Law of 6 August 2015 'for business growth and equal economic opportunities', known as the 'Macron law'), transforming it into ARAFER. Since 2019, the Authority's scope of competence has been extended to the regulation of airport fees. It is now called the *Autorité de régulation des transports* ('transport regulatory authority'—ART). The ART is the guarantor of the functioning of rail transport in keeping with conditions of competition. It has the power to advise on the documents of reference regarding the networks (DRR), which set forth the technical and contractual 'rules of the game', including fees, for access to rail infrastructure. This power enables it to monitor respect for equal access, transparency, and non-discrimination. Intended for applicants and users, the DRR provides the entire set of technical, commercial, and contractual information essential for the utilization of the rail network. The ART also issues a legally binding 'final assent' on the scheduling of fees for use, commonly known as railway charges. Article L. 2100-2 of the transport code specifies, moreover, that the state's powers in the rail transport system must be deployed 'in keeping with the principles of equity and non-discrimination'.

The ART, like industry regulatory authorities, regularly launches public consultations. The participation of regulated companies in the processes of regulation has been strongly accentuated in recent decades by means of 'participatory regulation' mechanisms.

These consultation procedures are not always framed by the legislation on the industry. The legislator has at times intervened with specific provisions. The first noteworthy and innovative initiative came from the law of 9 July 2004, which provided a framework for the consultative procedures used in the electronic communications sector: any measure 'having a significant impact on a market or affecting the interests of end users' must be published before adoption within a period allowing consultation of the interested parties of at least thirty days, barring in exceptional circumstances, in order to enable observations regarding the measure to be gathered. The outcome of the consultations is made public (Article L. 32-1-V of the CPCE, modified by ordinance No 2021-650 of 26 May 2021).

In the absence of specific rules applicable to consultations conducted in the rail transport sector, it may be appropriate to refer to general procedural law.

Indeed, in the face of the gaps in statute law, the administrative courts forged the regime of innominate consultations quite some time ago. They have been able to apply it, for example, in relation to the consultations conducted by the competition authority.[270] Traditionally the *Conseil d'Etat* has considered that the authorities can create ad hoc consultation procedures. However, these consultations are not exempt from the duty to respect legality. The administrative body may choose not to consult but, when it does consult, the consultation must be regular and respect legality.[271] In the aforementioned *Groupe Canal Plus* case, it was ruled that the parties, having obtained communication of the result of the consultation, had had sufficient time to be able to present their observations properly.

[270] CE, 21 December 2012, No 362347, *Groupe Canal Plus*.

[271] To recall a recent instance, CE, 19 July 2017, *Association citoyenne 'Pour Occitanie Pays catalan et autres'*.

The *Conseil d'Etat*, in a public report of 2011 entitled 'consult differently, participate effectively', had proposed a series of principles to better frame procedures for public participation: to respect time limits proportionate to the importance of the subject presented; to be circumscribed and to mention the main stakeholders; to be documented beforehand in a complete, precise, and objective manner; to be conducted impartially and, if possible, by a third party; to be subject to an assessment of the observations gathered; to specify the follow-up activity planned; a follow-up may possibly be planned after the entry into effect of the finally adopted measure. These proposals were not followed.

The CRPA, however, has led to progress in the state of the law. It has introduced a regime of general law to which any procedure for involving the public is subject when the authority decides, apart from the cases governed by legislative or regulatory provisions, to involve the public in drafting a reform, a project or a legal instrument (CRPA, Article L. 131-1): the authority must render public the modalities of the procedure and make the useful information available to the persons concerned, ensuring that they have a reasonable period of time to participate and that the outcome or the planned follow-up are made public at the appropriate time.

However, the law still offers insufficient protection. The public character of the procedure and the requirement of a 'reasonable time' are established. 'The making available of useful information' renders concrete a form of obligation of accessibility of information. However, the mere mention of 'persons concerned' neither gives the assurance that the opinions of all participants will be gathered nor guarantees respect for the representativeness of the consultation or the pluralism of opinions. Nor is there mention of the requirement of impartiality of the consultation, but this may, perhaps, be deduced from Article L. 100-2 of the CRPA, which requires the administrative body to guarantee 'everyone impartial treatment'.

With one important judgment, administrative case law has had the occasion to add supplementary safeguards.[272] Regularity of a consultation implies that the perimeter of the public consulted is pertinent as regards the purpose and ensures the sincerity of the consultation. The sincerity of consultation supposes that the modalities of the same prevent vitiation of the outcome by several opinions originating from one person or by opinions stated by persons from outside the defined perimeter. Sincerity constitutes a requirement deduced from the principles of equality and impartiality, general legal principles recalled by Article L. 100-2 of the CRPA.

Therefore, one may consider that, beyond the rules that may be applicable in the rail sector, the ministry's argument holding that the absence of an obligation to consult confers complete procedural freedom would not be accepted. The sincerity of the consultation seems impaired by the absence of pertinence of the perimeter of the public consulted and the marginalizing of one of the operators. Still, it will be recalled that since 2011, the administrative judge has adopted a case law policy of neutralizing procedural flaws,[273] particularly during consultation procedures. An irregularity can compromise the legality of the decision only if it has been exerted, in the case

[272] ibid.
[273] CE, ass, 23 December 2011, *Danthony et al*, prev.

concerned, an 'influence on the sense of the decision taken' or if it has deprived the interested parties of a 'safeguard'. Previous case law already restricted the annulment of spontaneous consultative procedures to cases in which irregularity had exercised an influence on the decision taken. It would therefore be appropriate to ascertain *in concreto* whether this was the case. It seems pertinent to consider the possible influence on the final decision, but this would indeed have to be the case. It is not certain that the consultation deprived the company of a 'safeguard' as understood in the Danthony decision. The notion of safeguard refers to the rights and freedoms guaranteed by the constitution or an international convention. However, there can be no question of invoking a violation of the rights of the defence, which in the present case are not applicable. The principle of equality?

D. Germany

DS

In Germany, the tariffs of the railway companies are not established by the regulatory authority (DT) but by the railway companies themselves in conformity, however, with certain legally established conditions (§ 12 *Allgemeines Eisenbahngesetz* of 27 December 1993). Nevertheless, according to German administrative law, the DT can enact administrative rules (*Verwaltungsvorschriften*) even without a particular legal basis, interpreting the law and binding the authority in its application of the legal criteria. As these rules have no legal basis, there is no duty to enter into consultations before implementing them.

On the other hand, these rules are not directly binding on courts, being subject only to statutory law (Article 97.1 *GG*). The courts, nevertheless, have to respect administrative rules as elements of the administrative practice and thus, as instruments guaranteeing the egalitarian application of the law.

From this point of view, the fact that, in preparing the rules, some stakeholders have been consulted and others have not, indicates bias on the part of the administration, thus acting in breach of the equality principle. Therefore, the court, applying the law and considering the interpretation of administrative rules, will have reason to doubt whether these rules are appropriate to guarantee the equal application of the law and may investigate a possible lack of information due to the lack of consultation in greater detail. The court has no power to annul the rules, which are binding directly only for an administration subordinated to the DT, but it is not bound by them, and the disparity in consultations reduces the informative and regulatory relevance of the rules.

E. Greece

TF

In the Greek legal order, there is no general obligation (save any explicit contrary provision) on the public administration to consult an interested party, despite the fact that it took into account the opinion of others. This is because the ensuing administrative act cannot be challenged on grounds of procedural *ultra vires* since the interested parties have no advisory power; on the other hand, there is no special provision to this end in the law.

Therefore, the competent Court would endorse the respondent's argument.

F. Italy

SV

In the case at issue, we understand that rail transport sector legislation does not establish any obligation to consult stakeholders and that, nonetheless, the Department of Transport decided of its own accord to consult only the two incumbents, causing the *de facto* exclusion of the newcomer, High-Speed Rail (HSR).

In such a situation, after acknowledging that neither the sector-specific legislation nor the Italian APA establishes the right to be consulted in the context of administrative procedures for adopting general administrative acts (in this specific case, fixing new tariffs), the Italian administrative court could take into consideration the administration's actual decision to electively carry out the consultation.

Nonetheless, after the Department of Transport has made the decision to conduct a consultation on the preliminary details of the measure regarding the implementation of new sectoral tariffs, it should not subsequently and unjustly exclude certain parties with a legitimate interest from participating in the process. In this case, the Italian administrative court could uphold High-Speed Rail (HSR)'s arguments and annul the tariff measure due to 'abuse of discretion' ('*excès de pouvoir*', ie a breach of the general principles of administrative action).

In particular, the complainant could argue a violation of the principle of impartiality established in Article 97(II) of the Italian Constitution, which is also echoed in Article 1(1) of the Italian APA. Furthermore, they could raise concerns about the absence of a thorough preliminary investigation and, in a broader sense, the irrationality of the decision to deny participation by the newcomer company, despite expressing the necessity to gather information from sector operators.

However, it should be noted that—as yet—there is no relevant case law on the matter, so no real prediction can be made on whether these objections would be upheld.

That said, Article 13(1) of the Italian APA states that the provisions regarding participation laid down in the act do not apply to activities conducted by administrative bodies with the intention of issuing legislative (administrative regulations), general administrative, or planning/programming acts, for which the special rules governing their formation apply.[274]

Administrative case law[275] has consistently clarified that tariff-setting measures constitute general administrative acts. This implies that, in accordance with the

[274] See Vaccari, Berti and Silvestri (n 86) para 3.

[275] See, among the many, Tuscany Regional Administrative Court, Florence, Div I, No 350, 8 March 2018; Lazio Regional Administrative Court, Rome, Div II, No 3666, 3 March 2015; Council of State, Div VI, No 2309, 17 April 2009; Council of State, Div VI, No 565, 1 February 2002; and Lazio Regional Administrative Court, Rome, Div II, No 657, 8 June 1993.

aforementioned Article 13 of Italian Law No 241/1990, these activities are not bound by the regulations on notifying individual users or other parties whose legal interests may be affected by the introduction of the new tariffs.

The legislator can therefore establish—on a case-by-case basis—forms of mandatory participation in individual sector-specific rules. In many cases, the guaranteed participation of sector operators in drawing up regulatory or general administrative acts is a means of reinforcing the principle of legality in procedural terms, so as to offset the lack of 'substantive' legality affecting the activity of many independent administrative authorities.[276]

However, when the sector-specific legislation does not oblige administrative bodies to comply with specific consultation requirements regarding the 'outlines' of general administrative acts, nothing in the case law grants potential stakeholders the right to be heard.

It has, however, been clarified in case law that administrative bodies have the discretion, based on the principle of sound administration, to allow for greater stakeholder consultation through non-conventional forms of participation. In such a scenario, the contributions provided by the participants are to be regarded as non-binding, and rejecting them does not necessitate an extensive and detailed statement of reasons.[277] If, albeit being under no obligation to do so, the administrative body decides to introduce these optional forms of participation, it must then comply with the general principles of administrative procedure mentioned above, as it may not breach the principle of impartiality or engage in irrational unequal treatment of stakeholders by inviting only some to contribute to the procedure and excluding others.

Lastly, it should be pointed out that, although this question assumes that there are no sector-specific rules establishing an obligation to consult stakeholders, in 2011 (Italian Decree Law No 201 of 6 December 2011) an independent transport sector authority was set up in Italy with regulatory and assurance functions (*Autorità di regolazione dei trasporti*—ART).

With Board Resolution No 5 of 16 January 2014, this authority introduced regulations for conducting the procedures within its competence and for stakeholder participation.

Regarding our specific objectives, Article 5 of these regulations stipules that, once procedures for implementing regulatory acts have begun, the authority is required to use its website to disseminate a stakeholder consultation document containing, in addition to the outline of the regulatory act in question, a range of information to stimulate the participation of all stakeholders:

(i) a description of the essential features of the regulatory act it intends to adopt;
(ii) the questions on which the authority invites the stakeholders to submit observations and proposals;
(iii) the procedures and the deadline for submitting observations and proposals.

[276] See, among the many, Lombardy Regional Administrative Court, Milan, Div II, No 1901, 20 August 2019; Council of State, Div VI, n. 2521, 2 May 2012; and Council of State, Div VI, No 7972, 27 December 2006.

[277] Council of State, Div IV, No 6172, 16 October 2006.

If account were taken of these sector-specific rules, it would be even more likely that High-Speed Rail (HSR)'s application would be upheld by the Italian administrative court.

G. Romania

D-C D

Consequently, the questions raised by the case study are (a) whether there are rules on identifying the 'interested parties', and (b) the failure to identify one of these can lead to the annulment of the regulation.

First, there are no rules on identifying the interested party other than through the register of interests kept by public authorities. It is within their discretion to determine the parties eligible for consultation. However, this process should adhere to the general principles of proportionality, transparency, equality, and impartiality as set out in the Administrative Code (Articles 6 to 13). In this context, if the authority knows that an interested party intends to enter the market, it should be obliged to invite that party to the consultation table. The selection of a limited number of participants may be justifiable only when there are many interested parties.

Second, when analysing such a procedural error, the courts may conclude that the result of the decision-making process would have been the same, and thus this procedural fault is not decisive for the annulment of the adopted regulation; the lack of consultation or the failure to conduct it correctly is not automatically a ground for annulment. However, if there are reasons to believe that the result would have been different, the court can annul the decision and order the proceeding to be resumed.

H. Serbia

MM

From the formulation of the case, it is assumed that the central issue is access to railway infrastructure and tariffs for its use. The Law on Railways[278] regulates access to railway infrastructure and services. Under Article 12 of the Law, railway companies have the right to access railway infrastructure under equal, non-discriminatory, and transparent conditions for the purpose of performing transport of goods and passengers in accordance with this Law. The Law further contains detailed provisions on the calculation of access prices and the allocation of railway infrastructure capacity, which, among other things, determine that the Government should adopt a methodology for this calculation and prescribes the role for the sectoral regulator—the Railways Directorate—in the various stages. However, according to Article 17 the Infrastructure Operator, *after consultation with interested parties*, must prepare and publish a *Network Statement*, containing, inter alia, the following information: a part on the principles of price calculation and price levels, which contains detailed

[278] The Law on Railways, Official Gazzette No 41/2018 and 62/2023. The analysis is done on the basis of law applicable at the time of writing in 2020.

information on the method of calculating prices, *as well as information on prices*, and other relevant information on access related to services. The information contains detailed methodologies, rules and, if necessary, scales in terms of costs and prices. According to the Law, it also comprises information on price changes which have already been decided or which are foreseen for the next five years, if any are available. It is explicitly underlined that the infrastructure operator will make the contents of the draft version of the Network Statement *available to interested parties* no later than ten days before the consultation.

In the Serbian context, and in this particular hypothetical case, High-Speed Rail would be excluded from this part of the consultation process. The company could initiate the procedure for reviewing the 'constitutionality and legality' of general acts by the Constitutional Court. Bearing in mind that this Network statement clearly falls within the broad scope of other general acts and that the procedure envisaged by the Law was not adhered to, it is likely that the Court would conclude that it is not in line with the legality requirement and strike down the act.

I. Spain

IMD

The Spanish legal system provides for three participation mechanisms: prior public consultation, public consultations, and the hearing for all stakeholders or parties concerned, although public bodies are allowed to establish additional participation mechanisms targeting individuals directly or through organizations and associations representing collective interests.

In the case at hand, it seems that the three market participants would be affected by the new tariffs. Therefore, in order to ensure their participation, after preparing the draft setting out the new tariffs, the DT should have conducted a hearing with them, as established by the general rules on administrative procedure. Act 38/2015 on the Railway Sector specifically requires (i) a consultation including all railway companies on the draft tariff framework (comprising the various fees payable by railway operators to the body responsible for the railway infrastructure), and (ii) that the National Commission on Markets and Competition issue a report. Provided that all railway operators qualify as stakeholders or parties concerned, and considering that consultations are mandatory, all of them should be involved. Even if the stakeholders or parties concerned fail to attend the consultation, they will still retain legal standing to file any appeals against the final decision (thus, they will always be entitled to make their pleas in law, although they will not be able to object in terms of timing), but since public consultation is mandatory, failure to conduct it constitutes grounds for annulment.

In any event, assuming that (i) there was no mandatory consultation under the applicable sector-specific legislation and that the consultation had to be conducted at an early stage of the procedure—ie there being no draft yet—and (ii) the DT had freely decided to carry out a consultation, the right to, and principle of, good or sound administration would apply. Under this principle and right, the DT would be required to duly consider the interests of all stakeholders. The principle of transparency would also apply, whereby the relevant public body would be required to ensure that potential addressees be actively involved in rulemaking, especially considering that this rule in particular affects public revenue. Also note that the decision-making body may open a public consultation via an announcement in the relevant official gazette, thereby allowing anyone to examine the relevant file or record.

Consequently, we would have to assess whether the third company (HSR), which was not individually invited to participate, could have participated through a general consultation mechanism. If we do not believe this was possible, ie if only the other two companies were consulted individually, there could have been a violation of the right to be heard. Otherwise, ie if HSR could have submitted its comments through the general public consultation mechanism, there would be no infringement or violation. This legal reasoning applies because participation qualifies—as stated by the Constitutional Court—as a procedural mechanism required to protect the parties potentially concerned.

There is an even more remarkable aspect in the case: the duty to consider all the necessary elements to make the decision, arising from the principle of participation within administrative procedures. Scholars have argued that this duty gives rise to an additional requirement, ie encouraging the greatest possible participation, assuming that, as participation increases, so does the social acceptance of rules and decisions.

The objectivity standard, falling under the principle of good administration, entails an additional requirement: investigating and weighing the facts of the case to make the most widely accepted decision. This, at the same time, requires public authorities to be aware of all the relevant circumstances and weigh them, as stated in Supreme Court judgments. Spanish legal scholarship has concluded that the objectivity standard does not only require that a procedure be conducted but also that it be adversarial to some extent, meaning that it must be open so as to allow the parties concerned to have a say and satisfy the general interest. The objectivity standard also entails that the equality principle be fulfilled or, in other words, that all the parties concerned or potential stakeholders be able to express themselves and participate on an equal footing.

In the case of HSR, there being three distinct operators, excluding one of them (which is also a company entering the market and thus possibly offering different inputs), we could argue that there has been a breach of the equality principle. Although public consultation was not mandatory, once the DT decided to hold it, the principle of equality would have to be fulfilled. The DT cannot arbitrarily discriminate against HRS.

J. Switzerland

AF

According to Article 29 para 1 of the Federal Constitution, requiring that '[e]very person has the right to equal and fair treatment in judicial and administrative proceedings', there is a right to 'equality of arms' between the parties. This right applies between the parties to a procedure and not between third parties.[279]

[279] ATF 127 I 73, c 3f/bb.

Under this right, each party to a proceeding must be treated in the same manner, particularly concerning the right to be heard, even if it is sometimes unavoidable that one party has more information than the other.[280]

In the case at hand, the competent court would endorse the newcomer's argument; if the regulator decides to consult some stakeholders, then it is constitutionally bound to consult them all.

K. United Kingdom

GA and CM

There are two overlapping ways in which HSR might challenge the tariffs in this case (that being its ultimate objective). The first would be to plead breach of consultation requirements, as envisaged by the scenario; while the second would be to plead breach of the right to a hearing given that the tariff presumably has direct implications for its business model. In reality, HSR would be likely to plead both a lack of consultation and a breach of hearing rights, thereby allowing the court to decide which route is conceptually best suited to their case.

The contours of the law on consultation have been outlined in response to the third of the general and introductory questions that address the position in UK law, which referenced the so-called '*Gunning*' criteria and the leading cases of *Reilly* and *Moseley*.[281] In this scenario, the issue is less about the quality of a consultation and more the fact that consultation did not occur, where HSR would challenge the decision as 'irrational' at common law. In the first instance, HSR would say that the failure to consult it breached the equality principle (which is a subset of irrationality) given that the two other providers were consulted.[282] While the common law accepts that a decision maker can justify differential treatment where two situations are not the same,[283] it is not at all clear why HSR was distinguished from the other providers in this scenario. While the DT might try to argue that it consulted the other two providers because they were established providers in the field, it is difficult to see how that argument would prevail given that HSR was to be directly affected by a decision that would affect a closed group of three providers. Nor could the fact that the consultation was undertaken on a voluntary basis assist the DT: the decision at hand would be a public law decision which must accord with the first principles of public law, including irrationality.

Irrationality would also allow HSR to make the point from the scenario about the regulator failing to obtain information from all relevant sources. The concept of irrationality includes not only equality but also a failure to take into account all relevant considerations, as well as a duty of due enquiry. As Lord Greene put it in the *Wednesbury Corporation* case:

[280] ATF 142 I 99, c 3.3.

[281] *R v Brent London Borough Council ex p Gunning* [1986] 84 LGR 168, 189; *Re Reilly's Application* [2013] UKSC 61, [2014] AC 1115; and *R (Moseley) v Haringey LBC* [2014] UKSC 56, [2014] 1 WLR 3947.

[282] On the relationship between equality and irrationality see *R (Gallaher) v Competition and Markets Authority* [2018] UKSC 25, [2019] AC 96.

[283] *Matadeen v Pointu* [1998] UKPC 9, [1999] 1 AC 98.

> The exercise of such a discretion must be a real exercise of the discretion. If, in the statute conferring the discretion, there is to be found expressly or by implication matters which the authority exercising the discretion ought to have regard to, then in exercising the discretion it must have regard to those matters.[284]

HSR may therefore have grounds for arguing that the wider statutory framework required the DT to have regard for the views of all economic actors affected by any new tariffs, particularly if there are only three such actors.

The above points could, as noted, alternatively be argued as aspects of breach of the right to a hearing, and it would be for the court to decide whether hearing rights (which are, of course, closely related to consultation requirements) would provide a better conceptual framework for determination of the case. Were the court to do so, HSR would argue that, as the decision at hand had direct implications for its business model, it was entitled to notification that the decision was under consideration, an opportunity to make representations, and reasons which explain why the final decision was taken. HSR might here also argue breach of the ECHR: its business model might be argued to come under Article 1 of Protocol 1 and thereby constitute a 'civil right' within the meaning of Article 6 ECHR.

One final point concerns HSR's view that the tariffs do not apply to it given that it was not consulted/given a hearing. HSR should here be advised that it would be better to observe the new tariffs pending any challenge, as public law measures are presumptively valid pending any grant of interim relief and/or any judicial ruling that they have been made in breach of public law principle.[285] Ignoring the tariff in advance of a challenge may leave HSR open to some form of regulatory sanction.

In sum: there is a strong argument that HSR should have been consulted given that the other providers were consulted, notably as there are only three providers in the field. The point might be advanced with reference to the irrationality principle and/or the right to a hearing. HSR should be advised to observe the new tariffs pending any judicial ruling on their legality.

L. Venezuela

FP-F

Based on the constitutional right to equality (Article 21), the requirement is established that in the exercise of its tasks and in making its decisions, the Public Administration must apply the same treatment and protection to persons and institutions that participate in the actions that are the object of their hearing.

Respect for the principle or subjective right to equality and non-discrimination is an obligation of the bodies and entities of all branches that make up the public authorities, which requires those who are in analogous or similar factual situations to be treated in the same way and that all citizens enjoy the right to be treated equally under the law.

[284] *Associated Provincial Picture Houses v Wednesbury Corporation* [1948] 1 KB 223, 228.
[285] *Smith v East Elloe* [1956] AC 736, 769, Lord Radcliffe.

The principle of equality under the law aims to prevent any discrimination arising in the application of legal norms by the public authorities, including the Public Administration, which, in addition to respecting this principle, is at the service of the citizens, so its actions must be based on the principles of honesty, participation, speed, effectiveness, efficiency, transparency, accountability, and responsibility in the exercise of public functions, with complete submission to the law and rights (Article 141 of the Constitution).

Furthermore, as we have already mentioned, Articles 140 and 141 of the Venezuelan regulations that regulate the organization and operation of the Public Administration (the Organic Law of Public Administration) establish the obligation for the organs or entities of the administration to publicly consult all the interested parties before approving regulatory projects, in order to promote and achieve the effective participation of organized society and the interested parties by receiving their proposals to ensure, among others, the principles of participation, effectiveness, efficiency, transparency, and accountability.

Public consultation in Venezuela is mandatory because without it, ie if the competent body or entity fails to send the draft project to the organized community and fails to inform all interested parties so that they can present observations or suggestions, the regulatory standard thus approved would be null and void.

In the case at hand, the Department of Transport (DT) indeed carries out prior consultation. Still, it discriminates by not consulting the three railway companies on the economic and other criteria that should be taken into account in establishing the new rates that will have to be applied.

Hence, we can conclude that the competent tribunal would support HSR's argument. Indeed, the fact that DT has not held a public consultation with the three companies that provide the railway service not only prevents it from having sufficient elements to establish rates in accordance with the needs and demands of those who will provide the service, to the detriment of administrative effectiveness and efficiency but also, and above all, it translates into a violation of the principle of equality with regard to High-Speed Rail (HSR).

X. Case 9—Failure to consult the affected community before building a new gas pipeline

A. Austria

SS

The administrative court will probably decide on the basis of sector-specific legislation but argue that the obligation of the DI to consult the community has its foundations in general principles. Assuming that there is no specific right of the municipality to be heard and, in particular, that such a right is not provided for a municipality by constitutional law, the administrative court will not apply by analogy a provision that does not regulate the concrete procedure.

However, the federation and the provinces ('*Länder*') are required to take account of the interests of the concerned communities ('*bundesstaatliches Berücksichtigungsgebot*'). From this perspective, there is an obligation to consult the community.[286]

B. China

XS

The court will decide the case on the basis of existing general legal principles and declare the DI's decision unlawful.

In China, gas pipeline constructions, as with other urban constructions, are governed by Urban and Rural Planning Law,[287] as well as by Administrative Authorization Law.[288]

Generally speaking, urbanization plans are considered as regulatory acts within the meaning of Article 13 of the Administrative Litigation Law, and cannot be challenged before the courts.[289] Otherwise, interested persons may challenge the detailed urban plans if their interests are actually affected.

Concerning the procedural legality of the decision relating to a detailed urban plan, two cases judged by the High People's Court of Guangdong province, in 2018[290] and 2019,[291] can provide some clarification. In these two cases, the local urban authority made a detailed urban plan without consulting the interested persons on the grounds that the local regulations did not specify the procedure of this kind of decision-making. The court rejected the argument of the urban authority and considered that even though there were no clear procedural rules on the making of urban detailed decisions, it did not mean that there were no procedural restrictions. It confirmed that the legality of the detailed urban plan depended on

286 VfSlg 15552/1999.
287 城乡规划法.
288 行政许可法.
289 Supreme People's Court, 30 March 2020, No 2019-10407 (2019最高法行申10407号).
290 High People's Court of Guangdong province, 5 March 2018, No 2017-1544 (2017粤行终1544号).
291 High People's Court of Guangdong province, 27 June 2019, No 2018-378 (2018粤行终378号).

whether this decision was made in compliance with the 'fundamental principles of fair procedure',[292] ie the principle of due process.[293] More precisely, the urban detailed decision had to be subjected to the procedural principles resulting from the Administrative Authorization Law.

Article 47 of this law provides:

> In the event that the administrative authorization is directly related to major interests of the applicant and others, the administrative authority shall, before making its decision, inform the applicant and the other interested persons of the right to a public hearing . . . [294]

The High People's Court of Guangdong province declared the urban detailed decision unlawful. Considering that the annulment of this decision was likely to harm the public interest of an entire neighbourhood, it did not quash the decision, but ordered the applicants be paid compensation.

C. France

SS

The gas sector has evolved significantly over the past fifteen years, namely in terms of liberalization, through the application of European directives, and the privatization of the traditional operator. The gas sector, like that of energy in general, rests on the dissociation of regulation depending on whether it concerns production, transmission, or distribution. The transmission networks make it possible to import gas. The transmission network, an infrastructure made up of pipelines and compressor stations, is structured in a principal network and regional networks that deliver natural gas to the distribution networks.

The transmission business in France is regulated (in addition to the European regulations) by the *Code de l'Energie* ('energy code'), which coexists with other codes such as the *Code général des collectivités territoriales* ('general local authorities code') and the *Code de l'environnement* ('environment code'—C env). The energy code, amongst its constraints, calls for the establishment of a ten-year investment plan, which must mention the principal transmission infrastructures to be built or significantly modified in the coming ten years and submitted for examination by the energy regulatory commission (*Code de l'Energie*, Article L. 431-6).

Since ordinance No 2010-418 of 27 April 2010, the energy code has devoted, above all, specific attention to the construction and operation of gas transmission structures. This is article L. 431-1 of the energy code, which refers to book V, title V, chapter V of the environment code. Gas transmission is regulated under a separate regime from that of electricity. The environment code thus contains particular provisions for

[292] 最基本公正程序原则.

[293] 正当程序原则.

[294] 行政许可直接涉及申请人与他人之间重大利益关系的，行政机关在作出行政许可决定前，应当告知申请人、利害关系人享有要求听证的权利.

pipelines carrying natural gas or similar gas, hydrocarbons, and chemical products (C env, Articles L. 555-1 to L. 555-30). Authorization is preceded by an impact study and a public inquiry so required under Book I, title II, chapter II or III of the environment code. The applicant for authorization will perhaps seek a declaration of public interest (C env, Article L555-25).

Consultations are also a requirement of the environment code. For information purposes, the prefect informs the public bodies in charge of the public domain areas affected by the project of the application for authorization (Article R. 555-13). He or she also sends information regarding the application, accompanied by a copy of the dossier, to the municipalities to be affected by the risks and inconveniences the pipeline may cause, or least to any municipalities through which the pipeline will pass or whose territory is situated within a certain distance, specified in the texts, from the pipeline's proposed route, requesting their opinion (Article R 555-14).

French legislation thus requires this consultation, as well as participation (public inquiries etc). In addition, gas transmission projects of 'national interest' are subject to the public debate procedure (C env, Article L. 121-1, para 1).

If the principle of participation is not specific to the area of the environment, it is here that it bears one of the strongest implications. The general law of administrative procedure presents no added value here and forms a less protective legal framework.

Nor is it certain that an invocation of the general principles of environmental law will be more effective than that of the infringement of the aforementioned specific provisions.

Indeed, among the internal sources, the principle of participation has been elevated by the legislator to a general principle of environmental law (Article L. 110-1, II, 5 of the environment code). However, it joins the already existing provisions since the principle is appreciated 'within the framework of the laws that define its scope'. The principle therefore corresponds to the procedures prescribed by law and is not intended to produce effects when the procedures do not exist.[295]

Its consecration by the environment charter (Article 7) also confers upon it a constitutional scope:

> Every person has the right, under the conditions and within the limits defined by law, to gain access to information regarding the environment held by the public authorities and to participate in the development of public decisions impacting on the environment.

The central notion is that of 'impact on the environment'. However, a strict interpretation of this which excludes decisions with no direct and significant impact on the environment has been adopted. One will note that a procedure for the consultation of mayors in a field other than that of the case to be examined, namely Article L. 562-2 of the environment code—which calls for consultation of the mayors of the municipalities concerned before the prefect may render some of the provisions of a draft plan for the prevention of foreseeable natural risks immediately applicable—has been held

[295] See CE, 26 June 2013, No 360466, *Commune de Roquefère et al*, in the wind power sector.

not to be a decision having an impact on the environment.[296] According to the *Conseil constitutionnel*, it is a consultation intended to ensure the safety of persons and property with regard to foreseeable risks.

From the point of view of litigation, this indicates two possibilities: either the omission of the public participation procedure has been total and will entail annulment after the ascertainment of 'external' legality and, more specifically, of a procedural defect; or it is a matter of irregularity arising, for example, from the mere absence of consultation with the municipality. In the second case, it is difficult to assess whether or not the administrative judge will deem the irregularity to be 'substantial' according to the principle drawn from the Danthony case law.[297] Only a substantial irregularity is likely to cause the annulment of the measure adopted following the inquiry.

Danthony, which modifies the judge's function and allows the neutralization of a procedural defect more widely than in the past, has already been applied to rulings with an impact on the environment that have followed a particular procedure for public participation.[298] In the area of public inquiries—which much resembles the case considered—it has been ruled that the opinions stated on the project, when rendered obligatory by a legislative or regulatory text prior to the opening of the inquiry, must also be mentioned in the dossier submitted for public inquiry. This case regarded the opinions of the local municipalities affected by the creation of a national park. Still, the breach of these obligations is such as to vitiate the procedure and therefore entail the illegality of the measure taken after the public inquiry only if it may have impaired the information of the entire set of persons with an interest in the operation or if it was such as to exert an influence over the results of the inquiry and, consequently, on the administrative body's decision.[299] The solution therefore rests on an appreciation of the circumstances specific to each matter.

In any event, we may note that, in French law, the mechanisms for public participation have only a limited impact on the final decision. The procedures do not produce pivotal effects on the decision's content. They never establish a co-decision. The effects of public inquiries and public debate procedures are limited.

D. Germany

DS

Concerning planning infrastructural enterprises, German law provides for a special planning decision procedure (*Planfeststellungsverfahren*, §§ 72-78 *VwVfG*), with an extensive consultation and participation procedure. However, this procedure takes place only if the law specifically requires it (§ 72.1 *VwVfG*). In this sense, sector-specific rules prevail. However, there is a procedure for both gas pipelines and electric plants in Germany (§ 43 *Energiewirtschaftsgesetz*).

[296] Cons Const, 9 September 2014, dec No 2014-411 QPC, *Cne Tarascon*.
[297] CE, 23 December 2011, No 335477, *Danthony*. See above, S Saunier in this book.
[298] See, eg, CE, 12 July 2019, No 424600, *Fé. nationale des chasseurs, procédure jugée irrégulière*.
[299] As in CE, 29 October 2013, No 360085, *Assoc Les amis de la rade et des calanques*.

If this were not the case for gas pipelines, applying the planning decision procedure and, consequently, the consultations included in it would be impossible. On the other hand, all the effects of this procedure, namely the concentration of decision-making for all the licences necessary for the project, would not take place. Most of these decisions—as administrative acts—would affect specific communities, citizens, and environmental associations etc. Therefore, all these subjects should be consulted according to the general rules of administrative procedure (§ 28 *VwVfG*); there appears to be no room for the exceptions allowed in this paragraph. The lack of consultation would violate the principles of the rule of law. The consultation could be recovered until the court decision and thus during the court procedure (§ 45 *VwVfG*), but the court would anyway review it.

E. Greece

TF

In the Greek legal order, except for an explicit contrary provision, the public administration has no general obligation to consult an interested party despite the fact that it took into account the opinion of others. This is so because the administrative act that will be issued cannot be challenged on the grounds of procedural *ultra vires*, since the interested parties have no advisory power; on the other hand, there is no special provision on the matter in the law.

Therefore, the competent Court would endorse the respondent's argument.

F. Italy

NB

If Italian legislation mandates consultation of the affected community solely in cases involving the construction of a new electricity plant, then in the specific case of the citizens' petition regarding the construction of a gas pipeline, the (administrative) court would probably dismiss the petition. The administration's decision not to publish documentation regarding the new plant on its website (as long as they are accessible upon request from any citizen, pursuant to Article 3-*sexies* of Italian Legislative Decree No 152 of 3 April 2006, the Environmental Code) and not to consult the affected community must be deemed lawful.

The Italian APA specifically exempts the provisions regarding stakeholder participation from applying to activities conducted by the public administration when issuing legislative (administrative regulations), general administrative, planning, and programming acts (Article 13). However, this exclusion does not affect the regulations on participation established by sector-specific provisions that govern the formulation of these types of acts. It is therefore necessary to refer on a time-by-time basis to the individual special provisions in order to establish whether or not the administration is obliged to publish projects and to consult the affected community beforehand (see General and introductory question I.3).

The Italian legal system has no general principle requiring the administration to consult the affected community before implementing general interest projects other than in the cases expressly established by law. Not even the general principles arising from Article 6 of the Aarhus Convention appear to have penetrated the Italian legal system to the point that case law will overturn the general exclusion of participation laid down by Article 13 of the general law on administrative procedure.

However, the decision in question could be deemed unlawful due to noncompliance with Directive No 2011/92/EU of the European Parliament and of the Council (amended by Directive 2014/52/EU), which establishes the fundamental principle of mandatory public participation in the EIA procedure, which applies to the construction of gas pipelines. Furthermore, the fact that Italian law imposes no obligation to consult the community before a gas pipeline is built could be deemed unconstitutional as it is incompatible with Article 6 of the Aarhus Convention, ratified by Italy with Law No 108 of 16 March 2001, the former committing the Member States to inform the public in a timely and effective manner and to allow citizens to play an active role early in the decision-making process with regard to a series of listed activities, including the construction of gas pipelines.

However, there are no decisions of this kind in Italian case law, since the Italian legal system is in complete accordance with European and international law regarding this issue, and it explicitly outlines the consultation obligations that have been breached in this case.

More specifically, Italian Legislative Decree No 152/2006 (Environmental Code) incorporates various mechanisms for public participation in procedures involving the planning, programming, and subsequent execution of projects regarding infrastructures likely to have significant environmental impact. An extensive list of infrastructures (including gas pipelines) is subject to 'strategic environmental assessment' (SEA) and 'EIA procedures, requiring a mandatory phase in which the project is published and the public consulted through a public inquiry at the request of public entities and associations (in addition to the institution of 'public debate' under Article 22 of the Public Contracts Code implemented by Prime Ministerial Decree No 76 of 10 May 2018). Lastly, implementing the provisions of the Aarhus Convention and Directive 2003/4/EC on public access to environmental information, Article 3-*sexies* of the Environmental Code states that anyone may access information on the state of the environment and the landscape in the national territory without being required to prove that they have a relevant legal interest.

G. Romania

D-CD

Public participation in decision-making on environmental issues is regulated by EGO 195/2005 on environmental protection as a matter of principle (Article 3(1) letter h)). Furthermore, Article 5(1) letter b) provides that the Romanian state recognizes the right of 'any person' to a healthy and ecologically balanced environment, ensuring access to environmental information and the right to be consulted in the decision-making process regarding environmental policy and regulations.

In addition to the national legislation, there are obligations to conduct an Environmental Impact Assessment for investments of this kind, so the EIA Directive[300] would also be applicable. One of the objectives of the Directive is to afford the public an important role in the decision-making process concerning projects. In this respect, it highlights the importance of public consultation and participation in the decision-making process with regard to several points. For instance, Recital 16 of the codified 2011 EIA Directive states that

> Effective public participation in decision-making allows the public to express their opinions and concerns, which the decision-maker can take into account, thereby increasing the accountability and transparency of the decision-making process and contributing to public awareness of environmental issues and support for the decisions made.

Moreover, Article 6 of the codified 2011 EIA Directive establishes the framework for public consultation during EIA procedures, and paragraph 4 of this article expressly provides that:

> The public concerned shall be given early and effective opportunities to participate in the environmental decision-making procedures referred to in Article 2(2) and shall, for that purpose, be entitled to express comments and opinions when all options are open to the competent authority or authorities before the decision on the request for development consent is taken.

Lastly, it is important to note that under Article 6(8) of the Aarhus Convention, to which Romania is a party, each signatory must ensure that public opinion is considered when final decisions are made.

Thus, in the specific circumstance described in the case study, there are clear legal grounds to conclude that if special legislation or regulation at the local level does not provide specifically for the right to participate in environmental decision-making, the general rules would still apply, and consultation would be mandatory.

H. Serbia

MM

In this hypothetical case, the preliminary issue in the Serbian (as in most other European) systems would be whether the environmental impact assessment (EIA) procedure providing for the wide participation of the public concerned would need to be performed prior to granting the permit to construct the gas pipeline. Serbia is party to the Aarhus Convention[301] and has thus undertaken to provide public, and

[300] Directive 2011/92/E of The European Parliament and of The Council of 13 December 2011 on the assessment of the effects of certain public and private projects on the environment [2012] OJ L 26/1.

[301] Law on the ratification of the Convention on access to information, public participation in decision-making and access to justice in environmental matters, Official Gazette of the Republic of Serbia—International documents, No 135/2004.

public-concerned (in this case, the affected community), participation in environmental decision-making processes. Furthermore, the Constitution of Serbia provides that everyone has the right to be informed accurately, fully, and in timely fashion about issues of public importance (Article 51). Following the definitions set in the Aarhus Convention, the Law on Environmental Impact Assessment,[302] the public concerned includes the public affected by, or likely to be affected by, a project. These include non-governmental organizations that promote environmental protection and are registered with the competent authority, and this protection is applicable to the project, ie to the execution of construction works, the installation of facilities, plants and equipment, their reconstruction, removal and/or change in terms of technology, work process technology, raw material, production material, energy, and waste. By law, the Government of the Republic of Serbia prescribes, 1) a list of projects for which an impact assessment is mandatory, and 2) a list of projects for which an impact assessment may be required. The Decree on establishing these lists[303] places in List I (projects for which impact assessment is mandatory) pipelines for the transport of gas, liquefied petroleum gas, and petroleum, and petroleum products or chemicals with a diameter of more than 800 mm and a length exceeding 40 km. List II (projects for which impact assessment may be required) contains gas pipelines, except internal factory pipelines, which are over 10 km long and over 150 mm in diameter. In both cases, the public concerned has to be informed during the early stages of the process. For the purpose of this case, we assume that the pipeline concerned would need to undergo the process of environmental impact assessment. According to the Law, a developer may not commence project implementation without having previously completed the impact assessment procedure and obtained the approval of the EIA study from the competent authority (Article 5). The competent authority has an obligation to inform the public of all the decisions taken during the procedure (Article 29). It is specifically established that the competent authority must inform the authorities, organizations, and the *public concerned* about its decision either to grant approval for the EIA Study or to refuse the application for approval within ten days from the date of adoption of the decision. The notice must contain: 1) the content of the decision, 2) the main reasons for the decision, and 3) the most important measures that the project developer must take to prevent, reduce, or eliminate adverse effects (Article 25). The decision of the competent authority is final. The applicant and the public concerned are entitled to initiate an Administrative Court proceeding against the decision of the competent authority referred to (Article 26). Furthermore, the competent authority must provide the authorities, organizations, and public concerned with full documentation relating to the impact assessment procedure for review within fifteen days from the date of receipt of their written request (Article 27). Bearing in mind the existing EIA standards, which would allow public access to all documents related to the project, if the public concerned is denied this access, it could challenge the rejection by the Department of Infrastructure in an administrative dispute, and it is expected that the Administrative Court would uphold this claim and order access to all relevant documents.

[302] Official Gazette of the Republic of Serbia, No 135/2004 and 36/2009.
[303] Official Gazette of RS, No 114/2008.

I. Spain

IMD

According to constitutional case law, public consultation takes place both by means of a citizen participation mechanism and a source of information for the decision-making body.

The applicable sector-specific legislation—in particular Act 34/1998 on Hydrocarbons—provides for mandatory planning requirements for all facilities in the natural gas basic grid and the secondary transport grid, and it also requires facilities to obtain prior authorization for the various actions related to natural gas distribution. Furthermore, it is expressly stated that the various authorization procedures must include public consultation. Act 34/1998 allows for projects regarding gas fuel facilities and infrastructure to be allocated for public use or declared 'of public utility' for expropriation or taking purposes, also requiring public consultation in this case. Public consultation is also mandatory if the project has to be subject to an environmental impact assessment.

Royal Decree 1434/2002 on the transport, distribution, commercialization, supply, and authorization procedures for natural gas facilities (RD 1434/2002) implements the aforesaid legislation. RD 1434/2002 requires all applications for facility authorizations to be subject to public consultation so that anyone (whether a stakeholder or not) may submit comments. There can be a single public consultation if the application and the public utility declaration are simultaneous. Therefore, when required by the applicable legislation, according to these provisions and the case law, failing to hold public consultations would invalidate the relevant administrative authorization or permit because public consultation qualifies as an indispensable procedural step.

Regarding transparency, Article 6 LTBG requires publication of the yearly and multi-year plans and programmes laying down specific targets, as well as the schedule, activities, and means to meet such targets. Also, Article 5 establishes that public authorities must make periodic and updated publications of all the information that could be relevant for ensuring transparency. Neither of these provisions would lead to the conclusion that information regarding a building project for a new gas pipeline must be published. However, Article 7 LTBG specifically requires the publication of 'all documents for which the applicable sector-specific legislation requires a public consultation' on the transparency platform. Non-compliance could carry a penalty for breaching these disclosure requirements but, in practice, penalties are rarely imposed in these cases.

Even assuming that this specific requirement did not exist, it would be necessary to respect the general provisions of the LPAC. As mentioned above, under Article 83, the competent bodies *may* hold public consultations 'if so required by the nature of the procedure'. Therefore, public authorities enjoy broad scope for decision-making when it comes to deciding whether or not to carry out public consultations. The case at hand does not involve draft regulations, ie rule-making, so the DI is not required to hold public consultations. Consequently, it is unlikely that a court of justice would invalidate the decision. Only if, considering the circumstances, it became obvious that the nature of the procedure called for public consultation, would failing to have one entail the annulment of the procedure, also considering the applicability of the right to, and principle of, good or sound administration, which requires careful consideration of all relevant elements to make the best possible decision.

J. Switzerland

AF

The Convention on access to information, public participation in decision-making, and access to justice in environmental matters (Aarhus Convention) of 25 June 1998 entered into force for Switzerland on I June 2014. This requires pipelines for the transport of gas, oil, or chemicals with a diameter of more than 800 mm and a length of more than 40 km (annex I 14 of the Convention) to be subject to the obligation of public participation as defined in the Convention:

> The public concerned shall be informed, either by a public notice or individually as appropriate, early in an environmental decision-making procedure, and in an adequate, timely and effective manner.[304]

There is also a general principle of public participation, set out in Article 4 of the Federal Act on Spatial Planning of 22 June 1979, according to which the authorities responsible for planning must ensure that the public can participate adequately in the spatial planning process.

Here, Article 21*b* of the Federal law on installations for transporting liquid or gaseous fuels or combustibles by pipeline of October 4 1963 applies specifically. It establishes a thirty-day public inquiry period for pipeline plans. If this special rule did not exist in Swiss law, the legislator would violate the Aarhus Convention.

K. United Kingdom

GA and CM

This is a difficult scenario to address as there is no obvious comparator from existing UK case law that indicates how it might be resolved. While the environmental associations would almost certainly have standing to challenge the decision—the UK has a long tradition of facilitating public interest litigation, including in the area of the environment[305]—first principles would suggest that their argument about consultation under the statute is an ambitious one. The following points might be made:

i. The associations' argument ultimately reduces to one about statutory interpretation, where the applicants would be asking the court to read into the legislation mandatory requirements about consultation in relation to unspecified areas of activity. While it is true that UK courts routinely read legislation in a purposive

[304] Art 6 para 2 of the Convention.

[305] See G Anthony, 'Public Interest and the Three Dimensions of Judicial Review' (2013) 64 Northern Ireland Legal Quarterly 125.

manner, they have made it clear that they will not assume the role of the legislature when doing so.[306] In this scenario, that appears to be precisely what they would be invited to do, as the applicants would be seeking consultation rights under a statute that manifestly does not give them such rights beyond named areas. It is unlikely that the courts would be attracted to this argument as it could result in a consultation requirement in relation to almost any matter that touches upon the statute. (For an instance of a narrow approach to the interpretation of statute in the environmental field see *R (Friends of the Earth) v Secretary of State for Transport*[307].)

ii. The applicants' related point about DI's interpretation frustrating the legislator's intention in relation to transparency would be unlikely to advance their position. While there is no doubt that the legislature has sought to enhance transparency, the term is specifically linked to electricity plants and there is nothing to suggest that it is to be used to impose a much broader set of consultation obligations. To hold otherwise would, again, take the court towards the realm of impermissible judicial legislation.

Does this mean that the applicants would be unable to raise legal arguments? Not necessarily, for two reasons. First, and in terms of consultation, it may be that they could raise a point about a procedural legitimate expectation of consultation if the DI has previously had a practice of consulting on such matters, even in the absence of a statutory duty to do so. While there is nothing in the facts to suggest that there ever was such a practice, the common law will require consultation with individuals and/or groups if they have previously been consulted about such issues. In that instance, the court would require the DI to consult, subject to there being any reason of public interest why it should not do so.[308]

The second reason is that it may be possible for associations to challenge the DI's decision as *ultra vires* the legislation at hand and/or as a use of power for an improper purpose. The key here is whether the legislation specifically references new gas pipelines or whether it makes express mention of electricity plants. If it refers only to the latter, the applicants could argue that the DI has no power to process applications in relation to gas pipelines as that would be to stray beyond the statutory framework. The argument could also be presented in terms of purposes: the legislation grants powers in relation to electricity plants and use of those powers in relation to gas pipelines is an improper use of those powers.[309]

To summarize: it is unlikely that the associations would be able to advance an argument about consultation under the statute though they may be able to rely upon the common law (depending on the fuller factual context) and/or argue that the DI's decision is *ultra vires* that legislation in question.

[306] On the purposive approach see *General Dynamics v State of Libya* [2021] UKSC 22, para 132, Lord Stephens.

[307] [2020] UKSC 52, [2021] PTSR 190.

[308] See, most famously, *Council of Civil Service Unions v Minister for the Civil Service* [1985] AC 374.

[309] On improper purposes see *R (Palestine Solidarity Campaign) v Secretary of State for Housing, Communities and Local Government* [2020] UKSC 16, [2020] 1 WLR 1774.

L. Venezuela

FP-F

In addition to establishing the right to public participation in matters of general interest, the Venezuelan Constitution establishes the need to guarantee such involvement with respect to activities related to the environment since the state is obliged to inform and consult the public precisely to ensure such participation (Article 128 of the Constitution).

As mentioned above, the Organic Law of Public Administration, a general rule applicable to all public administrations, requires competent bodies and entities to publicly consult interested persons and civil society on decisions that may affect the community.

In addition to the above, the environmental legislation that builds on the content of Article 128 of the Constitution states that all interested persons have the right to participate in the administrative procedure related to the protection of the environment; in other words, they not only have the right to information about the projects but to propose recommendations and actively participate in their preparation.

In this sense, Article 40 of the current Organic Law of the Environment provides that:

> The National Executive, through the ministry with jurisdiction over environmental matters, shall regulate the mechanisms to make effective the legitimate exercise of the right to citizen participation in the formulation, adoption, execution and control of policies, plans, projects and other measures for the conservation of the environment.

Since the construction of new power plants would affect the environment, even if the Organic Law of Public Administration and the Organic Law of the Environment were not in force, the tribunal with jurisdiction in the matter would decide in favour of the environmental organizations, applying Article 128 of the Constitution, which expressly envisages the participation of citizens when the Public Administration intends to execute projects in which the environment may be affected.

XI. Case 10—Refusal to give access to an algorithm

A. Austria

SS

It makes no difference if a municipality, a province (*'Land'*), or the Federation (*'Bund'*) decides whose name will be engraved on the plaque (Bund). However, this depends on whether the decision is a private or public law act.

Here, it can be assumed that the decision is a private law act because the municipality is executing no law and because the selection itself does not infringe on any fundamental rights of people or have to be executed using sanctions or coercion.

Although the municipality has not made the decision itself but has followed the suggestions made by the computer program, these suggestions are the responsibility of the municipality because it mandated the selection process to the program.

As the selection is a private law act, neither the right to be heard nor other rights guaranteed in the AVG apply.

Hector could ask the municipality to provide him with the relevant information; however, it remains doubtful that his enquiry will result in a successful outcome for him. While § 1 (Obligation to give Information Act (*'Auskunftspflichtgesetz'*)[310] gives everybody a right to obtain information from an authority, and this law also applies to private law issues,[311] it is nevertheless limited: The right to get information only applies to the knowledge that the authority already possesses. Therefore, an enquiry will only be successful if the authority already knows why the algorithm did not select Hector.

Irrespective of the foregoing, the decision about which names will be written on the plaque must not be arbitrary. If the authority cannot state the reason for the selection because it does not know, it may provide information regarding the basis the computer program uses to make the selection. However, excessively strict standards cannot be applied here as it would not be illegal for the authority to make a selection by drawing lots.

B. China

XS

For the court, it makes no difference whether the decision was taken by a local authority. But we cannot be sure that the court would order the administration to give reasons for its decision, which was based on an algorithm.

[310] *Bundesgesetz vom 15. Mai 1987 über die Auskunftspflicht der Verwaltung des Bundes und eine Änderung des Bundesministeriengesetzes 1986—Auskunftspflichtgesetz* (Federal Freedom of Information Act), Orig Vers: BGBl No 287/1987 for tasks of the federation; *Gesetz über die Auskunftspflicht—Wiener Auskunftspflichtgesetz* (Vienna Freedom of Information Act), Orig Vers: LGBl No 20/1988 for tasks of the province (here: Vienna).

[311] 41 of the attachment to the government bill, XVII legislative period, to § 1.

According to the Constitution, local acts are subject to laws and regulations issued by the State Council.

Indeed, Article 57 of the Constitution makes the National People's Congress the supreme organ of the State, and the Standing Committee of the National People's Congress its permanent organ. According to Article 67 of the Constitution, the Standing Committee of the National People's Congress has the power to 'interpret the Constitution and supervise its application',[312] to 'interpret the law',[313] to 'annul regulations, decisions or orders made by the State Council which are not in compliance with the Constitution or the law',[314] and 'to annul local regulations or decisions made by the authorities of provinces, autonomous regions and municipalities which are not in compliance with the Constitution, the law or the national regulations'.[315]

Article 110 of the Constitution provides for a double submission of local executives both to the local People's Congresses from which they arise and to the superior government. All local governments are 'under the unified leadership of the State Council and are subordinate to it'.[316]

In two judgments concerning municipal acts,[317] the Supreme People's Court cited the Programme relating to the general implementation of the principle of legality in the administrations, as a legal reference, and confirmed that 'the administrative authority must abide by the principle of due process in its actions, strictly follow legal procedures, and guarantee to interested persons and stakeholders the right to information, to participation, and to be compensated. Before making a decision, it must inform interested persons and stakeholders and give them the opportunity to make a statement and defend themselves.'[318]

So there is no doubt that the court will review the local authority's decision, as well as a national one. But it is not sure that the court would accept to review the decision, which is based on an algorithm.

The first question is whether the algorithm used by the administration can constitute an exception of disclosure, as 'internal administrative information' or 'in-process information' within the meaning of Article 16 of the Regulation on Open Government Information.

As said before, in Cases 6 and 7, in-process information is not an absolute exception from disclosure. Once the decision is made, the information that was under investigation, discussion, and processing is no longer in-process information. The algorithm used by the administration will be in this situation.

312 解释宪法，监督宪法的实施.

313 解释法律.

314 撤销国务院制定的同宪法、法律相抵触的行政法规、决定和命令.

315 撤销省、自治区、直辖市国家权力机关制定的同宪法、法律和行政法规相抵触的地方性法规和决议.

316 全国地方各级人民政府都是国务院统一领导下的国家行政机关，都服从国务院.

317 Supreme People's Court, 2 July 2019, No 2018-8767 (2018最高法行申8767号), 4 July 2019, No 2018-8769 (2018最高法行申8769号).

318 行政机关实施行政行为应当遵守程序正当原则，要严格遵循法定程序，依法保障行政管理相对人、利害关系人的知情权、参与权和救济权，作出对行政管理相对人、利害关系人不利的行政决定之前，应当告知并给予其陈述和申辩的机会。

Concerning the question of internal administrative information, as we showed in Case 7, if the information could have an impact on the rights and duties of the interested person, it will not be considered an internal administrative information.

Furthermore, Article 5 of the Regulation on Open Government Information states that:

> The disclosure of information by the administration shall be a routine release to the public, and the non-disclosure shall be an exception. Administrative authorities must disclose information according to the principles of fairness, equity, lawfulness, and convenience for the citizens.[319]

According to Article 36 (3) of the same regulation, if 'an administrative authority decides not to disclose requested information in accordance with this regulation, it shall inform the requester that such information cannot be disclosed, together with an explanation of the reasons'.[320] Article 37 states that

> if the requested information includes content that shall not be disclosed or that is not Government Information, but this content can be distinguished, the administrative authority shall provide the requester with the disclosable part of the request information and explain the reasons for the non-disclosed content.[321]

However, under Chinese administrative law, there are no special rules on algorithmic decision-making, even though the algorithm is used more and more in administrative decisions.[322] More precisely, there are no rules enshrining the right to an explanation for output from an algorithm. The courts have to decide the case on the basis of the Regulation on Open Government Information. A case concerning the enrolment of primary and secondary school students[323] could provide some clarification.

In this case, the applicant asked the local education authority to provide a legal basis and justifications for the delimitation of several local school districts, as well as explanations for the systematic admission of students from certain primary schools to certain middle schools. The education authority provided him with information relating to the concerned schools and the basis for the delimitation of local school districts, but without explanations for the systematic admission. For the court, the reply of the administrative authority 'fulfilled the duty to disclose information and was in compliance with legal procedural rules'.[324] In a way, the court admitted that the

319 行政机关公开政府信息，应当坚持以公开为常态、不公开为例外，遵循公正、公平、合法、便民的原则。

320 行政机关依据本条例的规定决定不予公开的，告知申请人不予公开并说明理由.

321 申请公开的信息中含有不应当公开或者不属于政府信息的内容，但是能够作区分处理的，行政机关应当向申请人提供可以公开的政府信息内容，并对不予公开的内容说明理由。

322 Especially in the areas of administrative authorizations, administrative penalty, distribution of social assistance, and the enrolment of primary and secondary school students. Currently, algorithms are amply used in the fight against Covid-19, such as the Digital QR Code.

323 High People's Court of Heilongjiang province, 7 December 2020, No 2020-530 (2020黑行终530号).

324 履行了信息公开职责，且程序符合法律规定.

administrative authority only had to provide information relating to the treatment parameters, and had no obligation to explain the data processing.

With regard to this situation, scholars have noted possible conflicts between algorithmic automated decision-making and administrative due process[325]. Indeed, the requirements of due process could be bypassed by algorithmic decision-making. Thus, the use of algorithms may call into question the transparency of a decision[326] and infringe procedural rights such as the right to be heard, the right to defend oneself, and the right to an explanation.[327] Some have suggested setting up an algorithmic accountability system[328] or a principle of 'Technological Due Process'.[329]

Two bills relating to the rules of data processing are being discussed and submitted for public consultation: Law on the Protection of Personal Information (Draft)[330] and Data Security Law (Draft).[331]

Article 25 of the Law on the Protection of Personal Information (Draft) provides:

> The use of personal information for automated decision-making should ensure the transparency of decision making and guarantee the fair and reasonable results of the decision.[332]
>
> [...]
>
> The interested person has the right to request the decision maker to give explanations for the decision made by automated decision-making that have a significant impact on individual rights and personal interests and has the right to refuse that the decision be only made by automated decision-making.[333]

[325] L Zhang (张凌寒), 'Confrontation and Articulation between Algorithmic Automated Decision-making and Administrative Due Process (算法自动化决策与行政正当程序制度的冲突与调和)' (2020) 6 Oriental Law (东方法学) 4–17.

[326] E Zhang (张恩典), 'Challenge of Artificial Intelligence Algorithmic Decision to Rule of Administrative Law and Legal Countermeasures (人工智能算法决策对行政法治的挑战及制度因应)' (2020) 4 Administrative Law Review (行政法学研究) 34–45.

[327] Y MA (马颜昕), 'Administrative Penalties under Automated Administration (自动化行政方式下的行政处罚: 挑战与回应)' (2020) 4 Political Science and Law (政治与法律) 139–48; Y Qin (秦梅玉), 'The Rise of Automated Administration and its Legal Problems (自动化行政的兴起及其法律挑战)' (2021) 2 Dynamics of Social Sciences (社会科学动态) 5–12; Z Xie (解正山), 'Regulating Algorithmic Decision: Focusing on the Right to Explanation of Algorithm (算法决策规制——以算法"解释权"为中心)' (2020, January) 42(1) Modern Law Science (现代法学) 179–93.

[328] Q Wang (汪庆华), 'The Multiple Dimensions of Algorithmic Transparency and Algorithmic Accountability (算法透明的多重维度和算法问责)' (2020) 6 Journal of Comparative Law (比较法研究) 163–73; Xie (解正山) (n 327).

[329] D Liu (刘东亮), 'Technological Due Process: The Double Variation of Procedural Law & Programming Algorithms in the Age of AI (人工智能时代程序法和算法的双重变)' (2020) 5 Journal of Comparative Law (比较法研究) 64–79.

[330] 个人信息保护法（草案）, Legislative Affairs Commission of the National People's Congress Standing Committee, 21 October 2020.

[331] 数据安全法（草案）, Legislative Affairs Commission of the National People's Congress Standing Committee, 3 July 2020.

[332] 利用个人信息进行自动化决策,应当保证决策的透明度和结果公平合理。

[333] 通过自动化决策方式作出对个人权益有重大影响的决定,个人有权要求个人信息处理者予以说明,并有权拒绝个人信息处理 者仅通过自动化决策的方式作出决定。

Article 37 of the Data Security Law (Draft) provides:

> The collection and use of data by administrative authorities to perform their statutory duties shall be carried out in compliance with the conditions and procedures prescribed by laws and administrative regulations.[334]

Article 40 of this same bill states that:

> Under the principles of Justice, Fairness, and Convenience for the citizens, administrative authorities should disclose administrative data in a timely and accurate manner.[335]

The adoption of these bills will strengthen the judicial review of decisions based on the algorithm.

C. France

SS

Today, 'algorithms' are used to ground administrative decisions, as in the case of the matter now analysed. The framework for their use under French law is contained in the general law of administrative procedure constituted by the CRPA. In France, there is no dedicated text similar to the 'digital administration codes' of some countries.

The right of access to the rules defining the algorithmic processing used by public bodies in taking their individual decisions and the principal characteristics of implementation is a creation of Law No 2016-1321 of 7 October 2016 ('Law for a digital Republic'). This regulatory text applies to all authorities governed by the code, including local authorities. It pursues a goal of administrative transparency which, to date, hardly seems to have been attained. It raises significant difficulties of implementation for local authorities.

This right is proclaimed in article L. 311-3-1 of the CRPA:

> An individual decision taken on the basis of an algorithmic processing bears an explicit mention in informing the interested party. The rules defining this processing and the principal characteristics of its implementation are communicated by the authority to the interested party if the latter so requests.

This right of access does not concern the algorithm itself but the rules defining the algorithmic processing and the source codes (CRPA, Article L. 300-2).

Mention of the use of an algorithm must be accompanied by that of the right to know the rules governing the processing and the principal characteristics of its

334 国家机关为履行法定职责的需要收集、使用数据，应当在其履行法定职责内依照法律、行政法规规定的条件和程序进行。

335 国家机关应当遵循公正、公平、便民的原则，按照规定及时、准确地公开政务数据。

implementation, as well as how this right to access and referral, as the case may be, to the CADA may be exercised (CRPA, Article 311-3-1-1).

The authority will inform the party against whom an individual decision is taken on the basis of an algorithm, at the latter's request, in an intelligible form, and respecting legally protected secrets, of a set of information: the mode and degree to which the algorithm contributed to the decision; the data processed and their sources; the parameters of the processing and, where applicable, their weighting, applied to the situation of the data subject; and lastly, the operations effected by the processing (CPRA, Article R. 311-3-1-2).

Moreover, Article L. 312-1-3 of the CRPA requires authorities to publish on their websites the rules governing the principal algorithmic processing used in the conduct of their tasks when they state the reasons for individual decisions.

It may be feared that the authorities' discretionary power and consequently their power of evaluation will end up weakened by the use of algorithmic processes. Some consider that the authorities would then be in a situation of circumscribed powers. Hector's remark is pertinent. There is no precise answer to this question.

Still, regarding the right of access, there also arises the question of the juncture between this general regime and the special derogation regimes. This received a first answer in case law from the suit originating from the use of the Parcours Sup platform, intended to gather and manage prospective University students' placement preferences. The *Conseil d'Etat* ruled in favour of applying the regime prescribed by the education code (Article L. 612-3) for providing information regarding the higher education establishments' local algorithmic processes. According to the *Conseil d'Etat*, it followed from Article L. 612-3 of the education code and the preparatory work for the law that the legislator intended to govern this right of access through 'particular provisions'. These special provisions derogate from the CRPA.[336] As a result, the Universities need not grant access to third parties, and in particular the student unions, the documents regarding the algorithmic processing they use. The *Conseil constitutionnel* then heard the same matter and for the first time established a constitutional right of access to administrative documents on the basis of Article 15 of the DDHC.[337] However, the Council admitted that this right could be the subject of restrictions as long as these had no disproportionate adverse effect on the public interest objective pursued. In order to protect the assessment of each application, it held that the legislator had pursued the public interest in protecting the secrecy of the teaching teams' deliberations. The restriction was necessary and proportionate. The *Conseil constitutionnel* stated, however, that after the pre-registration procedure, the Universities must publish the criteria according to which applications were examined.

To date, a solution through derogation of this type has not been issued with regard to algorithms used by local authorities. They are therefore subject to the general law as it emerges from the CRPA. However, the state of the law is under construction.

[336] CE, 12 June 2019, Nos 427916 and 427919, *Université des Antilles*.
[337] Cons Const, 3 April 2020, No 2020-834 QPC, *UNEF* (n 203).

D. Germany

DS

According to the traditional description of administrative tasks, the construction of a monument and, thus, of a funeral plaque is part of the activities that do not create individual rights or duties; therefore, there is no case for bringing a claim before the administrative court. There is neither a 'regulation' contained in an administrative act nor a legal relationship between the administration and the citizen; the statement of historical facts is not a question of law. Therefore, it could be argued that a complaint before the administrative court would be inadmissible (§§ 42.2, 43 *VwGO*). The question of whether an algorithm, and especially one built by a private company, may be taken as the basis for the plaque does not take into account the rights of the citizens and the object of a legal controversy between them and the administration.

Nevertheless, this argumentation may be considered questionable, especially if the plaque mentions those who 'contributed most to their nation' and if membership of this category is controversial. Then one may argue that the failure to mention a member of Hector's family is a discriminating inequality that violates Hector's right, and that he may defend this right for equal treatment. From this point of view, the construction of the funeral plaque could be qualified as a general administrative act (*Allgemeinverfügung*, § 35 phr. 2 *VwVfG*) regulating the plaque, or the sum of various administrative acts either mentioning or omitting the merits of certain citizens, or the statement of a legal relationship between Hector and the local authority. On these grounds, Hector could motivate his complaint as a violation of his rights (§ 42.2, 43 *VwGO*).

On this basis, the mayor of Two Rivers will have to explain why the member of Hector's family and the citizens mentioned on the plaque have been treated differently. This raises the question of the use of an algorithm and the construction of this algorithm by a private company.

Algorithms cannot be excluded as a means of technical support for the administration, but the information collected in this way is nothing more than a sum of facts. How to evaluate them and decide on the persons mentioned on the plaque is an additional and essential step, and this decision only constitutes the administrative act. Only if there were a legal norm delegating this decision to an algorithm could the result of its use substitute the administrative act. The administration's margin of discretion cannot justify the lack of a concrete administrative decision and its abandonment in favour of an algorithm. In reality, § 35a *VwVfG* permits, in principle, fully automated administrative decisions, but only if (1) a legal norm envisages it and (2) the administration has no margin of discretion. Both conditions are missing. Therefore, the mayor of Two Rivers has to justify his decision.

Because the algorithm cannot replace the administrative decision, the fact that a private company has developed it is irrelevant. The administration may use algorithms as technical support, including those provided by private sources, but it must assume its own responsibility concerning the application of the law.

The situation would be no different in the case of a decision by a national authority.

E. Greece

TF

Regarding the first question, local government authorities are constitutionally organized as public law legal persons enjoying both administrative and financial independence. However, the Constitution does not grant the local government agencies full autonomy in the form of the power to introduce their own binding rules. For this reason, the state, under the provisions of Article 102 para 4 of the Constitution provides for the supervision of local authorities, but it must consist exclusively of a review of legality. Consequently, the sum of the rules governing the action of the Public Administration according to the rule of law principle equally binds the legal action of the local authority. As stated earlier, the local authorities may not proceed to issue legal acts except based on the competence granted by law and within the limits of that competence.

As for the second question, in the context of the Greek legal order, according to the case law, the use of algorithms in the administrative process is not subject to judicial review.[338] On the contrary, the only form of control of the administration's action is limited to its internal control, through administrative appeals, which must be expressly provided for. However, public administration is governed by the principle of transparency. Failure to comply with this fundamental principle of administrative law, which seeks to ensure the legality of administrative action, creates major constitutional problems. Thus, the administration must seek every appropriate means so that, being duly informed, citizens can anticipate the administration's reactions and plan their activity on the basis of predictability. In this context, the algorithm constitutes the justification of the administrative act, which the recipients of the act should be able to understand, in order to effectively exercise their rights. Therefore, should the choices of the algorithm be found to be discriminatory, the administration is obliged to review and replace or improve the algorithm in order to bring it into conformity with the principle of legality. Furthermore, it should be pointed out that when it is deemed necessary to resort to an algorithm or other mathematical formula, the prior hearing of the interested party, which may contribute to the improvement of the formula in question, is a fundamental principle, so this right evolves into a form of co-operation between the administration and the citizenry, especially when it comes to applying new technological data which directly affect a person's legal position and, in particular, the exercise of fundamental rights.

In conclusion, it must be said that modern technological developments require the revision of basic institutions of administrative and procedural law in order to effectively protect the citizen. In order to achieve this, it is necessary to respect the fundamental rules governing administrative action so that the rights of the citizen will be protected. This protection is all the more important in cases where the algorithm is used by private operators. Therefore, in order to provide more complete protection, the legislator should take action to establish rules, particularly when private bodies process personal data using automated means, so that the citizen can enjoy the necessary protection. This position is reinforced in Article 25 para 1 of the Constitution,

[338] See Rulings No 2632/2001, 2768/2020 of the Council of State.

which states that the public administration is obliged to ensure the unhindered and effective exercise of citizens' rights, and these rights also apply to the relations between private parties to which they relate. According to this provision, fundamental rights are invested with additional normative power, so that they can overturn or modify rules of law that infringe constitutionally guaranteed rights. In this sense, individual rights are not transformed into mere guidelines for the interpretation of legal rules, but, on the basis of their direct normative force, they dynamically penetrate legal relations, shaping, revising, and enriching them, in the context of their interpretation, with new content suited to emerging socio-economic developments.

F. Italy

SV

In the case at hand, the Italian administrative court would grant Hector the right to access the algorithm on which the decision of the municipality of Two Rivers was based, as the discretionary nature of the powers of the administrative body and the fact that it is a local authority are immaterial.

Once Hector learns the criteria used to select the names that have been selected to appear on the plaque, Hector could dispute their substantive lawfulness—again before the administrative court—accusing the authority of abuse of discretion ('*excès de pouvoir*'), and, referring to the general principles governing the acts of public bodies, challenging any instances of irrational, discriminatory, or unequal treatment.

To substantiate these conclusions, we should firstly remark that, in recent years, Italian administrative case law[339] has stated that the public administration must also be able to exploit the significant potential offered by the 'digital revolution'.

In many cases, the use of algorithms enables the correction of a number of typical imperfections inherent to cognitive processes and human-made choices, so that the final decision may be more neutral and impartial, being the result of rational data-based calculations.

Using software to make administrative decisions is a way to achieve this goal, especially with regard to 'serial' or 'standardised' procedures. The procedure involves processing large numbers of applications together with the acquisition of specific objectively provable data, and the absence of discretionary evaluations.

In addition, the use of algorithms adheres to the fundamental rules of efficiency and economy of administrative action (Article 1 of Law No 241/1990) which, in compliance with the constitutional principle of sound administration (Article 97 of the Italian Constitution), requires the administration to pursue its objectives without wasting resources and carrying out its procedures expeditiously.

In any case, even if it is simpler to use algorithms for non-discretionary administration, there is nothing to prevent the same objectives being achieved also in relation to

339 See, in particular, Council of State, Div VI, No 881, 4 February 2020; Council of State, Div VI, No 8472, 13 December 2019; and Council of State, Div VI, No 2270, 8 April 2019; Lazio Regional Administrative Court, Rome, Div III-*bis*, No 9230, 10 September 2018.

decisions involving discretion. In this case, administrative discretion, which obviously cannot be delegated to software, is exercised during the development of digital tools, in accordance with the instructions issued by the public administration.

The administrative court has observed that the use of computerized procedures can never justify bypassing the principles underpinning the legal system and governing the conduct of administrative activity. Algorithms function as organizational modules, providing a useful support for investigations and decision-making. Nevertheless, they remain subject to the standard checks that apply to any administrative procedure. The technical regulations governing each algorithm are considered general administrative rules, created by humans rather than machines. This confirms its full legal status, indicating that it is subject to the general principles of administrative activity (Article 1 of Law No 241/1990), including those of public notification and transparency, reasonableness, proportionality, and others.

Administrative case law has established two essential guarantees applying to every potential use of algorithms by the public administration. These guarantees are the possibility to obtain full knowledge of the algorithm and the criteria for its 'construction', as well as the possibility to attribute the decision to the relevant entity.

The first guarantee stems from the principle of transparency and entails the right to access the algorithm (considered to be a 'computerised administrative act')[340] in its entirety. This right enables verification of whether the criteria, conditions, and outcomes of the automated process comply with the provisions and objectives established both in law and by the administration. Access cannot be denied merely by citing the grounds of the confidentiality of the companies creating the algorithms. Once these tools have been used for the benefit of the authority, the principle of transparency takes precedence.

The second guarantee is that, in the context of algorithm-based administrative decisions, it must always be possible to identify the entity or centre responsible for making the decision (the principle of non-'exclusiveness' of the algorithm-based decision).

This requirement also responds to the fundamental need to conduct a full and effective review of how power is exercised and represents a direct statement of the citizen's right to defence, as no one can be denied the chance to know the procedures (automated or otherwise) that have led to a decision that will adversely affect their rights. This is the only effective way to conduct an assessment (also at the case-law level) of the lawfulness of an administrative decision with the same level of intensity as an assessment of power exercised in a traditional manner.

These conclusions also extend to territorial authorities other than the state itself. In the Italian legal system, these authorities include municipalities, provinces, metropolitan cities, and regions. Article 29(2-*bis*) of Law No 241/1990 stipulates that the provisions of the Italian APA regarding the obligations of public bodies to ensure access to administrative dossiers pertain to the essential levels of service for civil and social rights that must be uniformly guaranteed nationwide.[341] Furthermore, subsequent

[340] See ruling No 3742 of the Lazio Regional Administrative Court, Rome, 21 March 2017.

[341] See art 117(II)(m) of the Italian Constitution; Vaccari, Berti, Silvestri (n 86) para 1.

paragraph 2-*quater* states that when regulating administrative procedures within their sphere of influence, local authorities may not set lower safeguards than those available to private citizens through the provisions concerning the essential service levels mentioned in paragraphs 2-*bis* and 2-*ter*, as they may only establish higher levels of protection.

G. Romania
D-CD

In Romania, there is no distinction between a national or local authority regarding decision-making. Law No 554/2004 on Administrative Judicial Review contains common provisions for challenging decisions at both national and local levels. When reviewing a decision, a court examines whether an abuse of power had taken place, taking into account that decisions by the local authorities entail a margin of discretion. For a discussion of bound competence and discretion in Romanian law, refer to Romania, Case 1 above.

However, when exercising discretionary powers, the administration is still bound by principles such as equality, proportionality, impartiality and transparency (Articles 6 to 13 of the Administrative Code).[342] Thus, such a decision must consider any individual who could fall into the category of servicemen who have 'contributed most to their nation'.

For instance, the principle of equality enshrined in Article 7 of the Administrative Code provides that

> beneficiaries of the operation of public administration authorities and institutions have the right to be treated equally, in a non-discriminatory manner, in conjunction with the obligation of public administration authorities and institutions to treat all beneficiaries equally, without discrimination based on legally specified criteria.

The algorithm, developed by a private company, should have been adopted by the municipality through an administrative act, so the algorithm itself needs to observe the principles mentioned above. Moreover, when a public task is delegated to a private company (for instance, building an algorithm or its practical application), all these principles must be respected. The algorithm was developed for use by a public authority, so it is not exempt from applying general principles.

The question here is whether the applicant has a right or a mere interest. In my opinion, it constitutes a subjective right deriving from the administrative act that sets the parameters of the content of the plaque. The right stems from the fact that the name of anyone meeting the specified criteria should be included on the monument, not only those determined by an algorithm.

Consequently, the refusal to consider Hector's arguments can be challenged in court on the grounds of lack of proportionality, equality, and impartiality.

[342] Available at <http://legislatie.just.ro/Public/DetaliiDocumentAfis/215925> accessed June 2023.

H. Serbia

MM

In a particular case, the fact that a decision was made by a local rather than national authority is not relevant in terms of the ability to challenge the decision before the relevant courts or other competent bodies. In the Serbian case, there would be two issues to analyse. The first is access to information, in this case the algorithm that determined the names; the second is the very decision to use an algorithm and its character as a decision taken in administrative procedure or as a decision taken by the local council within its powers to adopt general acts. According to the Serbian constitution, everyone has the right to access information kept by state bodies and organizations with delegated public powers in accordance with the law (Article 51). As can be concluded from the facts of the case, it is centred on access, or denial thereof, to information of public importance—in this case an algorithm. The Law on Free Access to Information of Public Importance[343] stipulates that information of public importance, within the meaning of that Law, is information held by a public authority, created during or relating to the operation of such a body, which is contained in a document and concerns anything the public has a justified interest in knowing. For information to be considered of public importance, it must be *irrelevant* whether the source of information is a public authority or another person, *the medium used for the document containing the information* (paper, tape, film, electronic media, etc), on which date the information was created, or in which way the information was obtained, nor may any other similar properties of such information bear any relevance for this purpose (Article 2). The Law further provides for a comprehensive yet effective procedure to protect access to rights in cases where requests are rejected or not answered by lodging a complaint with the Commissioner for Information of Public Importance and Personal Data Protection. In this case, the Commissioner would be expected to order the local municipality to provide the information, ie the algorithm.

As to the second issue, the character of the decision, it should first be determined whether it represents an administrative act to which administrative procedure would apply. Yugoslav legal theory developed the concept of 'administrative matter', and in the decades-long case law, only the decisions falling into the definition of 'administrative matter' could be challenged in the court. The troublesome aspect, however, is that the Law on General Administrative Procedure and the Law on Administrative Disputes define 'administrative matter' in different ways.[344] The LGAP defines it as a situation in which an authority, in directly applying laws, other regulations, and statutory instruments, legally or factually affects the position of a party by passing administrative acts, passing letters of guarantee, concluding administrative agreements, or undertaking administrative actions, and providing public services (Article 2). The Law on Administrative Disputes, on the other hand, defines 'administrative matter' as an individual indisputable situation of public interest in which the need to

[343] Official Gazette of RS, No 120/04, 54/07, 104/09 i 36/10, and 105/2021.

[344] Lilić specifically points to this, see further: S Lilić, *Law on General Administrative Procedure—Anatomy of a Legislative Project with the Model for the General Reconstruction of LGAP* (YUKOM, Dosije 2019)(in Serbian).

authoritatively legally determine the future behaviour of a party arises directly from the legislation (Article 5). The decision on how to choose the names to appear on the plaque cannot be considered to fall into any of the categories above in either of the two laws. The Mayor's claim to the 'greatest margin of discretion' implies that the decision to use an algorithm to choose the names of those included on the plaque is in essence a political decision or policy choice (most probably adopted as a general act of local council). As already examined in case 3, the Law on Local Self-government[345] stipulates that local self-government bodies manage public affairs of *direct, common, and general interest to the local population*. It also prescribes the right and obligation of such bodies to plan, regulate, and manage public affairs which are in their jurisdiction and of interest to the local population (Article 2). Therefore, all that could be challenged in the Constitutional Court is whether the decision to use an algorithm falls within the competences of the local self-government body, which it evidently does. According to Article 167—Control of Constitutionality and Legality, if the Court determines that the decision was within the remits given to the local municipality, the policy choice to use an algorithm could not be challenged.

I. Spain

IMD

The Spanish legal system makes no distinctions based on government levels for a case like this. It makes no difference whether a local, regional, or national authority uses an algorithm designed by a private company that has been awarded a public contract, and the same holds true from the exercise of discretionary powers. Also, Spanish law has no specific regulations on the use of algorithms for administrative decision-making. However, this does not prevent the application of the general provisions on administrative procedure.

This case requires examination of the two sides of the same coin: on the one hand, the exercise of discretionary powers or prerogatives; on the other, the decision to exercise discretionary power through an algorithm, also considering the role of transparency.

Firstly, although there is broad scope for discretion, all the procedural and rule-based aspects involved in the exercise of discretionary powers must be subject to review or control. In the case at hand, relying on an algorithm designed by a private company to make the decision entails the applicability of (i) public procurement law and (ii) the requirements for automated administrative decision-making laid down in Act 40/2015 on the Legal Regime applicable to Public Authorities (LRJSP) regarding the approval and operation of the algorithm. Indeed, Article 41 LRJSP implements the transparency standard as follows:

> Automated administrative action or decision-making means any act fully performed through electronic means by a public authority within an administrative procedure where there is no direct involvement of any public official.

[345] Law on Local Self-government (Official Gazette of RS, No 129/2007, 83/2014—other law, 101/2016—other law, 47/2018, and 111/2021—other law).

Article 41 adds that

> the competent body/bodies should be previously established on a case-by-case basis to define the specifications, schedule, maintenance, monitoring and quality assurance controls and, if appropriate, the audit procedure for the algorithm's information system and source code. Also, there must be a designated body responsible for challenges or appeals.

We could debate whether the case involves an automated action or an artificial intelligence-driven decision (which we cannot infer with regard to the facts of the case), but there is no doubt that Article 41 applies. Thus, from a procedural perspective, the said requirements must be met. Before making a decision, the municipality of Two Rivers would have to issue an administrative decision specifying the above-mentioned aspects. Otherwise, the decision could be found voidable on the grounds of non-compliance with an indispensable procedural requirement directly tied to the potential stakeholders' rights of defence.

Second, it should be recalled that there is a requirement to give reasons in discretionary decisions, ie the decision-making body must briefly state the reasons, mentioning relevant facts and supporting arguments for its decision, in order to secure the stakeholders' rights of defence and the fulfilment of the right to, and principle of, good or sound administration. It is unlikely that a court could consider the decision well-founded by simply referring to the output of the algorithm based on the available data. At the very least, it would be essential to know the origin of the data and how the algorithm works in order to determine which soldiers to honour and acknowledge on the plaque. The transparency standard requires these aspects to be disclosed and accessible unless otherwise required on grounds of overriding legal reasons.[346] There being no such reasons, the decision would be voidable as ill-founded. Lastly, the fact that the parties concerned have no knowledge of the algorithm's underlying rationale is also relevant, since this unawareness affects their rights of defence.

Considering these circumstances, there being no major differences arising from the use of an algorithm for decision-making, if a party concerned was rendered defenceless, the court would uphold Hector's appeal and would declare the decision voidable.

J. Switzerland

AF

Article 21 of the new Data Protection Act of 25 September 2020 (DPA) now provides a duty to inform in the case of automated individual decisions taken by a federal

[346] In Spain, several individuals have exercised their right of access to know an algorithm's source code, and after the public authorities had dismissed their claims, brought the case before specific oversight authorities, who granted total or partial access to the code. See Resolution 200/2017, of 21 June, issued by the Catalonia Committee tasked with Securing the Right of Access to Public Information. At the national level, regarding the public service requirement in the electric sector (discount tariff), see Resolution 701/2018 issued by the national Transparency and Good Governance Council. This resolution granted partial access but was challenged, and the judicial decision is still pending.

authority. If the data subject so requests, the controller must allow him to express his point of view, and the data subject may demand that a natural person review the automated individual decision.

The situation is not the same for municipal and cantonal authorities, as not all cantonal laws on this subject provide such explicit rules yet, but they will be gradually revised in the coming years.

Article 9 para 1(a) a of the Modernized Convention for the Protection of Individuals with Regard to the Processing of Personal Data of the Council of Europe (CETS No 223), not yet in force, should also be mentioned:

> Every individual shall have a right not to be subject to a decision significantly affecting him or her based solely on an automated processing of data without having his or her views taken into consideration.

However, in the absence of special rules on algorithmic decisions or in anticipation of such rules, the general requirement to state reasons arising from the right to be heard under art 29 para 2 Cst (see above Switzerland case 7 'The unjustified denial of a licence') should apply to decisions made with the help of an algorithm.

The present case is complicated by the fact that erecting a memorial plaque is, in principle, a 'material act' and not a ruling in Swiss administrative law. As a result, the persons concerned do not have a right to be heard, as would be the case if it were a ruling.[347] If it were to be assumed that Hector would be seriously prejudiced by this measure, a formal ruling would have to be rendered, and Hector would be able to demand a proper motivation on the basis of the general right to be heard.

K. United Kingdom

GA and CM

This scenario poses two questions, both of which can be answered in short order.

The first question is whether it makes any difference that the decision is taken by a local authority as opposed to a national authority. The short answer here is 'no'. While the courts can look more or less closely at a decision depending on whether it is taken by a central or local authority—where the nature and extent of discretion can be relevant[348]—all public decision makers must always act in accordance with the first principles of public law. The courts will thus potentially intervene in any case to ensure that the rule of law is upheld.

The second question is whether it makes any difference that the decision is based on an algorithm. This is an issue that has attracted commentary in recent years in the UK (as elsewhere), as it is well-known that there can be concerns about whether algorithms are consciously or unconsciously biased and whether they guarantee

[347] See A Flückiger, 'Switzerland' in this book, para 3.

[348] See, *International Transport Roth GmbH v Home Secretary* [2003] QB 728, 765–66, paras 81–85, Laws LJ.

procedural fairness.[349] The matter has not, as yet, been litigated to any significant extent in the UK, so any challenge would be made to the decision of the local authority as the decision maker that made use of the algorithm. The focus of any such challenge might include arguments about the reasonableness and legality of entrusting an exercise of discretion to an automated actor.

L. Venezuela

FP-F

Regarding this last proposed case, we can assume that the competent tribunal would not accept the reasons put forward by the Municipality since the decision to select the names to be included on the plaque had to be justified, regardless of whether it came from a municipal, regional, or national public administration. Nor is it relevant whether the method used is digital or not because the need to justify the administrative act remains. Furthermore, in Venezuela, the Law of Government Information requires free software; hence the algorithm code should be open and auditable.

[349] For some of the corresponding issues see P Craig, *Administrative Law* (9th edn, Sweet and Maxwell 2021) ch 10; and C Harlow and R Rawlings, *Law and Administration* (4th edn, Cambridge UP 2022) 248ff.

PART IV
COMPARATIVE ANALYSIS

15
About the Way General Principles Combine with Sector-Specific Rules in Administrative Procedural Law

Jean-Bernard Auby

I. General principles and their functions in general

The purpose of this chapter is to propose some elements of reflection concerning how general principles of procedure are combined with procedural rules laid down by specific legislation in the various administrative laws.

The approach adopted here is to start from some remarks concerning general principles and their functions in general (I) and some observations on the particular dimensions that general principles and their functions may have in the context of administrative law, and more specifically, in procedural administrative law (II), before suggesting an analytical model for how general procedural principles and specific rules combine in practice, as shown by comparative analysis (III).

Let us start by putting together some ideas about what it is that we call general principles and what types can be discerned (A), then about the functions these norms assume (B), and lastly, about the distinction between these and sector-specific rules (C).

A. The concept of general principles and categories of general principles

One comprehensive definition of general principles is that they are 'rules, norms or constructs that serve as the basis for the law, as sources of its creation, application or interpretation'.[1]

General principles are at the interface between positive and natural law and often reflect the latter's inspiration.

Nevertheless, they are an integral component of any body of law, even if they are apparent to differing degrees. As Dworkin words it,

> when lawyers reason or dispute about legal rights and obligations, particularly in those hard cases when our problems with these concepts seem most acute, they make

[1] A-J Arnaud (ed), *Dictionnaire encyclopédique de théorie et de sociologie du droit* (Librairie Générale de Droit et de Jurisprudence 1993)at Principes du droit.

Jean-Bernard Auby, *About the Way General Principles Combine with Sector-Specific Rules in Administrative Procedural Law*
In: *General Principles and Sector-Specific Rules in European Administrative Laws.* Edited by: Giacinto della Cananea and Jean-Bernard Auby, Oxford University Press. © Jean-Bernard Auby 2024. DOI: 10.1093/oso/9780198867579.003.0015

use of standards that do not function as rules, but operate differently as principles, policies and other sorts of standards.[2]

That said, among the principles inspiring a given body of law, a distinction can, and should, be made between those that remain underlying and do not acquire the status of norms recognized by that body and those explicitly raised to that status. As Kelsen writes, certain principles of morality, politics, or morals influence the creation of legal norms by the competent legal authorities, but they must be clearly distinguished from the legal norms whose content is consistent with them.[3]

To ensure the clarity of the analysis we propose in this chapter, it seems necessary to stick to principles that have been raised to the status of positive norms in the system in question.

However, an essential distinction must be made here, contrasting principles formally proclaimed in a written source of law—be it a treaty, the constitution, a statute, etc—with those that happen to be highlighted by judges independently of any written source in order to fill gaps in such sources.

This distinction is of great practical importance, as it implies a hierarchy: judges will typically refrain from giving principles that they deduced by themselves from the spirit of the legal system precedence over explicit written norms.

Further distinctions can be made concerning the general principles. For example, they are general to a greater or lesser degree. Some are highly versatile: eg all those related to equality. Others have a more specific purpose, as they have emerged to address particular problems that their broader counterparts could not deal with. In practice, in a given system, general principles often tend towards a lesser degree of generality.[4]

Another type of distinction can be drawn concerning the objects of different principles, eg:

- principles of a procedural nature and those related to substance (legal situations, the legal nature of an institution, and so on);
- principles conferring rights on the people—citizens, consumers—and principles conferring powers on public institutions; etc.

B. The functions fulfilled by general principles

Bodies of law contain various general principles recognized as norms of positive law. The following are contrasting examples. In public international law, one can identify a consistent set of general principles, some of which are inspired by national laws (estoppel, respect for acquired rights, etc). In contrast, others are derived from international law itself (the principle of humanity, freedom of maritime navigation, etc), to which the norms of '*jus cogens*' must be added, which are distinct and superior.[5]

[2] R Dworkin, *Taking Rights Seriously* (Duckworth 2004) 22.
[3] H Kelsen, *Théorie générale des normes* (Presses Universitaires de France 1996) 153.
[4] D de Bechillon, *Qu'est-ce qu'une règle de droit?* (Editions Odile Jacob 1997) 50.
[5] A Kaczorovska-Ireland, *Public International Law* (Routledge 2015) 325.

In contrast, a relatively recently developed body of law, such as global administrative law, still contains only few general principles. The doctrinal work and jurisprudential developments likely to bring them to light are still in progress.[6]

Domestic legal cultures—leaving aside their specific administrative law dimension, which our analysis will focus on later—are variously welcoming to general principles. In the common law world, for example, general principles tend to breed a certain distrust due to the widely shared conviction that their concrete consequences are difficult to anticipate.

On the other hand, it can be argued that every legal system contains general principles, more or less explicitly, and these general principles generally play an important role both as a source of inspiration for the whole system and as a default reference when explicit norms within it are lacking.[7]

Beyond this, not all general principles fulfil the same function. There are different kinds of general principles, sometimes reflecting functional differences. In this respect, an important distinction is to be made between those that constitute primary norms and those that constitute secondary norms, according to the terms of Hart's theory:[8] ie between principles with a direct bearing on a legal regime and those playing the indirect role of secondary norms.

C. General principles as distinct from sector-specific rules

A few words about the distinction between general principles and sector-specific rules are in order.

That a norm is a general principle does not necessarily mean it would be universally applicable to all possible legal situations. It may simply signify that it applies broadly in a given legal corpus: a given branch of law, a given legislation.

In contrast, norms which, within a given body of law, apply only to certain materially defined situations (matter-specific), or only to certain persons or authorities (person-specific or agency-specific), or only in certain places (territorially specific) may be regarded as 'sector-specific'.

II. Specific orientations of the issue in administrative law and procedural administrative law

It may be that the distinction between general principles and specific rules has particular resonance, a particular meaning, in administrative law in general (A) or procedural administrative law in particular (B). This needs to be briefly verified.

[6] G Anthony, J-B Auby, J Morison, and T Zwart (eds), *Values in Global Administrative Law* (Hart Publishing 2010); S Cassese, *An Introduction to Global Administrative Law* (Edward Elgar 2021).

[7] eg J-L Bergel, *Théorie générale du droit* (Dalloz 2004) 106.

[8] The latter tending to become dominant in contemporary legal systems: M van de Kerchove and F Ost, *Le système juridique entre ordre et désordre* (Presses Universitaires de France 1988) 231.

A. General principles and sector-specific rules in administrative law in general

1. Administrative law is, overall, very rich in general principles. This is primarily due to its historical development in the modern era, a period of considerable growth of administrative power and increasing sensitivity to the need to protect citizens against abuses of public power. The very *raison d'être* of administrative law naturally calls for the formulation of certain types of general principles. This is associated with what the American authors of a recent book aptly term the '*morality of administrative law*'.[9] This is also essential for its coherence, as some Spanish authors explain.[10]

This observation allows us to understand, for example, how it was possible for John Griffith and Harry Street to publish a book on the 'Principles of Administrative Law' in 1952[11] at a time when the dominant scholarship still denied the existence of administrative law in Great Britain, and how the Court of Justice could refer to the 'general rules of administrative law' in a case of 1960[12] when the existence of administrative law within the European law was not yet recognized either.

It is true, but this does not negate the phenomenon these examples illustrate, that the various national administrative laws have followed the path of recourse to general principles in different ways.

Where the construction of administrative law evolved mainly by way of case law, it was the judges who, at various times, referred to general principles of recourse to case law to regulate problems that the existing law did not cover correctly and, in particular, to ensure protection vis-à-vis public authorities that the existing law did not sufficiently provide. This was the scenario in French administrative law, where administrative judges went so far as to invent general principles without feeling obliged to point to any external basis in the legal order.[13] The same occurred in common law countries, but their judges looked to the common law for general principles specifically to apply them to emerging administrative law issues.[14]

Regarding national administrative laws constructed more on the basis of written law, administrative judges have sought general principles in statutes and constitutions.

In fact, constitutions increasingly contain principles relating to administrative procedure: either they concern it explicitly, or they regard more general norms from which constitutional case law has drawn consequences for it. A salient example is the rule of 'due process', which appears in Article 5 of the American Constitution

[9] C Sunstein and A Vermeule, *Law & Leviathan. Redeeming the Administrative State* (Harvard UP 2020).

[10] J M Rodríguez de Santiago, G Doménech Pascual, and L Arroyo Jiménez (eds), *Tratado de derecho administrativo* (Marcial Pons 2021) 26, 777ff.

[11] J Griffith and H Street, *Principles of Administrative Law* (Pitman 1952).

[12] Case 43/59, *Eva von Lachmüller, Bernard Peuvrier, Roger Ehrhardt v Commission of the European Economic Community* [1960] ECLI:EU:C:1960:37.

[13] See, eg, Jacques Petit and Pierre-Laurent Frier, *Droit administratif* (Librairie Générale de Droit et de Jurisprudence 2020) 122ff.

[14] See G Anthony, 'United Kingdom' in this book.

and is also found in the Constitutions of Paraguay, Brazil, and Taiwan, and various other states. Another is the principle of good administration, which is present in the Finnish Constitution, or the analogous principle of '*buon andamento*', which appears in Article 97 of the Italian Constitution, as well as the rules contained in Article 103 of the Spanish Constitution:

> The public administration shall serve the general interest in a spirit of objectivity and shall act in accordance with the principles of efficiency, hierarchy, decentralization, deconcentration and coordination in full submission to the law.[15]

Incidentally, it is evident that the constitutionalization of administrative law principles—associated with the fact that many general principles of administrative law derive from international and European sources of standards protecting fundamental rights—is tending to blur the distinction between administrative laws mainly based on case law and those more rooted in written law.

2. Does the distinction between general principles and sectoral rules have a particular scope in administrative law?

This may be true insofar as the contemporary history of administrative law shows a proliferation of specific regulations. Some govern large fields, such as tax law, customs law, local government, digital administration, and so on. Others more restrictively cover various concrete areas of public authority intervention: from social assistance to urban planning, economic intervention, environmental protection,[16] etc. These regulations come to form an enormous 'special administrative law', against which the general principles—elements of 'general administrative law'—often have to struggle to impose themselves.[17]

B. General principles and sector-specific rules in procedural administrative law

1. First of all, it must be emphasized that among general principles accepted by the various administrative laws, there are always a significant number that concern procedure.

These include wide-encompassing principles such as due process, transparency, respect for acquired rights, and so on, but also more narrow-targeted ones like those concerning time limits for administrative procedures, the right to call for witnesses, and so on.[18]

[15] J-B Auby (ed), *Codification of Administrative Procedure* (Bruylant 2014) 11.

[16] See, eg, S Storr, 'Austria' in this book.

[17] See, eg, de Santiago, Pascual, and Jiménez (eds) (n 10) 67ff.

[18] J-B Auby (ed), *Droit comparé de la procédure administrative* (Comparative Law of Administrative Procedure) (Bruylant 2016).

Such principles of procedural administrative law are often partly constitutionalized. Contributions to this book provide a range of examples concerning, in particular, Austria,[19] Italy,[20] Serbia,[21] Switzerland,[22] Venezuela,[23] and China, its constitution bringing a rather specific group of principles to the fore, however.[24] By contrast, the Rumanian Constitution simply mentions the right to judicial review and does not contain principles relating to administrative procedure itself.[25]

Some are guaranteed by international or European sources concerning the protection of fundamental rights: eg the important principle of good administration, proclaimed by the European Charter.

In a growing number of legal systems, this is supplemented by a general law of administrative procedure, which contains all the general principles accepted in the country's administrative procedural law—except those considered sufficiently protected by higher sources. We might call them 'general administrative procedure acts'.[26]

This type of general statute on administrative procedure is now becoming more widespread. In this book we find, in particular, the examples of Austria, with its famous model dating back to 1925,[27] Serbia,[28] Italy,[29] and Spain.[30] Venezuela even has three laws on administrative procedure[31]

In the European sphere, only the United Kingdom and Ireland have not adopted one. French administrative law overcame its traditional reluctance towards this kind of instrument in 2018.[32]

2. Perhaps paradoxically, the existence of a general legislation on administrative procedure does not eliminate all forms of sector-specific procedural rules.

In fact, to take into account particular social or economic contexts and/or accommodate certain bureaucratic practice, specialized regulations frequently establish their own procedural schemes, deviating more or less from those established by the general legislation. The natural tendency of administrations to try and impose their own procedural preferences is sometimes offset by rules which only allow them to do so when duly motivated.[33]

[19] Storr (n 16).
[20] S Vaccari, N Berti, and M Silvestri, 'Italy' in this book.
[21] M Milenković, 'Serbia' in this book.
[22] A Flückigel, 'Switzerland' in this book.
[23] F Pesci-Feltri, 'Venezuela' in this book.
[24] See X Sun, 'China' in this book.
[25] See D Dragoş, 'Romania' in this book.
[26] See Auby (ed), *Codification of Administrative Procedure* (n 15).
[27] See Z Kmieciak (ed), *Administrative Procedure in the Habsburg Succession Countries* (Lodz University and Wolters Kluwer Polska 2021).
[28] Milenković (n 21).
[29] Vaccari, Berti, and Silvestri (n 20).
[30] See I M Delgado, 'Spain' in this book.
[31] Pesci-Feltri (n 23).
[32] See S Saunier, 'France' in this book.
[33] See Auby (ed), *Droit comparé de la procédure administrative* (n 18) 483f.

III. Practical modes of combination as illustrated by comparison

In the light of the above, we can now venture some hypotheses as to how, in practice, general principles and specific rules come to combine in administrative procedural law. First, this requires us to acknowledge that there are situations in which the two types of norms do not meet (A). It will then be seen that, when a general principle and a specific rule coexist, the most frequent solution is that one of the two has priority (B). Nevertheless, it should be added that they sometimes tend to apply cumulatively (C).

A. Situations in which no conjunction between general principles and sector-specific rules occurs

This hypothesis may appear paradoxical: norms of a general character should apply to every situation pertaining to the corresponding body of law. However, things are a little more complex for at least two opposite reasons.

First, a particular specialized field of administrative law can be exempt from any specific procedural requirement and thus be submitted only to the general procedural rules. This is not infrequent.

In fact, such situations are provided for in some legal systems in the form of provisions that give general laws of administrative procedure a subsidiary character: the general law then acts as a default rule, applicable to all procedures not governed by specific texts. This is how the relationship between the 1976 German General Administrative Procedure Act and specific statutes is organized, the former being, according to its Article 1, applicable 'when no federal law or federal regulation contains similar or contrary provisions'.

The subsidiary application of the general law may be confined to certain areas: the Spanish general law does not usually apply in the field of taxation, but it is allowed to play a suppletive role in the event of gaps in the tax legislation.

The second reason concerns situations which should, in principle, be covered by both general principles and specific rules but which the legislation subtracts from the former and subjects only to the latter:[34] thus, making the specific regulation impermeable vis-à-vis general procedural rules.

This can be seen, for example, in the relationship established between the 2012 Estonian General Administrative Procedure Act and the law applicable to public procurement: according to its Article 2:

> For the purposes of this Act, the procedure for … public procurement and adjudication of challenges for the purposes of the Public Procurement Act … are not administrative procedure.

[34] In fact, China also shows an example of situations not covered by either general principles or specific ones. There are proceedings concerning civil servants: see Sun (n 24).

B. The most common solution: one norm takes priority over the other

We must then consider the cases where one procedural administrative law issue is potentially subject to two general principles and sector-specific rules, with no superior norm overriding the former.

To begin with, let us note that solutions to this kind of conflict between norms can be found in two ways. They can be explicitly provided in written law: many general administrative procedure acts envisage their combination with specific laws. They can also come from some jurisprudence, an example of which is the position of common law courts, to which we will return shortly.

1. Competition between a general principle and sector-specific rules often results in one type of norm prevailing: either general principles trump the sector-specific rules or the reverse.

Rationally, the second solution should be dominant, in accordance with the old legal adage '*lex specialis derogat generalibus*'. And indeed, this is what happens in some administrative laws. A clear example can be found in the 2017 Swedish General Administrative Procedure Act, whose section 4 states:

> If another act or an ordinance contains a provision that differs from this Act, that provision is applied.

A particular version of this solution appears when some of the administrations typically falling within the scope of the general principles are given the right to disregard them in order to apply their own rules. Thus, in Portuguese law, many provisions of the general administrative procedure act are optional, and agencies can override them if they consider them inappropriate.

On the other hand, priority may be given to general principles. This is well illustrated by English-type systems, in which the common law principles concerning the procedural rights of citizens can only be restricted by pieces of specialized legislation if they are provided for in express and unambiguous language and if they are compatible with the 1998 Human Rights Act.[35] Similarly, Italian case law has stated that any provision restricting stakeholder participation in administrative procedure has to be interpreted narrowly.[36]

Obviously, the preferential application of either general principles or sector-specific rules is also conditioned by their respective positions in the normative hierarchy. Where administrative procedural rules are embedded in the constitution or international treaties, they will generally retain primacy over sector-specific rules unless they also have constitutional or international rule status.

Sometimes the relationship between the general law and specific legislation is variable. Thus, in Czech law, the application of specific legislation sometimes precludes applying general law, whereas the general law typically plays a subsidiary role in relation

[35] Anthony et al (n 6).
[36] Vaccari, Berti, and Silvestri (n 20).

to special legislation. In Estonian law, the general law is, in principle (Article 112), applicable in a field covered by special legislation only if the latter provides for it: but case law has accepted that reference to the general law is only necessary when the special law has the same level of specificity as the general law, whereas, when the special law covers a more limited field, the general law is applicable even without reference to it.[37]

2. Comparative examination of procedural administrative laws shows that the conflict between general principles and sector-specific rules may be resolved in a more nuanced way.

Sometimes, when faced with competition between general principles and sector-specific rules, judges will decide which of these norms should have priority depending on the context and the issues at stake.

A variant of this solution concerns cases where judges are given, or give themselves, the authority to weigh up the interests protected by the general principle and the specific rule in order to decide which should prevail.

C. Cumulative application

The relationship between general principles and sector-specific rules may be one of addition: both apply cumulatively to produce a higher level of general protection for citizens.

Sometimes, cumulative application will simply reflect the fact that precisely the same norm has the status of a general principle and is also a rule stated in the specific legislation concerned. The chapter on Romania[38] gives an example of this concerning the principle of impartiality, reiterated in the legislation concerning the asylum application procedure.

In some jurisdictions, the relationship between general acts of administrative procedure and specific legislation is based on the fact that their respective provisions may be applied cumulatively if this creates added value. This is the principle established in Chilean, Portuguese, and Swiss law. Finnish law also adopts this formula in its combinations with municipal law, which contains special provisions on procedural rules applicable to local authorities.[39]

This combined application implies an assessment of the interests borne by the general principles and the specific rules, respectively. This assessment is necessary to determine whether or not their combined application produces added value.

One issue in particular needs to be considered. In some cases, the specific laws that must be coordinated with the general law are neither matter-specific nor territorially specific; instead, they are specific to an administrative entity or a group of administrative entities (organ-specific or agency-specific). In the American system, for example, general procedural law is strongly complemented by specific laws governing procedures before each agency.

[37] See Auby (ed), *Droit comparé de la procédure administrative* (n 18) 490.
[38] Dragoş (n 25).
[39] ibid.

A key question is thus whether the administrations in question have the right to supplement or even adapt the rules of the general law themselves.

In the German system, authorities sometimes have room for manoeuvre to adapt the procedure to the more or less complex nature of the situation being administered.

In other systems, administrations seem to have an even greater latitude to regulate their procedures: in Estonia, they have extensive freedom over procedural details, and the same seems to be the case in Taiwan.

* * *

The subject we have addressed here introduces us to an issue that is much more complex than it appears, namely the structure of legal systems and the role that principles play in that structure.[40] A somewhat simple pyramid view sometimes prevents us from grasping the extent of the phenomenon.

The subject of the combination of general principles and specific rules in administrative procedural law illustrates this well. One would be inclined to think that the former should naturally take priority because of the greater richness of their meaning and their often high rank in the normative hierarchy. We have seen that things are, in practice, a little more complicated.

This reflects the fact that the formal landscape offered by a legal system sometimes hides underlying logic that does not necessarily fit with it.

It also reflects realities specific to administrative law, especially procedural administrative law. Administrative regulations are, in a way, sectorally produced. Each of them is inspired by an administration—a ministry or group of ministries—with its own understanding of the realities to be regulated, its own procedural practices.

Each particular administration will try to impose its own procedural rules, with which it feels comfortable. It will then be up to governmental coordination authorities, the legislator, and perhaps judges, to bring them back to common principles where this seems desirable.

[40] See, eg, Académie Internationale de Droit Comparé, *La structure des systèmes juridiques* (Bruylant 2003).

16
General Principles at the European Level

Mads Andenas

I. General principles relevant for resolving the hypothetical cases

This chapter addresses the general principles at the European level. In the interlocking European legal order, general principles are applied at all levels, including that of the European Union (EU), European human rights, and nation states. General principles at different levels contribute to the formation and application of principles at other levels. Domestic law at the nation state level contributes to the formation of principles at the levels of the EU, European human rights, and international law. In the other direction, from the European law level to the domestic, these supranational level principles influence the principles at the domestic level, and create an influential interaction between the interlocking legal orders. This also includes an interaction with international law, which not only will have its direct impact, but its impact at any of these levels. General principles are open-textured, and open for influences that may not formally or jurisdictionally fit into doctrines of autonomy of the jurisdiction in question, or its doctrine on sources of law. The general principles are strengthened through such impact at all the different levels and their interaction. That goes so far that law from other jurisdictions, including domestic law from states outside the European jurisdictions or regional international law, may enter at any of the levels.

In his introduction, Giacinto della Cananea has explained the focus on the relationship between general principles and sector-specific rules, and why this relationship is such an interesting subject for a comparative analysis.[1] He also explains the main outcomes of the project of this book in the final chapter, 'Same Problems, Same Solutions?'.

We turn first to the general principles relevant for resolving the hypothetical cases, as these general principles have been enumerated in the national reports.

We begin by discussing how general principles of EU law are applied in the national reports of the cases in A. immediately below. In B. we turn to the application of general principles of European human rights law, and in C. to international law.

[1] G della Cananea, 'Introduction' in this book.

Mads Andenas, *General Principles at the European Level* In: *General Principles and Sector-Specific Rules in European Administrative Laws.* Edited by: Giacinto della Cananea and Jean-Bernard Auby, Oxford University Press.
 DOI: 10.1093/oso/9780198867579.003.0016

A. General principles of EU law

General principles of EU law are general principles of law applied by the European Court of Justice (ECJ) and the national courts of the Member States when determining the lawfulness of legislative and administrative measures within the EU. In the first European Economic Areas Agreement (EEA) opinion of the ECJ, Opinion 91/1,[2] the ECJ explains that the EU treaty constitutes the constitutional charter of a Community based on the rule of law. At the core are the principles of primacy and direct effect of EU law:

> The essential characteristics of the Community legal order which has thus been established are in particular its primacy over the law of the Member States and the direct effect of a whole series of provisions which are applicable to their nationals and to the Member States themselves.

General principles of EU law may have reached a constitutional level which protects them against treaty amendment (such as primacy and direct effect established in Opinion 1/91). They may be amended by treaty. They may also—at the other end—fill in where there is no secondary legislation providing an answer. They may be general in the sense that they apply across the legal order, or they may be limited to a legal or a policy sector.

The interaction on general principles between the states as treaty makers and the ECJ has not been without tensions. Proportionality has been developed based on the treaties and secondary legislation. It sets limits to Member State action, but also to the actions of EU institutions. The existence of the principle has thus not been controversial.

Subsidiarity has been more controversial. Subsidiarity had no treaty base and had the potential to circumscribe EU competencies. It was not wholly embraced by the EU courts. Already the Single European Act,[3] signed in 1986, incorporated subsidiarity into environmental policy, but without referring to it explicitly as such. It is indicative of the judicial reception that in 1995, the Court of First Instance of the European Communities[4] stated that the principle of subsidiarity was not a general principle of law, against which the legality of Community action should have been tested, prior to the entry into force of the Treaty on the European Union (TEU). The principle of subsidiarity was formally taken into the treaties by the TEU in 1992. The TEU referred to the principle in the Treaty establishing the European Community (TEC). The Treaty of Amsterdam in 1997 kept the wording of the reference to the principle of subsidiarity in the renumbered Article 5, second paragraph, of the TEC. It also annexed to the

[2] *Opinion 91/1* [1991] ECR I-06079, ECLI:EU:C:1991:490, in para 219. Full title: *Opinion of the Court of 14 December 1991 on the draft agreement between the Community, on the one hand, and the countries of the European Free Trade Association, on the other, relating to the creation of the European Economic Area.*

[3] Single European Act, OJ L 169, 29 June1987.

[4] Case T-29/92 *Vereniging van Samenwerkende Prijsregelende Organisaties in de Bouwnijverheid and others v Commission of the European Communities*, 21 February 1995 [1995] European Court Reports II-00289, ECLI:EU:T:1995:34.

TEC a Protocol on the application of the principles of subsidiarity and proportionality. This 1997 Protocol had thirteen articles clarifying the legal nature of the principles of subsidiarity and proportionality, and emphasizing the duty to provide reasons. The first five made clear the extent to which the principles were to be restricted within the principles developed by the ECJ:

(1) In exercising the powers conferred on it, each institution shall ensure that the principle of subsidiarity is complied with. It shall also ensure compliance with the principle of proportionality, according to which any action by the Community shall not go beyond what is necessary to achieve the objectives of the Treaty.
(2) The application of the principles of subsidiarity and proportionality shall respect the general provisions and the objectives of the Treaty, particularly as regards the maintaining in full of the acquis communautaire and the institutional balance; it shall not affect the principles developed by the Court of Justice regarding the relationship between national and Community law, and it should take into account Article F(4) of the Treaty on European Union, according to which 'the Union shall provide itself with the means necessary to attain its objectives and carry through its policies'.
(3) The principle of subsidiarity does not call into question the powers conferred on the European Community by the Treaty, as interpreted by the Court of Justice. The criteria referred to in the second paragraph of Article 3b of the Treaty shall relate to areas for which the Community does not have exclusive competence. The principle of subsidiarity provides a guide as to how those powers are to be exercised at the Community level. Subsidiarity is a dynamic concept and should be applied in the light of the objectives set out in the Treaty. It allows Community action within the limits of its powers to be expanded where circumstances so require, and conversely, to be restricted or discontinued where it is no longer justified.
(4) For any proposed Community legislation, the reasons on which it is based shall be stated with a view to justifying its compliance with the principles of subsidiarity and proportionality; the reasons for concluding that a Community objective can be better achieved by the Community must be substantiated by qualitative or, wherever possible, quantitative indicators.
(5) For Community action to be justified, both aspects of the subsidiarity principle shall be met: the objectives of the proposed action cannot be sufficiently achieved by Member States' action in the framework of their national constitutional system and can therefore be better achieved by action on the part of the Community.

Articles 2 and 3 make specific reference to the jurisprudence of the ECJ, which the 1997 Protocol builds upon, and which these references made explicitly clear that were to be upheld under the 1997 Protocol.

In 2007 the Treaty of Lisbon, amending the TEU and TEC, incorporated the principle of subsidiarity into Article 5(3) of the TEU, retaining in this TEU article the words of the corresponding TEC article. It also added references to the regional and local dimension of subsidiarity and a new role for the national parliaments in compliance with subsidiarity.

General principles of EU law that give effect to the rule of law may be derived from common legal principles in the various EU Member States, or general principles found in international law or other EU law sources. General principles are applied to avoid the denial of justice, fill gaps in EU law, and strengthen the coherence of EU law.

Article 6(3) of the Treaty on European Union provides for fundamental rights:

> Fundamental rights, as guaranteed by the European Convention for the Protection of Human Rights and Fundamental Freedoms and as they result from the constitutional traditions common to the Member States, shall constitute general principles of the Union's law.

In the EU treaties there is an express reliance on the general principles in the laws of the Member States for the liability of EU institutions. Article 340 of the Treaty on the Functioning of the European Union (TFEU) maintained the original provision in the former Article 215 of the Treaty establishing the European Economic Community (EEC) (in words unamended from the Treaty of Rome of 1957). Article 215 provides for the application of the 'general principles common to the laws of the Member States' in the case of non-contractual liability.

General principles of EU law have been developed in the ECJ's case law, and in many instances have been taken into the EU treaties. In addition to fundamental rights, proportionality, and subsidiarity as discussed above, they include legal certainty, equality before the law, and the precautionary principle in environmental policy. The precautionary principle is a sectoral principle with increasing reach outside environmental policy.

The ECJ has relied on domestic law in the identification and development of general principles of EU law.[5] This was the case also for the early case law on the liability of EU institutions under Article 340 of the TFEU based on Article 215 of the Treaty establishing the EEC (as already mentioned, in words unamended from the Treaty of Rome of 1957). In the extension and application of this case law, the opinions of the Advocates General in the important cases on Member State liability for breach of EU law contained sophisticated analysis of domestic law, which were relied upon by the ECJ in the seminal judgments in the 1990s.[6] The case law on liability for breach of EU law, has later been applied by the ECJ without any reliance on domestic law, or 'the laws of the Member States'. It gives effect to the principle of full reparation for damage by breach of the law, in a regime that combines civil liability and state or public authority liability.[7]

[5] As explained by K Lenaerts and K Gutman, 'Comparative Law and the Court of Justice of the European Union: Interlocking Legal Orders Revisited' in M Andenas and D Fairgrieve (eds), *Comparative Law in the Courts* (OUP 2015) 141–76.

[6] Joined cases C-6/90 and C-9/90 *Francovich* [1991] European Court Reports I-05357, ECLI:EU:C:1991:428ECLI:EU:C:1991:428 and Joined cases C-46/93 and C-48/93 *Brasserie du Pêcheur SA v Bundesrepublik Deutschland and The Queen v Secretary of State for Transport, ex parte: Factortame Ltd and others*, [1996] European Court Reports I-01029, ECLI:EU:C:1996:79.

[7] Applying the general principle of international law of full reparation as confirmed by the Permanent Court of Justice, the forerunner to the International Court of Justice, in *Factory at Chorzow (Germany v Poland)*, 1927 P.C.I.J. (ser. A) No 9. The International Court has in its modern jurisprudence relied on the damages jurisprudence of the ECtHR, in particular in *Ahmadou Sadio Diallo (Republic of Guinea v Democratic Republic of the Congo)*, Compensation, Judgment, ICJ Reports 2012, 324.

The principles of EU law are referred to and relied upon in domestic courts and in the European Court of Human Rights (ECtHR), which in return reciprocate by relying on the others.

The ECJ is different from national courts and the ECtHR in that it does not rely on domestic law, or 'the laws of the Member States', except in the identification of principles. Domestic courts would occasionally rely on courts from other Member States in their application of EU law. In the classic judgment from the first years of UK EU membership, in *Bulmer v Bullinger*,[8] Lord Denning cited judgments of German and Dutch courts on the application of Article 267 of the TFEU (formerly Article 177 EEC and Article 234 EC) on references from national courts to the ECJ. And in *Techna SA*,[9] the French *Conseil d'Etat* made a reference to a decision by the English High Court concerning labelling requirements under EU law, explicitly citing an English case in support of suspending a directive.[10] *Techna* may help explain why the ECJ remains so reluctant to acknowledge the domestic case law on EU law. In *Techna SA* the French *Conseil d'Etat* sought support from the English courts to suspend a directive, and in a way the ECJ would not itself have sanctioned. The application of EU law in domestic courts, by higher courts in different countries citing one another where they could not find a clear solution in the ECJ jurisprudence, could in such cases challenge the supremacy of the ECJ and the effectiveness of EU law.[11] Thus the ECJ would never cite a domestic court as an authority on any point of EU law. This restraint in the use of domestic law is very different from the ECtHR which may give domestic courts much space and attention in its judgments. The ECtHR would seem to attach weight on the domestic courts' interpretation of the European Convention on Human Rights (ECHR) rights, and this could include an individual judgment from a domestic court that has set out its interpretation on the acceptable reach of a specific right. This is in addition to the assessment of the formation of principles, or in particular a 'national consensus' which applies to the very core of the ECtHR's treaty competence in a way that has no parallel in the ECJ.

The EU does not have doctrines on a national margin of appreciation or a proceduralization by which the national margin has been extended under the case law of the ECtHR.[12] The ECJ does not refer to any 'consensus' between Member States when it determines which groups are covered by the protection for rights under the treaties.[13] Subsidiarity in EU law[14] is primarily for the legislator, and not any effective ground of judicial review of legislation or administrative action, or even as an interpretative principle.

[8] *Bulmer v Bullinger* [1974] Ch 401.

[9] *Techna SA*, the French *Conseil d'Etat* 29 October 2003 No 260768.

[10] M Andenas and D Fairgrieve, 'In Search of Common Language for Open Legal Systems' in Andenas and Fairgrieve (n 5) 2–22.

[11] This is set out in several of the contributions in M Andenas and F Jacobs (eds, with a Foreword by Lord Bingham), *European Community Law in the English Courts* (OUP) 1998).

[12] See, for a recent analysis, A Stone Sweet, W Sandholz, and M Andenas, 'The Failure to Destroy the Authority of the European Court of Human Rights: 2010–2018' (2022) 21 Law Pract Int Courts Trib 244–77.

[13] Case C-13/94 *P v S and Cornwall County Council* [1996] European Court Reports I-02143, ECLI:EU:C:1996:170.

[14] As introduced in art 5(3) of the Treaty on European Union (TEU) and Protocol (No 2) on the application of the principles of subsidiarity and proportionality.

The ECJ framed its gradually emerging case law on a range of issues as a matter of literal interpretation of the treaty provisions or other EU legislation. This applies to the protection of transsexuals or gender reassigned. In *P v S and Cornwall County Council*,[15] the employer, and the UK with support of other states, declared that dismissing a person after gender reassignment was not gender discrimination. The employer said it would have dismissed the person whatever gender they were reassigned to. The ECJ ruled that the Equal Treatment Directive, it was asked to interpret, precluded dismissal for a reason related to gender reassignment. The ECJ simply declared that as long as they were fired because of the gender reassignment, that certainly revealed that gender or sex was the ground of the dismissal. It constituted a breach of the narrow prohibition on sex discrimination in employment, and the wider discrimination ban. This was primarily framed as a matter of literal interpretation of the Treaty and other EU legislation. This literal interpretation was also an expression of a fundamental principle of equality. The ECJ's judgments had an important impact on the ECtHR. Throughout the 1980s and 1990s, the ECtHR had stuck to a narrow interpretation of the protection of privacy in Article 8 of the ECHR, the right to marry, and also the prohibition of discrimination in Article 14 ECHR. Only in the 2002 Grand Chamber judgment of *Goodwin*[16] did the ECtHR follow and extended Article 8 protection of the personal sphere of individual to transsexuals, including the right to establish details of their identity as individual human beings. It had in several judgments indicated that this right was about to achieve the necessary 'national consensus', and several years after the ECJ, the ECtHR could declare that protection had to be extended also under the ECHR.

The ECJ's incremental case law on free movement of goods provide another example. It concerns treaty provisions prohibiting any form of quantitative restrictions on imports and exports and any measure having the equivalent effect of quantitative restrictions (today in Articles 34 and 35 of the TFEU). Joseph Weiler and others have analysed the case law by the ECJ where it plainly asks whether there is a restriction that could make movement burdensome or less attractive, not requiring any form of discrimination, as 'transformational' and radical.[17] In the earlier case law, the ECJ had made the application of the prohibition subject to a gradually hardening discrimination requirement, going from a less burdensome test on state regulation towards a more demanding test. In *Dassonville*, measures having the equivalent effect of quantitative restrictions was defined as 'all trading rules enacted by a member state which are capable of hindering, directly or indirectly, actually or potentially, intra-community trade'.[18] *Dassonville* and the preceding cases on customs tariffs could instead be seen as providing a literal interpretation of the free movement provisions of the treaty, setting out what constitutes a measure having the equivalent effect of quantitative restrictions. This follows the public international law method on treaty interpretation according to

[15] Case C-13/94 *P v S and Cornwall County Council* [1996] European Court Reports I-02143, ECLI:EU:C:1996:170.

[16] *Christine Goodwin v the United Kingdom* (Application no 28957/95) ECtHR 11 July 2002.

[17] J H H Weiler, 'The Transformation of Europe' (1991) 100 Yale LJ 2403–483. In the years that followed, Weiler developed this line of analysis in several publications, and also applied it to the seminal decisions of the WTO Appellate Body on what constituted restrictions or restrictions having equivalent effect.

[18] Case 8/74 *Procureur du Roi v Dassonville* [1974] ECR 837, ECLI:EU:C:1974:82.

the Vienna Convention on the Law of Treaties (VCLT). What breaks with the traditional canons of treaty interpretation would be the reading down of the free movement requirements that ended with a requirement of discrimination. This could be explained as incrementally giving direct effect to free movement.[19] What is interesting for our purposes is that the ECJ provided the incrementally hardening discrimination test and eventually did away with it, giving direct effect to the restrictions requirement (the literal interpretation). The ECJ did so without relying on any margin of national discretion, national consensus, or acquitting states that had undertaken a review of the measures satisfying certain procedural requirements or provided reasons, or after any wider balancing of considerations. The ECJ's approach was not based on the same interaction between national law and national court we find in the jurisprudence of the ECtHR, based on the principles of ECHR law that the latter court had developed.

The EU courts, with the ECJ as the supreme judicial organ of the EU, has a role in upholding the treaties which has worked out differently from the way in which the ECtHR operates. The ECJ would in important cases rule against submissions by the Member States, even a large majority of them, or all of them. EU law is not determined by submissions by the Member States who can only amend the treaties or other EU law through appropriate procedures, to the extent that these are available to them. This is a difference from the ECtHR, which never rules against a large majority of states. It is not wholly explained by the existence of the European Commission that has no real counterpart in the system under the ECHR.

The ECJ would rely on domestic law, or 'the laws of the Member States', in the identification of general principles, both where the treaties required it, and elsewhere. When these are established as principles of EU law, they become autonomous or independent from on the domestic law, or 'the laws of the Member States', on which their introduction into EU law were based. The ECJ would not make subsequent references to judgments by domestic courts.[20] As explained above, the ECJ would not refer to domestic courts on any EU law matter at all, except in its review of their compliance with EU law under an obligation to comply as bodies of Member States.[21]

The courts of the Member States implement EU law, and are under a duty to do so. Member State courts vary in the way in which they rely on EU law and the case law of the ECJ, at least in the way in which they discuss the ECJ jurisprudence in their judgments. Courts in all Member States will have an extensive jurisprudence on European principles of law. The application of proportionality is a pressing problem in all national jurisdictions. In the UK Supreme Court, Lord Reed has in several judgments restated the proportionality test that applies in EU and ECHR law, and compared how domestic courts should apply them, as seen in his judgments in *Bank Mellat* and *Lumsdon*.[22] There are intense judicial discussions also about how the domestic

[19] M Andenas, 'The Reach of Free Movement and the Gradualist Approach of the CJEU' in M Andenas, T Bekkedal, and L Pantaleo (eds), *The Reach of Free Movement* (T.M.C. Asser Press and Springer 2017) 1–17, and M Andenas, 'Sovereignty' in C Baudenbacher (ed), *The Fundamental Principles of EEA Law* (Springer 2017) 90–109.

[20] As explained by Lenaerts and Gutman (n 5).

[21] Andenas and Jacobs (eds, with a Foreword by Lord Bingham) (n 11).

[22] *Bank Mellat v HM Treasury (No 2)* [2013] UKSC 39, [2014] AC 700 and *R (Lumsdon) v Legal Services Board* [2015] UKSC 41, [2016] AC 697.

judgments can be reconciled, and about what the underlying principles ought to be—see for instance Lord Sales 2020 lecture.[23]

It is interesting to note the extent to which the courts of the Member States apply EU law and the case law of the ECJ also when the applicable law is not strictly speaking EU law, and there is no obligation to apply EU law (as we will discuss below). Member State courts will apply the proportionality test as part of EU and ECHR law, but this test will also influence the general test of judicial review in what remains of domestic public law outside the reach of EU and ECHR law.[24] This will apply also to other principles.

An important feature of the relationship between domestic courts and the ECJ is the preliminary rulings procedure under which domestic courts have wide options to refer with the exception of courts of last instance which have a more narrowly defined duty to refer questions of EU law to the ECJ.[25]

Article 267 of the TFEU provides:

> The Court of Justice of the European Union shall have jurisdiction to give preliminary rulings concerning:
> (a) the interpretation of the Treaties;
> (b) the validity and interpretation of acts of the institutions, bodies, offices or agencies of the Union.

As we will see below, a similar procedure has been added to the ECHR for domestic courts to refer questions to the ECHR. To date, the ECtHR has delivered six opinions compared to the many thousands by the ECJ.

In the EU there is no general procedural code. There are, as in some Member States, detailed procedural rules on the exercise of EU administrative powers, including in agricultural, competition, and state aid policy. General principles of EU law constitute one way in which these sectoral rules are used to fill gaps and generate rules where none have been directly provided. Principles of EU law may also directly apply to Member States in their exercise of EU law, powers, or authority, or in the application of EU legislation such as the extensive EU directives on environmental impact assessment that also transposes international obligations such as the Aarhus Convention.

Sector-specific rules has developed in many fields of EU law. One instance is in the rights of the defence jurisprudence developed in competition law where the EU had competences to enforce the law directly against individual citizens and companies. The interaction with the rights under Article 6 of the European Convention, the EU Charter of Rights, and treaty reform, has moved the rights of defence up to the general level.

[23] Lord Sales, 'Proportionality review in appellate courts: a wrong turning?' (November 2020), <https://www.supremecourt.uk/docs/speech-181120.pdf> accessed 15 February 2024.

[24] Lord Bingham of Cornhill, 'A New Common Law for Europe' in B S Markesinis (ed), *The Coming Together of the Common Law and the Civil Law* (Hart/Bloomsbury 2000) 2, citing M Andenas in *English Public Law and the Common Law of Europe* (Key Haven Publications 1998) 8 on the impact on domestic judicial review of EU and ECHR proportionality test.

[25] M Andenas, *Article 177 References to the European Court—Policy and Practice* (Butterworths 1994).

Article 6 ECHR has developed into the central pillar of European human rights protection and also of a common constitution based on the EU and ECHR legal orders. The ECJ has developed a distinct jurisprudence on 'rule of law', 'judicial protection', and 'loyalty'/'sincere cooperation' in the judgments against Poland and Hungary.[26] The ECJ rulings on Poland are quite remarkable in their express reliance on the ECtHR, see *A K v Krajowa Rada Sądownictwa*.[27]

Turning back to Part III of this book: general principles of EU law are applied in the national reports of the cases in different ways. The general principles of EU law may determine the procedure or the outcome directly, or they may influence the application of domestic law that falls outside the EU jurisdiction in a direct manner. One example of the latter is in the Spanish report on the application of the principle of good administration.

As already set out at the beginning of this section, the environmental impact assessment rules are referred to in the Austrian, French, and Romanian reports. The Romanian report refers to the EU general principle of the rights of the defence and the Spanish report to the Charter of Fundamental Rights with regard to the concept of good administration.

Here are the mentions that general principles of EU law got in the national reports:

a) Austrian report mentions the provisions concerning the environmental impact assessment (see page 28 above).
b) The French report refers to the case law of the CJEU (case No 5). It also refers to EU directives on the delivery of public services and EU regulations on the environment (case No 9, see page 218 above).
c) The Greek report refers to the case law of the CJEU (case No 5, see page 165 above).
d) The Italian report refers to the case law of the CJEU (case No 5, see page 167 above).
e) The Romanian report refers to the EU general principle of the rights of the defence (case No 6, see page 182 above) and to EU regulations on the environment (case No 9, see page 223 above).

[26] Most importantly: Joined Cases C-615/20 and C-671/20, *YP and Others and M M* ECLI:EU:C:2023:562 for the remedies (eg paras 57–58) and principles of supremacy and sincere cooperation in paras 73, 74, 80, 81, 93; C-156/21 *Hungary v Parliament and Council*, EU:C:2022:97, para 232, on Art 2 TEU being not merely a statement of policy guidelines or intentions, but containing values which are an integral part of the very identity of the European Union as a common legal order, values which are given concrete expression in principles containing legally binding obligations for the Member States; C-791/19, EU:C:2021:596, para 52 and Case C-204/21, *European Commission, supported by Kingdom of Belgium, Kingdom of Denmark, Kingdom of the Netherlands, Republic of Finland, Kingdom of Sweden as interveners v Republic of Poland*, ECLI:EU:C:2023:442, para 69 on the principle of the effective judicial protection of individuals' rights under EU law, Art 19(1) TEU, as 'a general principle of EU law stemming from the constitutional traditions common to the Member States, which has been enshrined in Articles 6 and 13 ECHR and which is now reaffirmed by Article 47 of the Charter' (Commission v Poland (Disciplinary regime for judges).

[27] See Joined Cases C-585/18, C-624/18, and C-625/18, *A v Krajowa Rada Sądownictwa*, ECLI:EU:C:2019:982, paras 126, 127, 128, 129, 130, 133, 137, 145. Koen Lenaerts' contribution to the 'Special Issue of the CJEL on the rule of law', https://cjel.law.columbia.edu/print/latest-issues/ and at the FIDE report on mutual trust, mutual recognition, and rule of law—the institutional report contains some useful points and references: https://cic.events/fide/fide-publications-vol-1.pdf, 67 ff.

f) The Spanish report refers to Article 41 of the Charter of Fundamental Rights with regard to the concept of good administration (see page 65 above).
g) The Serbian report refers to the Serbian adjustment to EU law in the introductory part (see page 63 above).
h) The UK report mentions initially the 'historical influence of EU law' on general principles, now applicable under the guise of 'retained EU law' (see page 78 above). It also refers to EU on state aids (case No 2, see page 88 above).

B. ECHR law

Most of the national reports from Member States make reference to Article 6 ECHR, and most of them in the report on case No 5. This is not surprising, as this is the provision about due process. The Austrian report case No 1 refers not only to Article 6 but also to Article 10 ECHR on freedom of expression.

General principles of European human rights law are general principles of law applied by the ECHR in Strasbourg and the national courts of the Member States when reviewing the compliance of national measures with the ECHR.

The ECtHR has developed principles on several core issues, and the one core principle that only applies to the ECtHR is the margin of appreciation.[28] This goes back to the *Belgian Linguistics* case of 1968, and was entrenched in the *Handyside* case of 1976.[29] The ECtHR has an extensive jurisprudence on proportionality and balancing, and a range of other principles.

Individuals can make direct complaints. States can also bring complaints against other states. Previously individuals could only complain to the European Commission of Human Rights which would decide on whether to bring the complaint forward to the ECtHR. The Member States of the Council of Europe adopted Protocol No 11 in 1998 which provided individuals with a right to complain directly about a Member State in the ECtHR for violations of their ECHR rights. The Commission was abolished. The mechanism to regulate the relationship to domestic legal process and courts, is the requirement that domestic remedies must be exhausted. This exhaustion requires that the complainant has brought the case before domestic courts, and up to the court of final appeal. This allows the domestic legal system, also at the judicial review stage, to give effect to the principles of subsidiarity. At the beginning of the century, all Member States had incorporated the ECHR into domestic law such that it could be enforced by domestic courts.

Until recently, the ECtHR had no preliminary rulings procedure as the one under which domestic courts could refer questions of EU law to the ECJ as provided for by Article 267 of the TFEU. In addition to the references to the ECJ, many Member States has reference procedures under which domestic courts can refer questions to a higher court. If a German court considers a statute to be unconstitutional and its decision depends on this statute, it suspends the proceedings and refers the matter to the Federal

[28] There is no parallel doctrine in public international law, and the UN Human Rights Committee has explicitly rejected it for the application of the ICCPR.

[29] *Belgian Linguistics* ECtHR 23 July 1968; *Handyside v the United Kingdom* ECtHR 7 December 1976.

Constitutional Court for decision.[30] The Federal Constitutional Court receives some 100 references annually. In France any party to a trial may raise a priority question of constitutionality (QPC) at any point in the proceedings.[31] The *Conseil constituionnel* delivers some 50 preliminary rulings annually on the issue of constitutionality. But also in countries without any formalized reference system there are often ways in which questions can proceed to the higher courts without a full trial of the facts.

Protocol No. 16 to the Convention, adopted in 2013 and entered into force on 1 August 2018, enabled the highest national courts, as designated by the Member States concerned, to request the ECtHR to give advisory opinions. This applies to questions of principle relating to the interpretation or application of the rights and freedoms defined in the ECHR. The ECtHR has discretion to accept or refuse a request. Advisory opinions are delivered by the ECtHR Grand Chamber; they contain reasons and are 'not binding'. There is every reason to expect these advisory opinions to be considered as authoritative as Grand Chamber judgments on the matters of law that they pronounce. To date, the ECtHR has delivered six opinions. It is clear that the advisory opinion procedure under Protocol No 16 will enhance the Court's role as a constitutional court, while bolstering the Court's view on the importance of inter-judicial dialogue to the subsidiarity principle.

Subsidiarity and the margin of appreciation was added to the ECHR Preamble by Protocol No 15, also adopted in 2013 and entering into force in 2021:

> Affirming that the High Contracting Parties, in accordance with the principle of subsidiarity, have the primary responsibility to secure the rights and freedoms defined in this Convention and the Protocols thereto, and that in doing so they enjoy a margin of appreciation, subject to the supervisory jurisdiction of the European Court of Human Rights ...

The official explanatory report declares that this reform 'is intended ... to be consistent with the doctrine of the margin of appreciation as developed by the Court in its case law'.[32] As with subsidiarity in the treaty process of the EU, some states had an aim of holding the court back, see the discussion above under A. Some authors are of the view that Protocol 15 would lead to a turn to greater national margins of appreciation.[33] Others are of the view that Protocol 15 simply does as it says, and only accepts and reinforces the Court's established interpretation of the margin of appreciation.

The ECtHR has complemented its doctrine on the national margin of appreciation by a doctrine of proceduralization. In this way the national margin has been extended.[34]

[30] Art 100(1) of the Basic Law and §§ 80 ff of the Federal Constitutional Court Act.

[31] Introduced under the constitutional reform of 2008 in Art 61-1 of the French Constitution.

[32] Explanatory Report to Protocol No 15 to the ECHR (2013), available at <www.echr.coe.int/Documents/Protocol_15_explanatory_report_ENG.pdf> accessed February 2024. The Parliamentary Assembly of the Council of Europe underlined that the 'reference to the principle of subsidiarity and the doctrine of the margin of appreciation' strictly means 'as developed in the Court's case law': Parliamentary Assembly of the Council of Europe, Opinion 283 (2013), available at <http://assembly.coe.int/nw/xml/XRef/Xref-XML2HTMLen.asp?fileid=19723&lang=en> accessed July 2023.

[33] See, for example, M Rask Madsen, '"Unity in Diversity" Reloaded: The European Court of Human Rights' Turn to Subsidiarity and its Consequences' (2021) 15(1) The Law & Ethics of Human Rights 93–123.

[34] Stone Sweet, Sandholz, and Andenas (n 12) 244–77.

The ECtHR has made extensions of the group of protected groups dependent on a 'consensus' between Member States. *Dudgeon* (1981)[35] held that criminalizing homosexual acts was in breach of the ECHR. The ECtHR cited in support of its interpretation of Article 8 (privacy) 'an emerging consensus' across Member States that consensual homosexuality between adults in private ought not to be considered a crime. It developed an argument about the rule of law itself depending on a moral consensus. Another example is *Goodwin*,[36] where the ECtHR Grand Chamber unanimously found violations of Article 8 (right to respect for privacy and family life) and Article 12 (right to marry and to found a family). The ECtHR had in a series of cases from the 1980s and 1990s signalled that a sufficient consensus was in the process of emerging in the Member States so that the court itself could extend the protections of the Convention to transsexuals. The ECJ protected transsexuals under EU law several years earlier and relying on the words of the EU law written sources. As discussed above, the ECJ framed its gradually emerging case law on a range of issues as a matter of literal interpretation of the treaty provisions or other EU legislation. We have discussed *P v S and Cornwall County Council*[37] above. This ECJ judgment helped the ECtHR establish the national consensus it required to extend the protection to transsexuals.

The ECJ's approach was not based on the same interaction with national law and national courts we find in the jurisprudence of the ECtHR, based on the principles of ECHR law that the latter court had developed.

This provides an interesting contrast not only to the ECJ's discrimination jurisprudence. As discussed above, the ECJ's incremental case law on free movement of goods provide another example of how the ECJ approached the issues as matters of EU law, without relying on any national consensus or limiting the effect of EU law on any national margin of appreciation. At the same time, this limits the role of national courts, and also the exchanges between the European Court (here the ECJ) and national courts. A national consensus requirement may provide input to the formulation of the substantive rule. A national margin of appreciation increases the independent role of national courts in applying and giving effect to the European (ECHR) norms.

While national consensus, margin of appreciation, and proceduralization has been used as a deference mechanism, and to acquit states, such doctrines are overtly political. So even if such deference has been exercised to avoid conflicts with states, it is not clear if the method increases legitimacy among critics from the national side. It may be that the ECtHR judgment in *Christine Goodwin v the United Kingdom*[38] and the ECJ judgment in *P v S and Cornwall County Council*[39] illustrate that a more literal interpretation that may lend the court a greater authority or legitimacy. The ECtHR postpones or refuses the application and enforcement of rights based on doctrines

[35] *Dudgeon v. the United Kingdom* (Application no 7525/76) ECtHR 1981.

[36] *Christine Goodwin v the United Kingdom* (Application no 28957/95) ECtHR 2000.

[37] Case C-13/94 *P v S and Cornwall County Council* [1996] European Court Reports I-02143, ECLI:EU:C:1996:170.

[38] *Christine Goodwin v the United Kingdom* (Application no 28957/95).

[39] Case C-13/94 *P v S and Cornwall County Council* [1996] European Court Reports I-02143, ECLI:EU:C:1996:170.

of deference such as waiting for a national consensus to emerge, a varying margin of national appreciation, and proceduralization under which national measures are not censured because national authorities or courts have undertaken a balancing exercise referring to the Convention and the ECtHR's jurisprudence. When then a set of political tests are satisfied, the critical state would easily focus exactly on those political criteria and not the words of the Convention that, as in *Christine Goodwin*'s case, under a literal interpretation should protect Ms. Goodwin.

The ECtHR has developed a doctrine of the ECHR as 'a living instrument', which is to be interpreted 'in the light of present-day conditions'.[40] This ECtHR doctrine is not all that different from the ECJ's teleological interpretation. The ECtHR explains that it must take account of 'evolving norms of national and international law in its interpretation of Convention norms'.[41] One difference in the approach of the ECJ and the ECtHR is in the way the latter will take account of norms of national and international law in its interpretation of Convention norms. As discussed, the ECtHR would cite domestic courts in their application of the ECHR. This promotes a relationship that the ECJ with its approach cannot foster in the same way.

We have already discussed how Lord Reed in the UK Supreme Court in several judgments has restated the proportionality test that applies in EU and ECHR law, and compared how domestic courts should apply them, as seen in his judgments in *Bank Mellat* and *Lumsdon*.[42]

There will be a lively discussion in most jurisdictions about national courts going further in the interpretation of rights provisions of the ECHR than the ECtHR has done.[43]

The effect of ECHR norms and the case law of the ECtHR outside the jurisdictional reach of the ECHR in national courts is no less important than for EU law and the ECJ. Many national constitutions will have provisions that are similar or even identical to those of the ECHR. The pressing issue will often be if these domestic constitutional provisions should be given at least the reach of the ECHR, and what scope should be left to use national sources and traditions to go further.

Member State courts will not only apply the proportionality test as part of EU and ECHR law, but these tests will also influence the general test of judicial review in what remains of domestic public law outside the reach of EU and ECHR law.[44] This is pressing in jurisdictions in which the domestic standards of review are less exacting than under the ECHR (or EU) standards of review or remedies required. This will apply also to other principles.

Turning back to the national reports in Part III of this book: general principles of ECtHR law are applied in the national reports of the cases in different ways. As for EU

[40] *Tyrer v the United Kingdom*, 5856/72, ECtHR 25 April 1978, para 31, *Christine Goodwin v the United Kingdom* (Application no 28957/95) ECtHR 11 July 2002, para 74–75.

[41] *Demir and Baykara v Turkey*, Grand Chamber, 34503/97, ECtHR 12 November 2008, para 68.

[42] *Bank Mellat v HM Treasury (No 2)* [2013] UKSC 39, [2014] AC 700 and *R (Lumsdon) v Legal Services Board* [2015] UKSC 41, [2016] AC 697.

[43] See eg M Andenas and E Bjorge, 'Ambrose: Is the Ullah Principle Wrong?' (2012) 128 LQR 319, 322–23.

[44] Lord Bingham of Cornhill (n 24) 8, on the impact on domestic judicial review of EU and ECHR proportionality test.

law, the general principles of ECHR law may determine the procedure or the outcome directly, or they may influence the application of domestic law that falls outside the ECHR jurisdiction in a direct manner.

As already set out in the introduction, most of the national reports from Member States make reference to Article 6 ECHR, and most of them in the report on case No 5. This is not surprising, as this is the provision about due process. The Austrian report case No 1 refers not only to Article 6 but also article 10 ECHR on freedom of expression.

Article 6 ECHR has developed into the central pillar of European human rights protection and also of a common constitution based on the EU and ECHR legal orders. The discussion under A. above shows the use by the ECJ of Article 6 ECHR and the ECtHR case law.

The other way, after *Bosphoros*,[45] there are several ECtHR cases on the relationship to the ECJ. In *Moraru*[46] the ECtHR reinforced compliance with the ECJ jurisprudence and the coherence of fundamental rights in Europe. The ECtHR let it provide a ground for violations that domestic courts had failed to 'meaningfully engage' with the relevant case law of the ECJ which the applicant had invoked before them, and which the ECHR also extensively quoted.[47]

Here are the mentions of the ECHR and the ECtHR in the national reports in Part III of this book:

a) Austria: Article 6 ECHR extended by the Administrative Court (*Verwaltungsgerichtshof*) to administrative proceedings and article 10 ECHR (case No 1), (see page 27 and 93 above).
b) The French report refers to Article 6 ECHR (case No 5), (see page 162 above).
c) The German report refers to Article 6 ECHR (case No 5), (see page 164 above).
d) The Greek report refers to Article 6 ECHR (case no. 5), (see page 165 above).
e) The Italian report refers to Article 6 ECHR (case no. 5), (see page 167 above).
f) The Romanian report refers to Article 6 ECHR (case No 4), (see page 152 above).
g) The Spanish report refers to the case law of the ECtHR (case No 5), (see page 179 above).
h) The Swiss report refers to Article 6 ECHR in the introduction, as well as with regard to cases Nos 1 and 5, (see page 103 and 172 above).
i) The UK report refers to Article 6 ECHR (case No 5), (see page 173 above).

[45] *Bosphorus Hava Yolları Turizm ve Ticaret Anonim Şirketi v Ireland* (Application no 45036/98) ECtHR 30 June 2005: in line with previous case law, Member States of an international organization such as the EU are still liable under the ECHR for 'all acts and omissions of its organs regardless of whether the act or omission in question was a consequence […] of the necessity to comply with international legal obligations' (para 153). In light of 'the growing importance of international cooperation and of the consequent need to secure the proper functioning of international organisations' (para 150), the ECtHR established the presumption of equivalent protection of ECHR rights by the EU. This applies even though the EU is not a party to the ECHR.

[46] *Moraru v Romania* (Application no 42103/15) ECtHR 8 November 2022.

[47] Including C-409/16 *Ypourgos Esoterikon and Ypourgos Ethnikis paideias kai Thriskevmaton v Maria-Eleni Kalliri* ECLI:EU:C:2017:767, 18 October 2017 §§ 24 and 54.

C. International law principles

International law principles are cited in several of the national reports in Part III of this book. The Aarhus Convention on environmental impact assessments is mentioned the most.

There is currently much attention on the role of general principles in international law.[48]

Article 38 of the Statute of the International Court of Justice provides in Article 38(c) for general principles of law as a source of international law:

1. The Court, whose function is to decide in accordance with international law such disputes as are submitted to it, shall apply:
   a. international conventions, whether general or particular, establishing rules expressly recognized by the contesting states;
   b. international custom, as evidence of a general practice accepted as law;
   c. the general principles of law recognized by civilized nations;
   d. ... judicial decisions and the teachings of the most highly qualified publicists of the various nations, as subsidiary means for the determination of rules of law.

Article 38(d) establishes 'judicial decisions' as a secondary source of international law, and opens up for the use of judgments as a means of identifying general principles of law.[49]

In the current debate over general principles of international law, the different positions have been clarified and set out in the context for the UN International Law Commission's (ILC) work on general principles of law. The ILC has adopted, on first reading, eleven draft conclusions on general principles of law, together with commentaries. They are now submitted to consultation with a view to adoption early 2025.[50]

According to one restrictive approach general principles of law are strictly limited to those national in origin, widespread among the globe's well-functioning legal systems, and to be distinguished from principles of customary international law and treaty law. To the holders of this restrictive approach it is a major problem that that general principles of law are unwritten legal norms that judges choose to recognize. For that reason it is part of the restrictive approach to advocate methodological constraints.

[48] See, for a current analysis of the role and controversies over general principles of international law, A Stone Sweet and M Andenas, 'The Law and Politics of the General Principles of Law in the Twenty-First Century' (23 November 2022) University of Hong Kong Faculty of Law Research Paper No 2022/56, available at SSRN: <https://ssrn.com/abstract=4284293> or <http://dx.doi.org/10.2139/ssrn.4284293> accessed July 2023 (under publication in Columbia Journal of Transnational Law).

[49] See M Andenas and J R Leiss, 'The Systemic Relevance of "Judicial Decisions" in Article 38 of the ICJ Statute' (2018) 77 Zeitschrift für ausländisches öffentliches Recht 907–72.

[50] See the ILC official record of its 74th session (from 24 April to 2 June and from 3 July to 4 August 2023) on its web site, <https://legal.un.org/ilc/sessions/74/> accessed February 2024. See in particular 'General principles of law' (Summary <https://legal.un.org/ilc/summaries/1_15.shtml> accessed February 2024, and 'Analytical Guide' <https://legal.un.org/ilc/guide/1_15.shtml> accessed February 2024. On the consultation, see <http://legal.un.org/docs/?path=../ilc/reports/2023/english/chp4.pdf&lang=EFSRAC> accessed February 2024, of the 2023 ILC Report and Comments by Governments <http://legal.un.org/ilc/guide/1_15.shtml#govcoms> accessed February 2024.

To require a comparative showing of a principle's status across the major legal systems of the world is but one way in which to tightly restrict any form of law-making.

A less restrictive approach entails that general principles of law can overlap with principles of customary international law and treaty law, may originate either in international or domestic legal orders, and that international courts possess broad, inherent authority to construct and apply them.

Both approaches accept that general principles may play an important role in promoting coherence in a fragmenting international legal system.[51] But advocates of the restrictive approach are concerned that this could allow excessive use of general principles which could outweigh any positive coherence. For some the fragmentation of international law is less problematic. They see fragmented regimes as a consequence of states using their treaty-making powers, and do not wish courts and tribunals to seek coherence by means such as general principles. That could tend to free courts from the strictures of state consent and literal interpretation.

Most ground their arguments in how international courts actually evolve and deploy general principles of law. But the restrictive approaches would emphasize state consent, and find deeply problematic judicial reliance on general principles of law produced in the absence of consent or mechanisms of ongoing state control.

Proportionality is developed as a principles not only by the ECJ and the ECtHR but in several different other regional and international courts and tribunals. In the ICJ case law, the proportionality principle remains relatively inchoate as it develops in different specialized fields.[52] The ICJ has referred to the principle in certain areas, most often with reference to maritime boundary disputes,[53] the use of force,[54] or the legality of peaceful countermeasures.[55] Every other powerful international court has worked to codify the principle as an analytical framework consisting of a sequence of distinctive stages or tests for much wider purposes than the ICJ. This is done in order to adjudicate the qualified rights in human rights law with the ECtHR in the lead. It is also done in the application of the derogation clauses in economic law (with a similar

[51] M Andenas and L Chiussi, 'Cohesion, Convergence and Coherence of International Law' in M Andenas, M Fitzmaurice, A Tanzi, and J Wouters (eds), *General Principles and the Coherence of International Law* (Brill 2019) 9–34, 17 and A Stone Sweet and M Andenas, 'The Law and Politics of the General Principles of Law in the Twenty-First Century' (23 November 2022) University of Hong Kong Faculty of Law Research Paper No 2022/56, available at SSRN: <https://ssrn.com/abstract=4284293> or <http://dx.doi.org/10.2139/ssrn.4284293> accessed 17 July

[52] ibid.

[53] Here the issue has been the relationship between the relative length of a state's coastline and the shelf awarded to that state. Should it be proportional to their coastline? In *North Sea Continental Shelf* cases, the ICJ considered what constituted a reasonable degree of proportionality. The ICJ ruled that delimitation carried out in accordance with equitable principles ought to bring about a reasonable degree of proportionality between the extent of the continental shelf areas of the coastal state and the length of its coast. *North Sea Continental Shelf Cases (Federal Republic of Germany v Denmark; Federal Republic of Germany v Netherlands)*, 1969 ICJ Rep 3 (February 20), at 54.

[54] International and humanitarian lawyers are often concerned to distinguish the proportionality requirement here. Proportionality 'is here not strictly used as an "ends–means" balancing test between competing interests. Instead it is used as a means of limiting harm against others in situations of armed conflict', see E Crawford, 'Proportionality', in Max Planck Encyclopedia of Public International Law (2012), available at <http://www.opil.ouplaw.com> accessed July 2023.

[55] In *Gabčíkovo–Nagymaros Project (Hungary v Slovakia)*, 1997 ICJ Rep 7 (25 September), at 56, the ICJ states: 'the effects of a countermeasure must be commensurate with the injury suffered, taking account of the rights in question'.

role for the ECJ). Investment treaty arbitration and WTO law are important fora for the development of the principle of proportionality.

As already discussed in the introduction to this section, international law principles are cited in several of the national reports in Part II of this book. The Aarhus Convention on environmental impact assessments is mentioned the most.

Here are the mentions of international law principles in the national reports in Part II of this book:

a) The German report refers to international treaties (case No 1), (see page 96).
b) The Greek report refers to customary international law and treaties in the introductory part, (see page 44).
c) The Italian report refers to international law and EU law, with regard to the international protection of refugees (case No 1), (see page 98), to the ICPPR (case No 5), (see page 167) and to the Aarhus Convention (case No 9), (see page 222).
d) The Romanian report refers to the Aarhus Convention (case No 9), (see page 223).
e) The Serbian report refers to international law and EU law, with regard to the international protection of refugees (case No 1), (see page 101), and to the Aarhus Convention (case No 9), (see page 223).
f) The Swiss report mentions the Aarhus Convention (case No 9), (see page 226), and Article 9 para 1(a) of the Modernised Convention for the Protection of Individuals with Regard to the Processing of Personal Data of the Council of Europe (CETS No 223) (case No 10), (see page 243).
g) The Venezuelan report refers to international treaties with regard to case No 1.

The upshot of all this is that, although the ECHR and international law have a different legal status across the national legal systems included in our comparative analysis, together with EU law they reflect or even constitute a core minimum of process rights. This applies especially clearly in some areas, such as the protection of the environment. As a result, even when public authorities take highly discretionary decisions, which may adversely affect the interests of individuals or firms, the process rights that constitute the core minimum—such as the right to be heard and to obtain the reasons of an adverse decision—must be respected. There may, in addition, be judicial discretion as to how the rights included in the core minimum must be interpreted in other areas, where public authorities enjoy less discretion. It will be for the courts to specify the more detailed constraints flowing from those rights. The advantages and disadvantages of administrative procedure legislation have been discussed elsewhere, but the existence of this core minimum of process rights is at the very least important progress for the rule of law and sound governance.

17
The Legal Relevance and Significance of Administrative Procedure Legislation

Angela Ferrari Zumbini

I. Introduction

This chapter aims to address the question of whether having a code of administrative procedure actually makes a difference,[1] so, to this end, a comparative analysis of the solutions will be carried out between countries with an Administrative Procedure Act (APA) and those without.

First, a few words to explain the choice of countries selected and the cases used in the study may be in order.

Most of the countries considered have a general law on administrative procedure. As a result, the selection focused on three countries, each with distinct laws adopted at different points in time. The Austrian *Allgemeine Verwaltungsverfahrensgesetz* (*AVG*), the first administrative procedure law passed in 1925 and later amended in 1991, focuses on procedure. The German *Verwaltungsverfahrensgesetz* (*VwVfG*) dates from 1976 and, in line with Otto Mayer's approach, focuses on the end product of the procedure, ie the administrative act. The Italian *Nuove norme in materia di procedimento amministrativo e di diritto di accesso ai documenti amministrativi* was passed in 1990 but has undergone very profound changes in recent years, making it something of a hybrid (as can be seen even from the title, literally 'New rules on administrative procedure and the right of access to administrative documents'). This approach allows us to examine whether the mere existence of an APA actually makes a difference and leads to uniform solutions despite the different characteristics of the APAs.

There are very few European countries that lack an APA. The UK famously has neither a written constitution nor an APA, and Romania too does not have an APA, being one of the three out of the 27 EU members lacking one.

As for the choice of cases selected for comparative analysis, the aim was to examine both first-generation and second-generation proceedings, to use Barnes' well-known distinction.[2] More specifically, three individual proceedings were chosen, each relating to a fundamental principle of administrative procedure: the right to a hearing (case 3), access to files (case 6), and the obligation to give reasons (case 7). The selection criterion for the second-generation proceedings was the same, analysing the

[1] Recalling—albeit in a different field—the question posed by C J Cowton and P Thompson, 'Do Codes Make a Difference? The Case of Bank Lending and the Environment' (2000) 24 J Bus Ethics 165.

[2] J Barnes, 'Three Generations of Administrative Procedures' in S Rose-Ackerman and others (eds), *Comparative Administrative Law* (Elgar 2017).

Angela Ferrari Zumbini, *The Legal Relevance and Significance of Administrative Procedure Legislation* In: *General Principles and Sector-Specific Rules in European Administrative Laws*. Edited by: Giacinto della Cananea and Jean-Bernard Auby, Oxford University Press. © Angela Ferrari Zumbini 2024. DOI: 10.1093/oso/9780198867579.003.0017

obligation to consult all stakeholders equally (case 8) and the requirement to consult the general public (case 9). The case involving automated administrative decision-making (case 10) was selected because of the striking contemporary topic of public authorities using algorithms, and it is interesting to see whether having an APA also makes a difference in innovative cases that pose new challenges to judicial review.

Before carrying out a comparative analysis of the cases (Section IV), some considerations will be discussed regarding the shared background and distinctive traits among the countries selected for analysis (Section II), as well as the overall importance and significance of having an APA in general (Section III). Lastly, some concluding remarks are drawn in Section V.

II. Background commonalities and distinctive traits

Some very quick background commonalities and distinctive traits need to be underlined from the outset. These include constitutional provisions, supranational legal orders, and legal traditions.

First of all, it may be appropriate to recall one fundamental, but trivial, aspect: if the discipline of administrative procedure is codified, then this discipline is subject to constitutional review by the constitutional courts (where they exist).

Austria and Germany share the fundamental *Rechtsstaatsprinzip*, but while this is explicitly stated in the German *Grundgesetz* (Article 20), it is found as a general fundamental principle in Austria.

In Italy, Article 97(2) of the Constitution stipulates that public bodies must be organized in a manner prescribed by law to ensure sound and impartial administration. Doctrine and jurisprudence have derived three fundamental constitutional 'pillars' of public administration from this provision: the principles of legality, impartiality, and sound administration.[3] However, there is no mention of the principle of procedural fairness in the Constitution, and it is not considered a constitutional principle. Nevertheless, it is considered a general principle of law and a 'guiding principle' for legislators and interpreters of the law.[4]

As the UK lacks a written constitution, the fundamental procedural rights stem from the common law rules of fairness and natural justice.[5]

One fundamental commonality among all five selected countries is that they are signatories of the European Convention of Human Rights (ECHR), which necessitates a comprehensive assessment of its impact and significance. Consequently, they must all comply with Article 6 of the Convention, which ensures fairness in court trials.[6] It is important to note that the ECHR holds constitutional status in Austria.

[3] M Cartabia and N Lupo, *The Constitution of Italy. A Contextual Analysis* (Hart 2022).

[4] See S Vaccari, N Berti, and M Silvestri, 'Italy' in this book.

[5] See G Anthony, 'United Kingdom' in this book.

[6] On the complex question of the applicability of art 6 to some administrative proceedings, see C Teleki, *Due Process and Fair Trial in EU Competition Law. The Impact of Article 6 of the European Convention on Human Rights* (Brill 2021). For an Italian perspective, see M Gnes, 'The Application of the European Convention on Human Rights in Italian Administrative Law' (2001) 13 Eur Rev Publ L 529.

One important distinctive trait concerns Romania, which experienced a prolonged period under the Soviet rule and was therefore subjected to a communist regime. This historical context may have left a lasting legacy in the country's legal culture.

Lastly, it is important to note that after Brexit the UK is no longer an EU Member State, which has significant consequences regarding the application of European legislation and its legacies.[7] In particular, Article 41(2)(a) of the Union's Charter of Fundamental Rights (CFR) recognizes and protects 'the right of every person to be heard before any individual measure which would affect him or her adversely is taken'. After the Lisbon Treaty came into force in 2009, the Charter has had the same legal value as the European Union treaties. Hence, four of the countries selected for analysis continue to be subject to Article 41 CFR, while the UK, after Brexit, is no longer bound by it.[8]

III. The relevance and significance of having an APA in general

A. Discussions before codification

Considering the relevance and significance of having an APA in general, it is pertinent to revisit the discussions that preceded codifications in the countries chosen for this comparative analysis.

1. Austria

From a historical perspective, the parliamentary discussion surrounding the approval of the law that established the *Verwaltungsgerichtshof* (*VwGH*) in 1875 generated much criticism regarding the complete absence of administrative procedure regulation at the time. Indeed, several members of the two chambers emphasized the need to codify administrative law, as at that time there was 'no regulation of administrative procedure, which is completely unregulated and left to the arbitrariness of the administrations'.[9] When the law establishing the *Verwaltungsgerichtshof* was adopted, many

[7] For a detailed analysis of the process that led to the UK leaving the Union, along with the consequences, see P Craig, 'Brexit, A Drama: The Endgame—Part I' (2020) ELR, Oxford Legal Studies Research Paper No 10/2020, available at SSRN: https://ssrn.com/abstract=3541896.

[8] Section 5(4) of the 2018 European Union Withdrawal Act states that 'The Charter of Fundamental Rights is not part of domestic law on or after exit day'. However, many commentators affirm that the CFR will continue to have some influence and will have certainly effects, mainly through judicial decisions. B McCloskey, 'The Charter of Fundamental Rights' in C McCrudden (ed), *The Law and Practice of the Ireland-Northern Ireland Protocol* (Cambridge UP 2022) claims that the extinction of the CFR from UK law was a clear intention of the UK government. Nevertheless, the author suggests 'The multiple components of the Brexit legal architecture, not less than complex, having been finalized and activated, it is not clear that this apparent intention has been achieved.' Indeed, in December 2022, the Upper Tribunal (Administrative Appeal Chamber) has found that the EU Charter of Fundamental Rights continues to apply to certain EU citizens residing in the UK, who are within the scope of the EU–UK Withdrawal Agreement (Case No: UA-2022-001067-USTA).

[9] The quoted sentence is from Ernst von Plener, a member of the *Abgeordnete Haus*, pronounced during the session of 18 March 1875, reported in P Gautsch von Frankenthurn, *Die Gesetze vom 22. October 1875, R.G.B. Nr. 36 und 37, Jahr- gang 1876 über den Verwaltungsgerichtshof: mit Materialien* (Manz'sche k.k. Verlag 1876). The quoted sentence is on p 175 '*keine Vorschriften, keine Normen für das administrative Verfahren. Das administrative Verfahren unserer Behörden ist vollständig regellos, der reinen Willkür der Behörden überlassen*'.

criticized the provision that administrative acts could be annulled due to the lack of essential forms relating to the procedure since the law provided neither a definition nor a list of the essential forms.[10]

Many exponents of both academia and the government administration called for the codification of procedural rules. Between the close of the nineteenth century and the beginning of the twentieth, several works were published arguing for the utility, if not the necessity, of reform (and thus a codification) of administrative procedure. Lemayer, the founding father of the *Verwaltungsgerichtshof*, published his apologetic studies on administrative jurisdiction in 1896;[11] Brunstein's study of 1900 focused precisely on administrative procedure reform,[12] and Tezner drew up a draft law on administrative procedure in 1902.[13]

Legislative intervention was called for (largely) to implement two distinct but coherent fundamental requirements of the rule of law.

At government level, the studies and drafts for an outline of the APA were explicitly inspired by what was defined as the primary purpose of any procedural rule, namely legal certainty (*Rechtssicherheit*).

There was also broad academic consensus on the desirability of codifying administrative procedures. In addition to the principle of *Rechtssicherheit*, scholars also based their arguments on the basic principle of making the parties to the procedure subjects of rights by law.

Through its case law, the *VwGH* granted an essential series of rights to the addressees of measures. However, the growing case law did not allow for a systematic and formal attribution of the status of 'subject of rights' to the parties and did not necessarily guarantee uniform and constant application.[14]

Codification was (also) intended to formally grant citizens subject-of-rights status during administrative procedures[15] without the possibility of heterogeneous and diverse application. This purpose is clearly consistent with the complementary principle of legal certainty but not necessarily a consequence of it, since legal certainty could also aim (primarily) to ensure the legality of administrative action, leaving the protection of individual legal subjectivity in the background.

Lastly, the decisive impetus for adopting a law on administrative procedure stemmed from post-war circumstances. In particular, a decisive factor for the codification of administrative procedure was the so-called *Genfer Reformbeschlüsse* concluded in 1922 between a defeated Austria, on the one hand, and a victorious UK, France, Italy, and Czechoslovakia, on the other.[16]

[10] T Olechowski, *Die Einführung der Verwaltungsgerichtsbarkeit in Österreich* (Manz 1999).

[11] K Lemayer, *Apologetische Studien zur Verwaltungsgerichtsbarkeit* (Hoelder 1896).

[12] J L Brunstein, *Das Administrativ-Verfahren und seine Reform* (Manz 1900).

[13] F Tezner, 'Praktische Vorschläge zur Reform des österreichischen Administrativverfahrens' (1902) 53 Allgemeine österreichische Gerichtszeitung 51.

[14] E Mannlicher, *Die österreichische Verwaltungsreform des Jahres 1925* (Springer 1926).

[15] H Schäffer, 'Administrative Procedure in Austria. 80 Years of Codified Procedure Law' (2005) 17 ERPL 871ff.

[16] E C Hellbling, *Österreichische Verfassungs- und Verwaltungsgeschichte: ein Lehrbuch für Studierende* (Springer 1956) esp 449ff.

In this international treaty, signed after the close of the First World War, the new Austrian Republic, which had emerged from the ashes of the Austro-Hungarian Empire, had to introduce a law to simplify administration in order to reduce Austria's expenditure and give it access to a loan from the League of Nations totalling around 690 million gold crowns (*Goldkronen*) over 20 years.[17]

2. Germany

The German *Grundgesetz* (GG) establishes the principle that public administration is bound to the parliamentary legislator (Article 20(3) GG). In addition, Article 19(4) enshrines the principle of *Rechtsschutz*, since anyone who believes a public authority has infringed his or her rights can seize a court to protect them.

After the GG came into force, there was intense academic debate about the feasibility and desirability of codifying the regulation of administrative procedure, among other topics.[18] One of the terms of reference was the Austrian law of 1925, which had explicitly established numerous citizens' rights, including the right to be heard. Many scholars held that the protections afforded to citizens in the Austrian law already existed in the German legal system. Indeed, protection of the citizen in dealings with the authorities is 'amply, perhaps too amply, but in any case sufficiently, provided by the administrative and constitutional courts'.[19] Echoing Mayer's theories, many scholars considered administrative case law to be a sufficient source for protecting the rights of individuals in their relations with the administration.[20] Even among scholars who advocated for codified legislation with a broader *Rechtsschutz*, which would include access and participation rights, the idea that case law could remedy any procedural shortcomings for safeguarding individuals was firmly established. Ule's successful *je-desto* formula summarizes the reciprocal relationship between administrative proceedings and administrative judicial protection.[21]

After extensive debate, the *VwVfG* was enacted in 1976, implementing the constitutional principles of legality and *Rechtsschutz* within the framework of a federal law.

3. Italy

In Italy, too, administrative courts—even in the absence of a legislative discipline on administrative procedure—had been enucleating a series of principles on administrative action aimed at protecting the rights of individuals since the end of the

[17] It is not certain exactly what the final amount paid out by the League of Nations was, but it is known that Austria received at least 650 million *Goldkronen*. cf G Strejcek, 'Vor 90 Jahren flossen Österreich aus einer Völkerbund-Anleihe rund 650 Millionen Goldkronen zu. Die folgende Sanierung des Staatshaushaltes brachte aber keine nachhaltige politische Stabilität' *Wiener Zeitung* (Wien, 13–14 October 2012) <https://www.wienerzeitung.at/nachrichten/wissen/geschichte/493525-Rettungsschirm-des-Jahres-1922.html> accessed 17 February 2022.

[18] H Hill and others (eds), *35 Jahre Verwaltungsverfahrensgesetz—Bilanz und Perspektiven* (Dunker & Humblot 2011).

[19] K A Bettermann, 'Das Verwaltungsverfahren' in *Veröffentlichungen der Vereinigung der Deutschen Staatsrechtslehrer* (De Gruyter 1959). The cited sentence is on p 168. My own translation; the original text is '*das Schutz des Bürgers gegenüber der Verwaltung ist in reichlichem, vielleicht in allzu reichem, jedenfalls aber ausreichendem Maße durch die Verwaltungs-und Verfassungsgerichte gewährt*'.

[20] O Bachof, 'Nochmals: Verwaltungsverfahren und Verwaltungsgerichtsbarkeit' (1958) DVBl 6.

[21] C H Ule, 'Verwaltungsverfahren und Verwaltungsgerichtsbarkeit' (1957) DVBl (1957) 597.

nineteenth century.[22] However, the regulation of administrative action was chaotic and fragmented.[23]

In 1940, A M Sandulli dedicated a monograph to the subject of administrative procedure,[24] undertaking a work of legal definition and systematization, also highlighting the importance of the notion of administrative procedure.[25]

As mentioned earlier, the Constitution affirmed the principles of impartiality and sound administration. Some scholars highlighted a lack of effectiveness in terms of the adaptation of administrative law to constitutional law. The principle of impartiality refers expressly to the organization of the public authorities, but it was interpreted (and not only by the Constitutional Court) as a principle that would conform the entire administrative activity. After the Constitution came into force, the importance of having a comprehensive law on administrative procedure became evident. This need arose not merely in order to translate constitutional principles but primarily to organize and systematize administrative proceedings. Indeed, the draft of a general law on administrative procedure prepared in 1948 by the Commission chaired by Ugo Forti contained 'only the normative formulation of those principles that are firmly based on authoritative and undisputed scholarship in a constant jurisprudence'.[26]

The legislative process that culminated in the adoption of a law on administrative procedure was particularly long and arduous despite the general consensus on its necessity.

The scheme proposed by the Forti Commission did not pass, nor did the subsequent bill presented by Lucifredi in 1958, which substantially reproduced it. In the early 1980s, a new Commission, led by Mario Nigro, was set up to draft a new bill. Almost a decade and several amendments later, the draft was approved and became Law No 241 of 7 August 1990, entitled 'New rules on administrative procedure and the right of access to administrative documents'. This law codified essential principles of administrative action and granted numerous rights to private individuals. It contains (as of its original version in 1990) an entire section devoted to the participation of private parties in administrative proceedings and one devoted to the right of access to files.

B. APAs and the extent of judicial power

One of the major arguments against the codification of administrative procedure rules has always been that of the 'paralysing corset', meaning that codification would shrink

[22] A Sandulli, 'Il procedimento amministrativo' in S Cassese (ed), *Trattato di diritto amministrativo*, Vol II (Giuffrè 2003); A Bassani, 'Initial Investigation on Excess of Power: Judicial Review of Administrative Action in Italy (1890–1910)' in G della Cananea and S Mannoni (eds), *Administrative Justice Fin de siècle. Early Judicial Standards of Administrative Conduct in Europe* (1890–1910) (OUP 2021).

[23] F Benvenuti, 'L'attività amministrativa e la sua disciplina generale' in G Pastori (ed), *La procedura amministrativa* (Neri Pozza 1964).

[24] A M Sandulli, *Il procedimento amministrativo* (Giuffrè 1940).

[25] The notion of administrative procedure had already been elaborated in Austria by Friedrich Tezner in his book *Das Handbuch des österreichischen Administrativverfahrens* (Manz 1896).

[26] Presidency of the Council of Ministers, Commission for Administrative Reform, The General Law on Public Administration (1948). My own translation; the original text is '*unicamente la formulazione normativa di quei principi che trovano la loro conferma in un'autorevole ed incontrastata dottrina, in una costante giurisprudenza*'.

the creative power of the courts. However, the research carried out in this book shows that codification did not prevent courts from recalling general principles of law when the APA had no provision for specific cases or even when courts wanted to broaden individual rights vis-à-vis public authorities.

Indeed, administrative courts have played a major role in shaping and framing the rules governing administrative procedures in every country. The creative power of administrative judges was noticeable before the APAs were adopted (in those countries where they were indeed adopted). Due to the scarcity of general rules on administrative action, the courts developed a range of general principles regarding administrative action, encompassing legality, equality, impartiality, transparency, reasonableness, and proportionality. However, the 'law-making' activity of administrative courts did not cease with codification; quite to the contrary. Even after adopting the APAs, administrative courts continued to shape and construe individual and collective procedural rights.

It is interesting to highlight two further observations regarding the role played by courts, comparing the evolutionary paths of two legal systems that exhibit a strong judicial imprint in their administrative law.

First of all, the notion of administrative procedure emerged in Austria through the work of the administrative court. When ruling on the lawfulness of specific acts, the court examined the procedure followed for their adoption, attaching equal (if not greater) importance to the 'path' followed rather than the final outcome. Indeed, the *Verwaltungsgerichtshof* developed a very well-structured system of safeguards protecting individuals during administrative proceedings as early as the close of the nineteenth century.[27] The principles elaborated by the Austrian administrative court were then codified in the 1925 *AVG*.[28]

This evolution contrasts with the development of the traditionally better-known (at least in Europe) administrative court, the *Conseil d'État*. Of course, in France too,[29] administrative law is rooted mainly in case law,[30] especially as far as general principles are concerned. However, the *Conseil d'État* has always prioritized judicial review, leaving procedural aspects in the background. Indeed, with some notable exceptions, even French legal scholarship has never placed administrative procedure at the heart of its interests.

In France, the origins of administrative law rooted in jurisprudence have resulted in the diminished significance of the legislative regulation of administrative procedure in favour of the centrality of judicial control. Conversely, in Austria, this same development has led to the emergence of the notion of procedure, with its consequent legislative codification but in precisely the opposite direction.

[27] A Ferrari Zumbini, 'Standards of Judicial Review of Administrative Action in the Austro-Hungarian Empire' in G della Cananea and S Mannoni (eds), *Administrative Justice Fin de siècle. Early Judicial Standards of Administrative Conduct in Europe* (1890–1910) (OUP 2021).

[28] G della Cananea, A Ferrari Zumbini, O Pfersmann (eds), *The Austrian Codification of Administrative Procedure. Diffusion and Oblivion* (1920–1970) (OUP 2023).

[29] J-B Auby, 'General Report' in J-B Auby (ed), *Codification of Administrative Procedure* (Bruylant 2014); J-M Auby and R Drago, *Traité de contentieux administratif* (3rd edn, Librairie générale de droit et de jurisprudence 1984).

[30] G Vedel and P Devolvé, *Droit administratif* (9th edn, PUF 1984).

This curious discrepancy can be interpreted in the light of the different approaches underlying administrative law in the two legal systems.[31] In France, it is manifested in an objective[32] form of judicial protection, seeking to ensure the lawfulness of administrative action. In contrast, Austria predominantly embraces a subjective type of protection, focusing on safeguarding the rights of individuals vis-à-vis the public authorities.

In any event, it should be noted that the origins of administrative law in case law do not necessarily lead to favouring the judicial review aspect over the procedural one and the rights associated with it.

IV. The relevance and significance of having an APA in specific cases

A. First-generation procedures (adjudication)

1. The right to a hearing (case 3)

This case concerns a local authority's withdrawal of a licence *inaudita altera parte*.

In Austria, the *AVG* explicitly requires the authority to enable the affected parties to claim their rights and legal interests. Moreover, Article 45(3) requires the parties to be able to know about the outcome based on the evidence presented and to comment on it. Hence, in Austria, there would be no need to rely on general principles here as the law clearly states the parties' rights. However, *Parteiengehör* is a fundamental general principle in Austrian law and has foundational value.[33] The *Verwaltungsgerichtshof* had already stated in 1884[34]—well before the *AVG* was adopted—that participation was part of the Nature of Things, so the fact that the law did not explicitly provide for this requirement was not decisive. This was a general unwritten principle rooted in natural justice.

The German APA too explicitly establishes the right to a hearing in § 28 (1), which states that before an administrative act affecting the rights of a participant may be executed, the latter must be allowed to comment on the facts pertinent to the decision.

Similarly, participation and the right to be heard are also considered general principles of law in Italy. Moreover, Article 7 of the Italian APA (Law 241/1990)[35] stipulates that those who will be directly affected by the final measure must be notified of the commencement of a procedure, granting them the right to be heard and to submit relevant documents. However, Article 21-*octies* APA states that failure to notify the

[31] J-B Auby, 'Why France Was Unaffected by the Austrian Codification of Administrative Procedure' in G della Cananea, A Ferrari Zumbini, and O Pfersmann (eds), *The Austrian Codification of Administrative Procedure. Diffusion and Oblivion* (1920–1970) (OUP 2023).

[32] É Laferrière, *Traité de la juridiction administrative et des recours contentieux* (Librairie générale de droit et de jurisprudence 1989) (reprint of 1st edn 1887–1888) states that it is not '*un procès fait à une partie, c'est un procès fait à un acte*' vol II, 534.

[33] On this theory, see A Stone Sweet and G della Cananea, 'Proportionality, General Principles of Law, and Investor-State Arbitration: A Response to Alvarez' (2014) 46 NYU JILP 911.

[34] Judgment No 2263 of 24 October 1884 Sammlung der Erkenntnisse des k.k. Verwaltungsgerichtshofes of 1884, pp 493–95.

[35] The Italian APA has been translated in English by C de Rienzo in (2010) 2 It J Publ L 371.

commencement of a procedure will not affect the decision if the court finds that the final content of the measure could not have been different or because the right to defence had not been breached in practical terms.

Turning now to the countries that do not have an APA, the solutions do not appear to be any different in the UK. Indeed, the absence of a legal framework defining procedural guarantees becomes irrelevant, as the common law's procedural protections would apply. Those protections include the duty of public authorities to give prior notification of the proposed decision and grant the affected party the right to make both oral and written submissions before the decision is taken. The court would thus quash the decision.

The solution would be totally different in Romania. As we have seen, it is one of the few remaining European States without an APA. No right to be heard is established in sector-specific legislation either when issuing or withdrawing authorization. Moreover, there is no general principle in Romanian administrative law establishing a right to a hearing. Law 52/2003 regulates transparency in decision-making but guarantees participation rights only during administrative proceedings to issue general normative administrative acts. There is no obligation to hear the affected party before an individual administrative act is issued. Interestingly, the right to be heard is explicitly provided for in tax procedures, whereas Italy still does not guarantee it.

This total divergence between Romania and the other legal systems under consideration demonstrates that the mere presence or absence of an APA is not entirely decisive. Other fundamental elements, such as legal traditions, must also be considered. Indeed, one could hypothesize—although this would require further verification and investigation—that the lesser degree of protection afforded to individual rights vis-à-vis the public authorities in Romania might be a cultural legacy stemming from the prolonged existence of a communist regime in the country after the Second World War, during which Romania was under Soviet rule.

In some other countries, the right to a prior hearing is enshrined in the most significant piece of legislation, their respective constitutions, such as Article 20(2) of the Greek Constitution and in Article 105 of the Spanish Constitution.

It is interesting to note that also in China the court would quash the decision due to a violation of due process. The right of the person to be heard before an adverse decision is made appears to be a fundamental principle of the common core of administrative law systems, except in Romania.

2. Access to files (case 6)

This case concerns the decision of a tax authority to apply certain specific financially less favourable provisions of tax legislation than the general provisions to a taxpayer while also refusing to provide him or her with access to the necessary dossiers or documentation.

Here again, in Austria there is no need to rely on general principles as the law clearly states the parties' rights. Article 90(1)1 of the Tax Proceedings Act[36] rules that the tax authority must allow the parties to inspect and copy any files or parts of files necessary

[36] See S Storr, 'Austria' in this book.

to claim or defend their tax law interests or fulfil their tax law obligations. A similar right to inspect files is protected by § 17 *AVG* for administrative proceedings in general.[37] However, as the Austrian report clearly states, even if there were no specific legal provisions on the right to inspect files, 'it can be safely assumed that the competent court would deduce such a right from the right to be heard and the principle of a fair trial'.[38]

Tax law proves to be a somewhat unique domain. In fact, the German APA grants citizens a general right of access to personal data during an administrative proceeding (§ 29 *VwVfG*). However, the procedural code for cases concerning taxation (*Abgabenordnung—AO*) contains no corresponding right.[39] This difference has been interpreted as an intentionally different regulation established by the legislator. However, applying the general due process principle, the authority must disclose the document during proceedings in courts.

In Italy, too, the taxpayer can obtain access to the files only during proceedings in court. The APA expressly excludes taxation procedures from the right to access documents, for which the specific rules governing them remain unaffected (Article 24(1)(b)). There is no general provision in the sector-specific laws granting a taxpayer the right to access documents during the procedure. Courts have tried—very gradually and with fluctuating and inconsistent jurisprudence[40]—to limit the scope of the exception provided for in Article 24 APA, recalling general principles, stating that access to documents in tax matters may only be excluded while the procedure is in progress. Once the proceeding has been concluded (and the tax assessment notice has been adopted), investigative secrecy can no longer justify denying access.

The solution to this case is straightforward in the UK, as the taxpayer will be granted access to the files. The right of access will be based on the 2018 Data Protection Act, which establishes certain disclosure exclusions that do not apply in this case. Additionally, it falls under the general 'duty of candour' that public bodies should adhere to during their proceedings.[41]

The European legal order was crucial in introducing taxpayers' rights to access their files in Romania.[42] Here, sector-specific legislation fails to guarantee this right, and in the past, the courts did not uphold the taxpayers' grievances as they did not recognize the right to access the documents during the investigation procedure. In 2016, a national court referred to the European Court of Justice (ECJ) for a preliminary ruling on whether denial of access to files during tax proceedings was compatible with the principle of respect for the right of the defence. The ECJ declared that 'the general principle of EU law of respect for the rights of the defence'[43] must be interpreted as requiring the taxpayer to be granted access to the relevant documents during tax investigations. Following this ruling, the High Court of Cassation and Justice issued now-confirmed

[37] ibid.
[38] ibid.
[39] See D Schefold, 'Germany' in this book.
[40] A Ferrari Zumbini, 'The Power to Tax without Due Process of Law' (2019) 11 It J Publ L 119.
[41] See Anthony (n 5).
[42] See D Dragoş, 'Romania', in this book.
[43] C-298/16 *Ispas v Direcţia Generală a Finanţelor Publice Cluj* ECLI:EU:C:2017:843 (Judgment of the Court (Third Chamber) of 9 November 2017) para 39.

case law annulling tax decisions issued without prior hearing of the affected person and obligating the National Fiscal Authority to allow full access to the file.[44]

It is interesting to note that in the UK, the fact that the case concerns a tax proceeding does not appear to be relevant. Moreover, the final decision is also grounded on a written code—the Data Protection Act—which is derived from and gives effect to the EU General Data Protection Regulation, making Brexit irrelevant in this case.

3. The duty to give reasons (case 7)

This case originates from a public tender procedure to grant national television broadcasting rights on terrestrial frequencies. The authority denies a licence to a tenderer with no explanation for the rejection.

Also in this case, the *AVG*—which applies to these procedures, too—stipulates in § 58(2), that whenever the party's viewpoint is not fully shared or decisions are made based on objections or submissions from individuals involved, the reasons for such decisions must be stated in the administrative decision.

In Germany, both the sector-specific law and the APA require administrative decisions to be justified, so the court would quash the denial.

In the Italian APA, the requirement to give reasons is a cornerstone. Article 3 states that every administrative measure must include a statement of reasons. The statement of reasons must indicate the factual assumptions and the legal reasons that determined the administration's decision in relation to the findings of the preliminary investigation. Therefore, the court will annul the administrative decision.

In the UK, surprisingly, there is no general common law obligation to give reasons. However, relying upon the principle of fairness, the court could impose such a duty in consideration of the specific context, which involves a public interest.

In Romania, no general duty to give reasons is stipulated in written law. However, courts view it as an essential element of due process, and they quash decisions that lack sufficient reasoning. Even if sector-specific legislation does not envisage such a requirement, the general principles of due process, transparency, and proportionality would make the decision unlawful.

The duty to give reasons appears to be another fundamental element of the common core of administrative law throughout the various jurisdictions. This consistency may imply the likelihood of stronger convergence in the principles derived from judicial sources compared to legislative ones.

B. Second-generation procedures (administrative procedures aimed at issuing measures having a normative, general administrative, planning, or programming function)

1. The duty to consult all stakeholders equally (case 8)

This case regards the failure to consult a stakeholder before setting new tariffs.

In Austria, this would be a difficult case to conclude. However, for the purpose of our analysis, a crucial element emerges: even if there were no general or sector-specific

[44] See Dragoş (n 42).

law requiring all stakeholders to be consulted, the obligation of equal treatment would be derived from the constitutional principle of equal treatment laid down in Article 7 of the Federal Constitution and Article 20 of the Charter of Fundamental Rights of the European Union.

In Germany, railway company tariffs are not established by the regulator. Nevertheless, it can enact some administrative rules (*Verwaltungsvorschriften*) without having to enter into consultations before implementing them. Moreover, the court has no power to annul the rules, marking a significant difference with regard to the other countries.

In Italy, the APA expressly excludes the right to participate in the activities of the public authorities for issuing general administrative measures (such as the adoption of new tariffs, for which the special rules governing their formation remain unaffected (Article 13)). However, the court could annul the decision, citing general principles of law, such as impartiality (Article 97 of the Constitution), the requirement for a thorough preliminary investigation, and the prohibition of arbitrarily unequal treatment of stakeholders.

In the UK, the duty to consult is founded in the common law. Over time, courts have established criteria for the consultations to be respected, and the Supreme Court has identified consultation requirements 'with a higher quality of decision-making and ideas of justice, participation, and democracy'.[45] Interestingly, a tariffs' setting decided after consulting only two stakeholders out of three would be deemed to be irrational. Indeed, a breach of the equality principle is a subset of irrationality, and every public law decision must accord with the fundamental principles of public law, including rationality.

In Romania, the aforementioned Transparency Act 52/2003 requires public authorities to consult citizens with an interest before adopting general acts. However, should the court find that the content of the decision would have been the same in any event, the lack of consultation would not lead to annulment. This judicial doctrine is the same as the provisions of the German and Italian APAs regarding individual acts. Article 46 of the German *VwVfG* treats procedural defects as irrelevant if a *Kausalitätsprüfung* shows that the error clearly did not affect the merits of the decision. Very similarly, Article 21-*octies* (2) of the Italian APA states that the administrative measure cannot in any event be annulled simply for failure to give notice of the commencement of proceedings if the administration proves in court that the content of the measure could not have been different from that actually adopted.

To highlight the commonalities better, it is worth noting that this case would not arise in China due to the absence of private providers in the rail transport sector. Rail services in China are exclusively provided by a single state-owned company.

2. The duty to consult the general public (case 9)

This case concerns the failure to consult the affected community before building a new gas pipeline.

The resolution of this case in Austria is of particular interest. If the sector-specific legislation does not mandate consultations with the affected community, and even if

[45] See Anthony (n 5).

such consultations are required in a very similar case, the court will not apply a provision that does not regard the specific case by recourse to analogy. Rather, the court will affirm that such consultation duty is grounded in general unwritten principles.

The resolution of this case in Germany is also particularly interesting. The sector-specific law provides for a wide consultation and participation procedure, but this is not the most important element. If the sector-specific rule did not exist or did not provide for consultation, the general APA would apply in any case. In Article 28(2) of the German APA, exceptions to the hearing requirement are permitted when the authority intends to issue a general order, ie an administrative act directed towards a group of individuals defined or identifiable based on general characteristics or relating to the public law aspect of a matter or its use by the public at large. However, in the sphere of planning, the APA envisions a comprehensive and extensive participation process in the form of public consultation (§§ 72–78 *VwVfG*).

The Italian approach to this case would be quite unique. As previously mentioned, Article 13 of the Italian APA specifies that participation and consultation rights do not apply to the work of public authorities aimed at issuing regulatory, general administrative, planning, and programming acts, whose specific rules governing their formation remain unaffected. Moreover, in the Italian legal system, no general principle requires the administration to consult the community concerned before carrying out projects of general interest, except in cases expressly established by law. Hence, in this case, since the sector-specific law does not provide for any consultation rights, the court would not use general principles to annul the decision, as none have become firmly established in Italian law despite some attempts in this direction. However, the court could quash the decision because it is incompatible with EU law and the Aarhus Convention. In fact, Directive 2011/92/EU of the European Parliament and of the Council (amended by Directive 2014/52/EU) establishes the principle of compulsory public involvement in the Environmental Impact Assessment (EIA) procedure, which applies to the construction of gas pipelines. Article 6 of the Aarhus Convention, ratified by Italy with Law No 108 of 16 March 2001, commits states to informing the public in a timely and effective manner and enabling their effective and timely participation in the decision-making process regarding a number of listed activities, including pipelines. In this case, the Italian court would deem the decision unlawful, not because of general principles but due to the breach of supranational laws.

In the UK, the right of citizens' environmental associations to be consulted would not be affirmed by a broad interpretation of the statute. Courts typically interpret statutes in a 'purposive manner',[46] but extending an existing rule to cases not explicitly mentioned would exceed their authority and encroach upon that of the lawmaker. However, consultation rights might be successful under common law through the concept of 'procedural legitimate expectation'[47] if the authority had consulted the public on similar issues on previous occasions.

In Romania, public consultation in decisions involving environmental issues is provided for in the sector-specific legislation (Act 195/2005). Additionally, such

[46] ibid.
[47] ibid.

participation rights are protected by the aforementioned EIA Directive and the Aarhus Convention.

The obligation to consult the general public in planning procedures appears to be another fundamental shared element of the common core of administrative law, although this principle originates from different sources in various legal systems (such as domestic general principles, European legislation, and national APAs). In China, too, the courts would annul a decision that had been taken without consultation. They would rely on general principles of law, ie the fundamental principles of fair procedure enshrined in due process.

3. Access to the algorithm used by the public administration (case 10)

This case concerns the denial of access to an algorithm used by a public authority to select individuals who made significant contributions to their nation during the Second World War and inscribe their names on a funeral plaque in the town's central square.

In Austria, such a decision would fall within the domain of private law activity, since it neither infringes any fundamental right nor requires enforcement through sanctions or coercion, and the authority is not involved in executing a law. Therefore, none of the rights provided by the APA are protected.

In Germany—setting aside the debate over whether the construction of a monument is an administrative decision that can be challenged in an administrative court—the APA allows, in principle, for an administrative act to be issued entirely by automatic means, only if (1) it is permitted by law and (2) no discretion or discretionary power is involved. Since both these requisites are absent, the decision must be adequately motivated.

In Italy, recent administrative case law has established that public authorities should be permitted to adopt automated decisions, as algorithms enhance efficiency and align with the constitutional requirement of sound administration. In these recent cases, the courts have further asserted that automated decisions should adhere to all the general principles of administrative activity, including those of publicity and transparency. Therefore, relying on these general principles, the courts would grant access to the algorithm, providing full transparency regarding its structure and development criteria.

How this solution would be decided in the UK is uncertain, as the issue has not yet been fully litigated and resolved. The party's challenge could be based on grounds of reasonableness and legality, but the outcome would be uncertain.

In Romania too, the solution would not be straightforward; however, the right to access could be justified on the grounds of proportionality, equality, and impartiality.

V. Concluding remarks

Following careful examination, certain conclusions can be drawn.

A number of commonalities and divergences emerge, starting from the adjudication stage.

Firstly, in countries with a codified administrative procedure, the courts would probably also invoke the corresponding general principle even when the APA and/

or sector-specific legislation establish individual procedural rights. The right to a hearing, the right to access documents, and the requirement to give reasons are fundamental and foundational principles that would be used to fill any gaps when necessary, but they would be invoked even when none arise.

Secondly, the right to a prior hearing is well established in all APAs and UK common law. Some countries even include it in their constitutions. Surprisingly, it is not considered a general principle in Romanian administrative law. Hence, the resolution of case No 3 differs in Romania (the act would not be annulled because there is no obligation to hear the aggrieved party). This difference does not stem from the absence of an APA (as general principles might—and are—used to fill the gaps) but rather from the distinct content of general principles from country to country. This difference could also be explained by considering the different legal tradition coming from a long legacy of past Soviet domination.

Thirdly, tax matters are governed by a differentiated discipline, and there are some restrictions on individual rights. For instance, in Italy and Germany, taxpayers can access their files only *ex-post*, during the court proceeding, not during the administrative procedure. Conversely, in Austria and the UK, sector-specific rules also allow access to the files during the procedure. In Romania, courts rely on the EU general principle of respect for the right of the defence to establish taxpayers' rights to access the file. Once again, we can observe the application of a European principle since the corresponding rule is absent from Romanian national law.

Lastly, the case regarding the obligation to give reasons would be resolved in the same way in all five countries; this duty is acknowledged as a general principle (also in Romania) and proves to be a fundamental element in the common core of administrative law.

Turning now to the second-generation procedures, handling the cases is more complex and varied in the numerous countries under consideration.

Firstly, the duty to consult all stakeholders equally is derived from the constitutional principle of equality in Austria, the constitutional principle of impartiality in Italy, and the common law in the UK. In Germany, there is no express obligation, while in Romania, the Transparency Act does establish one, although the courts would not annul the act if the decision would have been the same in any event.

Secondly, the duty to consult the general public in planning procedures appears to be another fundamental element in the common core of administrative law, although its grounds differ in the various countries. In Germany and Romania, it is clearly stated in the law (the APA in the former and sector-specific legislation in the latter). In Austria, the duty to consult is a general unwritten principle that the court will use to fill the gap since they do not implement the consultation duties provided for in similar cases. Similarly, in the UK, courts would not go too far in interpreting written laws in a 'purposive manner', preferring to rely upon the common law principle of procedural legitimate expectations. In Italy, such a duty is derived from EU law, as it is not yet an established principle in the national legal order.

Lastly, the case regarding rights of access to the algorithm used by the public administration appears to be where the greatest number of divergences between countries emerge. In Austria, the case falls within the scope of private law, where none of the rights provided by the APA are guaranteed. In Germany, it is doubtful whether the administrative decision could even be challenged in an administrative court. In Italy, access will probably be granted relying on the principles of publicity and transparency. In the UK and Romania, how the case would be handled is particularly uncertain, and access may be guaranteed by relying on the principles of reasonableness and legality in the former and the principles of proportionality, equality, and impartiality in the latter. Automated administrative decisions pose new threats to the procedural rights of the individuals affected, and have repercussions on transparency; the solutions provided vary significantly across countries. Thus, there is a need for further comparative analysis in this field.

18
Same Problems, Same Solutions?

Giacinto della Cananea

I. Introduction

The preceding two parts of the book have presented an overview of the legal systems examined in our comparative research and illustrated the solutions to the hypothetical cases at the heart of our 'factual analysis' that would be adopted in those systems. This closing section aims to discuss these solutions and will concentrate on the common and distinctive features that emerge from all the reports in Part III.

The chapter is structured in the following manner. The first section will briefly illustrate the method used in our 'factual analysis'. The subsequent section will examine the solutions presented in the national reports, and the closing section will touch on the relevance and significance of this analysis for our broader investigation into the common core of European administrative laws.

II. From problems to solutions

The methodology used in our research, which has been illustrated earlier,[1] can be summarized as follows. Rather than describing the various national legal institutions, we have attempted to understand how specific problems would be addressed within the selected legal systems. These problems are formulated in factual terms, in the form of hypothetical cases, which is precisely what makes ours a 'factual analysis'. However, it remains to be explored how the variations among the legal systems included in our comparison impinge on the way problems are defined and their respective solutions.

A. Diversity of context

The reasons for choosing the legal systems for our comparison have already been explained,[2] so the current discussion will consider some implications that arise from the selection.

Ideally, a comparative inquiry can be conducted on either relatively or radically different legal systems. If we compare, for example, the administrative procedure

[1] G della Cananea, 'Introduction' in this book, Section III B.
[2] ibid Section III C.

Giacinto della Cananea, *Same Problems, Same Solutions?* In: *General Principles and Sector-Specific Rules in European Administrative Laws*. Edited by: Giacinto della Cananea and Jean-Bernard Auby, Oxford University Press.
 DOI: 10.1093/oso/9780198867579.003.0018

legislation adopted at the state level in the United States, it will come as no surprise to find several common traits since such legislation is adopted within the same federation, and there is a Model State APA, even though it is not binding on the states.[3] Similarly, if we compare the judicial review of administration in England and other Westminster-like democracies that once formed part of the British Empire, it will not be surprising to discover that the fundamental structures—such as how the legal control of discretion is shaped—are largely similar, if not the same.[4] A different choice is made when legal comparison involves four very diverse democracies, such as the US, the UK, France, and Germany.[5] An even wider-ranging option is to compare not only legal systems within the EU but also other European legal orders, such as Switzerland (which, following various agreements, is part of the single market), Serbia (which has applied for membership and is implementing the so-called 'pre-accession' strategy), and those of China and Venezuela.

It may be helpful to look a little more closely at two examples of this diversity. The first concerns a general principle that is part of our shared constitutional traditions in Europe, namely, the right to effective judicial protection from the executive branch.[6] In Venezuela, the effectiveness of judicial protection was undermined after the constitutional crisis that began under Chavez. In China, judicial protection is excluded in certain matters; for instance, civil servants cannot bring actions against acts that adversely affect them.[7] As a result, one could argue that in Europe judicial remedies against the executive have increased over the last two or three decades, and that there is an evident disparity between the Chinese legal system and those of countries such as Italy and the UK, which are members of the Council of Europe and subject to the European Convention on Human Rights (ECHR). However, the changes occurred in China as a consequence of membership of global legal regimes should not be neglected. The second example pertains to administrative procedure legislation. Among the 27 EU Member States, 24 have adopted some form of general legislation on administrative procedure or similar frameworks. However, no such legislation exists in Ireland or Belgium, where private law was codified as early as 1804. Nor is there any such legislation in Romania, although a general code has been adopted.[8] Interestingly, Venezuela implemented general legislation on administrative procedure just a few years after Germany, but the diminishing independence of the judiciary affects its effectiveness. This confirms that *législation comparée*—ie the mere study of national legislation—does not provide an adequate understanding of commonality and diversity.

[3] See, for further observations, A E Bonfield, 'The Federal APA and State Administrative Law' (1986) 72 Virginia L Rev 297.

[4] See, eg, P Daly, *Understanding Administrative Law in the Common Law World* (OUP 2022).

[5] See S Rose-Ackerman, *Democracy and Executive Power. Policymaking Accountability in the US, the UK, Germany, and France* (Yale UP 2021).

[6] Case 222/84 *Johnston v Chief Constable of the Royal Ulster Constabulary* [1986] ECR 1651, para 18 (holding that judicial protection 'reflects a general principle of law which underlies the constitutional traditions common to the member States').

[7] X Sun, 'China' in this book.

[8] D Dragoș, 'Romania' in this book.

B. Defining problems

The preceding discussion has highlighted the influence of context on the sources and principles of administrative law. However, the extent to which it influences the resolution of the problems faced by public authorities in the discharge of administrative functions and powers is quite another matter. This complex debate can only be briefly addressed here and involves a number of fundamental issues that have ramifications for the role of government in our societies. There is a balance to be struck between efficiency and legality, as well as between uniformity of standards and appropriacy in particular cases. Ambiguous terms such as 'citizen participation' and 'openness' also require careful interpretation. It is tempting, therefore, to seek one-size-fits-all answers. But, as we know, generalizations are either false or at least questionable.[9] Moreover, one runs the risk of assuming that similar or even identical legislative provisions will produce similar effects regardless of the different contexts in which they are applied.

This is why our comparative inquiry has been based on factual analysis, within which participants have responded to a series of individual hypothetical cases showing the different ways in which public authorities work. Although we explained this methodology at the outset, its importance warrants some consideration in relation to at least two aspects. First, the formulation of the hypothetical cases had to be set out in terms that would be comprehensible within all the selected legal systems selected for comparison. Thus, for example, even though the specific mechanisms of expropriation may be shaped differently across legal systems (requiring or not requiring judicial authorization), it always concerns the transfer of property rights without the consent of their holder. The questionnaire was only finalized after ensuring that the hypothetical cases were understandable to the experts on each legal system. Moreover, a new case was discussed and added during the workshop. The questionnaire can thus be seen as a collective enterprise.

Secondly, it is precisely because the analysis concerned a variety of legal systems and focused on general principles that such hypotheticals had to be formulated in terms that would allow not only a simple answer such as, for example, whether the rule *audi alteram partem* did or did not apply within a certain legal system but also at what level it could be applied. In other words, the hypothetical scenario could not be presented as excessively black or white. Shades of grey can—and do—exist, and balancing exercises can be shaped in more ways than one. In some cases, the general rule can be deemed satisfied if a minimum of procedural justice is upheld by providing notification and an opportunity to present a defence against a certain course of action. In such cases, a hearing based on written submissions may be sufficient and fair.[10] In other cases, the aggrieved individual may be entitled to an oral hearing, to submit evidence, and to address or cross-examine witnesses. Of course, previous government practice is relevant to this end. Let us consider a scenario where a statute grants a public authority administrative powers without specifying the procedures it must follow when exercising

[9] P Craig, *Administrative Law* (5th edn, Sweet & Maxwell 2003) 265.

[10] See, eg, the decision of the UK Privy Council in *Local Government Board v Arlidge* [1915] AC 120 HL.

them, and someone is dissatisfied with how the authority has interpreted the general rule. In this case, the reviewing court could be satisfied in the following instances: (i) if the authority adhered to the minimum requirements of procedural justice, as mentioned earlier, (ii) if the minimum requirements of procedural justice were fulfilled, as in other cases, and (iii) if the public authority deviated from its usual approach but provided adequate reasons for doing so. The argument from equality is grounded on a premise widely accepted in liberal democracies, namely that public authorities must treat like cases alike.[11] However, this principle does not preclude the possibility that individual cases may warrant a partially different course of action. Nevertheless, deviations from precedents often entail public authorities providing adequate reasons, as exemplified in case No 8, regarding the duty to consult all stakeholders equally.

C. Comparing solutions

The discussion thus far also calls for one or two words about the solutions. In a comparative inquiry involving different legal systems, some of which belong to radically different legal traditions, encountering a diversity of solutions should come as no surprise. However, this eventuality must be qualified in both theoretical and practical terms.

As a starting point, it is highly unlikely that two legal systems will have the exact 'same' rule or principle, because even if they adopt the same precept or linguistic proposition with binding effects, they will operate in a different context, if only due to language considerations. Similarly, it is highly improbable that the facts of two cases will be identical, as there can be variations in the factual elements involved. Consequently, the solutions envisioned within different legal systems are likely to diverge in more than one respect. In brief, even though context is not everything, it matters much.

From a theoretical viewpoint, a distinction must be made between identity, sameness, and *a fortiori* similarity. While in many ordinary language contexts, sameness and identity are regarded as synonymous, some scholars distinguish between identity, viewed as the absence of differences, and sameness, viewed as 'the belonging together of what is distinct' in one or more respects[12] but sharing certain properties. Others

[11] Carl Schmitt's *Verfassungslehre* (1924), J Seitzer (trl), *Constitutional Theory* (Duke UP 2008) 194 explained why in the nineteenth century equality was consubstantial to the concept of *Rechtsstaat*. See also B Jeanneau, *Les principes généraux du droit dans la jurisprudence administrative* (Sirey 1954) 7 (observing that equality was regarded by the French *Conseil d'Etat* as a general principle of law, especially after 1945). For further remarks, see L L Tammelo, 'Equality as the Core of Justice' (1966) 52 ARSP 135 (observing that in the history of Western civilization, 'doctrines that have conceived of "equality" as the core of justice have politically become those most influential, and along with the victory of democratic ideas and ideals it has acquired a good intellectual standing'). But see also the contrary view of P Westen, 'The Empty Idea of Equality' (1982) 95 Harvard L Rev 537 (arguing that 'statements of equality logically entail ... simpler elements of rights'). As regards Europe, see B De Witte, 'New Institutions for Promoting Equality in Europe: Legal Transfers, National Bricolage, and European Governance' (2012) 60 AJCL 49 (illustrating the spread, within the EU, of institutions entrusted with the task of promoting equal treatment).

[12] This sentence is taken from Martin Heidegger, quoted by D A White, 'Heidegger on Sameness and Difference' (1980) 11 Southwest J Philos 107, 112 (noting that whereas identity is a purely logical concept, which can be predicated of a being with respect to itself, sameness is a notion that applies only to certain types of being).

distinguish between partial (or respective) and overall similarity, the former referring to some aspects and the latter concerning the resemblance of two or several objects, all things considered. It is important, therefore, to analyse the characteristics of two or more objects of study to understand which factors determine diversity and which make it possible to gather them together. Thus, for example, it is one thing if, in a given legal system, public authorities are not required to give reasons for their decisions, even if they are detrimental to individuals and legal entities. It is quite another if, elsewhere, public authorities are required to give reasons that can vary in both extent and level of detail. Expanding on our example, there is a similarity in the sense that both cases have a property in common, because public authorities are required to furnish reasons. But there is also, qualitatively, a distinction between a purely procedural obligation to give (albeit brief or standardized) reasons and a more substantive requirement to provide adequate or even compelling reasons.

Furthermore, from a practical perspective, the range of possible solutions within the legal systems included in our comparative inquiry is not unlimited. In Europe, with the notable exception of Russia, all legal systems are bound by the European Convention of Human Rights (ECHR) and must respect the right to a fair hearing enshrined in Article 6, including the right to an impartial tribunal and a fair procedure.[13] As a result, the notion of diversity must be qualified, as there are differences that can be justified, for instance, through the doctrine of the margin of appreciation and others that cannot be tolerated within a convention that safeguards certain rights. This is why the European Court of Human Rights (ECtHR) is likely to condemn 'egregious' violations of these rights. Moreover, the ECHR has a broader influence as it shapes how national courts interpret the due process rights established by constitutional and legislative provisions. Thus, for example, Swiss courts have invoked Article 6 of the ECHR to strengthen procedural requirements, eg impartiality and the right to be heard. The Court's rulings are also increasingly quoted by other courts in the world. On the other hand, greater diversity may be more evident in non-European legal systems, such as those of China and Venezuela.

III. Commonality and diversity

Based on these preliminary remarks, the subsequent discussion will focus on the solutions provided in the national reports. The first aspect to be addressed is a longstanding principle known by the Latin *nemo judex in causa sua* maxim (meaning 'no one should be a judge in his own case'). Following that, the procedural requirements pertaining to administrative adjudication will be examined, including another traditional maxim, *audi alteram partem* (literally, 'hear the other side'). Lastly, the analysis will extend to solutions regarding non-adjudicatory procedures and the challenges posed by digitalized administration.

[13] For a comparative analysis, see A Stone Sweet and H Keller, 'Assessing the Impact of the ECHR on National Legal Systems' in A Stone Sweet and H Keller (eds), *A Europe of Rights. The Impact of the ECHR on National Legal Systems* (OUP 2008) 677.

A. The impartial and unbiased adjudicator requirement

This principle, established long ago by Roman jurists, codified by Justinian, and acknowledged—together with the *audi alteram partem* maxim—as one of the fundamental premises of natural justice, is also known as the rule against bias, so the decision maker must have an impartial and unprejudiced mind on the question he or she is called upon to decide. Consequently, recusal is inevitable if a judge or a prosecutor has a possible conflict of interest or there is the risk of a lack of impartiality on political or religious grounds. As Judge Barak aptly notes, 'absence of bias is crucial to the judicial process; hence the imagery of blindfolded justice'.[14] It is important to add, first of all, that in modern legal systems, this principle applies not only to the administration of justice but also to administrative adjudication. Secondly, it is precisely because this is a fundamental principle of law that what matters is not merely whether a decision is clearly influenced by partiality and prejudice, for example, because the adjudicator has a personal interest conflicting with that of the applicant seeking authorization or a licence, but also the appearance of bias.

The example we use for our hypothetical case is immigration. We suppose that Fatima is a Sudanese national who fled her country in order to save her life and entered a European country illegally. Here, she applies for asylum. However, her asylum request is rejected by a three-member board presided over by a man who frequently provides interviews to newspapers, stating that the board's role is to prevent the invasion of African migrants. Fatima challenges the rejection of her application before the appropriate court, claiming that the president of the board exhibited clear bias, thereby influencing the entire procedure, and that the final decision should be annulled. This raises two questions. The first is whether each legal system included in our comparative enquiry defines a general principle against bias. The second is whether any violation of this principle would result in the nullification of the disputed decision.

The national reports indicate a combination of sector-specific legislation and general principles regarding asylum procedures. Virtually all legal systems have adopted specific rules regarding the asylum procedure, and their interpretation varies in relation to general principles, such as those established by Articles 6 and 10 ECHR.[15] There are, however, significant differences. On the one hand, in most of the legal systems examined, courts only have the power to invalidate an unlawful decision, while in Austria they may also replace the board's decision. Additionally, courts across the various legal systems examined follow different approaches. Three of them can be distinguished as follows. First, in France and Italy, for example, although there is no prohibition on publicly expressing ideas about how power should be exercised, doing so would affect the level of obligation to abstain from taking part in a procedure where there is even the slightest potential for bias or prejudice. Interestingly, a similar

[14] A Barak, 'The Role of a Supreme Court in a Democracy' (2002) 116 Harvard L Rev 55 (for whom 'it is not his own subjective values that the judges imposes on the society in which he operates'). See also M H Redish and L C Marshall, 'Adjudicatory Independence and the Values of Procedural Due Process' (1986) 95 Yale LJ 455 (critiquing the positivist argument that the legislative determination of what type of process is due should satisfy the constitutional requirement of due process and arguing that a 'floor' is necessary).

[15] For a broader analysis of the impact of the EU in this field, see European Council on Refugees and Exiles, *The Application of the EU Charter of Fundamental Rights to Asylum Procedures* (2014).

solution would be applied in China. Then, particularly in legal systems like that of Germany, where administrative decisions are invalidated only if procedural deficiencies affect their substance, a statement expressing concerns about an 'invasion of African migrants' would raise reasonable doubts about the bias of the president of the board. Thirdly, in Spain and, probably, Romania, the courts would be unlikely to overturn the decision solely based on the president's remarks, but they would consider whether they actually influenced the decision.

That being said, the crucial point is that even though administrative bodies operate differently from courts in the execution of administrative functions and powers, the distinction regarding the rule against bias has been diminished. Whether it is now a difference of degree rather than kind is another question. What matters is that the impartiality of the adjudicator remains an essential requisite for the proper discharge of administrative functions and powers. Moreover, in this case, not only is the appearance of bias reinforced by its racial dimension, but Fatima might even be able to argue that the decision was affected by actual, rather than apparent, bias. Lastly, it should be noted that while in other cases the courts may balance the competing interests of public bodies, such as maintaining order and security, this is not the case when the adjudicator's impartiality is at stake. If the courts find that the denial of the asylum application is influenced by prejudice, they will quash the administrative authority's decision.

B. Standardless adjudication?

In our second hypothetical case, we examine a scenario that could be regarded as a worst-type scenario: ie a situation which, until a few years ago, was considered a demonstration of the profound divergence between the civil law and common law systems. This situation concerns the exercise of discretion. On the one hand, UK courts adhered to what was called the no-fettering rule.[16] On the other hand, German and Italian administrative courts required public authorities to exercise their discretionary powers within a structured framework. Giannini underscored this difference in his preface to the translation of Wade's textbook. He took a positive view of the no-fettering rule, as it gave public administrations considerable flexibility in their decision-making processes.[17] Few years later, Davis dissented from this point of view.[18] He argued that police officers, border control officers, and prosecutors exercised extensive discretionary powers and argued that, in order to avoid arbitrariness, it was necessary for them to limit their discretion and establish a structured framework for its exercise, thus

[16] See the House of Lord's ruling in *British Oxygen Co Ltd v Board of Trade* [1971] AC 610. For further remarks, see P Daly, Understanding Administrative Law (OUP 2021) 57 (for whom the no-fettering doctrine should be viewed as a principle, as opposed to a rule).

[17] Giannini, 'Prefazione' in W Wade, *Diritto amministrativo inglese* (Giuffrè 1965) xv–xvi. See also G Antony, 'United Kingdom' in this book (on the debate concerning policies and legitimate expectations and noting that there would be only weak grounds for arguing that public consultation was necessary).

[18] K C Davis, *Discretionary Justice. A Preliminary Inquiry* (Greenwood Press 1969) 31. See also S Koslow, 'Standardless Administrative Adjudication' (1970) 22 Admin L Rev 407 (observing that courts have increasingly assumed responsibility for formulating standards where the legislature has failed to do so).

ensuring accountability.[19] This was an important step beyond the simplistic notion of eliminating discretion, and paved the way for new thinking on the interplay between rules and discretion.

In our hypothetical case, we assume that legislation allows for allocating public money to the toy industry for a specific purpose without specifying the means to be employed. When the administration decides to establish certain rules of practice before allocating public money, its decision is challenged on the grounds that there is no legislative provision mandating the adoption of any rule or policy.

Interestingly, all the European legal systems examined acknowledge the existence of legal rules that do not directly affect the rights and interests of individuals but instead regulate and define the exercise of discretionary powers granted to public authorities. They recognize the validity of adopting such rules and make due distinctions. It is one thing to establish that administrative rules are inflexible insofar as they leave no discretion to decision makers, for instance, by indicating a mandatory process rather than a recommended albeit optional one,[20] but it is quite another when rules are conditional or flexible, allowing officials to take certain actions if specific circumstances are met. This approach is close to the idea of how discretion should be exercised 'normally'—but not in every instance. Furthermore, the importance of following a proper procedure is universally recognized.[21]

There are, however, variations in this area; firstly, the question of whether there is a general duty to establish predetermined standards of administrative conduct. In Italy, this duty has been codified by administrative procedure legislation, which does not exist elsewhere.[22] Secondly, it is compulsory to consult stakeholders before adopting rules that aim to interpret or implement legislation, as well as the binding nature of implementing rules.[23] Additionally, the behaviour of the courts differs. In the UK, unless there is something in the wording of the statute that indicates Parliament's intent to grant the public authority the power to issue guidelines or rules, the courts will most probably quash the challenged rule. The reason for this is that the rule is meant to be applied as a rigid and mandatory requirement leaving no room for discretion on the part of government officials. In other words, it is entirely binding on decision makers. Last but not least, even though the €50 threshold could be defended as significant in some way, it could be objected that it is an arbitrary figure.

[19] Davis (n 18) 219.

[20] See G della Cananea and M Andenas, 'Administrative Procedure and Judicial Review: A 'Common Core' Research' in G della Cananea and M Andenas (eds), *Judicial Review of Administration in Europe. Procedural Fairness and Propriety* (OUP 2021) 14 (distinguishing irregularity from annullability and nullity). See also J Evans, 'Mandatory and Directory Rules' (1982) 1 Legal Studies 227 (explaining why mandatory rules are those procedural rules the breach of which necessarily invalidates administrative action, while this is not the case for directive rules).

[21] See, eg, in the UK, the ruling of the House of Lords in *R v Secretary of State for Health, ex parte US Tobacco International Inc* [1992] QB 353, in which a ban on tobacco was held to be invalid because the company was not told the scientific grounds on which the ban was based during the procedure.

[22] Art 12 of the Italian APA requires public authorities to pre-establish the 'criteria and ways' in which they will act.

[23] For example, the French *Conseil d'Etat* held that certain acts of general applicability, such as circulars and guidelines, may not be contested judicially if they have no binding effects: CE, Sect, 12 June 2020, *GISTI* No 418142, Rec.

On the other hand, a Greek or Romanian court would probably invalidate the rules established by the DTI, citing the lack of authority to establish such rules. In other legal systems, such as those of Italy and Serbia, the court would probably be satisfied with ascertaining that a standard of administrative conduct has been predetermined and adhered to in the specific case. Although this aspect does not directly concern the rule itself (but its application), it should not be overlooked as it implies the existence of an enforceable legitimate expectation. In still other legal systems, a court may deem that if there is a procedural flaw, it can be rectified and may instruct the public authority to conduct a consultation before the conclusion of the judicial process.

However, all this should not prevent an adequate understanding of the development of the law over time. It is evident that the regulation of discretion has not remained static. In fact, it has changed in a manner that goes beyond the rigid distinction between a no-fettering (inflexible) rule and the obligation to establish criteria and standards beforehand, without which individual administrative acts would be deemed invalid.

C. Administrative adjudication: procedural requirements

As a third step, our discussion revolves around a set of hypothetical cases addressing various procedural requirements and different types of administrative functions and powers. Among these requirements, we see numerous standards of administrative conduct that must be followed *before* a public authority makes a final decision that affects an individual, social group, or legal entity. One of the most obvious procedural requirements in this category concerns issuing a notice signalling the commencement of a procedure. This is required and is traditionally considered in two contexts: the dismissal of civil servants and the withdrawal of licences. In the former, this requirement is examined alongside the right to be heard and to obtain legal assistance, while in the latter, it is assessed in conjunction with the duty to give reasons. Moreover, while the former is very similar to one of the most famous cases on natural justice in the UK, *Ridge v Baldwin*, the latter has much in common with the well-known dispute in which the French *Conseil d'Etat* first expressly invoked the existence on general principles such as those concerning the right of the defence.[24] Two additional requirements are then considered: the right to access documentation held by a public authority and the right to remain silent during an administrative procedure (as per another Latin maxim, *nemo tenetur se detegere*). Lastly, there is a fundamental requirement that applies *after* a decision has been made and justifies it—namely, the requirement to give reasons. The requirements also vary in terms of the areas to which they apply. Access to dossiers is examined in a context often unjustly neglected by administrative lawyers: tax law. The right to remain silent is analysed in the context of the rules governing financial markets, which, in Europe, fall under single-market legislation. Similarly, the duty to give reasons pertains to electronic communications, which is the subject of the last hypothetical case.

[24] See House of Lords, *Ridge v Baldwin* [1964] AC 40 and Craig (n 9) 415; *Conseil d'Etat*, judgment of 5 May 1944, *Dame veuve Trompier-Gravier*. For further discussion, see Jeanneau (n 11) 180.

How would these hypothetical cases be resolved in practice? To what extent would they confirm the initial conjecture that European administrative laws exhibit both differences and similarities? Furthermore, can these similarities be expressed not only as general principles but also as mid-level standards of administrative action? If so, which standards are shared by most, if not all, legal systems?

It must be said from the outset that anyone seeking simple answers risks disappointment in more than one way. Firstly, understanding how these hypothetical cases would be resolved is no easy task. For example, the scenario concerning the withdrawal of a licence *inaudita altera parte*, raises the question of whether, in addition to sector-specific rules adopted at the national level, there are also local rules and customs that must be adhered to. Moreover, it raises concerns about the complexity of balancing interests, as the respondent, in this case the local authority, argues that strict adherence to all procedural requirements in every instance would result in a waste of time and money. This argument has recently gained support from some legislatures (notably in Germany and Italy), worried about what they see as an excess of emphasis on procedural rights at the expense of administrative efficiency. Perhaps the only relatively straightforward case concerns the unfair dismissal of a civil servant, except when considering China, which will be revisited later.

Meanwhile, we may observe that this hypothetical case has two particular characteristics. The first is that it is an 'extreme' case in that it can be resolved even if the relevant principle is extremely general and the threshold for applying it is relatively high. This scenario has much in common with public law disputes that have been adjudicated by various courts for a considerable length of time, for example, in Italy and the UK.[25] Consistency in treatment and the rational development of principles hold significant importance. They are essential from the perspective of the individual coming before a court but also from the broader standpoint of legal certainty.

Secondly, when considering how these hypothetical cases would be resolved from the comparative perspective, it soon becomes apparent that there is a notable similarity among European legal systems regarding the first set of procedural requirements, traditionally analysed within the framework of the maxim *audi alteram partem*; specifically, the issuance of a notice and the opportunity to have a hearing. However, we can also observe diversity regarding another procedural requirement: the right to remain silent, as Table 18.1 shows.

In general terms, the *audi alteram partem* principle is now firmly established as one of the fundamental norms that administrative authorities must adhere to. In this respect, no divergence can be discerned between the EU legal systems and other European legal orders, such as those of Serbia, Switzerland, and the UK. The importance of Article 6 ECHR, broadly interpreted by the ECtHR, cannot be underestimated, even though its interpretation is not without difficulties.[26]

Interestingly, there is a striking difference vis-à-vis the Chinese legal system, where administrative decisions adversely affecting civil servants cannot be challenged before the courts. This difference can be interpreted as an indication of the enduring

[25] See the judicial decisions discussed in G della Cananea and S Mannoni (eds), *Administrative Justice Fin de siècle: Early Judicial Standards of Administrative Conduct in Europe (1890–1910)* (OUP 2021).

[26] See P Craig, 'The Human Rights Act, Article 6 and Procedural Rights' (2003) 56 Public L 753.

Table 18.1 Procedural requirements in administrative adjudication

Country	Notice and hearing	Legal assistance	Access to files	Right to remain silent	Duty to give reasons
Austria	3, 4	4	6		7
France	3, 4	4	6		7
Germany	3, 4	4	6	5	7
Greece	3, 4	4	6		7
Italy	3, 4	4	6	5	7
Romania	3, 4	4	6		7
Serbia	3, 4	4	6		7
Spain	3, 4	4	6		7
Switzerland	3, 4	4	6		7
UK	3, 4	4	6	5	7
China	3		6		7
Venezuela	3, 4	4	6	5	7

Source: Author

relevance of the distinction between liberal democracies and authoritarian governments. However, adopting a dynamic perspective, we can remark that the extent and intensity of judicial review have substantially improved over the last three decades, a change best seen through the lens of historical awareness, keeping in mind the severe limitations that numerous European systems of administrative justice have faced in the past.

While this result was, perhaps, predictable, an unexpected area of agreement has emerged regarding the other two requirements: access to files and the duty to give reasons. In the case of access to dossiers, we have imagined a scenario in which an individual argues that, regardless of the specific rules governing the power to tax, some form of access to the documentation held by the administration should be mandated. There appear to be three types of solution. The first is that sector-specific rules establish individuals' right to access the files, as in Austria. The second solution is that (eg in Germany) sector-specific rules do not grant individuals the right to access, and they take precedence over general provisions acknowledging it, although the refusal may be rectified during judicial proceedings. The third solution is that, even though sector-specific rules do not envision access, they must be interpreted in line with the principles of fairness and due process established either through constitutional provisions (as in Serbia and Switzerland)[27] or legislation. A further distinction can be made, based on whether a right of access to documents is defined by general legislation on administrative procedure or by open government legislation. Spain, for example, adopts general legislation on administrative procedure, while France uses

[27] Serbian Constitution, art 42 (4); Swiss Constitution, art 13.

open government legislation to define the right of access. Though these differences are significant, there is also common ground in the sense that excluding access based on sector-specific rules would amount to an improper exercise of discretion. This is particularly so where, as in this case, the applicant is adversely affected by the tax administration's decision.

Interestingly, within the EU, safeguarding the rights of the defence must be interpreted as a requirement that, in national administrative procedures concerning VAT assessment, public authorities must grant individuals the opportunity to access information and documents pertaining to them in the administrative file. However, this duty is not without limitations. As Advocate General Bobek observed in his opinion in the *Ispas* case,[28] national tax authorities are under no general obligation to provide automatic and complete access to files or to disclose documents and information supporting their intended decision. The ECJ aligned with its Advocate General's position and affirmed that while a right of access exists in EU law, the procedural autonomy of Member States must be upheld and respected. Accordingly, national rules apply so long as

> they are not less favourable than those governing similar domestic situations (principle of equivalence) and they do not render impossible in practice or excessively difficult the exercise of rights conferred by the European Union legal order (principle of effectiveness).[29]

Consequently, for the court,

> if the rights of the defence are to be genuinely respected, there must … be a real possibility of access to those documents and that information, unless objectives of public interest warrant restricting that access.[30]

The importance and relevance of both EU law and the ECHR become evident when considering the requirement to give reasons (as addressed in cases 3 and 7). In this regard, a contrast arises between the diversity that emerges at a broader level and the commonality found within our hypothetical scenarios. Even a brief examination of the legal systems under consideration reveals several differences. In some European legal systems, notably in the UK, there is no general obligation to provide reasons, although the historical origins of this practice remain obscure, and Article 6 ECHR will have implications for the rights it recognizes and protects.[31] In other legal orders, administrative procedure legislation establishes a general obligation, including both administrative acts with favourable and unfavourable effects on interested parties. In a few legal systems, the obligation is either laid down by constitutional provisions or at least derived from them.

[28] Opinion of AG Michal Bobek in Case C-298/16 *Ispas v Direcția Generală a Finanțelor Publice Cluj* ECLI:EU:C:2017:843 (Judgment of the Court (Third Chamber) of 9 November 2017) para 126.

[29] ibid para 29.

[30] ibid para 34.

[31] Craig (n 9) 437.

Additionally, there is diversity concerning the nature and strictness of the duty to give reasons. While some legal systems merely require that reasons be given, the general legislation on administrative procedure in the Netherlands sets a more ambitious requirement, namely to provide adequate reasons.[32] One might therefore expect to see an area of disagreement emerge regarding our hypothetical cases, but the outcomes are not as predictable as they initially seemed. In fact, an obligation to give reasons has been identified in both scenarios. In the case of the unjust dismissal of the civil servant—a police officer—even in the absence of sector-specific rules, the obligation to provide reasons is affirmed on the basis of the duties of legality and fairness imposed on public authorities. In the other case, which pertains to issuing licences to carry out electronic communications,[33] the prevailing viewpoint rejects the notion that if sector-specific rules do not explicitly establish a duty to provide reasons, it cannot be derived from the obligation to establish and adhere to objective criteria. In some legal systems, Germany and Switzerland for example, this duty is closely connected with the right to be heard, which holds constitutional significance. In others, including Greece, Italy, and Spain, the duty to give reasons is established through administrative procedure legislation. France, too, has had a requirement of this type since 1986, well before adopting the code that regulates the relationship between citizens and public authorities in 2016. In conclusion, regarding this aspect, there are enduring differences alongside a growing sense of commonality. This commonality can be observed through a narrow interpretation of Article 41(2)(c) of the Charter of Fundamental Rights of the EU, which acknowledges that the 'obligation of the administration to give reasons for its decisions' is universally recognized only for decisions—as opposed to rules—that have a detrimental effect on individuals or legal entities.

Conversely, while, as we shall see, it might be expected that an area of disagreement between legal systems could emerge with regard to the right to remain silent (case No 5), this is not so. This expectation might arise in the light of a dispute recently brought before the ECJ. The Italian Constitutional Court referred a preliminary question to the ECJ, seeking clarification on whether EU rules align with the national constitutional tradition according to which, even though national regulators require the collaboration of all those involved in the financial markets, such collaboration cannot be compelled under the threat of pecuniary sanctions, licence suspension, or revocation. In simpler terms, the national court recognizes the right to remain silent during the administrative procedure in accordance with shared constitutional traditions and the International Covenant on Civil and Political Rights.[34] Advocate General Pikamae's opinion, while critical of certain aspects of the preliminary question's formulation,

[32] Dutch GALA, Section 4: 16 'A decision shall be based on proper reasons'. For further remarks, see W den Ouden and T Barkhuysen, 'Netherlands' in J-B Auby (ed), *Codification of Administrative Procedure* (Bruylant 2014) 262 (observing that the Act focuses on decisions).

[33] In this sector, art 11(1) of the Framework Directive—Directive 2002/21/EC of the European Parliament and of the Council of 7 March 2002 on a common regulatory framework for electronic communications networks and services states that national regulatory authorities must act 'on the basis of transparent and publicly available procedures, applied without discrimination and without delay'.

[34] ICCP, art 14(3)(g) recognizes and protects everyone's right 'not to be compelled to testify against himself or to confess guilt'. For further discussion, see G della Cananea, 'Common Constitutional Traditions Taken Seriously: Process Rights' (2021) 33 Eur Rev Public L 81.

identified a solution within Article 52(3) of the Charter of Fundamental Rights. The distinction between natural and legal persons was deemed relevant in clarifying why the privilege against self-incrimination may be invoked by the former but not the latter. Based on this distinction, Member States are not required to penalize individuals who refuse to answer questions posed by the supervisory authority that could potentially establish their liability for an offence subject to administrative sanctions of a criminal nature. The ECJ endorsed the view of its Advocate General,[35] but it referred exclusively to the interpretation of the ECHR by the Strasbourg Court rather than relying on shared constitutional traditions.[36]

The question that arises is whether a shared constitutional tradition exists and can be identified in this regard. The least that can be said is that diversity reigns. Firstly, there are legal systems—such as in Serbia—where general legislation on administrative procedure recognizes and safeguards the right to refuse to testify if this would lead to self-incrimination in criminal proceedings. In the UK, too, the right to silence exists at common law, though it could be limited by parliamentary legislation. Secondly, there are legal systems where, although the right to remain silent is specifically established only for criminal proceedings, constitutional and administrative courts have extended its application to administrative procedures that may result in penalties. This is true not only in Italy but also in Greece, Spain, and to a certain extent, Switzerland. Thirdly, there are legal systems, such as those of Austria and Germany, where a judicial extension of the norm applicable to criminal proceedings is not ruled out, but it must be balanced with the duty to cooperate. Lastly, there are legal systems where the right to remain silent does not exist, such as Romania and possibly France. Nor does it exist in China, where it is argued that recognizing such a right would interfere with administrative efficiency. What emerges, therefore, is an area of disagreement.

IV. Beyond adjudicatory procedures

The discussion thus far has focused on the applicability and content of procedural requirements in the context of administrative adjudication. However, we must be cautious not to assume that adjudication standards are equally applicable to other forms of administrative action. Fuller's caveat remains valid:

> The great danger is that we will unthinkingly carry over to new conditions, traditional institutions and procedures ... As lawyers, we have a natural inclination to 'judicialise' every function of government. Adjudication is a process with which we are familiar and which enables us to show that adjudication is an ineffective instrument for economic management and governmental participation in allocating economic resources. It may be objected that without the guarantees afforded by adjudicative procedures, governmental power is subject to grave abuse. [...] In any

[35] Case C-481/19 *DB v Commissione Nazionale per le Società et la Borsa (Consob)* (CJEU, gd ch, 2 February 2020).

[36] ibid para 36.

event, in the search for institutional safeguards against abuse we need not to confine ourselves to adjudicative procedures in the strict sense.[37]

Coherently with this caveat, three hypothetical cases included in our questionnaire (Nos 8, 9, and 10) seek to shed light on how administrative functions and powers are discharged beyond 'adjudicative procedures in the strict sense', to borrow Fuller's phraseology. These cases involve, firstly, consulting stakeholders prior to determining new tariffs; secondly, the consultation of the general public prior to constructing a new gas pipeline; and thirdly, access to the algorithm used by a public body.

The first case is significant because, as public utilities expand and become liberalized, regulators have to protect and promote the public interest, at the same time striking a balance with the rights of private providers. Therefore, the procedure followed by these administrative bodies is a matter of paramount importance. The question at hand is not so much whether procedures should affect and limit the powers of regulators, but how they should do so. Should they incorporate the safeguards we traditionally associate with due process in a procedural sense, similar to those found in the context of adjudication, except when administrative action risks becoming arbitrary? This discussion focuses specifically on the requirements prescribed by the various legal systems to determine new tariffs. There is, however, an additional element to consider. In this scenario, we suppose the regulator chooses to consult with the stakeholders despite not being compelled to do so. However, it restricts the consultation process to only the two incumbents without involving the newcomer.

This additional element has proved crucial. On the one hand, while both liberalization and regulation are relevant to all the legal systems included in our comparison, apart from China, the specific procedural rules designed to ensure the protection of the rights of both providers and users are a matter for the domestic legal order of each Member State, in accordance with the principle of national procedural autonomy. Not surprisingly, these procedural rules vary. In some instances, there is no consultation with stakeholders at all. In most legal systems, we can find the authority to consult stakeholders, but not the duty. Moreover, once a consultation is conducted, there are shared criteria that dictate what evidence should be received and taken into account and what factual findings are necessary to support the regulator's conclusions.[38] It is unsurprising that administrative procedure should vary in this manner: disagreements of this kind are inevitable since rate-setting is part of rule-making, and in this respect, administrative procedure legislation tends to be more diverse than adjudication.

On the other hand, in most European legal systems, with the exception of Greece, even though public consultation is not mandatory, *if* the public authority opts for it, *then* the consultation must be conducted correctly and fairly. Consequently, all stakeholders must be consulted, and the regulatory authority must receive and consider all evidence, producing relevant findings based on the information gleaned. Otherwise, the principles of equality and reasonableness (or rationality) would be infringed, and, as a consequence, the tariffs established by the regulator may be annulled. The

[37] L Fuller, *The Morality of Law* (rev edn, Yale UP 1969) 176–77.

[38] A Benedetti, 'The Proceduralization of Public Decisions in Public Utilities: Issues from a Comparative Law Study' (2022) 34 Eur Rev Public L 341.

disagreement concerning the existence of a duty to consult stakeholders does not call into question the general point expressed earlier, namely that a public authority may exercise its discretion without consulting them. However, it may not do so in a way that implies treating undertakings competing in the same market differently.

In our second case, we shift our attention to consultation, but we focus on a different type of administrative procedure, concerning the construction of a new gas pipeline. We seek to understand whether there is an obligation to consult the affected local community. This form of administrative action has always posed challenges for applying conventional procedural justice requirements. The courts have grappled with the very nature of the decision-making process, which does not align with one of the primary features of adjudication, namely the triadic structure. The position of the administration, coupled with the broad range of policy considerations that must be taken into account, precludes it.

Moreover, identifying an 'opponent' in the traditional sense becomes challenging since courts may be hesitant to acknowledge the existence of an individual interest directly affected by the final decision. Hence, some legal systems allow social groups, such as committees and associations, to participate in the administrative procedure. Interestingly, this is the case also in the UK, where the legislative framework imposes requirement beyond what is imposed by natural justice.[39] Another increasingly used tool is the requirement for public authorities to conduct an environmental assessment before making the final decision. This serves to identify areas of concern and aspects of the project that are likely to harm collective interests. It can be observed that both these approaches suggest that the traditional paradigm may not necessarily be the most appropriate. It remains to be seen how they work in practical terms and whether they enable the achievement of procedural justice. It is worth noting that in Europe, this goal is pursued not only by EU law but also by the Aarhus Convention, which has been ratified by all the Member States of the Council of Europe and which recognizes and protects the right to know and the right to participate in administrative decision-making.[40]

In our hypothetical case, we suppose that while municipal rules mandate consultation of the general public before the authorities make any decision concerning the construction of new electricity plants by private companies, no such provision exists for new gas pipelines. The question thus arises as to whether general principles of fairness and transparency should remedy the absence of sector-specific rules. If so, the question then arises of whether a court would be willing to quash or modify a decision made in disregard of those principles.

The potential solutions to this question differ from various points of view. First of all, unlike European legal systems, the Chinese one does not provide for judicial

[39] See G Anthony, 'United Kingdom' in this volume.

[40] Convention on Access to Information, Public Participation in Decision-making and Access to Justice in Environmental Matters, adopted at Aarhus on 25 June 1998. The EU, too, is part of the Convention: see its Regulation No 1376/2006 of 6 September 2006 on the application of the provisions of the Aarhus Convention on Access to Information, Public Participation in Decision-making and Access to Justice in Environmental Matters to Community institutions and bodies. For further analysis, see P Bejchova, 'Aarhus Convention and the Right to Know' (2010) 11 Common L Rev 44; M Lee and C Abbot, 'The Usual Suspects—Public Participation under the Aarhus Convention' (2003) 66 Modern L Rev 80 a7 93 (noting that, though the Convention is a 'fairly weak legal document', access to information is the 'strongest pillar').

review of urban plans, which are considered regulatory acts and cannot, therefore, be challenged before the courts. Secondly, while in some European legal systems, such as those of Spain and Switzerland, consultation of the affected community is required by sector-specific legislation, this is not the case across all legal systems. For example, there is no such requirement in Greece. Nor is consultation always required by general legislation, unlike in France, where the building of infrastructures of 'national interest' that may have an impact on the environment is subject to public debate. This is also true of Germany, where administrative procedure legislation would apply. Where there is no such legislative framework, the courts will have recourse to general principles in one way or another. One approach is to invoke the Aarhus Convention. Interestingly, this solution would not only be applicable within the EU but also in Serbia, where failure to consult the public could result in the administrative court granting access to all available documents. Another solution, likely to be used in Austria, is to refer—as the Constitutional Court has already done—to the constitutional duty to consider the interests of the local communities affected. A variety of sector-specific rules thus coexist with a broader understanding of procedural justice, which emphasizes the importance of consulting the general public before making a final decision.

Digitalized administration provides another example of the matter under discussion. There are two reasons for choosing this example. On the one hand, the rapid advancement of digital technologies has affected almost every sphere of human life, including public administration. On the other hand, it is both important and interesting to explore the responses to the daily questions in the context of administrative functions.[41] It is important because public bodies increasingly rely on new technologies, in relation to making decisions on the allocation of civil servants, or complex issues regarding the use of police powers. Additionally, it is interesting to examine whether the use of new technologies aligns with traditional perspectives on administrative decision-making and the judicial review of administrative actions.

In our hypothetical case, we imagine a situation where a local authority decides to pay tribute to some of its former members by including their names on a funeral plaque installed in the town's central square. To select the names, the authority opts to gather information from civil and military archives and employs a specially developed algorithm provided by a private company. We seek to understand whether local community members have a right of access to the reasons for including some individuals and excluding others. Specifically, we explore whether a local authority can be made to grant access to the algorithm it used. Not surprisingly, in an area that is evolving rapidly, it is expected that solutions will evolve with them.

That being said, legal systems exhibit varying approaches, as Table 18.2 shows. While many legal orders would apply general principles that would ultimately force the local authority to grant access to the algorithm, others would not require any such disclosure.[42] Thus, for example, in Austria, Germany, Serbia, Spain, and Switzerland,

[41] For further analysis, see J-B Auby, 'Administrative Law Facing Digital Challenges' (2020) 1 Eur Rev Digital Adm & L 7; P Daly, J Raso, and J Tomlinson, 'Administrative Law in the Digital World' in C Harlow (ed), *Research Handbook on Administrative Law* (Elgar 2021) 255.

[42] See Auby (n 41) 12 (observing the variety of solutions adopted by national judges).

Table 18.2 Procedural requirements in non-adjudicative procedures

Country	Duty to equally consult stakeholders	Duty to consult the general public before deciding about infrastructure	Access to an algorithm held by an administration
Austria	8	9	10
France	8	9	
Germany	8	9	10
Greece	8	9	10
Italy	8	9	10
Romania	8	9	
Serbia	8	9	10
Spain	8	9	10
Switzerland	8	9	10
UK	8	9	10
China	8		
Venezuela	8	9	10

Source: Author

the local authority would have to give reasons for its decision and, if unable to do so because it has relied on the algorithm, it would be required to disclose information about it. In contrast, in France, sector-specific rules take precedence over general norms, and limitations on access may be permitted as long as they are not disproportionate.

V. Conclusion

Everything we have seen here suggests two concluding remarks. Firstly, we need to consider the nature of procedural safeguards against public authorities, taking into account the innovative characteristics of administrative decision-making and judicial review. Secondly, the level of assurance provided by general principles for this protection when sector-specific rules are either lacking or insufficient is an aspect of considerable importance from the comparative perspective.

From the first standpoint, the first set of hypothetical cases in our questionnaire focuses on administrative adjudication, examining both traditional scenarios (such as the dismissal of a civil servant) and some more contemporary situations (such as gathering information for financial market surveillance). In both cases, legal systems impose certain procedural limitations on administrative decision-making. The other hypothetical cases concentrate on non-adjudicative procedures, such as those related to consulting either stakeholders or the general public, as well as the sphere of digitalized administration. Before looking at how problems concerning these forms of administrative action would be solved in the legal systems selected for our comparative research, one thing is clear: more thought should be given to understanding the nature of decision-making processes beyond the conventional adjudication paradigm. There are questions of procedural fairness and propriety that cannot be fully understood within the confines of the existing paradigm. This suggests that further research is necessary in areas such as the rule-making and planning processes.

From a comparative perspective, three general points can be made. First, across all the European legal systems examined, the general principles of law are applied by the courts, regardless of old and new distinctions, such as civil law versus common law countries or EU Member States versus non-Member States. As observed initially,[43] general principles are mainly judicial creations, as they are developed by the courts, often without any written source, to meet contemporary legal demands. In the past, this has given rise to debates about judicial activism, but in several legal systems general principles have been codified by either constitutional or legislative provisions. Secondly, our focus is essentially on procedural requirements, including the duty to respect the procedure previously established, the right to be heard, and the duty to give reasons. These requirements are typically incorporated into balancing processes, where considerations of fairness, propriety, and transparency are weighed against concerns about administrative decision-making costs and the timely implementation of policies. This explains why the maximization of procedural requirements is particularly relevant in 'egregious' cases, where administrative powers are exercised arbitrarily and opaquely, while this is less likely to occur in other situations. Thirdly, and more importantly for the subject of this book, if we consider how administrative procedures operate at present, where sector-specific rules do not provide adequate solutions, general principles will provide the solutions. These principles manifest as mid-level but still comprehensive standards of administrative action, such as the right to be heard. It is in this sense, and within these limits, that common ground, or a common core between the European legal systems included in our comparison, can be found, while there is less convergence with legal systems in other regions of the world, such as East Asia. However, the usual caveat applies: extensive further analysis is necessary to test and validate these findings.

[43] della Cananea, 'Introduction' (n 1) para 2.

Selected Bibliography

Allegretti U, *L'imparzialità amministrativa* (Cedam 1965).

Anthony G, 'Transparency, Public Administration, and the Common Law' in A Pottakis (ed), *Transparency and Reform of Administrative Procedures* (Esperia Publications 2010) 187–202.

Anthony G, 'Public Interest and the Three Dimensions of Judicial Review' (2013) 64 Northern Ireland Legal Quarterly 125–42.

Araujo Suárez J, *Formal Administrative Law Treaty* (3rd edn, Vadell Hermanos Editores 1998).

Arroyo Jiménez L and Utrilla Fernández-Bermejo M D (eds), *La adjudicación administrativa de recursos escasos: ordenación sectorial y reconstrucción sistemática* (Tirant lo Blanch 2018).

Auby J-B (ed), *Codification of Administrative Procedure* (Bruylant 2014).

Benvenuti F, 'Funzione amministrativa, procedimento, processo' (1952) II Rivista trimestrale di diritto pubblico 118–45.

Brewer Carías A R, *Administrative Law Treaty. Public Law and Latin America. The Administrative Procedure*, vol IV (Civitas, Thomson Reuters 2013).

Bull H P and Mehde V, *Allgemeines Verwaltungsrecht mit Verwaltungslehre* (9th edn, CF Müller 2015).

Costaş C F, 'Access to File: Right(s) of the Defence or Defence of the Right(s)?' (2018) 5 Cluj Tax Forum Journal 17–23.

Costaş C F, 'Towards a Magna Carta of Taxpayers' Rights in the Times of the Hunger Games?' in M Tofan, I Bilan, and A-M Bercu (eds), *EUFIRE 2018* (Editura Universităţii 'Alexandru Ioan Cuza' 2018) 427–33.

Craig P, *Administrative Law* (9th edn, Sweet and Maxwell 2021).

della Cananea G, 'Equivalent Standards under Domestic Administrative Law: A Comparative Perspective', Paper for the BIICL conference on 'Fair and equitable treatment in investment treaty law', London, 9 September 2005.

della Cananea G and Mannoni S (eds), *Administrative Justice Fin de siècle. Early Judicial Standards of Administrative Conduct in Europe* (1890–1910) (OUP 2021).

della Cananea G, Ferrari Zumbini A, and Pfersmann O (eds), *The Austrian Codification of Administrative Procedure. Diffusion and Oblivion* (1920–1970) (OUP 2023).

Donnelly C, Hare I, Woolf H, and Jowell J, *De Smith's Judicial Review* (8th edn, Sweet and Maxwell 2020).

Dragoş D C, Neamtu B, and e Veliscu R, 'Judicial Review in Romania between Tradition and Dialogue' in R Caranta and A Gerbrandy (eds), *Traditions and Change in European Administrative Law* (Europa Law Publishing 2011) 189–236.

Dragoş D C, Neamtu B, and Cobârzan B V, 'Procedural Transparency in Rural Romania: Linking Implementation with Administrative Capacity?' (2012) 78 International Review of Administrative Sciences 134–57.

Dragoş D C, Neamtu B, and Suciu R, 'The Allocation of Gambling Licences, Radio Frequencies and CO2 Emission Permits in Romania' in P Adriaanse, F van Ommeren, W den Ouden, and J Wolswinkel (eds), *Scarcity and the State II. Member State Reports on Gambling Licences, Radio Frequencies and CO2 Emission Permits* (Intersentia 2016) 203–41.

Ehlers D and Pünder H (eds), *Allgemeines Verwaltungsrecht* (16th edn, CF Müller 2022).

Erbguth W and Gockelberger A, *Allgemeines Verwaltungsrecht* (10th edn, Nomos 2020).

Fuchs C and Thalmann P, 'Förderungs- und Beihilfenrecht' in B Raschauer, D Ennöckl, and N Raschauer (eds), *Grundriss des österreichischen Wirtschaftsrechts* (4th edn, Manz 2021) 627–704.

Gamero Casado E (ed), *Tratado del Procedimiento Administrativo Común y del Régimen Jurídico Básico del Sector Público* (Tirant lo Blanch 2018).

González Pérez J, *Administrative Procedure Treaty* (Cívitas 2000).

Guichot Reina E, Barrero Rodríguez C, *El derecho de acceso a la información pública* (Tirant lo Blanch 2020).

Harlow C and Rawlings R, *Law and Administration* (4th edn, Cambridge UP 2022).

Hengstschläger J and Leeb D (eds), [Commentary on the] *AVG* (Manz status 1.1.2014, rdb.at).

Hernández J I, *Administrative Procedure Lessons* (Fundación de Estudios de Derecho Administrativo 2012).

Kahl W and Ludwigs M (eds), *Handbuch des Verwaltungsrechts*, 12 vol, forthcoming, esp vol 4: *Status des Einzelnen und Verfahren* (CF Müller 2022).

Lilić S, *Law on General Administrative Procedure—Anatomy of a Legislative Project with the Model for the General Reconstruction of LGAP* (YUKOM, Dosije 2019) (in Serbian).

Lilić S, *Administrative Law in Serbia* (University of Belgrade—Faculty of Law 2022).

Lilić S and Milenković M, 'Administrative Procedure in Former Yugoslavia and the Austrian Administrative Procedure Act' in della Cananea G, Ferrari Zumbini A, and Pfersmann O (eds), *The Austrian Codification of Administrative Procedure. Diffusion and Oblivion (1920–1970)* (OUP 2023) 119–34.

Martín Delgado I, 'Automation, Artificial Intelligence and Sound Administration. A Few Insights in the Light of the Spanish Legal System' (2022) 3 European Review of Digital Administration & Law 9–30.

Maurer H and Waldhoff C, *Allgemeines Verwaltungsrecht* (20th edn, CH Beck 2020).

Milosavljević B, *Administrative Law* (Union Faculty of Law, Official Gazette 2019) (in Serbian).

Pastori G (ed), *La procedura amministrativa* (Neri Pozza 1964).

Pautsch A and Hoffmann L, *VwVfG. Kommentar* (2nd edn, Erich Schmidt 2020).

Pesci Feltri F, *Violations of the Due Process in the Venezuelan Sanctioning Procedure*. Colección Monográfica, No 9, Centro para la Integración y el Derecho Público (Editorial Jurídica Venezolana 2018).

Ponce Solé J, *Deber de buena administración y derecho al procedimiento administrativo debido. Las bases constitucionales del procedimiento administrativo y del ejercicio de la discrecionalidad* (Lex Nova 2001).

Sala G, *Potere amministrativo e principi dell'ordinamento* (Giuffrè 1993).

Schulev-Steindl E, *Verwaltungsverfahrensrecht* (6th edn, Verlag Österreich 2018).

Spiliotopoulos Ep, *Greek Administrative Law*, Preface by Prof J Jowel QC (Bruylant) 2004.

Spiliotopoulos Ep and Fortsakis Th, *Constitutional Law in Greece* (3rd edn, Kluwer Law International 2017).

Stoicescu R and Stan O, 'Equity capital markets in Romania: a regulatory overview' (Thomson Reuters Practical Law, 1 January 2022) <https://uk.practicallaw.thomsonreuters.com/w-023-8817?originationContext=document&transitionType=DocumentItem&contextData=(sc.Default)&firstPage=true> accessed June 2023.

Storr S, 'Allgemeiner Teil' in B Raschauer, D Ennöckl, and N Raschauer (eds), *Grundriss des österreichischen Wirtschaftsrechts* (4th edn, Manz 2021) 1–123.

Sun X, 'La déontologie des fonctionnaires sous la République Populaire de Chine' (2016) 38 *Annuaire Européen d'Administration Publique 2015* 39–57.

Sun X, 'La notion de parti politique en Chine' (2018) 16 Les partis politiques (*Cahiers de la Recherche sur les Droits Fondamentaux*) 59–67.

Sun X, 'Les raisons de l'absence de recours à la notion de démocratie par les juridictions de la République Populaire de Chine' in M Rota (ed), *Le recours à la notion de démocratie par les juridictions* (Collection 'Colloque & Essais', Institut Universitaire Varenne 2018) 99–108.

Sun X, 'La réforme de la loi sur la sanction administrative de la République Populaire de Chine' (2021) 43 *Annuaire Européen d'Administration Publique 2020* 426–41.

Sun X, 'L'adaptation des juridictions chinoises à la crise sanitaire liée à l'épidémie de COVID-19' in R Maurel (ed), *L'éthique des procédures contentieuses en temps de pandémie. Approches de droits international et comparé, coll. Droit administratif/Administrative Law* (Bruylant 2022) 455–68.

Tomić Z, *General Administrative Law* (University of Belgrade—Faculty of Law 2018) (in Serbian).

Travi A, 'Giurisprudenza amministrativa e principio di legalità' (1995) I Diritto Pubblico 91–123.

Travi A, *Pubblica amministrazione. Burocrazia o servizio al cittadino* (*Vita e Pensiero* 2022).

Voßkuhle A, Eifert M, and Möllers C (eds, former eds: Hoffmann-Riem, Wolfgang/Schmidt-Aßmann, Eberhard), *Grundlagen des Verwaltungsrechts*. 2 vol (3rd edn, CH Beck 2022).

Wielinger G, *Einführung in das österreichische Verwaltungsverfahrensrecht und in das Recht der österreichischen Verwaltungsgerichtsbarkeit* (2nd edn, Leykam 2019).

Index

For the benefit of digital users, indexed terms that span two pages (e.g., 52–53) may, on occasion, appear on only one of those pages.

Tables are indicated by an italic *t* following the page number